Sri Aurobindo

A Greater Psychology

An Introduction to
Sri Aurobindo's Psychological Thought

Edited by A. S. Dalal

JEREMY P. TARCHER / PUTNAM
a member of Penguin Putnam Inc.
New York

Most Tarcher/Putnam books are available at special quantity discounts for bulk purchases for sales promotions, premiums, fund-raising, and educational needs. Special books or book excerpts also can be created to fit specific needs. For details, write Putnam Special Markets, 375 Hudson Street, New York, NY 10014.

Jeremy P. Tarcher/Putnam
a member of
Penguin Putnam Inc.
375 Hudson Street
New York, NY 10014
www.penguinputnam.com

Library of Congress Cataloging-in-Publication Data
Dalal, A. S.
A greater psychology : an introduction to Sri Aurobindo's
psychological thought / A. S. Dalal.
p.   cm.
Includes biblographical references and index.
ISBN 1-58542-089-1
1. Ghose, Aurobindo, 1872–1950.   2. Ghose, Aurobindo,
1872–1950—Knowledge—Psychology.   3. Psychology and
Religion.   4. Spiritual life—Psychology.   I. Ghose,
Aurobindo, 1872–1950.

BL1273.892.G56 D35   2001   00-064780
150'.92—dc21

Printed in the United States of America

1   3   5   7   9   10   8   6   4   2

This book is printed on acid-free paper. ∞

Contents

PART TWO
ESSAYS ON SRI AUROBINDO'S PSYCHOLOGICAL THOUGHT

...the greater psychology awaiting its hour...
Sri Aurobindo

Foreword

by Ken Wilber

Sri Aurobindo Ghose was India's greatest modern philosopher-sage, flowing out of a country that is one of the most astonishing and profound geographical sources of spiritual awareness on the planet. But Aurobindo's genius was not merely that he captured the profundity of India's extraordinary spiritual heritage. He was the first great philosopher-sage to deeply grasp the nature and meaning of the modern idea of evolution. And thus, in Aurobindo, we have the first grand statement of an evolutionary spirituality that is an integration of the best of ancient wisdom and the brightest of modern knowledge. It wasn't that other great thinkers had not seen that evolution is basically Spirit-in-action (it was obvious to Schelling and Hegel, for example). Nor was Aurobindo necessarily the most enlightened spirit in modern India (many would point to the illustrious Sri Ramana Maharshi in that regard). But nobody combined both philosophical brilliance and a profoundly enlightened consciousness the way Aurobindo did. His enlightenment informed his philosophy; his philosophy gave substance to his enlightenment; and that combination has been rarely equaled, in this or any time.

There is no question about it: the modern world has ir-reversibly discovered the fact that the world evolves — Matter evolves, life evolves, mind evolves. And Spirit evolves — or, we might say, Spirit is the entire evolutionary process of its own unfolding, from matter to life to mind to the higher and su-perconscient realms of Spirit's own being. This evolutionary unfolding of Spirit — as it plays out in psychology, anthropology, religion, politics, the arts, and spiritual practice itself — is the central message of Aurobindo's voluminous writings.

As such, Aurobindo's message is still far ahead of its time.

The world remains, to speak in very general terms, divided into two highly contentious camps: those who believe in the ancient wisdom traditions (and therefore tend to completely distrust the modern notion of evolution), and those who believe the modern scientific view of evolution (which completely dispenses with any notions of Spirit). Both of those views are terribly partial and fragmented, even though both claim to have the inside track on truth. But as Aurobindo saw — probably more clearly than anybody before or since — the scientific account of evolution, which relies on nothing but frisky dirt, dynamic matter, and process systems (e.g., chaos theories, far-from-equilibrium dissipative structures, autopoiesis, etc.) cannot even begin to explain the extraordinary series of transformations that brought forth life from matter and mind from life, and that is destined to bring forth, in just the same way, higher mind and overmind and supermind: Spirit alone can account for the astonishment that is the glory of evolution. Likewise, there is nothing that authentic religion should fear in the notion of evolution. Real spirituality is not a theory about how to make the beans grow, nor is it an empirical account of anthropological data. It is not about whether or not Moses actually parted the Red Sea. It is about whether or not you can awaken to the Spirit in you which is beyond you, and that therefore plugs you straight into the Source and Suchness of the entire Kosmos. That you can develop your own contemplative abilities to recognize this Spirit is only to say that you can evolve into your own highest Estate — and that is yet another example of Aurobindo's message of evolutionary spirituality.

Aurobindo thus stands as one of the great founders of integral spirituality and integral practice. All subsequent attempts at such integrative efforts must, I believe, at least acknowledge Aurobindo's enduring genius and in many ways still unsurpassed efforts. His influence at home and abroad has been, and continues to be, enormous. At the very least, special mention should be made of the work of Mike Murphy (*The Future of the Body*);

Murphy and Leonard (*The Life We Are Given*); and my own *Integral Psychology*.

I would also like to take this opportunity to clear up an unfortunate slander that has been circulating about Aurobindo, namely, that some of his writings have a racist overtone. In particular, sections from The Human Cycle have been quoted to allegedly show that Aurobindo was advocating the superiority of certain races. In fact, as those passages make quite clear, Aurobindo was ridiculing and condemning those who think in that fashion. Less than honest critics have simply taken those sections out of context and presented them as Aurobindo's view, whereas they are clearly the view he is convicting. Aurobindo's integral embrace is, if anything, the opposite of racism.

When it comes to a "greater psychology"— one that includes body, mind, soul, and spirit, in both ascending/evolutionary and descending/involutionary currents — Aurobindo has much to teach us, as is clearly and beautifully documented in the book you now hold in your hands. A. S. Dalal has done a superb job in presenting a balanced sampling of Aurobindo's psychological writings. Because of its fair and representative nature, its comprehensive examples, and the clarity of Dalal's own commentary, this book is surely the finest overview of Aurobindo's psychological thought now available, and it will likely remain a classic reference for the foreseeable future. All of those who are deeply interested in a greater psychology — and what sane soul cannot be? — will find this book a wonderful companion, and I believe we can all thank A. S. Dalal for this noble effort. Aurobindo stands as a towering lighthouse signaling to all of us, through the stormy waves of life, that home can be found at the Source of that light, which, once found, transfigures everything.

Preface

Sri Aurobindo has been described by Ken Wilber as "India's greatest modern philosopher-sage" and also as "the greatest of all Vedantic philosophers". The aim of this book is to highlight another aspect of Sri Aurobindo, not that of a philosopher but of a mystic, for whom the ultimate Reality — popularly called God or Spirit — is not an abstract or philosophical concept but a concrete experience, "more concrete than anything sensed by ear or eye or touch in the world of Matter"(p. 190). The aim of the book is to present Sri Aurobindo as an Enlightened One whose view of the human being is based not on speculative theory nor on statistical inference but on self-realization. The aim is to present Sri Aurobindo as a Seer whose delineation of the future of the human being and of human society is not an ideative dream of what ought to be, but a spiritual pre-vision of what is already in the process of becoming.

It is significant that Wilber, whom an author has described as "the most comprehensive philosophical thinker of our times", bases his integral vision on the core model of the spectrum of consciousness, a model which underlies Sri Aurobindo's map of Reality.

Two features of Sri Aurobindo's psychological thought which have appealed to me most, and which I have tried to bring out in particular in this book, are its experiential basis and its integral nature.

Sri Aurobindo is among those few mystics who, based on a direct experience of the ultimate Reality, have given a systematic philosophical formulation of the nature of Reality founded on their experience. The mystical experience, states Sri Aurobindo, pertains to "a greater consciousness beyond Mind" (p. 182), and is therefore supra-intellectual. The mystic speaks about the supra-intellectual in philosophical or intellectual terms in order to communicate to "those who still live in the mental intelligence" (p. 183). Among such philosophies based on mystical experience, Sri Aurobindo's is perhaps the most comprehensive, permitting a synthesis and reconciliation of diverse insights which appear contrary because of their non-integral nature. In particular, Sri Aurobindo's integral psychological thought provides a framework for the integration of the conventional psychologies of the West — which study the outer personality — with the spiritual psychologies of the East which deal chiefly with the inner person.

While advocating a strictly scientific method in the pursuit of psychological knowledge, Sri Aurobindo points out the inherent limitations of a methodology based solely on reason and positivism, and argues for a spiritual approach to the study of experience which lies beyond the realm of reason, thus vindicating both science and spirituality.

In Sri Aurobindo's experience, the human being is one with and inseparable from the Being of the universe. Therefore in his thought, psychology is part of and intermingled with cosmology. The nature and development of the human being find an explanation in the light of the nature and evolution of the universe.

Sections in Part One of this book, consisting of passages from Sri Aurobindo's writings, follow a sequential development of thought (except for sections 14, 15, 19 and 20), and are, therefore, best read consecutively, unless one is already adequately familiar with Sri Aurobindo's thought.

The essays in Part Two of this book, originally written as independent articles, are meant to serve chiefly as an aid in understanding Sri Aurobindo's own writings contained in the anthology. They do not purport to be my expositions of Sri Aurobindo's thought but rather a faithful presentation of his thought, to a great extent in his own words. My comments are meant only to provide elucidations and to bring out the integral nature of the thought presented. Both the student and the scholar were kept in view in writing these essays. Therefore their contents pertain to different levels of understanding.

Sri Aurobindo never tried to systematize his psychological thought which is scattered throughout his various and numerous writings on yoga and philosophy. The essays aim at bringing out explicitly the system underlying his thought.

Sri Aurobindo's writings, based on spiritual experience rather than on intellectual theory, can convey not only their thought content but also something of the higher state of consciousness underlying the thought when read in a meditatively receptive way. This is but one reason why I have often chosen to quote Sri Aurobindo instead of paraphrasing him.

The reader, if not already familiar with the fact, will discover that Sri Aurobindo's writings cannot be understood by means of "speed reading". To read Sri Aurobindo with understanding is to engage in a sort of reflective meditation, dwelling on each sentence, sometimes re-reading a sentence.

The passages in the anthology have been drawn from a number of different sources, including Sri Aurobindo's letters on the same subject to different disciples. Therefore, although each passage under a given topic deals with a different aspect of the topic, certain ideas are repeated. Some repetitions will be found also in the essays. Generally, these repetitions serve to drive home salient or seminal ideas in Sri Aurobindo's thought.

A word regarding Sri Aurobindo's terminology. As do many original thinkers and persons who have had a unique experience, Sri Aurobindo, too, employs certain words of his own coinage, e.g. "supermind", "overmind", etc., and uses many common terms with an uncommon connotation, e.g. "transformation", "psychic", etc. Grasping well the meanings of such terms as used by Sri Aurobindo is indispensable to the understanding of his thought.

"Yoga", states Sri Aurobindo, "is nothing but practical psychology." For yoga as a method for the attainment of Self-realization and transformation of consciousness is merely the application of certain psychological principles. This book, which deals only with the theoretical aspects of Sri Aurobindo's psychological thought, is thus an introduction to the practical psychology underlying his yoga.

I am deeply grateful to Ken Wilber who offered helpful comments and valuable suggestions regarding the manuscript. His support and commendation have been a great encouragement to me in my hope to bring this book to a wide readership among those interested in a greater than conventional psychology.

I would like to take this opportunity to pay my tribute to Wilber for exercising the widest influence in highlighting the integral nature of Sri Aurobindo's thought. Thanks to Wilber's work, now published in twenty languages, almost everyone the world over interested in integral thought today is apt to be familiar with the name of Sri Aurobindo, whereas until a few decades ago, Sri Aurobindo was to a large extent unknown outside of India.

I am grateful also to Professor Arabinda Basu who has always been willing to give me his time whenever I needed help for clarifying philosophical points pertaining to Sri Aurobindo's psychological thought.

I wish to express my appreciation to Matthijs Cornelissen, M.D. and Lynn Crawford for their helpful suggestions and feedback and for their assistance in preparing the manuscript of this book.

A. S. D.

Introduction

I am glad of my association with this very important and remarkably scholarly book by Dr. A.S. Dalal, a valued friend and esteemed colleague. *A Greater Psychology* is a gathering together under one cover of all the salient aspects of Sri Aurobindo's psychological thought, thus providing an excellent introduction for psychology students and scholars as well as for the interested general reader.

The time for such a book has come and it is appearing at the right moment. For there is a growing interest in Indian yoga and spirituality in the Western world. Though much of this interest is not of the right kind it cannot be gainsaid that there are many people in Europe and North and South America whose interest is genuine, and the glamour of the exotic has little or no part in it. Nevertheless it cannot be denied that there is a good deal of misunderstanding about the nature of yoga.

This book is timely particularly because during recent years there has been an explosion of interest in the study of consciousness as evidenced by numerous journal articles and books on the subject by writers from several different disciplines. But Western thought has been concerned with the aspects and functions of consciousness rather than with the essential nature of consciousness. That is simply this that Consciousness is the Reality of all that is; it is self-existent and self-luminous. William James (whose book *Principles of Psychology* was admired by Sri Aurobindo) in his celebrated essay "Does Consciousness Exist?" answered the question by saying that consciousness is real but as a function, not as an entity. Sri Aurobindo says exactly the opposite: Consciousness is not only an entity but *the* Entity; its various aspects and functions are its self-expressions by the exercise of its own inherent Conscious Force.

It may well be asked what the subject of yoga has to do with

a book on Sri Aurobindo's psychological thought. The answer
lies in the fact that Sri Aurobindo was first and foremost an integral yogi and spiritual mystic. While he was also a philosopher
who formulated in rational terms — as far as that was possible
— a comprehensive system of experiential concepts about the
nature of the supreme Reality, the world, man, evolution of
consciousness in the world with which is connected the subject
of the role of consciousness in that evolution and the goal to
which it is moving, still it must be clearly pointed out that Sri
Aurobindo was first a yogi and then a philosopher. For on his
own admission the materials of his philosophy were provided
by yogic experiences obtained by the practice of certain psychological disciplines and not by speculative thinking. What then
is yoga? Normally, practices such as physical postures, breath
control, meditation, repeating a name of God or of a word or
group of words, a *mantra*, etc. are understood as yoga. But
these are particular disciplines and not the essence of yoga.
According to Sri Aurobindo, yoga has the same relation with
the inner nature and being of man as the natural sciences have
with the forces of external nature like, say, steam or electricity. Yoga studies by repeated observation and experiment the
forces and movements of the human psyche, its mental, vital
and physical aspects, their mutual relation and influence. In the
process of this inner exploration yoga discovers many capacities
for knowledge, action and enjoyment which are not known to
"empirical" psychology, for that deals with the surface nature
of man. True, there is depth psychology but yoga avers that
its depth is not deep enough, and that there is or should be a
"height" psychology and a "breadth" psychology as well. For
yoga includes not only methods of discovering depths of consciousness but also of heightening and widening it. These are
not empty notions but actual facts discovered and effectuated
by yoga.

Sri Aurobindo has said that real psychology is the science
of consciousness. But consciousness in his experience is not only

mental intelligence and feeling. For mind is only one level of the multi-level reality called Consciousness. This brings us to the philosophy of Sri Aurobindo. The basic elements of Sri Aurobindo's philosophy, briefly stated, are as follows. There is a supreme, sovereign Reality which depends on nothing for its being; this independent Reality is self-luminous, that is, it is not revealed by anything other than itself. It is dynamic and becomes everything in the world, arranging itself in a hierarchical system. As independent Being it is called Sat, Existence, or less abstractly, the Existent. It is the inmost Reality of everything and as such is termed Self. As a self-luminous reality, it is designated Consciousness which is self-conscious. As a dynamic reality, it is known as Consciousness-Force. As Consciousness-Force it manifests itself on many levels. It is life in plants, instinct in insects and animals, mental intelligence, will and feeling in human beings and powers higher than mind in yogis and mystics. It has the power of self-determination and self-limitation. By the exercise of this power it becomes determinate things. By self-limitation it seems to become progressively less conscious until it becomes what Sri Aurobindo designates the Inconscient, which conceals consciousness to such an extent that it seems non-existent there, though in truth it is existent but only unmanifest. As the Existent-Conscious, Reality has three self-determined aspects: Self, Soul and God the Lord. As Self it remains in the background of the process of self-manifestation of the Reality; as Soul it is the Conscious Being who sanctions the creative adventure of the Consciousness-Force, and as the Lord it controls the process of the self-manifestation of the Reality. The true being in man is a portion of the supreme Reality and is called the soul or psychic being by Sri Aurobindo. The psychic being is of the same essence as God and is other than body, life and mind.

Further, Consciousness, descended into and self-hidden in the Inconscient, progressively manifests itself. Another way of stating it is that it evolves its own higher levels which brings about the emergence of Matter, Life and Mind in the world. The evolution of Mind, or mental beings, is a stage in this process of the unfolding of consciousness of the supreme Reality. The process is continuing and is in travail of the manifestation of a level of consciousness higher than mind, for mind is a power which is a seeker of knowledge, and in so far as it has knowledge it is partial and even that too it does not properly possess. The higher level of consciousness which is in the process of manifestation is termed the Supermind by Sri Aurobindo. It is the Reality's integral self-knowledge and world-knowledge coupled with infallible will. The supermind is not only the Knowledge-Will of the Reality, it is the medium of its self-manifestation as and in the world. To all intents and purposes, Existence-Consciousness-Force as the supermind is at the core of everything through different levels of its own being and power. From the point of view of the world and man, which are respectively the venue and the medium of evolution of consciousness, the supermind is unfolding itself and its manifestation will bring about the emergence of a new race of beings here on this earth who will be equipped with true knowledge of the Reality and of the world and the will to effectuate the fulfilment of God here. Man is or can be a conscious and willing collaborator in this process of the evolution of the superman. Mind is the medium of the unfolding of the supermind and through that of the unveiled manifestation of the now-concealed and only partly revealed Divine Being.

This revelation requires the transformation of Nature so that on all its levels, physical, vital and mental it may become conscious and spiritualised. The life of the supramental race of beings will be the Life Divine. The means of attaining this goal of evolution is the Integral Yoga which Sri Aurobindo practised and expounded and taught, not merely by an intellectual exposition of it but practically also by opening up the being and consciousness of his disciples and followers. Many of them are discovering and developing new horizons of knowing, acting and enjoying and are evolving already existing but to them new levels of consciousness and thereby attaining them.

I have written on the philosophy of Sri Aurobindo and not on his psychology because Dr. Dalal's book has done that admirably. And here I will say a word about the main difficulty in understanding the philosophy and the yoga on which it is based. Sri Aurobindo had to find many technical terms to describe his yogic experiences and to formulate them philosophically. But apart from the novel nomenclature devised by him to explain the different levels of consciousness in the universe and their corresponding levels in human beings, even the more well-known terms have different significances from those they ordinarily have. Consciousness, Spirit, Self, Soul, Mind, Life, etc. mean very different things from what they are taken to mean by the general reader and in other spiritual literature. Of these terms "spirit" has some affinity with the Christian notion of God. But the meaning of the others and of many other words in Sri Aurobindo's writings must be understood as he uses them in order to avoid confusion and misunderstanding. Soul, for example, is not the animating principle of life, nor the seat of emotions, nor the total personality. Self, *atman*, both universal and individual, is an experiential concept of Vedanta and of Sri Aurobindo which has no parallel in Western thought or religious literature. All this will be clear to the readers of this most useful guide to Sri Aurobindo's philosophy and psychology of yoga.

One word at the end. This work is primarily on the psychology of Sri Aurobindo which he himself described as metaphysical psychology. And to get even a preliminary idea of it, it is essential to have an initial understanding of Consciousness. What then is Consciousness? Let Sri Aurobindo answer this crucial question:

"But here in our world of Matter the original and fundamental phenomenon we meet everywhere is a universal Inconscience, Consciousness appears to come in as only an incident, a development, a strange consequence of some ill-understood operations of Energy in inconscient Matter. It arises out of an original Inconscience, it dissolves or sinks back into the Inconscience. Once it has appeared it persists indeed but as a general phenomenon precariously manifested in individual living beings. It has the seeming either of an uncertain freak of inconscient Nature, — a disease some would conjecture, a phosphorescence playing upon the stagnant waters of inconscient being, active at certain points of animation, or a guest in a world in which it is alien, a foreign resident with difficulty able to maintain itself in a hardly amicable environment and atmosphere.

According to the materialist hypothesis consciousness must be a result of energy in Matter; it is Matter's reaction or reflex to itself in itself, a response of organised inconscient chemical substance to touches upon it, a record of which that inconscient substance through some sensitiveness of cell and nerve becomes inexplicably aware. But such an explanation may account, — if we admit this impossible magic of the conscious response of an inconscient to the inconscient, — for sense and reflex action [yet it] becomes absurd if we try to explain by it thought and will, the imagination of the poet, the attention of the scientist, the reasoning of the philosopher. Call it mechanical cerebration, if you will, but no mere mechanism of grey stuff of brain can explain these things; a gland cannot write Hamlet or pulp of brain work out a system of metaphysics. There is no parity, kinship or visible equation between the alleged cause or agent on the one side and on the other the effect and its observable process. There is a gulf here that cannot be bridged by any stress of forcible affirmation or crossed by any stride of inference or violent leap of argumentative reason. Consciousness and an inconscient substance may be connected, may interpenetrate, may act on each other, but they are and remain things opposite, incommensurate with each other, fundamentally diverse. An observing and active consciousness emerging as a character of an eternal Inconscience is a self-contradictory affirmation, an unintelligible phenomenon, and the contradiction must be healed or explained before this affirmation can be accepted. But it cannot be healed unless either the Inconscient has a latent power for consciousness — and then its inconscience is phenomenal only, not fundamental, — or else is the veil of a Consciousness which emerges out of a state of involution which appears to us as an inconscience."[1].

Arabinda Basu

[1] Sri Aurobindo, *Essays Divine and Human* (Pondicherry: Sri Aurobindo Ashram, 1994), pp. 288–89

Part One

An Anthology of
Sri Aurobindo's Writings

The integral knowledge admits the valid truths of all views of existence, valid in their own field, but it seeks to get rid of their limitations and negations and to harmonise and reconcile these partial truths in a larger truth which fulfils all the many sides of our being in the one omnipresent Existence.

Sri Aurobindo

It is not by "thinking out" the entire reality, but by a change of consciousness that one can pass from the ignorance to the Knowledge — the Knowledge by which we become what we know. To pass from the external to a direct and intimate inner consciousness; to widen consciousness out of the limits of the ego and the body; to heighten it by an inner will and aspiration and opening to the Light till it passes in its ascent beyond Mind; to bring down a descent of the supramental Divine through self-giving and surrender with a consequent transformation of mind, life and body — this is the integral way to the Truth.

Sri Aurobindo

1
Consciousness the Reality

Materialism indeed insists that, whatever the extension of consciousness, it is a material phenomenon inseparable from our physical organs and not their utiliser but their result. This orthodox contention, however, is no longer able to hold the field against the tide of increasing knowledge. Its explanations are becoming more and more inadequate and strained. It is becoming always clearer that not only does the capacity of our total consciousness far exceed that of our organs, the senses, the nerves, the brain, but that even for our ordinary thought and consciousness these organs are only their habitual instruments and not their generators. Consciousness uses the brain which its upward strivings have produced, brain has not produced nor does it use the consciousness. There are even abnormal instances which go to prove that our organs are not entirely indispensable instruments, — that the heart-beats are not absolutely essential to life, any more than is breathing, nor the organised brain-cells to thought. Our physical organism no more causes or explains thought and consciousness than the construction of an engine causes or explains the motive-power of steam or electricity. The force is anterior, not the physical instrument.

Momentous logical consequences follow. In the first place we may ask whether, since even mental consciousness exists where we see inanimation and inertia, it is not possible that even in material objects a universal subconscient mind is present although unable to act or communicate itself to its surfaces for want of organs. Is the material state an emptiness of consciousness, or is it not rather only a sleep of consciousness — even though from the point of view of evolution an original and not an intermediate sleep? And by sleep the human example teaches us that we mean not a suspension of consciousness, but its gathering inward away from conscious physical response to the impacts of external things. And is not this what all existence is that has not yet developed means of outward communication with the external physical world? Is there not a Conscious Soul, a Purusha who wakes for ever even in all that sleeps?

We may go farther. When we speak of subconscious mind, we should mean by the phrase a thing not different from the outer mentality, but only acting below the surface, unknown to the waking man, in the same sense if perhaps with a deeper plunge and a larger scope. But the phenomena of the subliminal self far exceed the limits of any such definition. It includes an action not only immensely superior in capacity, but quite different in kind from what we know as mentality in our waking self. We have therefore a right to suppose that there is a superconscient in us as well as a subconscient, a range of conscious faculties and therefore an organisation of consciousness which rise high above that psychological stratum to which we give the name of mentality. And since the subliminal self in us thus rises in superconscience above mentality, may it not also sink in subconscience below mentality? Are there not in us and in the world forms of consciousness which are submental, to which we can give the name of vital and physical consciousness? If so, we must suppose in the plant and the metal also a force to which we can give the name of consciousness although it is not the human or animal mentality for which we have hitherto preserved the monopoly of that description.

Not only is this probable but, if we will consider things dispassionately, it is certain. In ourselves there is such a vital consciousness which acts in the cells of the body and the automatic vital functions so that we go through purposeful movements and obey attractions and repulsions to which our mind is a stranger. In animals this vital consciousness is an even more important factor. In plants it is intuitively evident. The seekings and shrinkings of the plant, its pleasure and pain, its sleep and its wakefulness and all that strange life whose truth an Indian scientist has brought to light by rigidly scientific methods, are all movements of consciousness, but, as far as we can see, not of mentality. There is then a sub-mental, a vital consciousness which has precisely the same initial reactions as the mental, but is different in the constitution of its self-experience, even as that which is superconscient is in the constitution of its self-experience different from the mental being.

Does the range of what we can call consciousness cease with the plant, with that in which we recognise the existence of a sub-animal life? If so, we must then suppose that there is a force of life and consciousness originally alien to Matter which has yet entered into and occupied Matter, — perhaps from another world.... The ancient thinkers believed in the existence of such other worlds,...[1] which perhaps sustain life and consciousness in ours or even call it out by their pressure, but do not create it by their entry. Nothing can evolve out of Matter which is not therein already contained.

But there is no reason to suppose that the gamut of life and consciousness fails and stops short in that which seems to us purely material. The development of recent research and thought seems to point to a sort of obscure beginning of life and perhaps a sort of inert or suppressed consciousness in the metal and in the earth and in other "inanimate" forms, or at least the first stuff of what becomes consciousness in us may be there. Only while in the plant can we dimly recognise and conceive the thing that I have called vital consciousness. The consciousness of Matter, of the inert form, is difficult indeed for us to understand or imagine, and what we find it difficult to understand or imagine we consider it our right to deny. Nevertheless, when one has pursued consciousness so far into the depths, it becomes incredible that there should be this sudden gulf in Nature. Thought has a right to suppose a unity where

---

[1] Supraphysical planes of existence. "Evolution comes by the unceasing pressure of the supra-material planes on the material compelling it to deliver out of itself their principles and powers which might conceivably otherwise have slept imprisoned in the rigidity of the material formula." — Sri Aurobindo (Ed.)

that unity is confessed by all other classes of phenomena and in one class only, not denied, but merely more concealed than in others. And if we suppose the unity to be unbroken, we then arrive at the existence of consciousness in all forms of the Force which is at work in the world. Even if there be no conscient or superconscient Purusha inhabiting all forms, yet is there in those forms a conscious force of being of which even their outer parts overtly or inertly partake.

Necessarily, in such a view, the word consciousness changes its meaning. It is no longer synonymous with mentality but indicates a self-aware force of existence of which mentality is a middle term; below mentality it sinks into vital and material movements which are for us subconscient; above, it rises into the supramental which is for us the superconscient. But in all it is one and the same thing organising itself differently. This is, once more, the Indian conception of Chit which, as energy, creates the worlds. Essentially, we arrive at that unity which materialistic Science perceives from the other end when it asserts that Mind cannot be another force than Matter, but must be merely development and outcome of material energy. Indian thought at its deepest affirms on the other hand that Mind and Matter are rather different grades of the same energy, different organisations of one conscious Force of Existence.

But what right have we to assume consciousness as the just description for this Force? For consciousness implies some kind of intelligence, purposefulness, self-knowledge, even though they may not take the forms habitual to our mentality. Even from this point of view everything supports rather than contradicts the idea of a universal conscious Force. We see, for instance, in the animal, operations of a perfect purposefulness and an exact, indeed a scientifically minute knowledge which are quite beyond the capacities of the animal mentality and which man himself can only acquire by long culture and education and even then uses with a much less sure rapidity. We are entitled to see in this general fact the proof of a conscious Force at work in the animal and the insect which is more intelligent, more purposeful, more aware of its intention, its ends, its means, its conditions than the highest mentality yet manifested in any individual form on earth. And in the operations of inanimate Nature we find the same pervading characteristic of a supreme hidden intelligence, "hidden in the modes of its own workings".

The only argument against a conscious and intelligent source for this purposeful work, this work of intelligence, of selection, adaptation and seeking is that large element in Nature's operations to which we give the name of waste. But obviously this is an objection based on the limitations of our human intellect which seeks to impose its own particular rationality, good enough for limited human ends, on the general operations of the World-Force. We see only part of Nature's purpose and all that does not subserve that part we call waste. Yet even our own human action is full of an apparent waste, so appearing from the individual point of view, which yet, we may be sure, subserves well enough the large and universal purpose of things. That part of her intention which we can detect, Nature gets done surely enough in spite of, perhaps really by virtue of her apparent waste. We may well trust to her in the rest which we do not yet detect.

For the rest, it is impossible to ignore the drive of set purpose, the guidance of apparent blind tendency, the sure eventual or immediate coming to the target sought, which characterise the operations of World-Force in the animal, in the plant, in inanimate things. So long as Matter was Alpha and Omega to the scientific mind, the reluctance to admit intelligence as the mother of intelligence was an honest scruple. But now it is no more than an outworn paradox to affirm the emergence of human consciousness, intelligence and mastery out of an unintelligent, blindly driving unconsciousness in which no form or substance of them previously existed. Man's consciousness can be nothing else than a form of Nature's consciousness. It is there in other involved forms below Mind, it emerges in Mind, it shall ascend into yet superior forms beyond Mind. For the Force that builds the worlds is a conscious Force, the Existence which manifests itself in them is conscious Being and a perfect emergence of its potentialities in form is the sole object which we can rationally conceive for its manifestation of this world of forms.

The Life Divine, pp. 85-90

Consciousness is not, to my experience, a phenomenon dependent on the reactions of personality to the forces of Nature and amounting to no more than a seeing or interpretation of these reactions. If that were so, then when the personality becomes silent and immobile and gives no reactions, as there would be no seeing or interpretative action, there would therefore be no consciousness. That contradicts some of the fundamental experiences of yoga, e.g., a silent and immobile consciousness infinitely spread out, not dependent on the personality but impersonal and universal, not seeing and interpreting contacts but motionlessly self-aware, not dependent on the reactions, but persistent in itself even when no reactions take place. The subjective personality itself is only a formation of consciousness which is a power inherent, not in the activity of the temporary manifested personality, but in the being, the Self or Purusha.

Consciousness is a reality inherent in existence. It is there even when it is not active on the surface, but silent and immobile; it is there even when it is invisible on the surface, not reacting on outward things or sensible to them, but withdrawn and either active or inactive within; it is there even when it seems to us to be quite absent and the being to our view unconscious and inanimate.

Consciousness is not only power of awareness of self and things, it is or has also a dynamic and creative energy. It can determine its own reactions or abstain from reactions; it can not only answer to forces, but create or put out from itself forces. Consciousness is Chit but also Chit Shakti.

Consciousness is usually identified with mind, but mental

consciousness is only the human range which no more exhausts all the possible ranges of consciousness than human sight exhausts all the gradations of colour or human hearing all the gradations of sound — for there is much above or below that is to man invisible and inaudible. So there are ranges of consciousness above and below the human range, with which the normal human has no contact and they seem to it unconscious, — supramental or overmental and submental ranges.

When Yajnavalkya says there is no consciousness in the Brahman state, he is speaking of consciousness as the human being knows it. The Brahman state is that of a supreme existence supremely aware of itself, *svayamprakāśa* , — it is Sachchidananda, Existence-Consciousness-Bliss. Even if it be spoken of as beyond That, *parātparam*, it does not mean that it is a state of Non-existence or Non-consciousness, but beyond even the highest spiritual substratum (the "foundation above" in the luminous paradox of the Rig Veda) of cosmic existence and consciousness. As it is evident from the description of Chinese Tao and the Buddhist Shunya that that is a Nothingness in which all is, so with the negation of consciousness here. Superconscient and subconscient are only relative terms; as we rise into the superconscient we see that it is a consciousness greater than the highest we yet have and therefore in our normal state inaccessible to us and, if we can go down into the subconscient, we find there a consciousness other than our own at its lowest mental limit and therefore ordinarily inaccessible to us. The Inconscient itself is only an involved state of consciousness which like the Tao or Shunya, though in a different way, contains all things suppressed within it so that under a pressure from above or within all can evolve out of it — "an inert Soul with a somnambulist Force."

The gradations of consciousness are universal states not dependent on the outlook of the subjective personality; rather the outlook of the subjective personality is determined by the grade of consciousness in which it is organised according to its typal nature or its evolutionary stage.

It will be evident that by consciousness is meant something which is essentially the same throughout but variable in status, condition and operation, in which in some grades or conditions the activities we call consciousness can exist either in a suppressed or an unorganised or a differently organised state; while in other states some other activities may manifest which in us are suppressed, unorganised or latent or else are less perfectly manifested, less intensive, extended and powerful than in those higher grades above our highest mental limit.

Letters on Yoga, pp. 233-35

Consciousness is a fundamental thing, the fundamental thing in existence — it is the energy, the motion, the movement of consciousness that creates the universe and all that is in it — not only the macrocosm but the microcosm is nothing but consciousness arranging itself. For instance, when consciousness in its movement or rather a certain stress of movement forgets itself in the action it becomes an apparently "unconscious" energy; when it forgets itself in the form it becomes the electron, the atom, the material object. In reality it is still consciousness that works in the energy and determines the form and the evolution of form. When it wants to liberate itself, slowly, evolutionarily, out of Matter, but still in the form, it emerges as life, as animal, as man and it can go on evolving itself still farther out of its involution and become something more than mere man. If you can grasp that, then it ought not to be difficult to see further that it can subjectively formulate itself as a physical, a vital, a mental, a psychic consciousness — all these are present in man, but as they are all mixed up together in the external consciousness with their real status behind in the inner being, one can only become fully aware of them by releasing the original limiting stress of the consciousness which makes us live in our external being and become awake and centred within in the inner being. As the consciousness in us, by its external concentration or stress, has to put all these things behind — behind a wall or veil, it has to break down the wall or veil and get back in its stress into these inner parts of existence — that is what we call living within; then our external being seems to us something small and superficial, we are or can become aware of the large and rich and inexhaustible kingdom within. So also consciousness in us has drawn a lid or covering or whatever one likes to call it between the lower planes of mind, life, body supported by the psychic and the higher planes which contain the spiritual kingdoms where the self is always free and limitless, and it can break or open the lid or covering and ascend there and become the Self free and wide and luminous or else bring down the influence, reflection, finally even the presence and power of the higher consciousness into the lower nature.

Now that is what consciousness is — it is not composed of parts, it is fundamental to being and itself formulates any parts it chooses to manifest — developing them from above downward by a progressive coming down from spiritual levels towards involution in Matter or formulating them in an upward working in the front by what we call evolution. If it chooses to work in you through the sense of ego, you think that it is the clear-cut individual "I" that does everything — if it begins to release itself from that limited working, you begin to expand your sense of "I" till it bursts into infinity and no longer exists or you shed it and flower into spiritual wideness. Of course, this is not what is spoken of in modern materialistic thought as consciousness, because that thought is governed by science[2] and sees consciousness only as a phenomenon that emerges out of inconscient Matter and consists of certain reactions of the system to outward things. But that is a phenomenon of consciousness, it is not consciousness itself, it is even only a very small part of the possible phenomenon of consciousness and can give no clue to Consciousness the Reality which is of the very essence of existence.   *Letters on Yoga, pp. 236-38*

---

[2] "Science" is here used in the narrow sense of what is based on positivism (Ed.)

2
The Manifold Being

Self-knowledge is impossible unless we go behind our surface existence, which is a mere result of selective outer experiences, an imperfect sounding-board or a hasty, incompetent and fragmentary translation of a little out of the much that we are, — unless we go behind this and send down our plummet into the subconscient and open ourself to the superconscient so as to know their relation to our surface being. For between these three things our existence moves and finds in them its totality.

The Life Divine, p.223

...he [man] is aware only of a small part of his own being: his surface mentality, his surface life, his surface physical being is all that he knows and he does not know even all of that; below is the occult surge of his subconscious and subliminal mind, his subconscious and his subliminal life impulses, his subconscious corporeality, all that large part of himself which he does not know and cannot govern, but which rather knows and governs him. For, existence and consciousness and force being one, we can only have some real power over so much of our existence as we are identified with by self-awareness; the rest must be governed by its own consciousness which is subliminal to our surface mind and life and body. And yet, the two being one movement and not two separate movements, the larger and more potent part of ourselves must govern and determine in the mass the smaller and less powerful; therefore we are governed by the subconscient and subliminal even in our conscious existence and in our very self-mastery and self-direction we are only instruments of what seems to us the Inconscient within us.

The Life Divine, p. 212

...what we know of ourselves, our present conscious existence, is only a representative formation, a superficial activity, a changing external result of a vast mass of concealed existence. Our visible life and the actions of that life are no more than a series of significant expressions, but that which it tries to express is not on the surface; our existence is something much larger than this apparent frontal being which we suppose ourselves to be and which we offer to the world around us. This frontal and external being is a confused amalgam of mind-formations, life-movements, physical functionings of which even an exhaustive analysis into its component parts and machinery fails to reveal the whole secret. It is only when we go behind, below, above into the hidden stretches of our being that we can know it; the most thorough and acute surface scrutiny and manipulation cannot give us the true understanding or the completely effective control of our life, its purposes, its activities; that inability indeed is the cause of the failure of reason, morality and every other surface action to control and deliver and perfect the life of the human race. For below even our most obscure physical consciousness is a subconscious being in which as in a covering and supporting soil are all manner of hidden seeds that sprout up, unaccountably to us, on our surface and into which we are constantly throwing fresh seeds that prolong our past and will influence our future, — a subconscious being, obscure, small in its motions, capriciously and almost fantastically subrational, but of an immense potency for the earth-life. Again behind our mind, our life, our conscious physical there is a larger subliminal consciousness, — there are inner mental, inner vital, inner more subtle physical reaches supported by an inmost psychic existence which is the connecting soul of all the rest; and in these hidden reaches too lie a mass of numerous pre-existent personalities which supply the material, the motive-forces, the impulsions of our developing surface existence. For in each one of us here there may be one central person, but also a multitude of subordinate personalities created by the past history of its manifestation or by expressions of it on these inner planes which support its present play in this external material cosmos. And while on our surface we are cut off from all around us except through an exterior mind and sense-contact which delivers but little of us to our world or of our world to us, in these inner reaches the barrier between us and the rest of existence is thin and easily broken; there we can feel at once — not merely infer from their results, but feel directly the action of the secret world-forces, mind-forces, life-forces, subtle physical forces that constitute universal and individual existence; we shall even be able, if we will but train ourselves to it, to lay our hands on these world-forces that throw themselves on us or surround us and more and more to control or at least strongly modify their action on us and others, their formations, their very movements. Yet again, above our human mind are still greater reaches superconscient to it and from there secretly descend influences, powers, touches which are the original determinants of things here and, if they were called down in their fullness, could altogether alter the whole make and economy of life in the material universe.

The Synthesis of Yoga, pp.170-72

...there are three elements in the totality of our being: there is the submental and the subconscient which appears to us as if it were inconscient, comprising the material basis and a good part of our life and body; there is the subliminal, which comprises the inner being, taken in its entirety of inner mind, inner life, inner physical with the soul or psychic entity supporting them; there is this waking consciousness which the subliminal and the subconscient throw up on the surface, a wave of their secret surge. But even this is not an adequate account of what we are; for there is not only something deep within behind our normal self-awareness, but something also high above it: that too is ourselves, other than our surface mental personality, but not outside our true self; that too is a country of our spirit. For the subliminal proper is no more than the inner being on the level of the Knowledge-Ignorance luminous, powerful and extended indeed beyond the poor conception of our waking mind, but still not the supreme or the whole sense of our being, not its ultimate mystery.   *The Life Divine, pp. 560-61*

...as Being is one yet multiple, so also the same law prevails in ourselves and our members; the Spirit, the Purusha is one but it adapts itself to the formations of Nature. Over each grade of our being a power of the Spirit presides; we have within us and discover when we go deep enough inwards a mind-self, a life-self, a physical self; there is a being of mind, a mental Purusha, expressing something of itself on our surface in the thoughts, perceptions, activities of our mind-nature, a being of life which expresses something of itself in the impulses, feelings, sensations, desires, external life-activities of our vital nature, a physical be-ing, a being of the body which expresses something of itself in the instincts, habits, formulated activities of our physical nature. These beings or part selves of the self in us are powers of the Spirit and therefore not limited by their temporary expression, for what is thus formulated is only a fragment of its possibilities; but the expression creates a temporary mental, vital or physical personality which grows and develops even as the psychic being or soul-personality grows and develops within us. Each has its own distinct nature, its influence, its action on the whole of us; but on our surface all these influences and all this action, as they come up, mingle and create an aggregate surface being which is a composite, an amalgam of them all, an outer persistent and yet shifting and mobile formation for the purposes of this life and its limited experience.

But this aggregate is, because of its composition, a hetero-geneous compound, not a single harmonious and homogeneous whole. This is the reason why there is a constant confusion and even a conflict in our members which our mental reason and will are moved to control and harmonise and have often much difficulty in creating out of their confusion or conflict some kind of order and guidance; even so, ordinarily, we drift too much or

are driven by the stream of our nature and act from whatever in it comes uppermost at the time and seizes the instruments of thought and action, — even our seemingly deliberate choice is more of an automatism than we imagine; our co-ordination of our multifarious elements and of our consequent thoughts, feelings, impulses, actions by the reason and will is incomplete and a half- measure. In animal being Nature acts by her own mental and vital intuitions; she works out an order by the compulsion of habit and instinct which the animal implicitly obeys, so that the shiftings of its consciousness do not matter. But man cannot altogether act in the same way without forfeiting his prerogative of manhood; he cannot leave his being to be a chaos of instincts and impulses regulated by the automatism of Nature: mind has become conscious in him and is therefore self-compelled to make some attempt, however elementary in many, to see and control and in the end more and more perfectly harmonise the manifold components, the different and conflicting tendencies that seem to make up his surface being. He does succeed in setting up a sort of regulated chaos or ordered confusion in him, or at least succeeds in thinking that he is directing himself by his mind and will, even though in fact that direction is only partial; for not only a disparate consortium of habitual motive-forces but also newly emergent vital and physical tendencies and impulses, not always calculable or controllable, and many incoherent and inharmonious mental elements use his reason and will, enter into and determine his self-building, his nature-development, his life action. Man is in his self a unique Person, but he is also in his manifestation of self a multiperson; he will never succeed in being master of himself until the Person imposes itself on his multipersonality and governs it: but this can only be imperfectly done by the surface mental will and reason; it can be perfectly done only if he goes within and finds whatever central being is by its predominant influence at the head of all his expression and action. In inmost truth it is his soul that is this central being, but in outer fact it is often one or other of the part beings in him that rules, and this representative of the soul, this deputy self he can mistake for the inmost soul-principle.

This rule of different selves in us is at the root of the stages of the development of human personality... and we can reconsider them now from the point of view of the government of the nature by the inner principle. In some human beings it is the physical Purusha, the being of body, who dominates the mind, will and action; there is then created the physical man mainly occupied with his corporeal life and habitual needs, impulses, life-habits, mind-habits, body-habits, looking very little or not at all beyond that, subordinating and restricting all his other tendencies and possibilities to that narrow formation. But even in the physical man there are other elements and he cannot live altogether as the human animal concerned with birth and death and procreation and the satisfaction of common impulses and desires and the maintenance of the life and the body: this is his normal type of personality, but it is crossed, however feebly, with influences by which he can proceed, if they are developed, to a higher human evolution. If the inner subtle-physical Purusha insists, he can arrive at the idea of a finer, more beautiful and perfect physical life and hope or attempt to realise it in his own or in the collective or group existence. In others it is the vital self, the being of life, who dominates and rules the mind, the will, the action; then is created the vital man, concerned with self-affirmation, self-aggrandisement, life-enlargement, satisfaction of ambition and passion and impulse and desire, the claims of his ego, domi-nation, power, excitement, battle and struggle, inner and outer adventure: all else is incidental or subordinated to this movement and building and expression of the vital ego. But still in the vital man too there are or can be other elements of a growing mental or spiritual character, even if these happen to be less developed than his life-personality and life-power. The nature of the vital man is more active, stronger and more mobile, more turbulent and chaotic, often to the point of being quite unregulated, than that of the physical man who holds on to the soil and has a certain material poise and balance, but it is more kinetic and creative: for the element of the vital being is not earth but air; it has more movement, less status. A vigorous vital mind and will can grasp and govern the kinetic vital energies, but it is more by a forceful compulsion and constraint than by a harmonisation of the being. If, however, a strong vital personality, mind and will can get the reasoning intelligence to give it a firm support and be its minister, then a certain kind of forceful formation can be made, more or less balanced but always powerful, successful and effective, which can impose itself on the nature and environment and arrive at a strong self-affirmation in life and action. This is the second step of harmonised formulation possible in the ascent of the nature.

At a higher stage of the evolution of personality the being of mind may rule; there is then created the mental man who lives predominantly in the mind as the others live in the vital or the physical nature. The mental man tends to subordinate to his mental self-expression, mental aims, mental interests or to a mental idea or ideal the rest of his being: because of the difficulty of this subordination and its potent effect when achieved, it is at once more difficult for him and easier to arrive at a harmony of his nature. It is easier because the mental will once in control can convince by the power of the reasoning intelligence and at the same time dominate, compress or suppress the life and the body and their demands, arrange and harmonise them, force them to be its instruments, even reduce them to a minimum so that they shall not disturb the mental life or pull it down from its ideative or idealising movement. It is more difficult because life and body are the first powers and, if they are in the least strong, can impose themselves with an almost irresistible insistence on the mental ruler. Man is a mental being and the mind is the leader of his life and body; but this is a leader who is much led by his followers and has sometimes no other will than what they impose on him. Mind in spite of its power is often impotent before the inconscient and subconscient which obscure its clarity and carry it away on the tide of instinct or impulse; in spite of its clarity it is fooled by vital and emotional suggestions into giving sanction to ignorance and error, to wrong thought and to wrong action, or it is obliged to look on while the nature follows what it knows to be wrong, dangerous or evil. Even when it is strong and clear and dominant, Mind, though it imposes a certain, a considerable mentalised harmony, cannot integrate the whole being and nature. These harmonisations by an inferior control are, besides, inconclusive, because it is one part of the nature which dominates and fulfils itself while the others are coerced and denied their fullness. They can be steps on the way, but not final; therefore in most men there is no such sole dominance and effected partial harmony, but only a predominance and for the rest an unstable equilibrium of a personality half formed, half in formation, sometimes a disequilibrium or unbalance due to the lack of a central government or the disturbance of a formerly achieved partial poise. All must be transitional until a first, though not a final, true harmonisation is achieved by finding our real centre. *The Life Divine, pp. 896-900*

3
The Surface Being
and the Inner Being

The very first step in getting out of the ignorance is to accept the fact that this outer consciousness is not one's soul, not oneself, not the real person, but only a temporary formation on the surface for the purposes of the surface play. The soul, the person is within, not on the surface — the outer personality is the person only in the first sense of the Latin word *persona* which meant originally a mask.   *Letters on Yoga, pp. 304-05*

Our surface existence is only a surface and it is there that there is the full reign of the Ignorance; to know we have to go within ourselves and see with an inner knowledge. All that is formulated on the surface is a small and diminished representation of our secret greater existence. The immobile self in us is found only when the outer mental and vital activities are quieted; for since it is seated deep within and is represented on the surface only by the intuitive sense of self-existence and misrepresented by the mental, vital, physical ego-sense, its truth has to be experienced in the mind's silence. But also the dynamic parts of our surface being are similarly diminished figures of greater things that are there in the depths of our secret nature. The surface memory itself is a fragmentary and ineffective action pulling out details from an inner subliminal memory which receives and records all our world-experience, receives and records even what the mind has not observed, understood or noticed. Our surface imagination is a selection from a vaster more creative and effective subliminal image-building power of consciousness. A mind with immeasurably wider and more subtle perceptions, a life-energy with a greater dynamism, a subtle-physical substance with a larger and finer receptivity are building out of themselves our surface evolution. A psychic entity is there behind these occult activities which is the true support of our individualisation; the ego is only an outward false substitute: for it is this secret soul that supports and holds together our self-experience and world-experience; the mental, vital, physical, external ego is a superficial construction of Nature. It is only when we have seen both our self and our nature as a whole, in the depths as well as on the surface, that we can acquire a true basis of knowledge.

The Life Divine, p. 523

A superficial observation of our waking consciousness shows us that of a great part of our individual being and becoming we are quite ignorant; it is to us the Inconscient, just as much as the life of the plant, the metal, the earth, the elements. But if we carry our knowledge farther, pushing psychological experiment and observation beyond their normal bounds, we find how vast is the sphere of this supposed Inconscient or this subconscient in our total existence, — the subconscient, so seeming and so called by us because it is a concealed consciousness, — and what a small and fragmentary portion of our being is covered by our waking self-awareness. We arrive at the knowledge that our waking mind and ego are only a superimposition upon a submerged, a subliminal self, — for so that self appears to us, — or, more accurately, an inner being, with a much vaster capacity of experience; our mind and ego are like the crown and dome of a temple jutting out from the waves while the great body of the building is submerged under the surface of the waters.

This concealed self and consciousness is our real or whole being, of which the outer is a part and a phenomenon, a selective formation for a surface use. We perceive only a small number of the contacts of things which impinge upon us; the inner being perceives all that enters or touches us and our environment. We perceive only a part of the workings of our life and being; the inner being perceives so much that we might almost suppose that nothing escapes its view. We remember only a small selection from our perceptions, and of these even we keep a great part in a store-room where we cannot always lay our hand upon what we need; the inner being retains everything that it has ever received and has it always ready to hand. We can form into co-ordinated understanding and knowledge only so much of our perceptions and memories as our trained intelligence and mental capacity can grasp in their sense and appreciate in their relations: the intelligence of the inner being needs no training, but preserves the accurate form and relations of all its perceptions and memories and, — though this is a proposition which may be considered doubtful or difficult to concede in its fullness, — can grasp immediately, when it does not possess already, their significance. And its perceptions are not confined, as are ordinarily those of the waking mind, to the scanty gleanings of the physical senses, but extend far beyond and use, as telepathic phenomena of many kinds bear witness, a subtle sense the limits of which are too wide to be easily fixed. The relations between the surface will or impulsion and the subliminal urge, mistakenly described as unconscious or subconscious, have not been properly studied except in regard to unusual and unorganised manifestations and to certain morbidly abnormal phenomena of the diseased human mind; but if we pursue our observation far enough, we shall find that the cognition and will or impulsive force of the inner being really stand behind the whole conscious becoming; the latter represents only that part of its secret endeavour and achievement which rises successfully to the surface of our life. To know our inner being is the first step towards a real self-knowledge.   *The Life Divine, pp. 555-57*

There is an inner as well as an outer consciousness all through our being, upon all its levels. The ordinary man is aware only of his surface self and quite unaware of all that is concealed by the surface. And yet what is on the surface, what we know or think we know of ourselves and even believe that that is all we are, is only a small part of our being and by far the larger part of us is below the surface. Or, more accurately, it is behind the frontal consciousness, behind the veil, occult and known only by an occult knowledge. Modern psychology and psychic science have begun to perceive this truth just a little. Materialistic psychology calls this hidden part the Inconscient,[1] although practically admitting that it is far greater, more powerful and profound than the surface conscious self, — very much as the Upanishads called the superconscient in us the Sleep-self, although this Sleep-self is said to be an infinitely greater Intelligence, omniscient, omnipotent, Prajna, the Ishwara. Psychic science calls this hidden consciousness the subliminal self, and here too it is seen that this subliminal self has more powers, more knowledge, a freer field of movement than the smaller self that is on the surface. But the truth is that all this that is behind, this sea of which our waking consciousness is only a wave or series of waves, cannot be described by any one term, for it is very complex. Part of it is subconscient, lower than our waking consciousness, part of it is on a level with it but behind and much larger than it; part is above and superconscient to us. What we call our mind is only an outer mind, a surface mental action, instrumental for the partial expression of a larger mind behind of which we are not ordinarily aware and can only know by going inside ourselves. So too what we know of the vital in us is only the outer vital, a surface activity partially expressing a larger secret vital which we can only know by going within. Equally, what we call our physical being is only a visible projection of a greater and subtler invisible physical consciousness which is much more complex, much more aware, much wider in its receptiveness, much more open and plastic and free.   *Letters on Yoga, pp. 348-49*

There are always two different consciousnesses in the human being, one outward in which he ordinarily lives, the other inward and concealed of which he knows nothing. When one

---

[1] The "unconscious" in modern psychology connotes "a level of mind lacking in awareness". (Arthur S. Reber, *The Penguin Dictionary of Psychology* (Ed.)

does sadhana, the inner consciousness begins to open and one is able to go inside and have all kinds of experiences there. As the sadhana progresses, one begins to live more and more in this inner being and the outer becomes more and more superficial. At first the inner consciousness seems to be the dream and the outer the waking reality. Afterwards the inner consciousness becomes the reality and the outer is felt by many as a dream or delusion, or else as something superficial and external. The inner consciousness begins to be a place of deep peace, light, happiness, love, closeness to the Divine or the presence of the Divine, the Mother. One is then aware of two consciousnesses, the inner one and the outer which has to be changed into its counterpart and instrument — that also must become full of peace, light, union with the Divine.   *Letters on Yoga, p. 307*

The outer consciousness is shut up in the body limitations and in the little bit of personal mind and sense dependent on the body — it sees only the outward, sees only things. But the inner consciousness can see behind the thing, it is aware of the play of forces, personal or universal — for it is in conscious touch with the universal action.   *Letters on Yoga, p. 312*

...nothing is more difficult than to bring home the greatness and uplifting power of the spiritual consciousness to the natural man forming the vast majority of the race; for his mind and senses are turned outward towards the external calls of life and its objects and never inwards to the Truth which lies behind them. This external vision and attraction are the essence of the universal blinding force which is designated in Indian philosophy the Ignorance. Ancient Indian spirituality recognised that man lives in the Ignorance and has to be led through its imperfect indications to a highest inmost knowledge. Our life moves between two worlds, the depths upon depths of our inward being and the surface field of our outward nature. The majority of men put the whole emphasis of life on the outward and live very strongly in their surface consciousness and very little in the inward existence. Even the choice spirits raised from the grossness of the common vital and physical mould by the stress of thought and culture do not usually get farther than a strong dwelling on the things of the mind. The highest flight they reach — and it is this that the West persistently mistakes for spirituality — is a preference for living in the mind and emotions more than in the gross outward life or else an attempt to subject this rebellious life-stuff to the law of intellectual truth or ethical reason and will or aesthetic beauty or of all three together. But spiritual knowledge perceives that there is a greater thing in us; our inmost self, our real being is not the intellect, not the aesthetic, ethical or thinking mind, but the divinity within, the Spirit, and these other things are only the instruments of the Spirit.   *The Foundations of Indian Culture, p. 139*

On the surface we know only so much of our self as is formulated there and of even this only a portion; for we see our total surface being in a general vagueness dotted and sectioned by points or figures of precision: even what we discover by a mental introspection is only a sum of sections; the entire figure and sense of our personal formation escapes our notice. But there is also a distorting action which obscures and disfigures even this limited self-knowledge; our self-view is vitiated by the constant impact and intrusion of our outer life-self, our vital being, which seeks always to make the thinking mind its tool and servant: for our vital being is not concerned with self-knowledge but with self-affirmation, desire, ego. It is therefore constantly acting on mind to build for it a mental structure of apparent self that will serve these purposes; our mind is persuaded to present to us and to others a partly fictitious representative figure of ourselves which supports our self-affirmation, justifies our desires and actions, nourishes our ego. This vital intervention is not indeed always in the direction of self-justification and assertion; it turns sometimes towards self-depreciation and a morbid and exaggerated

self-criticism: but this too is an ego-structure, a reverse or negative egoism, a poise or pose of the vital ego. For in this vital ego
there is frequently a mixture of the charlatan and mountebank,
the poser and actor; it is constantly taking up a role and playing
it to itself and to others as its public. An organised self-deception
is thus added to an organised self-ignorance; it is only by going
within and seeing these things at their source that we can get
out of this obscurity and tangle.

For a larger mental being is there within us, a larger inner
vital being, even a larger inner subtle-physical being other than
our surface body-consciousness, and by entering into this or
becoming it, identifying ourselves with it, we can observe the
springs of our thoughts and feelings, the sources and motives
of our action, the operative energies that build up our surface
personality. For we discover and can know the inner being that
secretly thinks and perceives in us, the vital being that secretly
feels and acts upon life through us, the subtle-physical being that
secretly receives and responds to the contacts of things through
our body and its organs. Our surface thought, feeling, emotion
is a complexity and confusion of impulsions from within and
impacts from outside us; our reason, our organising intelligence
can impose on it only an imperfect order: but here within we find
the separate sources of our mental, our vital and our physical
energisms and can see clearly the pure operations, the distinct
powers, the composing elements of each and their interplay in
a clear light of self-vision. We find that the contradictions and
the struggles of our surface consciousness are largely due to the
contrary or mutually discordant tendencies of our mental, vital
and physical parts opposing and unreconciled with each other
and these again to the discord of many different inner possibilities of our being and even of different personalities on each level
in us which are behind the intermixed disposition and differing
tendencies of our surface nature. But while on the surface their
action is mixed together, confused and conflicting, here in our
depths they can be seen and worked upon in their independent

and separate nature and action and a harmonisation of them by the mental being in us, leader of the life and body, — or, better, by the central psychic entity, — is not so difficult, provided we have the right psychic and mental will in the endeavour: for if it is with the vital-ego motive that we make the entry into the subliminal being, it may result in serious dangers and disaster or at the least an exaggeration of ego, self-affirmation and desire, an enlarged and more powerful ignorance instead of an enlarged and more powerful knowledge. Moreover, we find in this inner or subliminal being the means of directly distinguishing between what rises from within and what comes to us from outside, from others or from universal Nature, and it becomes possible to exercise a control, a choice, a power of willed reception, rejection and selection, a clear power of self-building and harmonisation which we do not possess or can operate very imperfectly in our composed surface personality but which is the prerogative of our inner Person. For by this entry into the depths the inner being, no longer quite veiled, no longer obliged to exercise a fragmentary influence on its outer instrumental consciousness, is able to formulate itself more luminously in our life in the physical universe. *The Life Divine, pp. 532-34*

4
The Inconscient

A spiritual evolution, an evolution of consciousness in Matter in a constant developing self-formation till the form can reveal the indwelling Spirit, is ... the key-note, the central significant motive of the terrestrial existence. This significance is concealed at the outset by the involution of the Spirit, the Divine Reality, in a dense material Inconscience; a veil of Inconscience, a veil of insensibility of Matter hides the universal Consciousness-Force which works within it, so that the Energy, which is the first form the Force of creation assumes in the physical universe, appears to be itself inconscient and yet does the works of a vast occult Intelligence. The obscure mysterious creatrix ends indeed by delivering the secret consciousness out of its thick and tenebrous prison; but she delivers it slowly, little by little, in minute infinitesimal drops, in thin jets, in small vibrant concretions of energy and substance, of life, of mind, as if that were all she could get out through the crass obstacle, the dull reluctant medium of an inconscient stuff of existence. At first she houses herself in forms of Matter which appear to be altogether unconscious, then struggles towards mentality in the guise of living Matter and attains to it imperfectly in the conscious animal. This consciousness is at first rudimentary, mostly a half subconscious or just conscious instinct; it develops slowly till in more organised forms of living Matter it reaches its climax of intelligence and exceeds itself in Man, the thinking animal who develops into the reasoning mental being but carries along with him even at his highest elevation the mould of original animality, the dead weight of subconscience of body, the downward pull of gravitation towards the original Inertia and Nescience, the control of an inconscient material Nature over his conscious evolution, its power for limitation, its law of difficult development, its immense force for retardation and frustration. This control by the original Inconscience over the consciousness emerging from it takes the general shape of a mentality struggling towards knowledge but itself, in what seems to be its fundamental nature, an Ignorance. Thus hampered and burdened, mental man has still to evolve out of himself the fully conscious being, a divine manhood or a spiritual and supramental supermanhood which shall be the next product of the evolution. That transition will mark the passage from the evolution in the Ignorance to a greater evolution in the Knowledge, founded and proceeding in the light of the Superconscient and no longer in the darkness of the Ignorance and Inconscience.   *The Life Divine, pp. 824-25*

The Inconscience is an inverse reproduction of the supreme superconscience: it has the same absoluteness of being and automatic action, but in a vast involved trance; it is being lost in itself, plunged in its own abyss of infinity. Instead of a luminous absorption in self-existence there is a tenebrous involution in it, the darkness veiled within darkness of the Rig Veda, *tama āsīt tamasā gūḍham*, which makes it look like Non-Existence; instead of a luminous inherent self-awareness there is a consciousness plunged into an abyss of self-oblivion, inherent in being but not awake in being. Yet is this involved consciousness still a concealed knowledge by identity; it carries in it the awareness of all the truths of existence hidden in its dark infinite and, when it acts and creates, — but it acts first as Energy and not as Consciousness, — everything is arranged with the precision and perfection of an intrinsic knowledge. In all material things reside a mute and involved Real-Idea, a substantial and self-effective intuition, an eyeless exact perception, an automatic intelligence working out its unexpressed and unthought conceptions, a blindly seeing sureness of sight, a dumb infallible sureness of suppressed feeling coated in insensibility, which effectuate all that has to be effected. All this state and action of the Inconscient corresponds very evidently with the same state and action of the pure Superconscience, but translated into terms of self-darkness in place of the original self-light. Intrinsic in the material form, these powers are not possessed by the form, but yet work in its mute subconscience.   *The Life Divine, p. 550*

The world is a manifestation of the Real and therefore is itself real. The reality is the infinite and eternal Divine, infinite and eternal Being, Consciousness-Force and Bliss. This Divine by his power has created the world or rather manifested it in his own infinite Being. But here in the material world or at its basis he has hidden himself in what seem to be his opposites, Non-Being, Inconscience and Insentience. This is what we nowadays call the Inconscient which seems to have created the material universe by its inconscient Energy, but this is only an appearance, for we find in the end that all the dispositions of the world can only have been arranged by the working of a supreme secret Intelligence. The Being which is hidden in what seems to be an inconscient void emerges in the world first in Matter, then in Life, then in Mind and finally as the Spirit. The apparently inconscient Energy which creates is in fact the Consciousness-Force of the Divine and its aspect of consciousness, secret in Matter, begins to emerge in Life, finds something more of itself in Mind and finds its true self in a spiritual consciousness and finally a supra-mental Consciousness through which we become aware of the Reality, enter into it and unite ourselves with it. This is what we call evolution which is an evolution of Consciousness and an evolution of the Spirit in things and only outwardly an evolution of species. Thus also, the delight of existence emerges from the original insentience, first in the contrary forms of pleasure and pain, and then has to find itself in the bliss of the Spirit or, as it is called in the Upanishads, the bliss of the Brahman.

Letters on Yoga, p. 44

...in its actual cosmic manifestation the Supreme, being the Infinite and not bound by any limitation, can manifest in Itself, in its consciousness of innumerable possibilities, something that

seems to be the opposite of itself, something in which there can
be Darkness, Inconscience, Inertia, Insensibility, Disharmony
and Disintegration. It is this that we see at the basis of the
material world and speak of nowadays as the Inconscient —
the Inconscient Ocean of the Rigveda in which the One was
hidden and arose in the form of this universe — or, as it is
sometimes called, the non-being, Asat. The Ignorance which
is the characteristic of our mind and life is the result of this
origin in the Inconscience. Moreover, in the evolution out of
inconscient existence there rise up naturally powers and beings
which are interested in the maintenance of all negations of the
Divine, error and unconsciousness, pain, suffering, obscurity,
death, weakness, illness, disharmony, evil. Hence the perversion
of the manifestation here, its inability to reveal the true essence of
the Divine. Yet in this very base of this evolution all that is divine
is there involved and pressing to evolve, Light, Consciousness,
Power, Perfection, Beauty, Love. For in the Inconscient itself and
behind the perversions of the Ignorance the Divine Consciousness lies concealed and works and must more and more appear,
throwing off in the end its disguises. That is why it is said that
the world is called to express the Divine.   *Letters on Yoga, p. 9*

All aspects of the omnipresent Reality have their fundamental
truth in the Supreme Existence. Thus even the aspect or power of
Inconscience, which seems to be an opposite, a negation of the
eternal Reality, yet corresponds to a Truth held in itself by the
self-aware and all-conscious Infinite. It is, when we look closely
at it, the Infinite's power of plunging the consciousness into a
trance of self-involution, a self-oblivion of the Spirit veiled in
its own abysses where nothing is manifest but all inconceivably
is and can emerge from that ineffable latency. In the heights of
Spirit this state of cosmic or infinite trance-sleep appears to our
cognition as a luminous uttermost Superconscience: at the other
end of being it offers itself to cognition as the Spirit's potency
of presenting to itself the opposites of its own truths of being,

— an abyss of non-existence, a profound Night of inconscience, a fathomless swoon of insensibility from which yet all forms of being, consciousness and delight of existence can manifest themselves, — but they appear in limited terms, in slowly emerging and increasing self-formulations, even in contrary terms of themselves; it is the play of a secret all-being, all-delight, all-knowledge, but it observes the rules of its own self-oblivion, self-opposition, self-limitation until it is ready to surpass it. This is the Inconscience and Ignorance that we see at work in the material universe. It is not a denial, it is one term, one formula of the infinite and eternal Existence.   *The Life Divine, pp. 318-19*

The body... is a creation of the Inconscient and itself inconscient or at least subconscient in parts of itself and much of its hidden action; but what we call the Inconscient is an appearance, a dwelling place, an instrument of a secret Consciousness or a Superconscient which has created the miracle we call the universe. Matter is the field and the creation of the Inconscient and the perfection of the operations of inconscient Matter, their perfect adaptation of means to an aim and end, the wonders they perform and the marvels of beauty they create, testify, in spite of all the ignorant denial we can oppose, to the presence and power of consciousness of this Superconscience in every part and movement of the material universe. It is there in the body, has made it and its emergence in our consciousness is the secret aim of evolution and the key to the mystery of our existence.

The Supramental Manifestation and Other Writings, pp.10-11

5
The Subconscient

The subconscious in us is the extreme border of our secret inner existence where it meets the Inconscient, it is a degree of our being in which the Inconscient struggles into a half-consciousness;... Or, from another viewpoint, this nether part of us may be described as the antechamber of the Inconscient.

The Life Divine, pp. 422-23

...we mean by the subconscient that quite submerged part of our being in which there is no wakingly conscious and coherent thought, will or feeling or organized reaction, but which yet receives obscurely the impressions of all things and stores them up in itself and from it too all sorts of stimuli, of persistent habitual movements, crudely repeated or disguised in strange forms can surge up into dream or into the waking nature. For if these impressions rise up most in dream in an incoherent and disorganized manner, they can also and do rise up into our waking consciousness as a mechanical repetition of old thoughts, old mental, vital and physical habits or an obscure stimulus to sensations, actions, emotions which do not originate in or from our conscious thought or will and are even often opposed to its perceptions, choice or dictates. In the subconscient there is an obscure mind full of obstinate Sanskaras, impressions, associations, fixed notions, habitual reactions formed by our past, an obscure vital full of the seeds of habitual desires, sensations and nervous reactions, a most obscure material which governs much that has to do with the condition of the body. It is largely responsible for our illnesses; chronic or repeated illnesses are indeed mainly due to the subconscient and its obstinate memory and habit of repetition of whatever has impressed itself upon the body-consciousness.

Letters on Yoga, p. 353

The subconscient in the ordinary man includes the larger part of the vital being and the physical mind and also the secret body-consciousness.   *Letters on Yoga, p. 898*

The subconscient is universal as well as individual like all the other main parts of the Nature. But there are different parts or planes of the subconscient. All upon earth is based on the Inconscient as it is called, though it is not really inconscient at all, but rather a complete "sub"-conscience, a suppressed or involved consciousness, in which there is everything but nothing is formulated or expressed. The subconscient lies between this Inconscient and the conscious mind, life and body. It contains the potentiality of all the primitive reactions to life which struggle out to the surface from the dull and inert strands of Matter and form by a constant development a slowly evolving and self-formulating consciousness; it contains them not as ideas, perceptions or conscious reactions but as the fluid substance of these things. But also all that is consciously experienced sinks down into the subconscient, not as precise though submerged memories but as obscure yet obstinate impressions of experience, and these can come up at any time as dreams, as mechanical repetitions of past thought, feelings, action, etc., as "complexes" exploding into action and event, etc., etc. The subconscient is the main cause why all things repeat themselves and nothing ever gets changed except in appearance. It is the cause why people say character cannot be changed, the cause also of the constant return of things one hoped to have got rid of for ever. All seeds are there and all Sanskaras of the mind, vital and body, — it is the main support of death and disease and the last fortress (seemingly impregnable) of the Ignorance. All too that is suppressed without being wholly got rid of sinks down there and remains as seed ready to surge up or sprout up at any moment.

Letters on Yoga, pp. 354-55

The subconscient is a concealed and unexpressed inarticulate consciousness which works below all our conscious physical activities. Just as what we call the superconscient is really a higher consciousness above from which things descend into the being, so the subconscient is below the body-consciousness and things come up into the physical, the vital and the mind-nature from there.

Just as the higher consciousness is superconscient to us and supports all our spiritual possibilities and nature, so the subconscient is the basis of our material being and supports all that comes up in the physical nature.

Men are not ordinarily conscious of either of these planes of their own being, but by sadhana they can become aware.

The subconscient retains the impressions of all our past experiences of life and they can come up from there in dream forms: most dreams in ordinary sleep are formations made from subconscient impressions.

The habit of strong recurrence of the same things in our physical consciousness, so that it is difficult to get rid of its habits, is largely due to a subconscient support. The subconscient is full of irrational habits.

When things are rejected from all other parts of the nature, they go either into the environmental consciousness around us through which we communicate with others and with universal Nature and try to return from there or they sink into the subconscient and can come up from there even after lying long quiescent so that we think they are gone.

When the physical consciousness is being changed,[1] the chief resistance comes from the subconscient. It is constantly maintaining or bringing back the inertia, weakness, obscurity, lack of intelligence which afflict the physical mind and vital or the obscure fears, desires, angers, lusts of the physical vital, or the illnesses, dullnesses, pains, incapabilities to which the body-nature is prone....

---

[1] In the process of sadhana or spiritual practice. (Ed.)

Vhen something is erased from the subconscient so completely that it leaves no seed and thrown out of the circumconscient so completely that it can return no more, then only can we be sure that we have finished with it for ever.

Letters on Yoga, pp. 356-357

The Muladhar is the centre of the physical consciousness proper, and all below in the body is the sheer physical, which as it goes downward becomes increasingly subconscient, but the real seat of the subconscient is below the body, as the real seat of the higher consciousness (superconscient) is above the body. At the same time, the subconscient can be felt anywhere, felt as something below the movement of the consciousness and, in a way, supporting it from beneath or else drawing the consciousness down towards itself. The subconscient is the main support of all habitual movements, especially the physical and lower vital movements. When something is thrown out of the vital or physical, it very usually goes down into the subconscient and remains there as if in seed and comes up again when it can. That is the reason why it is so difficult to get rid of habitual vital movements or to change the character; for, supported or refreshed from this source, preserved in this matrix your vital movements, even when suppressed or repressed, surge up again and recur. The action of the subconscient is irrational, mechanical, repetitive. It does not listen to reason or the mental will. It is only by bringing the higher Light and Force into it that it can change.

Letters on Yoga, p. 357

That part of us which we can strictly call subconscient because it is below the level of mind and conscious life, inferior and obscure, covers the purely physical and vital elements of our constitution of bodily being, unmentalised, unobserved by the mind, uncontrolled by it in their action. It can be held to include the dumb occult consciousness, dynamic but not sensed by us, which operates in the cells and nerves and all the corporeal stuff and adjusts their life process and automatic responses. It covers also those lowest functionings of submerged sense-mind which are more operative in the animal and in plant life; in our evolution we have overpassed the need of any large organised action of this element, but it remains submerged and obscurely at work below our conscious nature. This obscure activity extends to a hidden and hooded mental substratum into which past impressions and all that is rejected from the surface mind sink and remain there dormant and can surge up in sleep or in any absence of the mind, taking dream forms, forms of mechanical mind-action or suggestion, forms of automatic vital reaction or impulse, forms of physical abnormality or nervous perturbance, forms of morbidity, disease, unbalance. Out of the subconscious we bring ordinarily so much to the surface as our waking sense-mind and intelligence need for their purpose; in so bringing them up we are not aware of their nature, origin, operation and do not apprehend them in their own values but by a translation into the values of our waking human sense and intelligence. But the risings of the subconscious, its effects upon the mind and body, are mostly automatic, uncalled for and involuntary; for we have no knowledge and therefore no control of the subconscient. It is only by an experience abnormal to us, most commonly in illness or some disturbance of balance, that we can become directly aware of something in the dumb world, dumb but very active, of our bodily being and vitality or grow conscious of the secret movements of the mechanical subhuman physical and vital mind which underlies our surface, — a consciousness which is ours but seems not ours because it is not part of our known mentality. This and much more lives concealed in the subconscience.

The Life Divine, pp. 733-34

The sub-conscious is the evolutionary basis in us, it is not the whole of our hidden nature, nor is it the whole origin of what we are. But things can rise from the subconscient and take shape in the conscious parts and much of our smaller vital and physical instincts, movements, habits, character-forms has this source.

There are three occult sources of our action — the super-conscient, the subliminal, the subconscient, but of none of them are we in control or even aware. What we are aware of is the surface being which is only an instrumental arrangement. The source of all is the general Nature, — universal Nature individ-ualising itself in each person; for this general Nature deposits certain habits of movement, personality, character, faculties, dispositions, tendencies in us, and that, whether formed now or before our birth, is what we usually call ourselves. A good deal of this is in habitual movement and use in our known conscious parts on the surface, a great deal more is concealed in the other unknown three which are below or behind the surface.

But what we are on the surface is being constantly set in motion, changed, developed or repeated by the waves of the general Nature coming in on us either directly or else indirectly through others, through circumstances, through various agen-cies or channels. Some of this flows straight into the conscious parts and acts there, but our mind ignores its source, appropri-ates it and regards all that as its own; a part comes secretly into the subconscient or sinks into it and waits for an opportunity of rising up into the conscious surface; a good deal goes into the subliminal and may at any time come out — or may not, may rather rest there as unused matter. Part passes through and is rejected, thrown back or thrown out or spilt into the universal sea. Our nature is a constant activity of forces supplied to us out of which (or rather out of a small amount of it) we make what we will or can. What we make seems fixed and formed for good, but in reality it is all a play of forces, a flux, nothing fixed or stable; the appearance of stability is given by constant repetition and recurrence of the same vibrations and formations. That is why our nature can be changed in spite of Vivekananda's saying[2]

---

[2] Vivekananda said that human nature cannot be changed just as a dog's crooked tail can never be made straight. (Ed.)

and Horace's adage[3] and in spite of the conservative resistance of the subconscient, but it is a difficult job because the master mode of Nature is this obstinate repetition and recurrence.

As for the things in our nature that are thrown away from us by rejection but come back, it depends on where you throw them. Very often there is a sort of procedure about it. The mind rejects its mentalities, the vital its vitalities, the physical its physicalities — these usually go back into the corresponding domain of general Nature. It all stays at first, when that happens, in the environmental consciousness which we carry about with us, by which we communicate with the outside Nature, and often it persistently rushes back from there — until it is so absolutely rejected, or thrown far away as it were, that it cannot return upon us any more. But when what the thinking and willing mind rejects is strongly supported by the vital, it leaves the mind indeed but sinks down into the vital, rages there and tries to rush up again and reoccupy the mind and compel or capture our mental acceptance. When the higher vital too — the heart or the larger vital dynamis rejects it, it sinks from there and takes refuge in the lower vital with its mass of small current movements that make up our daily littleness. When the lower vital too rejects it, it sinks into the physical consciousness and tries to stick by inertia or mechanical repetition. Rejected even from there it goes into the subconscient and comes up in dreams, in passivity, in extreme *tamas*. The Inconscient is the last resort of the Ignorance. *Letters on Yoga, pp. 358-59*

A descent into the subconscient would not help us to explore this region, for it would plunge us into incoherence or into sleep or a dull trance or a comatose torpor. A mental scrutiny or insight can give us some indirect and constructive idea of these hidden activities; but it is only by drawing back into the subliminal or

---

[3] "*Video meliora proboque, Deteriora sequor.*" ("I see the better and approve of it, I follow the worse.") — Horace (Ed.)

by ascending into the superconscient and from there looking down or extending ourselves into these obscure depths that we can become directly and totally aware and in control of the secrets of our subconscient physical, vital and mental nature. This awareness, this control are of the utmost importance. For the subconscient is the Inconscient in the process of becoming conscious; it is a support and even a root of our inferior parts of being and their movements. It sustains and reinforces all in us that clings most and refuses to change, our mechanical re-currences of unintelligent thought, our persistent obstinacies of feeling, sensation, impulse, propensity, our uncontrolled fixities of character. The animal in us, — the infernal also, — has its lair of retreat in the dense jungle of the subconscience. To penetrate there, to bring in light and establish a control, is indispensable for the completeness of any higher life, for any integral trans-formation of the nature.   *The Life Divine, pp. 734-35*

For human beings who have not got deeper into themselves, mind and consciousness are synonymous. Only when one becomes more aware of oneself by a growing consciousness, then one can see different degrees, kinds, powers of consciousness, mental, vital, physical, psychic, spiritual.

Letters on Yoga, p. 686

Planes of the Mental Being

In mind itself there are grades of the series and each grade again is a series in itself; there are successive elevations which we may conveniently call planes and sub-planes of the mental consciousness and the mental being. The development of our mental self is largely an ascent of this stair; we can take our stand on any one of them, while yet maintaining a dependence on the lower stages and a power of occasional ascension to higher levels or of a response to influences from our being's superior strata. At present we still normally take our first secure stand on the lowest sub-plane of the intelligence, which we may call the physical-mental, because it depends for its evidence of fact and sense of reality on the physical brain, the physical sense-mind, the physical sense-organs; there we are the physical man who attaches most importance to objective things and to his outer life, has little intensity of the subjective or inner existence and subordinates whatever he has of it to the greater claims of exterior reality. The physical man has a vital part, but it is mainly made up of the smaller instinctive and impulsive formations of life-consciousness emerging from the subconscient, along with a customary crowd or round of sensations, desires, hopes, feelings, satisfactions which are dependent on external things and external contacts and concerned with the practical, the immediately realisable and possible, the habitual, the common and average. He has a mental part, but this too is customary, traditional, practical, objective, and respects what belongs to the domain of mind mostly for its utility for the support, comfort, use, satisfaction and entertainment of his physical and sensational existence. For the physical mind takes its stand on matter and the material world, on the body and the bodily life, on sense-experience and on a normal practical mentality and its experience. All that is not of this order, the physical mind builds up as a restricted superstructure dependent upon the external sense-mentality. Even so, it regards these higher contents of life as either helpful adjuncts or a superfluous but pleasant luxury of imaginations, feelings and thought-abstractions, not as inner realities; or, even if it receives them as realities, it does not feel them concretely and substantially in their own proper substance, subtler than the physical substance and its grosser concreteness, — it treats them as a subjective, less substantial extension from physical realities. It is inevitable that the human being should thus take his first stand on Matter and give the external fact and external existence its due importance; for this is Nature's first provision for our existence, on which she insists greatly: the physical man is emphasised in us and is multiplied abundantly in the world by her as her force for conservation of the secure, if somewhat inert, material basis on which she can maintain herself while she attempts her higher human developments; but in this mental formation there is no power for progress or only for a material progress. It is our first mental status, but the mental being cannot remain always at this lowest rung of the human evolutionary ladder.

Above physical mind and deeper within than physical sensation, there is what we may call an intelligence of the life-mind, dynamic, vital.... The vital man... is the man of desire and sensation, the man of force and action, the man of passion and emotion, the kinetic individual: he may and does lay great stress on the material existence, but he gives it, even when most preoccupied with its present actualities, a push for life-experience, for force of realisation, for life-extension, for life-power, for life-affirmation and life-expansion which is Nature's first impetus towards enlargement of the being; at a highest intensity of this life-impetus, he becomes the breaker of bonds, the seeker of new horizons, the disturber of the past and present in the interest of the future. He has a mental life which is often enslaved to the vital force and its desires and passions, and it is these he seeks to satisfy through the mind: but when he interests himself strongly in mental things, he can become the mental adventurer, the opener of the way to new mind-formations or the fighter for an idea, the sensitive type of artist, the dynamic poet of life or the prophet or champion of a cause. The vital mind is kinetic and therefore a great force in the working of evolutionary Nature.

Above this level of vital mentality and yet more inly extended, is a mind-plane of pure thought and intelligence to which the things of the mental world are the most important realities; those who are under its influence, the philosopher, thinker, scientist, intellectual creator, the man of the idea, the man of the written or spoken word, the idealist and dreamer are the present mental being at his highest attained summit. This mental man has his life-part, his life of passions and desires and ambitions and life-hopes of all kinds and his lower sensational and physical existence, and this lower part can often equibalance or weigh down his nobler mental element so that, although it is the highest portion of him, it does not become dominant and formative in his whole nature: but this is not typical of him in his greatest development, for there the vital and physical are controlled and subjected by the thinking will and intelligence. The mental man cannot transform his nature, but he can control and harmonise it and lay on it the law of a mental ideal, impose a balance or a sublimating and refining influence, and give a high consistency to the multipersonal confusion and conflict or the summary patchwork of our divided and half-constructed being. He can be the observer and governor of his own mind and life, can consciously develop them and become to that extent a self-creator.

...to live in mind and the things of the mind, to be an

intelligence rather than a life and a body, is our highest position, short of spirituality, in the degrees of Nature. The mental man, the man of a self-dominating and self-formative mind and will conscious of an ideal and turned towards its realisation, the high intellect, the thinker, the sage, less kinetic and immediately effective than the vital man, who is the man of action and outer swift life-fulfilment, but as powerful and eventually even more powerful to open new vistas to the race, is the normal summit of Nature's evolutionary formation on the human plane. These three degrees of mentality, clear in themselves, but most often mixed in our composition, are to our ordinary intelligence only psychological types that happen to have developed, and we do not discover any other significance in them; but in fact they are full of significance, for they are the steps of Nature's evolution of mental being towards its self-exceeding, and, as thinking mind is the highest step she can now attain, the perfected mental man is the rarest and highest of her normal human creatures. To go farther she has to bring into the mind and make active in mind, life and body the spiritual principle.   *The Life Divine, pp. 717-20*

The Physical Mind

The true thinking mind does not belong to the physical, it is a separate power. The physical mind is that part of the mind which is concerned with the physical things only — it depends on the sense-mind, sees only objects, external actions, draws its ideas from the data given by external things, infers from them only and knows no other Truth until it is enlightened from above.

Letters on Yoga, p. 327

The physical mind is that which is fixed on physical objects and happenings, sees and understands these only, and deals with them according to their own nature, but can with difficulty respond to the higher forces. Left to itself, it is sceptical of the existence of supraphysical things, of which it has no direct experience and to which it can find no clue; even when it has spiritual experiences, it forgets them easily, loses the impression and result and finds it difficult to believe.

Letters on Yoga, pp. 347-48

That is the nature of the mental physical to go on repeating without use the movement that has happened. It is what we call the mechanical mind — it is strong in childhood because the thinking mind is not developed and has besides a narrow range of interests. Afterwards it becomes an undercurrent in the mental activities.

Letters on Yoga, p. 329

The Vital Mind

There is a part of the nature which I have called the vital mind; the function of this mind is not to think and reason, to perceive, consider and find out or value things, for that is the function of the thinking mind proper, *buddhi*, — but to plan or dream or imagine what can be done. It makes formations for the future which the will can try to carry out if opportunity and circumstances become favourable or even it can work to make them favourable. In men of action this faculty is prominent and a leader of their nature; great men of action always have it in a very high measure. But even if one is not a man of action or practical realisation or if circumstances are not favourable or one can do only small and ordinary things, this vital mind is there. It acts in them on a small scale, or if it needs some sense of largeness, what it does very often is to plan in the void, knowing that it cannot realise its plans or else to imagine big things, stories, adventures, great doings in which oneself is the hero or the creator.

Letters on Yoga, pp. 334-35

The vital mind is that part of the vital being which builds, plans, imagines, arranges things and thoughts according to the life-pushes, desires, will to power or possession, will to action, emotions, vital ego reactions of the nature. It must be distinguished from the reasoning will which plans and arranges things according to the dictates of the thinking mind proper, the discriminating reason or according to the mental intuition or a direct insight and judgment. The vital mind uses thought for the service not of reason but of life-push and life-power and when it calls in reasoning it uses that for justifying the dictates of these powers, imposes their dictates on the reason instead of governing by a discriminating will the action of the life-forces.

Letters on Yoga, p. 341

The Thinking Mind

But there is still another clearer reflective mentality behind the dynamic and vital which is capable of escaping from this absorption in life and views itself as assuming life and body in order to image out in active relations of energy that which it perceives in will and thought. It is the source of the pure thinker in us; it is that which knows mentality in itself and sees the world not in terms of life and body but of mind; it is that[1] which, when we get back to it, we sometimes mistake for the pure spirit as we mistake the dynamic mind for the soul. This higher mind is able to perceive and deal with other souls as other forms of its pure self; it is capable of sensing them by pure mental impact and communication and no longer only by vital and nervous impact and physical indications; it conceives too a mental figure of unity, and in its activity and its will it can create and possess more directly — not only indirectly as in the ordinary physical life — and in other minds and lives as well as its own. But still even this pure mentality does not escape from the original error of mind. For it is still its separate mental self which it makes the judge, witness and centre of the universe and through it alone strives to arrive at its own higher self and reality; all others are

---

[1] The mental being, *manomaya puruṣa*.

"others" grouped to it around itself: when it wills to be free, it has to draw back from life and mind in order to disappear into the real unity. For there is still the veil created by Avidya between the mental and supramental action; an image of the Truth gets through, not the Truth itself. *The Life Divine, pp. 169-70*

For the human thinking mind there are always many sides to everything and it decides according to its own bent or preference or to its habitual ideas or some reason that presents itself to the intellect as the best. It gets the real truth only when something else puts a higher light into it — when the psychic or the intuition touches it and makes it feel or see. *Letters on Yoga, p. 1247*

Manas, Buddhi

I don't use these terms [Manas, etc.] myself as a rule — they are the psychological phraseology of the old yoga.

Letters on Yoga, p. 331

The terms Manas, etc. belong to the ordinary psychology applied to the surface consciousness. In our yoga we adopt a different classification — based on the yogic experience. What answers to this movement of the Manas there would be two separate things — a part of the physical mind communicating with the physical-vital. It receives from the physical senses and transmits to the Buddhi — i.e., to some part or other of the Thought-Mind. It receives back from the Buddhi and transmits idea and will to the organs of sensation and action. All that is indispensable in the ordinary action of the consciousness. But in the ordinary consciousness everything gets mixed up together and there is no clear order or rule. In the yoga one becomes aware of the different parts and their proper action, and puts each in its place and to its proper action under the control of the higher Consciousness.... *Letters on Yoga, p. 330*

...we have to make clear the distinction, ignored in ordinary speech, between the *manas*, mind, and *buddhi*, the discerning intelligence and the enlightened will. Manas is the sense mind. Man's initial mentality is not at all a thing of reason and will; it is an animal, physical or sense mentality which constitutes its whole experience from the impressions made on it by the external world and by its own embodied consciousness which responds to the outward stimulus of this kind of experience. The Buddhi only comes in as a secondary power which has in the evolution taken the first place, but is still dependent on the inferior instrument it uses; it depends for its workings on the sense mind and does what it can on its own higher range by a difficult, elaborate and rather stumbling extension of knowledge and action from the physical or sense basis. A half-enlightened physical or sense mentality is the ordinary type of the mind of man.   *The Synthesis of Yoga, p. 636*

We may distinguish three successive gradations of the action of this intelligence. There is first an inferior perceptive understanding which simply takes up, records, understands and responds to the communications of the sense-mind, memory, heart and sensational mentality. It creates by their means an elementary thinking mind which does not go beyond their data, but subjects itself to their mould and rings out their repetitions, runs round and round in the habitual circle of thought and will suggested by them or follows, with an obedient subservience of the reason to the suggestions of life, any fresh determinations which may be offered to its perception and conception. Beyond this elementary understanding, which we all use to an enormous extent, there is a power of arranging or selecting reason and will-force of the intelligence which has for its action and aim an attempt to arrive at a plausible, sufficient, settled ordering of knowledge and will for the use of an intellectual conception of life.

In spite of its more purely intellectual character this secondary or intermediate reason is really pragmatic in its intention.

It creates a certain kind of intellectual structure, frame, rule into which it tries to cast the inner and outer life so as to use it with a certain mastery and government for the purposes of some kind of rational will. It is this reason which gives to our normal intellectual being our set aesthetic and ethical standards, our structures of opinion and our established norms of idea and purpose. It is highly developed and takes the primacy in all men of an at all developed understanding. But beyond it there is a reason, a highest action of the Buddhi which concerns itself disinterestedly with a pursuit of pure truth and right knowledge; it seeks to discover the real Truth behind life and things and our apparent selves and to subject its will to the law of Truth. Few, if any of us, can use this highest reason with any purity, but the attempt to do it is the topmost capacity of the inner instrument, the *antaḥkaraṇa*.   *The Synthesis of Yoga, pp. 624-25*

Mind and Sensory Experience

...our idea of sense action is governed by the limiting experience of the physical mind and we suppose that the fundamental thing in it is the impression made by an external object on the physical organ of sight, hearing, smell, touch, taste, and that the business of the mind, the present central organ of our consciousness, is only to receive the physical impression and its nervous translation and so become intelligently conscious of the object. ...we have to realise first that the mind is the only real sense even in the physical process: its dependence on the physical impressions is the result of the conditions of the material evolution, but not a thing fundamental and indispensable. Mind is capable of a sight that is independent of the physical eye, a hearing that is independent of the physical ear, and so with the action of all the other senses. It is capable too of an awareness, operating by what appears to us as mental impressions, of things not conveyed or even suggested by the agency of the physical organs, —

an opening to relations, happenings, forms even and the action of forces to which the physical organs could not have borne evidence. Then, becoming aware of these rarer powers, we speak of the mind as a sixth sense; but in fact it is the only true sense organ and the rest are no more than its outer conveniences and secondary instruments, although by its dependence on them they have become its limitations and its too imperative and exclusive conveyors.   *The Synthesis of Yoga, p. 833*

Manas, the sense mind, depends in our ordinary consciousness on the physical organs of receptive sense for knowledge and on the organs of the body for action directed towards the objects of sense. The superficial and outward action of the senses is physical and nervous in its character, and they may easily be thought to be merely results of nerve-action; they are sometimes called in the old books pranas, nervous or life activities. But still the essential thing in them is not the nervous excitation, but the consciousness, the action of the Chitta, which makes use of the organ and of the nervous impact of which it is the channel. Manas, sense-mind, is the activity, emerging from the basic consciousness, which makes up the whole essentiality of what we call sense. Sight, hearing, taste, smell, touch are really properties of the mind, not of the body; but the physical mind which we ordinarily use, limits itself to a translation into sense of so much of the outer impacts as it receives through the nervous system and the physical organs.   *The Synthesis of Yoga, p. 623*

...although it is the rule that when we seek to become aware of the external world, we have to do so indirectly through the sense-organs and can experience only so much of the truth about things and men as the senses convey to us, yet this rule is merely the regularity of a dominant habit. It is possible for the mind, — and it would be natural for it, if it could be persuaded to liberate itself from its consent to the domination of matter, — to take direct cognisance of the objects of sense without the aid of the sense-organs. This is what happens in experiments of hypnosis and cognate psychological phenomena. Because our waking consciousness is determined and limited by the balance between mind and matter worked out by life in its evolution, this direct cognisance is usually impossible in our ordinary waking state and has therefore to be brought about by throwing the waking mind into a state of sleep which liberates the true or subliminal mind. Mind is then able to assert its true character as the one and all-sufficient sense and free to apply to the objects of sense its pure and sovereign instead of its mixed and dependent action. Nor is this extension of faculty really impossible but only more difficult in our waking state, — as is known to all who have been able to go far enough in certain paths of psychological experiment.

The sovereign action of the sense-mind can be employed to develop other senses besides the five which we ordinarily use. For instance, it is possible to develop the power of appreciating accurately without physical means the weight of an object which we hold in our hands. Here the sense of contact and pressure is merely used as a starting-point, just as the data of sense-experience are used by the pure reason, but it is not really the sense of touch which gives the measure of the weight to the mind; that finds the right value through its own independent perception and uses the touch only in order to enter into relation with the object. And as with the pure reason, so with the sense-mind, the sense-experience can be used as a mere first point from which it proceeds to a knowledge that has nothing to do with the sense-organs and often contradicts their evidence. Nor is the extension of faculty confined only to outsides and superficies. It is possible, once we have entered by any of the senses into relation with an external object, so to apply the Manas as to become aware of the contents of the object, for example, to receive or to perceive the thoughts or feelings of others without aid from their utterance, gesture, action or facial expressions and even in contradiction of these always partial and often misleading data. Finally, by an utilisation of the inner senses, — that is to say, of the sense-powers, in themselves, in their purely mental or subtle activity as distinguished from the physical which is only a selection for the purposes of outward life from their total and general action, — we are able to take cognition of sense-experiences, of appearances and images of things other than those which belong to the organisation of our material environment. All these extensions of faculty, though received with hesitation and incredulity by the physical mind because they are abnormal to the habitual scheme of our ordinary life and experience, difficult to set in action, still more difficult to systematise so as to be able to make of them an orderly and serviceable set of instruments, must yet be admitted, since they are the invariable result of any attempt to enlarge the field of our superficially active consciousness whether by some kind of untaught effort and casual ill-ordered effect or by a scientific and well-regulated practice.   *The Life Divine, pp. 63-64*

Mind an Ignorance-Consciousness

...my experience is that there is something beyond Mind; Mind is not the last word here of the Spirit. Mind is an ignorance-consciousness and its perceptions cannot be anything else than either false, mixed or imperfect — even when true, a partial reflection of the Truth and not the very body of Truth herself.

Letters on Yoga, p. 52

At the outset man lives in his physical mind which perceives the actual, the physical, the objective and accepts it as fact and this fact as self-evident truth beyond question; whatever is not actual, not physical, not objective it regards as unreal or unrealised, only to be accepted as entirely real when it has succeeded in becoming actual, becoming a physical fact, becoming objective: its own being too it regards as an objective fact, warranted to be real by its existence in a visible and sensible body; all other subjective beings and things it accepts on the same evidence in so far as they can become objects of our external consciousness or acceptable to that part of the reason which builds upon the data supplied by that consciousness and relies upon them as the one solid basis of knowledge. Physical Science is a vast extension of this mentality: it corrects the errors of the sense and pushes beyond the first limitations of the sense-mind by discovering means of bringing facts and objects not seizable by our corporeal organs into the field of objectivity; but it has the same standard of reality, the objective, the physical actuality; its test of the real is possibility of verification by positive reason and objective evidence.

But man also has a life-mind, a vital mentality which is an instrument of desire: this is not satisfied with the actual, it is a dealer in possibilities; it has the passion for novelty and is seeking always to extend the limits of experience for the satisfaction of desire, for enjoyment, for an enlarged self-affirmation and aggrandisement of its terrain of power and profit. It desires, enjoys, possesses actualities, but it hunts also after unrealised possibilities, is ardent to materialise them, to possess and enjoy them also. It is not satisfied with the physical and objective only, but seeks too a subjective, an imaginative, a purely emotive satisfaction and pleasure. If there were not this factor, the physical mind of man left to itself would live like the animal, accepting his first actual physical life and its limits as his whole possibility, moving in material Nature's established order and asking for nothing beyond it. But this vital mind, this unquiet life-will comes in with its demands and disturbs this inert or routine satisfaction which lives penned within the bounds of actuality; it enlarges always desire and craving, creates a dissatisfaction, an unrest, a seeking for something more than what life seems able to give it: it brings about a vast enlargement of the field of physical actuality by the actualisation of our unrealised possibilities, but also a constant demand for more and always more, a quest for new worlds to conquer, an incessant drive towards an exceeding of the bounds of circumstance and a self-exceeding. To add to this cause of unrest and incertitude there comes in a thinking mind that inquires into everything, questions everything, builds up affirmations and unbuilds them, erects systems of certitude but finally accepts none of them as certain, affirms and questions the evidence of the senses, follows out the conclusions of the reason but undoes them again to arrive at different or quite opposite conclusions, and continues indefinitely if not *ad infinitum* this process. This is the history of human thought and human endeavour, a constant breaking of bounds only to move always in the same spirals enlarged perhaps but following the same or constantly similar curves of direction. The mind of humanity, ever seeking, ever active, never arrives at a firmly settled reality of life's aims and objects or at a settled reality of its own certitudes and convictions, an established foundation or firm formation of its idea of existence.

The Life Divine, pp. 413-15

Mind in its essence is a consciousness which measures, limits, cuts out forms of things from the indivisible whole and contains them as if each were a separate integer. Even with what exists only as obvious parts and fractions, Mind establishes this fiction of its ordinary commerce that they are things with which it can deal separately and not merely as aspects of a whole. For, even when it knows that they are not things in themselves, it is obliged to deal with them as if they were things in themselves; otherwise it could not subject them to its own characteristic activity. It is this essential characteristic of Mind which conditions the workings of all its operative powers, whether conception, perception, sensation or the dealings of creative thought. It conceives, perceives, senses things as if rigidly cut out from a background or a mass and employs them as fixed units of the material given to it for creation or possession. All its action and enjoyment deal thus with wholes that form part of a greater whole, and these subordinate wholes again are broken up into parts which are also treated as wholes for the particular purposes they serve. Mind may divide, multiply, add, subtract, but it cannot get beyond the limits of this mathematics. If it goes beyond and tries to conceive a real whole, it loses itself in a foreign element; it falls from its own firm ground into the ocean of the intangible, into the abysms of the infinite where it can neither perceive, conceive, sense nor deal with its subject for creation and enjoyment.

The Life Divine, pp. 162-63

A tree evolves out of the seed in which it is already contained, the seed out of the tree; a fixed law, an invariable process reigns in the permanence of the form of manifestation which we call a tree. The mind regards this phenomenon, this birth, life and reproduction of a tree, as a thing in itself and on that basis studies, classes and explains it. It explains the tree by the seed, the seed by the tree; it declares a law of Nature. But it has explained nothing; it has only analysed and recorded the process of a mystery. Supposing even that it comes to perceive a secret conscious force as the soul, the real being of this form and the rest as merely a settled operation and manifestation of that force, still it tends to regard the form as a separate existence with its separate law of nature and process of development. In the animal and in man with his conscious mentality this separative tendency of the Mind induces it to regard itself also as a separate existence, the conscious subject, and other forms as separate objects of its mentality. This useful arrangement, necessary to life and the first basis of all its practice, is accepted by the mind as an actual fact and thence proceeds all the error of the ego.

The Life Divine, p. 138

Mind cannot arrive at identity with the Absolute even when by a stretch of the intellect it conceives the idea, but can only disappear into it in a swoon or extinction: it can only have a kind of sense or an intimation of certain absolutes which it puts by the mental idea into a relative figure. It cannot grasp the universal, but only arrives at some idea of it through an extension of the individual or a combination of apparently separate things and so sees it either as a vague infinite or indeterminate or a half determined largeness or else only in an external scheme or constructed figure. The indivisible being and action of the universal, which is its real truth, escapes the apprehension of the mind, because the mind thinks it out analytically by taking its own divisions for units and synthetically by combinations of these units, but cannot seize on and think entirely in the terms, though it may get at the idea and certain secondary results, of the essential oneness. It cannot, either, know truly and thoroughly even the individual and apparently separate thing, because it proceeds in the same way, by an analysis of parts and constituents and properties and a combination by which it erects a scheme of it which is only its external figure. It can get an intimation of the essential inmost truth of its object, but cannot live constantly and luminously in that essential knowledge and work out on the rest from within outward so that the outward circumstances appear in their intimate reality and meaning as inevitable result and expression and form and action of the spiritual something which is the reality of the object.

The Synthesis of Yoga, pp. 758-59

Mind acts by representations and constructions, by the separation and weaving together of its constructed data; it can make a synthetic construction and see it as the whole, but when it looks for the reality of things, it takes refuge in abstractions — it has not the concrete vision, experience, contact sought by the mystic and the spiritual seeker. To know Self and Reality directly or truly, it has to be silent and reflect some light of these things or undergo self-exceeding and transformation, and this is only possible either by a higher Light descending into it or by its ascent, the taking up or immergence of it into a higher Light of existence.

Letters on Yoga, p. 245

Mind is only a preparatory form of our consciousness. Mind is an instrument of analysis and synthesis, but not of essential

knowledge. Its function is to cut out something vaguely from
the unknown Thing in itself and call this measurement or delim-
itation of it the whole, and again to analyse the whole into its
parts which it regards as separate mental objects. It is only the
parts and accidents that the Mind can see definitely and, after
its own fashion, know. Of the whole its only definite idea is an
assemblage of parts or a totality of properties and accidents.
The whole not seen as a part of something else or in its own
parts, properties and accidents is to the mind no more than
a vague perception; only when it is analysed and put by itself
as a separate constituted object, a totality in a larger totality,
can Mind say to itself, "This now I know." And really it does
not know. It knows only its own analysis of the object and the
idea it has formed of it by a synthesis of the separate parts and
properties that it has seen. There its characteristic power, its sure
function ceases, and if we would have a greater, a profounder
and a real knowledge, — a knowledge and not an intense but
formless sentiment such as comes sometimes to certain deep but
inarticulate parts of our mentality, — Mind has to make room
for another consciousness which will fulfil Mind by transcending
it or reverse and so rectify its operations after leaping beyond it:
the summit of mental knowledge is only a vaulting-board from
which that leap can be taken. The utmost mission of Mind is to
train our obscure consciousness which has emerged out of the
dark prison of Matter, to enlighten its blind instincts, random
intuitions, vague perceptions till it shall become capable of this
greater light and this higher ascension. Mind is a passage, not a
culmination.   *The Life Divine, pp. 127-28*

...when mind develops in life, its first functional aspect is a
mentality involved in action, in vital and physical needs and
preoccupations, in impulses, desires, sensations, emotions, unable to stand back from these things and observe and know
them. In the human mind there is the first hope of understanding, discovery, a free comprehension; here we might seem

to be coming to the possibility of self-knowledge and world-knowledge. But in fact our mind can at first only observe facts and processes and for the rest it has to make deductions and inferences, to construct hypotheses, to reason, to speculate. In order to discover the secret of Consciousness it would have to know itself and determine the reality of its own being and process; but as in animal life the emerging Consciousness is involved in vital action and movement, so in the human being mind-consciousness is involved in its own whirl of thoughts, an activity in which it is carried on without rest and in which its very reasonings and speculations are determined in their tendency, trend, conditions by its own temperament, mental turn, past formation and line of energy, inclination, preference, an inborn natural selection, — we do not freely determine our thinking according to the truth of things, it is determined for us by our nature. We can indeed stand back with a certain detachment and observe the workings of the mental Energy in us; but it is still only its process that we see and not any original source of our mental determinations: we can build theories and hypotheses of the process of Mind, but a veil is still there over the inner secret of ourselves, our consciousness, our total nature.

It is only when we follow the yogic process of quieting the mind itself that a profounder result of our self-observation becomes possible. For first we discover that mind is a subtle substance, a general determinate — or generic indeterminate — which mental energy when it operates throws into forms or particular determinations of itself, thoughts, concepts, percepts, mental sentiments, activities of will and reactions of feeling, but which, when the energy is quiescent, can live either in an inert torpor or in an immobile silence and peace of self-existence. Next we see that the determinations of our mind do not all proceed from itself; for waves and currents of mental energy enter into it from outside: these take form in it or appear already formed from some universal Mind or from other minds and are accepted by us as our own thinking. We can perceive also an occult or subliminal mind in ourselves from which thoughts and perceptions and will-impulses and mental feelings arise; we can perceive too higher planes of consciousness from which a superior mind energy works through us or upon us. Finally we discover that that which observes all this is a mental being supporting the mind substance and mind energy; without this presence, their upholder and source of sanctions, they could not exist or operate.   *The Life Divine, pp. 307-08*

Mind's Power for Truth

Mind has a power also for truth; it opens its thought-chamber to Vidya as well as to Avidya, and if its starting-point is Ignorance, if its passage is through crooked ways of error, still its goal is always Knowledge: there is in it an impulse of truth-seeking, a power, — even though secondary and limited, — of truth-finding and truth-creation. Even if it is only images or representations or abstract expressions of truth that it can show us, still these are in their own manner truth-reflections or truth-formations, and the realities of which they are forms are present in their more concrete truth in some deeper depth or on some higher level of power of our consciousness.   *The Life Divine, p. 496*

The visible imperfections and limitations of mind in the present stage of its evolution here we take as part of its very nature; but in fact the boundaries in which it is still penned are only temporary limits and measures of its still incomplete evolutionary advance; its defects of methods and means are faults of its immaturity and not proper to the constitution of its being; its achievement although extraordinary under the hampering conditions of the mental being weighed down by its instrumentation in an earthly body is far below and not beyond what will be possible to it in its illumined future. For mind is not in its very nature an inventor of errors, a father of lies bound down to a capacity of falsehood, wedded to its own mistakes and the leader of a stumbling life as it too largely is at present owing to our human shortcomings: it is in its origin a principle of light, an instrument put forth from the Supermind and, though set to work within limits and even set to create limits, yet the limits are luminous borders for a special working, voluntary and purposive bounds, a service of the finite ever extending itself under the eye of infinity.

The Supramental Manifestation and Other Writings, p. 53

(b) The Outer (Surface) Vital Being (Life-Nature)

Life then reveals itself as essentially the same everywhere from the atom to man, the atom containing the subconscious stuff and movement of being which are released in consciousness in the animal, with plant life as a midway stage in the evolution. Life is really a universal operation of Conscious-Force acting subconsciently on and in Matter; it is the operation that creates, maintains, destroys and re-creates forms or bodies and attempts by play of nerve-force, that is to say, by currents of interchange of stimulating energy to awake conscious sensation in those bodies. In this operation there are three stages; the lowest is that in which the vibration is still in the sleep of Matter, entirely subconscious so as to seem wholly mechanical; the middle stage is that in which it becomes capable of a response still submental but on the verge of what we know as consciousness; the highest is that in which life develops conscious mentality in the form of a mentally perceptible sensation which in this transition becomes the basis for the development of sense-mind and intelligence. It is in the middle stage that we catch the idea of Life as distinguished from Matter and Mind, but in reality it is the same in all the stages and always a middle term between Mind and Matter, constituent of the latter and instinct with the former.

The Life Divine, p. 186

There are four parts of the vital being — first, the mental vital which gives a mental expression by thought, speech or otherwise

to the emotions, desires, passions, sensations and other movements of the vital being; the emotional vital which is the seat of
various feelings, such as love, joy, sorrow, hatred, and the rest;
the central vital which is the seat of the stronger vital longings
and reactions, e.g. ambition, pride, fear, love of fame, attractions
and repulsions, desires and passions of various kinds and the
field of many vital energies; last, the lower vital which is occupied
with small desires and feelings, such as make the greater part of
daily life, e.g. food desire, sexual desire, small likings, dislikings,
vanity, quarrels, love of praise, anger at blame, little wishes of all
kinds — and a numberless host of other things. Their respective
seats are: (1) the region from the throat to the heart, (2) the
heart (it is a double centre, belonging in front to the emotional
and vital and behind to the psychic), (3) from the heart to the
navel, (4) below the navel. *Letters on Yoga, p. 334*

In the classification in which the mind is taken as something
more than the thinking, perceiving and willing intelligence, the
emotional can be reckoned as part of the mind, the vital in the
mental. In another classification it is rather the most mentalised
part of the vital nature. In the first case, the term 'higher vital'
is confined to that larger movement of the conscious life-force
which is concerned with creation, with power and force and conquest, with giving and self-giving and gathering from the world
for further action and expenditure of power, throwing itself out
in the wider movements of life, responsive to the greater objects of Nature. In the second arrangement, the emotional being
stands at the top of the vital nature and the two together make
the higher vital. As against them stands the lower vital which
is concerned with the pettier movements of action and desire
and stretches down into the vital physical where it supports the
life of the more external activities and all physical sensations,
hungers, cravings, satisfactions. The term 'lower' must not be
considered in a pejorative sense; it refers only to the position in
the hierarchy of the planes. For although this part of the nature in

earthly beings tends to be very obscure and is full of perversions, — lust, greed of all kinds, vanity, small ambitions, petty anger, envy, jealousy are its ordinary guests, — still there is another side to it which makes it an indispensable mediator between the inner being and the outer life.   *Letters on Yoga, pp. 338-39*

Vital... is a thing of desires, impulses, force-pushes, emotions, sensations, seekings after life-fulfilment, possession and enjoyment; these are its functions and its nature; — it is that part of us which seeks after life and its movements for their own sake and it does not want to leave hold of them if they bring it suffering as well as or more than pleasure; it is even capable of luxuriating in tears and suffering as part of the drama of life.
                                                  Letters on Yoga, p. 323

The nervous part of the being is a portion of the vital — it is the vital-physical, the life-force closely enmeshed in the reactions, desires, needs, sensations of the body. The vital proper is the life-force acting in its own nature, impulses, emotions, feelings, desires, ambitions, etc., having as their highest centre what we may call the outer heart of emotion, while there is an inner heart where are the higher or psychic feelings and sensibilities, the emotions or intuitive yearnings and impulses of the soul. The vital part of us is, of course, necessary to our completeness, but it is a true instrument only when its feelings and tendencies have been purified by the psychic touch and taken up and governed by the spiritual light and power.   *Letters on Yoga, p. 345*

...man can establish a mental control over his vital and in so far as he does it he is a man, — because the thinking mind is a nobler and more enlightened entity and consciousness than the vital and ought, therefore, to rule and, if the mental will is strong, *can* rule. But this rule is precarious, incomplete and held only by much self-discipline. For if the mind is more enlightened, the vital is nearer to earth, more intense, vehement, more directly able to touch the body. There is too a vital mind which lives by imagination, thoughts of desire, will to act and enjoy from its own impulse and this is able to seize on the reason itself and make it its auxiliary and its justifying counsel and supplier of pleas and excuses. There is also the sheer force of Desire in man which is the vital's principal support and strong enough to sweep off the reason, as the Gita says, "like a boat on stormy waters",...   *Letters on Yoga, p. 323*

Most people live in the vital. That means that they live in their desires, sensations, emotional feelings, vital imaginations and see and experience and judge everything from that point of view. It is the vital that moves them, the mind being at its service, not its master. In yoga also many people do sadhana from that plane and their experience is full of vital visions, formations, experiences of all kinds, but there is no mental clarity or order, neither do they rise above the mind. It is only the minority of men who live in the mind or in the psychic or try to live in the spiritual plane.   *Letters on Yoga, p. 1297*

As for the idea that the sadhana raises up things of the kind, the only truth in that is this: that, first, there are many things in the ordinary man of which he is not conscious, because the vital hides them from the mind and gratifies them without the mind realising what is the force that is moving the action — thus things that are done under the plea of altruism, philanthropy, service, etc. are largely moved by ego which hides itself behind these justifications; in yoga the secret motive has to be pulled out from behind the veil, exposed and got rid of. Secondly, some things are suppressed in the ordinary life and remain lying in the nature, suppressed but not eliminated;[2] they may rise

---

[2] "The difference between suppression and an inward essential rejection is the difference between moral control and spiritual purification." — Sri Aurobindo (Ed.)

up any day or they may express themselves in various nervous forms or other disorders of the mind or vital or body without it being evident what is their real cause. This has been recently discovered by European psychologists and much emphasised, even exaggerated in a new science called psycho-analysis. Here again, in sadhana one has to become conscious of these suppressed impulses and eliminate them — this may be called rising up, but that does not mean that they have to be raised up into action but only raised up before the consciousness so as to be cleared out of the being.   *Letters on Yoga, pp. 1297-98*

That [seeking enjoyment] is the attitude not of the whole vital but of the physical vital, the animal part of the human being. Of course it cannot be convinced by mental reasoning of any kind. In most men it is the natural and accepted attitude towards life varnished over with some conventional moralism and idealism as a concession to the mind and higher vital. In a few this part of the being is gripped and subordinated to the mental or the higher vital aim, forced to take a subordinate place so that the mind may absorb itself persistently in mental pursuits or idealisms or great political or personal ambitions (Lenin, Hitler, Stalin, Mussolini). The ascetic and the Puritan try to suppress it mostly or altogether. In our yoga the principle is that all must become an instrument of the Spirit and the parts of enjoyment taste the Ananda in things, not the animal enjoyment of the surface. But the Ananda will not come or will not stay so long as this part is not converted and insists on its own way of satisfaction.
          Letters on Yoga, p. 1294

Many men are not after happiness and do not believe it is the true aim of life. It is the physical vital that seeks after happiness, the bigger vital is ready to sacrifice it in order to satisfy its passions, search for power, ambition, fame or any other motive. If you say it is because of the happiness power, fame etc. gives, that again is not universally true. Power may give anything else, but it does not usually give happiness, it is something in its very nature arduous and full of difficulty to get, to keep or to use — I speak of course of power in the ordinary sense. A man may know he can never have fame in this life but works in the hope of posthumous fame or in the chase of it. He may know that the satisfaction of his passion will bring him everything rather than happiness — suffering, torture, destruction — yet he will follow his impulse. So also the mind as well as the bigger vital is not bound by the pursuit of happiness. It can seek Truth rather or the victory of a cause. To reduce all to a single hedonistic strain seems to me to be very poor psychology. Neither Nature nor the vast Spirit in things are so limited and one-tracked as that.

Letters on Yoga, p. 1295

(c) The Outer (Surface) Physical Being

...the physiological functionings of the body help to determine the mind's psychological actions: for the body is not mere unconscious Matter: it is a structure of a secretly conscious Energy that has taken form in it. Itself occultly conscious, it is, at the same time, the vehicle of expression of an overt Consciousness that has emerged and is self-aware in our physical energy-substance. The body's functionings are a necessary machinery or instrumentation for the movements of this mental Inhabitant; it is only by setting the corporeal instrument in motion that the Conscious Being emerging, evolving in it can transmit its mind formations, will formations and turn them into a physical manifestation of itself in Matter. The capacity, the processes of the instrument must to a certain extent reshape the mind formations in their transition from mental shape into physical expression; its workings are necessary and must exercise their influence before that expression can become actual. The bodily instrument may even in some directions dominate its user, it may too by a force of habit suggest or create involuntary reactions of the consciousness inhabiting it before the working Mind and Will can control or interfere. All this is possible because the body has a "subconscient" consciousness of its own which counts in our total self-expression; even, if we look at this outer instrumentation only, we can conclude that body determines mind, but this is only a minor truth and the major Truth is that mind determines body. In this view a still deeper Truth becomes conceivable; a spiritual entity ensouling the substance that veils it is the original determinant of both mind and body. On the other side, in the opposite order of process, — that by which the mind can transmit its ideas and commands to the body, can train it to be an instrument for new action, can even so impress it with its habitual demands or orders that the physical instinct carries them out automatically even when the mind is no longer consciously willing them, those also more unusual but well attested by which to an extraordinary and hardly limitable extent the mind can learn to determine the reactions of the body even to the overriding of its normal law or conditions of action, — these and other otherwise unaccountable aspects of the relation between these two elements of our being become easily understandable: for it is the secret consciousness in the living matter that receives from its greater companion; it is this in the body that in its own involved and occult fashion perceives or feels the demand on it and obeys the emerged or evolved consciousness which presides over the body.

The Life Divine, pp. 305-306

A great part of the body-consciousness is subconscient and the body-consciousness and the subconscient are closely bound together.

The body and the physical do not coincide — the body consciousness is only part of the whole physical consciousness.

Letters on Yoga, p. 1445

[Defects of the physical consciousness:] There are many — but mainly obscurity, inertia, tamas, a passive acceptance of the play of wrong forces, inability to change, attachment to habits, lack of plasticity, forgetfulness, loss of experiences or realisations gained, unwillingness to accept the Light or to follow it, incapacity (through tamas or through attachment or through passive reaction to accustomed forces) to do what it admits to be the Right and the Best.

Letters on Yoga, p. 1434

Apart from the individual difficulty there is a general difficulty in the physical earth-nature. Physical nature is slow and inert and unwilling to change; its tendency is to be still and take long periods of time for a little progress. It is very difficult for even the strongest mental or vital or even psychic will to overcome this inertia. It is only by bringing down constantly the consciousness and force and light from above that it can be done. Therefore there must be a constant will and aspiration for that and for the change and it must be a steady and patient will not tired out even by the utmost resistance of the physical nature.

Letters on Yoga, p. 1434

Dullness and dispersion are the two sides of the physical's resistance to the peace and concentrated power. They correspond to the inertia and the chaotic activity of physical Nature, that aspect of it which makes some scientists now say that all is brought about by chance and there is no certitude of things but only probability.

Letters on Yoga, p. 1436

In the physical being the power of past impressions is very great, because it is by the process of repeated impressions that consciousness was made to manifest in matter — and also by the habitual reactions of consciousness to these impressions, what the psychologists, I suppose, would call behaviour. According to one school consciousness consists only of these things — but that is the usual habit of stretching one detail of Nature to explain the whole of her.

Letters on Yoga, p. 1441

The physical consciousness or at least the more external parts of it are... in their nature inert — obeying whatever force they are habituated to obey, but not acting on their own initiative. When there is a strong influence of the physical inertia or when one is down in this part of the consciousness the mind feels like the material Nature that action of will is impossible. Mind and vital nature are on the contrary all for will and initiative and so when one is in mind or vital or acting under their influence will feels itself always ready to be active.   *Letters on Yoga, pp. 1441-42*

So far as it [living in the physical consciousness] can be said to be distinguishable by outward signs, it is a state of fundamental passivity in which one is and does what the forces of the physical plane make one be and do. When one lives in the mind, there is an active mental intelligence and mental will that tries to control and shape action and experience and life and everything else. When one is in the vital one is full of energy and enthusiasm and passion and force which may be right or wrong but is very much alive.   *Letters on Yoga, p. 1433*

Physical nature exists by constant repetition of the same thing — only a constant presentation of different forms of itself. This obstinate recurrence is therefore part of its nature when it is in activity; otherwise it remains in a dull inertia. When therefore we want to get rid of the old movements of physical nature, they resist by this kind of obstinate recurrence. One has to be very persistent in rejection[3] to get rid of it.

There are two aspects of physical Nature as of all Nature — the individual and the universal. All things come into one from the universal Nature — but the individual physical keeps some of them and rejects others, and to those it keeps it gives a personal form. So these things can be said to be both inside it and coming outside from within or created by it because it gives a special

---

[3] See footnote 2, p. 65. (Ed.)

form and also outside and coming in from outside. But when one wants to get rid of them, one first throws out all that is within into the surrounding Nature — from there the universal Nature tries to bring them back or bring in new and similar things of its own to replace them. One has then constantly to reject this invasion. By constant rejection, the force of recurrence finally dwindles and the individual becomes free and able to bring the higher consciousness and its movements into the physical being.

Letters on Yoga, pp. 1434-35

Classification

It must be remembered that while this classification is indispensable for psychological self-knowledge and discipline and practice, it can be used best when it is not made too rigid and cutting a formula. For things run very much into each other and a synthetical sense of these powers is as necessary as the analysis. Mind, for instance, is everywhere. The physical mind is technically placed below the vital and yet it is a prolongation of the mind proper and one that can act in its own sphere by direct touch with the higher mental intelligence. And there is too an obscure mind of the body, of the very cells, molecules, corpuscles.

Letters on Yoga pp.339-40

7
The Inner Being; the Subliminal (Self)

The Subliminal Distinguished from the Subconscient

...subliminal is a general term used for all parts of the being which are not on the waking surface. Subconscient is very often used in the same sense by European psychologists because they do not know the difference. But when I use the word [subconscient], I mean always what is *below* the ordinary physical consciousness, not what is behind it. The inner mental, vital, physical, the psychic are not subconscious in this sense, but they can be spoken of as subliminal.   *Letters on Yoga, p. 354*

The real subconscious is a nether diminished consciousness close to the Inconscient; the subliminal is a consciousness larger than our surface existence. But both belong to the inner realm of our being of which our surface is unaware, so both are jumbled together in our common conception and parlance.
                              The Life Divine, p. 223fn.

Ordinarily, we speak of a subconscious existence and include in this term all that is not on the waking surface. But the whole or the greater part of the inner or subliminal self can hardly be characterised by that epithet; for when we say subconscious, we think readily of an obscure unconsciousness or half-consciousness or else a submerged consciousness below and in a way inferior to and less than our organised waking awareness or, at least, less in possession of itself. But we find, when we go within, that somewhere in our subliminal part, — though not co-extensive with it since it has also obscure and ignorant regions, — there is a consciousness much wider, more luminous, more in possession of itself and things than that which wakes upon our surface and is the percipient of our daily hours; that is our inner being, and it is this which we must regard as our subliminal self and set apart the subconscient as an inferior, a lowest occult province of our nature. In the same way there is a superconscient part of our total existence in which there is what we discover to be our highest self, and this too we can set apart as a higher occult province of our nature. *The Life Divine, p. 557*

The Inner Being; the Psychical Consciousness

The inner being means the inner mind, inner vital, inner physical with the psychic behind as the inmost. *Letters on Yoga, p. 373*

There is an inner mental, an inner vital, an inner physical which connects the psychic and the external being.
Letters on Yoga, p. 1113

Most people live in their ordinary outer ignorant personality which does not easily open to the Divine; but there is an inner being within them of which they do not know, which can easily open to the Truth and the Light. But there is a wall which divides them from it, a wall of obscurity and unconsciousness. When it breaks down, then there is a release.... *Letters on Yoga, p. 995*

The subliminal self stands behind and supports the whole superficial man; it has in it a larger and more efficient mind behind the surface mind, a larger and more powerful vital behind the surface vital, a subtler and freer physical consciousness behind the surface bodily existence. And above them it opens to higher superconscient as well as below them to lower subconscient ranges. *Letters on Yoga, p. 1606*

...there is a "subliminal" self behind our superficial waking mind, not inconscient but conscient, greater than the waking mind, endowed with surprising faculties and capable of a much surer action and experience, conscient of the superficial mind, though of it the superficial mind is inconscient.

The Supramental Manifestation and Other Writings, p. 261

It [the subliminal] is, according to our psychology, connected with the small outer personality by certain centres of consciousness [Chakras] of which we become aware by yoga. Only a little of the inner being escapes through these centres into the outer life, but that little is the best part of ourselves and responsible for our art, poetry, philosophy, ideals, religious aspirations, efforts at knowledge and perfection.   *Letters on Yoga, pp. 1164-65*

Our subliminal self is not, like our surface physical being, an outcome of the energy of the Inconscient; it is a meeting-place of the consciousness that emerges from below by evolution and the consciousness that has descended from above for involution. There is in it an inner mind, an inner vital being of ourselves, an inner or subtle-physical being larger than our outer being and nature. This inner existence is the concealed origin of almost all in our surface self that is not a construction of the first inconscient World-Energy or a natural developed functioning of our surface consciousness or a reaction of it to impacts from the outside universal Nature, — and even in this construction, these functionings, these reactions the subliminal takes part and exercises on them a considerable influence. There is here a consciousness which has a power of direct contact with the universal unlike the mostly indirect contacts which our surface being maintains with the universe through the sense-mind and the senses. There are here inner senses, a subliminal sight, touch, hearing; but these subtle senses are rather channels of the inner being's direct consciousness of things than its informants: the subliminal is not dependent on its senses for its knowledge, they only give a form to its direct experience of objects; they do not, so much as in waking mind, convey forms of objects for the mind's documentation or as the starting-point or basis for an indirect constructive experience. The subliminal has the right of

entry into the mental and vital and subtle-physical pla
universal consciousness, it is not confined to the materia
and the physical world; it possesses means of communicati
with the worlds of being which the descent towards involution created in its passage and with all corresponding planes or
worlds that may have arisen or been constructed to serve the
purpose of the re-ascent from Inconscience to Superconscience.
It is into this large realm of interior existence that our mind and
vital being retire when they withdraw from the surface activities
whether by sleep or inward-drawn concentration or by the inner
plunge of trance.

Our waking state is unaware of its connection with the
subliminal being, although it receives from it, — but without any
knowledge of the place of origin, — the inspirations, intuitions,
ideas, will-suggestions, sense-suggestions, urges to action that
rise from below or from behind our limited surface existence.
Sleep like trance opens the gate of the subliminal to us; for
in sleep, as in trance, we retire behind the veil of the limited
waking personality and it is behind this veil that the subliminal has its existence. But we receive the records of our sleep
experience through dream and in dream figures and not in that
condition which might be called an inner waking and which
is the most accessible form of the trance state, nor through
the supernormal clarities of vision and other more luminous
and concrete ways of communication developed by the inner
subliminal cognition when it gets into habitual or occasional
conscious connection with our waking self. The subliminal... is
the seer of inner things and of supraphysical experiences; the
surface subconscious is only a transcriber. It is for this reason
that the Upanishad describes the subliminal being as the Dream
Self because it is normally in dreams, visions, absorbed states of
inner experience that we enter into and are part of its experiences, — just as it describes the superconscient as the Sleep Self
because normally all mental or sensory experiences cease when
we enter this superconscience.   *The Life Divine, pp. 425-27*

ull possession of a mind, a life-force,
: of things. It has the same capacities
tle sense and perception, a compre-
nd an intensive selecting intelligence,
t even though the same in kind, they
l, more sovereign. And it has other
ose of our mortal mind because of a
of the being, whether acting in itself or
turned upon its object, ... ich arrives more swiftly at knowledge,
more swiftly at effectivity of will, more deeply at understanding
and satisfaction of impulse. Our surface mind is hardly a true
mentality, so involved, bound, hampered, conditioned is it by the
body and bodily life and the limitations of the nerve-system and
the physical organs. But the subliminal self has a true mentality
superior to these limitations; it exceeds the physical mind and
physical organs although it is aware of them and their works
and is, indeed, in a large degree their cause or creator. It is only
subconscious in the sense of not bringing all or most of itself
to the surface, it works always behind the veil: it is rather a
secret intraconscient and circumconscient than a subconscient;
for it envelops quite as much as it supports the outer nature.
This description is no doubt truest of the deeper parts of the
subliminal; in other layers of it nearer to our surface there is a
more ignorant action and those who, penetrating within, pause
in the zones of lesser coherence or in the No-man's-land between
the subliminal and the surface, may fall into much delusion and
confusion:...   *The Life Divine, pp. 559-60*

The part of us that we have characterised as intraconscient and
circumconscient... includes the large action of an inner intelligence and inner sense-mind, of an inner vital, even of an
inner subtle-physical being which upholds and embraces our
waking consciousness, which is not brought to the front, which
is subliminal, in the modern phrase. But when we can enter
and explore this hidden self, we find that our waking sense

and intelligence are for the most part a selection from what we secretly are or can be, an exteriorised and much mutilated and vulgarised edition of our real, our hidden being or an upthrow from its depths. Our surface being has been formed with this subliminal help by an evolution out of the Inconscient for the utility of our present mental and physical life on earth; this that is behind is a formation mediating between the Inconscient and the larger planes of Life and Mind which have been created by the involutionary descent and whose pressure has helped to bring about the evolution of Mind and Life in Matter. Our surface responses to physical existence have at their back the support of an activity in these veiled parts, and often responses from them are modified by a surface mental rendering. But also that large part of our mentality and vitality which is not a response to the outside world but lives for itself or throws itself out on material existence to use and possess it, our personality, is the outcome, the amalgamated formulation of powers, influences, motives proceeding from this potent intraconscient secrecy.

Again, the subliminal extends itself into an enveloping consciousness through which it receives the shock of the currents and wave-circuits pouring upon us from the universal Mind, universal Life, universal subtler Matter-forces. These, unperceived by us on the surface, are perceived and admitted by our subliminal self and turned into formations which can powerfully affect our existence without our knowledge. If the wall that separates this inner existence from the outer self were penetrated, we could know and deal with the sources of our present mind-energies and life-action and could control instead of undergoing their results. But though large parts of it can be thus known by a penetration and looking within or a freer communication, it is only by going inward behind the veil of superficial mind and living within, in an inner mind, an inner life, an inmost soul of our being that we can be fully self-aware, — by this and by rising to a higher plane of mind than that which our waking consciousness inhabits. An enlargement and completion of our present evolutionary status, now still so hampered and truncated, would be the result of such an inward living; but an evolution beyond it can come only by our becoming conscious in what is now superconscient to us, by an ascension to the native heights of the Spirit.

The Life Divine, pp. 735-36

The external forms of our being are those of our small egoistic existence; the subliminal are the formations of our larger true individuality. Therefore are these that concealed part of our being in which our individuality is close to our universality, touches it, is in constant relation and commerce with it. The subliminal mind in us is open to the universal knowledge of the cosmic Mind, the subliminal life in us to the universal force of the cosmic Life, the subliminal physicality in us to the universal force-formation of Cosmic Matter;[1] the thick walls which divide from these things our surface mind, life, body and which Nature has to pierce with so much trouble, so imperfectly and by so many skilful-clumsy physical devices, are there, in the subliminal, only a rarefied medium at once of separation and communication.

The Life Divine, p. 221

The subliminal is separated from the cosmic through a limitation by the subtler sheaths of our being, its mental, vital, subtle-physical sheaths, just as the surface nature is separated from universal Nature by the gross physical sheath, the body; but the circumscribing wall around it is more transparent, is indeed less a wall than a fence. The subliminal has besides a formation of consciousness which projects itself beyond all these sheaths and forms a circumconscient, an environing part of itself, through which it receives the contacts of the world and can become aware of them and deal with them before they enter. The subliminal

---

[1] The subliminal is thus the link betweeen the individual and the universal (or the "transpersonal" as it would be called in the latest school of Western psychology). (Ed.)

is able to widen indefinitely this circumconscient envelope and more and more enlarge its self-projection into the cosmic existence around it. A point comes where it can break through the separation altogether, unite, identify itself with cosmic being, feel itself universal, one with all existence. In this freedom of entry into cosmic self and cosmic nature there is a great liberation of the individual being; it puts on a cosmic consciousness, becomes the universal individual. Its first result, when it is complete, is the realisation of the cosmic spirit, the one self inhabiting the universe, and this union may even bring about a disappearance of the sense of individuality, a merger of the ego into the world-being. Another common result is an entire openness to the universal Energy so that it is felt acting through the mind and life and body and the sense of individual action ceases. But more usually there are results of less amplitude; there is a direct awareness of universal being and nature, there is a greater openness of the mind to the cosmic Mind and its energies, to the cosmic Life and its energies, to cosmic Matter and its energies. A certain sense of unity of the individual with the cosmic, a perception of the world held within one's consciousness as well as of one's own intimate inclusion in the world consciousness can become frequent or constant in this opening; a greater feeling of unity with other beings is its natural consequence. It is then that the existence of the cosmic Being becomes a certitude and a reality and is no longer an ideative perception.

The Life Divine, pp. 541-42

The psychical consciousness is that of what is now often called the subliminal self, the subtle or dream self of Indian psychology, and its range of potential knowledge, almost infinite... includes a very large power and many forms of insight into both the possibilities and the definite actualities of past, present and future. Its first faculty, that which most readily attracts attention, is its power of seeing by the psychical sense images of all things in time and space. As exercised by clairvoyants, mediums and others this is often, and indeed usually, a specialised faculty limited though often precise and accurate in action, and implies no development of the inner soul or the spiritual being or the higher intelligence.[2] It is a door opened by chance or by an innate gift or by some kind of pressure between the waking and the subliminal mind and admitting only to the surface or the outskirts of the latter. All things in a certain power and action of the secret universal mind are represented by images, — not only visual but, if one may use the phrase, auditory and other images, — and a certain development of the subtle or psychical senses makes it possible, — if there is no interference of the constructing mind and its imaginations, if, that is to say, artificial or falsifying mental images do not intervene, if the psychical sense is free, sincere and passive, — to receive these representations or transcriptions with a perfect accuracy and not so much predict as see in its correct images the present beyond the range of the physical sense, the past and the future. The accuracy of this kind of seeing depends on its being confined to a statement of the thing seen and the attempt to infer, interpret or otherwise go beyond the visual knowledge may lead to much error unless there is at the same time a strong psychical intuition fine, subtle and pure or a high development of the luminous intuitive intelligence.

A completer opening of the psychical consciousness leads us far beyond this faculty of vision by images and admits us not indeed to a new time consciousness, but to many ways of the triple time knowledge. The subliminal or psychic[3] self can bring back or project itself into past states of consciousness and experience and anticipate or even, though this is less common, strongly project itself into future states of consciousness and

---

[2] The distinction between the psychical and the spiritual is an important contribution offered by Sri Aurobindo's psychological thought to transpersonal psychology. (Ed.)

[3] In his earlier (unrevised) writings, Sri Aurobindo sometimes used the term "psychic" as synonymous with "psychical". For different usages of the term "psychic", see the Glossary. (Ed.)

experience. It does this by a temporary entering into or identification of its being or its power of experiencing knowledge with either permanences or representations of the past and the future that are maintained in an eternal time consciousness behind our mentality or thrown up by the eternity of supermind into an indivisible continuity of time vision. Or it may receive the impress of these things and construct a transcriptive experience of them in the subtle ether of psychical being. Or it may call up the past from the subconscious memory where it is always latent and give it in itself a living form and a kind of renewed memorative existence, and equally it may call up from the depths of latency, where it is already shaped in the being, and similarly form to itself and experience the future. It may by a kind of psychical thought vision or soul intuition — not the same thing as the subtler and less concrete thought vision of the luminous intuitive intelligence — foresee or foreknow the future or flash this soul intuition into the past that has gone behind the veil and recover it for present knowledge. It can develop a symbolic seeing which conveys the past and the future through a vision of the powers and significances that belong to supraphysical planes but are powerful for creation in the material universe.

The Synthesis of Yoga, pp. 861-63

Sight, hearing, taste, smell, touch are really properties of the mind, not of the body; but the physical mind which we ordinarily use, limits itself to a translation into sense of so much of the outer impacts as it receives through the nervous system and the physical organs. But the inner Manas has also a subtle sight, hearing, power of contact of its own which is not dependent on the physical organs. And it has, moreover, a power not only of direct communication of mind with object, — leading even at a high pitch of action to a sense of the contents of an object within or beyond the physical range, — but direct communication also of mind with mind. Mind is able too to alter, modify, inhibit the incidence, values, intensities of sense impacts. These powers of the mind we do not ordinarily use or develop; they remain subliminal and emerge sometimes in an irregular and fitful action, more readily in some minds than in others, or come to the surface in abnormal states of the being. They are the basis of clairvoyance, clairaudience, transference of thought and impulse, telepathy, most of the more ordinary kinds of occult powers, — so called, though these are better described less mystically as powers of the now subliminal action of the Manas. The phenomena of hypnotism and many others depend upon the action of this subliminal sense-mind; not that it alone constitutes all the elements of the phenomena, but it is the first supporting means of intercourse, communication and response, though much of the actual operation belongs to an inner Buddhi.

The Synthesis of Yoga, pp. 623-24

The awakening of the psychical consciousness liberates in us the direct use of the mind as a sixth sense, and this power may be made constant and normal. The physical consciousness can only communicate with the minds of others or know the happenings of the world around us through external means and signs and indications, and it has beyond this limited action only a vague and haphazard use of the mind's more direct capacities, a poor range of occasional presentiments, intuitions and messages. Our minds are indeed constantly acting and acted upon by the minds of others through hidden currents of which we are not aware, but we have no knowledge or control of these agencies. The psychical consciousness, as it develops, makes us aware of the great mass of thoughts, feelings, suggestions, will impacts, influences of all kinds that we are receiving from others or sending to others or imbibing from and throwing into the general mind atmosphere around us. As it evolves in power, precision and clearness, we are able to trace these to their source or feel immediately their origin and transit to us and direct consciously and with an intelligent will our own messages. It becomes possible to be aware, more or less accurately and discerningly, of the activities of minds whether near to us physically or at a distance, to understand, feel or identify ourselves with their temperament, character, thoughts, feelings, reactions, whether by a psychic sense or a direct mental perception or by a very sensible and often intensely concrete reception of them into our mind or on its recording surface. At the same time, we can consciously make at least the inner selves and, if they are sufficiently sensitive, the surface minds of others aware of our own inner mental or psychic self and plastic to its thoughts, suggestions, influences or even cast it or its active image in influence into their subjective, even into their vital and physical being to work there as a helping or moulding or dominating power and presence.   *The Synthesis of Yoga, p. 847*

8
The Psychic Being

The inner being is composed of the inner mental, inner vital, inner physical, — but that is not the psychic being. The psychic is the inmost being and quite distinct from these. The word 'psychic' is indeed used in English to indicate anything that is other or deeper than the external mind, life and body, anything occult or supraphysical, but that is a use which brings confusion and error and we entirely discard it when we speak or write about yoga. In ordinary parlance we may sometimes use the word 'psychic' in the looser popular sense or in poetry, which is not bound to intellectual accuracy, we may speak of the soul sometimes in the ordinary and more external sense or in the sense of the true psyche.   *Letters on Yoga, p. 294*

The being of man is composed of these elements — the psychic behind supporting all, the inner mental, vital and physical, and the outer, quite external nature of mind, life and body which is their instrument of expression. But above all is the central being (Jivatma) which uses them all for its manifestation: it is a portion of the Divine Self; but this reality of himself is hidden from the external man who replaces this inmost self and soul of him by the mental and vital ego. It is only those who have begun to know themselves that become aware of their true central being; but still it is always there standing behind the action of mind, life and body and is most directly represented by the psychic which is itself a spark of the Divine. It is by the growth of the psychic element in one's nature that one begins to come into conscious touch with one's central being above. When that happens and the central being uses a conscious will to control and organize the movements of the nature, it is then that one has a real, a spiritual as opposed to a partial and merely mental or moral self-mastery.   *Letters on Yoga, pp. 301-02*

It is necessary to understand clearly the difference between the evolving soul (psychic being) and the pure Atman, self or spirit. The pure self is unborn, does not pass through death or birth, is independent of birth or body, mind or life or this manifested Nature. It is not bound by these things, not limited, not affected, even though it assumes and supports them. The soul, on the contrary, is something that comes down into birth and passes through death — although it does not itself die, for it is immortal — from one state to another, from the earth plane to other planes and back again to the earth-existence. It goes on with this progression from life to life through an evolution which leads it up to the human state and evolves through it all a being of itself which we call the psychic being that supports the evolution and develops a physical, a vital, a mental human consciousness as its instruments of world-experience and of a disguised, imperfect, but growing self-expression. All this it does from behind a veil showing something of its divine self only in so far as the imperfection of the instrumental being will allow it. But a time comes when it is able to prepare to come out from behind the veil, to take command and turn all the instrumental nature towards a divine fulfilment. This is the beginning of the true spiritual life. The soul is able now to make itself ready for a higher evolution of manifested consciousness than the mental human — it can pass from the mental to the spiritual and through degrees of the spiritual to the supramental state.   *Letters on Yoga, pp. 438-39*

The Jivatman, spark-soul and psychic being are three different forms of the same reality and they must not be mixed up together, as that confuses the clearness of the inner experience.

The Jivatman or spirit, as it is usually called in English, is self-existent above the manifested or instrumental being — it is superior to birth and death, always the same, the individual Self or Atman. It is the eternal true being of the individual.

The soul is a spark of the Divine which is not seated above the manifested being, but comes down into the manifestation to support its evolution in the material world. It is at first an undifferentiated power of the Divine Consciousness containing all possibilities which have not yet taken form, but to which it is the function of evolution to give form. This spark is there in all living beings from the lowest to the highest.

The psychic being is formed by the soul in its evolution. It supports the mind, vital, body, grows by their experiences, carries the nature from life to life. It is the psychic or *caitya puruṣa*. At first it is veiled by mind, vital and body, but as it grows, it becomes capable of coming forward and dominating the mind, life and body; in the ordinary man it depends on them for expression and is not able to take them up and freely use them. The life of the being is animal or human and not divine. When the psychic being can by sadhana become dominant and freely use its instruments, then the impulse towards the Divine becomes complete and the transformation of mind, vital and body, not merely their liberation, becomes possible.

The Self or Atman being free and superior to birth and death, the experience of the Jivatman and its unity with the supreme or universal Self brings the sense of liberation, it is this which is necessary for the supreme spiritual deliverance: but for the transformation of the life and nature the awakening of the psychic being and its rule over the nature are indispensable.

Letters on Yoga, pp. 282-83

The soul or psyche is immutable only in the sense that it contains all the possibilities of the Divine within it, but it has to evolve them and in its evolution it assumes the form of a developing psychic individual evolving in the manifestation the individual Prakriti and taking part in the evolution. It is the spark of the Divine Fire that grows behind the mind, vital and physical by means of the psychic being until it is able to transform the Prakriti of Ignorance into a Prakriti of Knowledge. This evolving psychic being is not therefore at any time all that the soul or essential psychic existence bears within it; it temporalises and individualises what is eternal in potentiality, transcendent in essence, in this projection of the spirit.

The central being is the being which presides over the different births one after the other, but is itself unborn, for it does not descend into the being but is above it — it holds together the mental, vital and physical being and all the various parts of the personality and it controls the life either through the mental being and the mental thought and will or through the psychic, whichever may happen to be most in front or most powerful in nature. If it does not exercise its control, then the consciousness is in great disorder and every part of the personality acts for itself so that there is no coherence in the thought, feeling or action.

The psychic is not above but behind — its seat is behind the heart, its power is not knowledge but an essential or spiritual feeling — it has the clearest sense of the Truth and a sort of inherent perception of it which is of the nature of soul-perception and soul-feeling. It is our inmost being and supports all the others, mental, vital, physical, but it is also much veiled by them and has to act upon them as an influence rather than by its sovereign right of direct action; its direct action becomes normal and preponderant only at a high stage of development or by yoga. It is not the psychic being which, you feel, gives you the intuitions of things to be or warns you against the results of certain actions; that is some part of the inner being, sometimes the inner mental, sometimes the inner vital, sometimes, it may be, the inner or subtle physical Purusha. The inner being — inner mind, inner vital, inner or subtle physical — knows much that is unknown to the outer mind, the outer vital, the outer physical, for it is in a more direct contact with the secret forces of Nature. The psychic is the inmost being of all; a perception of truth which is inherent in the deepest substance of the consciousness, a sense of the good, true, beautiful, the Divine, is its privilege.

Letters on Yoga, pp. 268-69

The true soul secret in us... this veiled psychic entity is the flame of the Godhead always alight within us, inextinguishable even by that dense unconsciousness of any spiritual self within which obscures our outward nature. It is a flame born out of the Divine and, luminous inhabitant of the Ignorance, grows in it till it is able to turn it towards the Knowledge. It is the concealed Witness and Control, the hidden Guide, the Daemon of Socrates, the inner light or inner voice of the mystic. It is that which endures and is imperishable in us from birth to birth, untouched by death, decay or corruption, an indestructible spark of the Divine. Not the unborn Self or Atman, for the Self even in presiding over the existence of the individual is aware always of its universality and transcendence, it is yet its deputy in the forms of Nature, the individual soul, *caitya puruṣa*, supporting mind, life and body, standing behind the mental, the vital, the subtle-physical being in us and watching and profiting by their development and experience. These other person-powers in man, these beings of his being, are also veiled in their true entity, but they put forward temporary personalities which compose our outer individuality and whose combined superficial action and appearance of status we call ourselves: this inmost entity also, taking form in us as the psychic Person, puts forward a psychic personality which changes, grows, develops from life to life; for this is the traveller between birth and death and between death and birth, our nature parts are only its manifold and changing vesture. The psychic being can at first exercise only a concealed and partial and indirect action through the mind, the life and the body, since it is these parts of Nature that have to be developed as its instruments of self-expression, and it is long confined by their evolution. Missioned to lead man in the Ignorance towards the light of the Divine Consciousness, it takes the essence of all experience in the Ignorance to form a nucleus of soul-growth in the nature; the rest it turns into material for the future growth of the instruments which it has to use until they are ready to be a luminous instrumentation of the Divine. It is this secret psychic entity which is the true original Conscience in us deeper than the constructed and conventional conscience of the moralist, for it is this which points always towards Truth and Right and Beauty, towards Love and Harmony and all that is a divine possibility in us, and persists till these things become the major need of our nature. It is the psychic personality in us that flowers as the saint, the sage, the seer; when it reaches its full strength, it turns the being towards the Knowledge of Self and the Divine, towards the supreme Truth, the supreme Good, the supreme Beauty, Love and Bliss, the divine heights and largenesses, and opens us to the touch of spiritual sympathy, universality, oneness. On the contrary, where the psychic personality is weak, crude or ill-developed, the finer parts and movements in us are lacking or poor in character and power, even though the mind may be forceful and brilliant, the heart of vital emotions hard and strong and masterful, the life-force dominant and successful, the bodily existence rich and fortunate and an apparent lord and victor. It is then the outer desire-soul, the pseudo-psychic entity, that reigns and we mistake its misinterpretations of psychic suggestion and aspiration, its ideas and ideals, its desires and yearnings for true soul-stuff and wealth of spiritual experience.[1] If the secret psychic Person can come forward into the front and, replacing the desire-soul, govern overtly and entirely and not only partially and from behind the veil this outer nature of mind, life and body, then these can be cast into soul images of what is true, right and beautiful and in the end the whole nature can be turned towards

---

[1] The word "psychic" in our ordinary parlance is more often used in reference to this desire-soul than to the true psychic. It is used still more loosely of psychological and other phenomena of an abnormal or supernormal character which are really connected with the inner mind, inner vital, subtle physical being subliminal in us and are not at all direct operations of the psyche. Even such phenomena as materialisation and dematerialisation are included, though, if established, they evidently are not soul-action and would not shed any light upon the nature or existence of the psychic entity, but would rather be an abnormal action of an occult subtle physical energy intervening in the ordinary status of the gross body of things, reducing it to its own subtle condition and again reconstituting it in the terms of gross matter.

the real aim of life, the supreme victory, the ascent into spiritual
existence.   *The Life Divine, p. 225-27*

It is the very nature of the soul or the psychic being to turn
towards the divine Truth as the sunflower to the sun; it accepts
and clings to all that is divine or progressing towards divinity
and draws back from all that is a perversion or a denial of it,
from all that is false and undivine. Yet is the soul at first but a
spark and then a little flame of godhead burning in the midst
of a great darkness; for the most part it is veiled in its inner
sanctum and to reveal itself has to call on the mind, the life-
force and the physical consciousness and persuade them, as best
they can, to express it; ordinarily, it succeeds at most in suffusing
their outwardness with its inner light and modifying with its pu-
rifying fineness their dark obscurities or their coarser mixture.
Even when there is a formed psychic being able to express itself
with some directness in life, it is still in all but a few a smaller
portion of the being — "no bigger in the mass of the body than
the thumb of a man"[2] was the image used by the ancient seers
— and it is not always able to prevail against the obscurity or
ignorant smallness of the physical consciousness, the mistaken
surenesses of the mind or the arrogance and vehemence of the
vital nature. This soul is obliged to accept the human mental,
emotive, sensational life as it is, its relations, its activities, its
cherished forms and figures; it has to labour to disengage and
increase the divine element in all this relative truth mixed with
a continual falsifying error, this love turned to the uses of the
animal body or the satisfaction of the vital ego, this life of an
average manhood shot with rare and pale glimpses of Godhead
and the darker luridities of the demon and the brute. Unerring in
the essence of its will, it is obliged often under the pressure of its
instruments to submit to mistakes of action, wrong placement
of feeling, wrong choice of person, errors in the exact form of

---

[2] *Katha Upanishad* (Ed.)

its will, in the circumstances of its expression of the infallible inner ideal. Yet is there a divination within it which makes it a surer guide than the reason or than even the highest desire, and through apparent errors and stumblings its voice can still lead better than the precise intellect and the considering mental judgment. This voice of the soul is not what we call conscience — for that is only a mental and often conventional erring substitute; it is a deeper and more seldom heard call; yet to follow it when heard is wisest: even, it is better to wander at the call of one's soul than to go apparently straight with the reason and the outward moral mentor. But it is only when the life turns towards the Divine that the soul can truly come forward and impose its power on the outer members; for, itself a spark of the Divine, to grow in flame towards the Divine is its true life and its very reason of existence. *The Synthesis of Yoga, pp. 144-45*

As the evolution proceeds, Nature begins slowly and tentatively to manifest our occult parts; she leads us to look more and more within ourselves or sets out to initiate more clearly recognisable intimations and formations of them on the surface. The soul in us, the psychic principle, has already begun to take secret form; it puts forward and develops a soul-personality, a distinct psychic being to represent it. This psychic being remains still behind the veil in our subliminal part, like the true mental, the true vital or the true or subtle physical being within us: but, like them, it acts on the surface life by the influences and intimations it throws up upon that surface; these form part of the surface aggregate which is the conglomerate effect of the inner influences and upsurgings, the visible formation and superstructure which we ordinarily experience and think of as ourselves. On this ignorant surface we become dimly aware of something that can be called a soul as distinct from mind, life or body; we feel it not only as our mental idea or vague instinct of ourselves, but as a sensible influence in our life and character and action. A certain sensitive feeling for all that is true and good and beautiful, fine and pure and noble, a response to it, a demand for it, a pressure on mind and life to accept and formulate it in our thought, feelings, conduct, character is the most usually recognised, the most general and characteristic, though not the sole sign of this influence of the psyche. Of the man who has not this element in him or does not respond at all to this urge, we say that he has no soul. For it is this influence that we can most easily recognise as a finer or even a diviner part in us and the most powerful for the slow turning towards some aim at perfection in our nature.

But this psychic influence or action does not come up to the surface quite pure or does not remain distinct in its purity; if it did, we would be able to distinguish clearly the soul element in us and follow consciously and fully its dictates. An occult mental and vital and subtle-physical action intervenes, mixes with it, tries to use it and turn it to its own profit, dwarfs its divinity, distorts or diminishes its self-expression, even causes it to deviate and stumble or stains it with the impurity, smallness and error of mind and life and body. After it reaches the surface, thus alloyed and diminished, it is taken hold of by the surface nature in an obscure reception and ignorant formation, and there is or can be by this cause a still further deviation and mixture. A twist is given, a wrong direction is imparted, a wrong application, a wrong formation, an erroneous result of what is in itself pure stuff and action of our spiritual being; a formation of consciousness is accordingly made which is a mixture of the psychic influence and its intimations jumbled with mental ideas and opinions, vital desires and urges, habitual physical tendencies. There coalesce too with the obscured soul-influence the ignorant though well-intentioned efforts of these external parts towards a higher direction; a mental ideation of a very mixed character, often obscure even in its idealism, sometimes even disastrously mistaken, a fervour and passion of the emotional being throwing up its spray and foam of feelings, sentiments, sentimentalisms, a dynamic enthusiasm of the life-parts, eager responses of the physical, the thrills and excitements of nerve and body, — all these influences coalesce in a composite formation which is frequently taken as the soul and its mixed and confused action for the soul-stir, for a psychic development and action or a realised inner influence. The psychic entity is itself free from stain or mixture, but what comes up from it is not protected by that immunity; therefore this confusion becomes possible.

Moreover, the psychic being, the soul-personality in us, does not emerge full-grown and luminous; it evolves, passes through a slow development and formation; its figure of being may be at first indistinct and may afterwards remain for a long time weak and undeveloped, not impure but imperfect: for it rests its formation, its dynamic self-building on the power of soul that has been actually and more or less successfully, against the resistance of the Ignorance and Inconscience, put forth in the evolution upon the surface. Its appearance is the sign of a soul-emergence in Nature, and if that emergence is as yet small and defective, the psychic personality also will be stunted or feeble. It is too, by the obscurity of our consciousness, separated from its inner reality, in imperfect communication with its own source in the depths of the being; for the road is as yet ill-built, easily obstructed, the wires often cut or crowded with communications of another kind and proceeding from another origin: its power to impress what it receives upon the outer instruments is also imperfect; in its penury it has for most things to rely on these instruments and it forms its push to expression and action on their data and not solely on the unerring perceptions of the psychic entity. In these conditions it cannot prevent the true psychic light from being diminished or distorted in the mind into a mere idea or opinion, the psychic feeling in the heart into a fallible emotion or mere sentiment, the psychic will to action in the life-parts into a blind vital enthusiasm or a fervid excitement: it even accepts these mistranslations for want of something better and tries to fulfil itself through them. For it is part of the work of the soul to influence mind and heart and vital being and turn their ideas, feelings, enthusiasms, dynamisms in the direction of what is divine and luminous; but this has to be done at first imperfectly, slowly and with a mixture. As the psychic personality grows stronger, it begins to increase its communion with the psychic entity behind it and improve its communications with the surface: it can transmit its intimations to the mind and heart and life with a greater purity and force; for it is more able to exercise a strong control and react against false mixtures; now more and more it makes itself distinctly felt as a power in the nature. But even so this evolution would be slow and long if left solely to the difficult automatic action of the evolutionary Energy; it is only when man awakes to the knowledge of the soul and feels a need to bring it to the front and make it the master of his life and action that a quicker conscious method of evolution intervenes and a psychic transformation becomes possible. *The Life Divine, pp. 893-95*

The psychic being is always there, but is not felt because it is covered up by the mind and vital; when it is no longer covered up, it is then said to be awake. When it is awake, it begins to take hold of the rest of the being, to influence it and change it so that all may become the true expression of the inner soul. It is this change that is called the inner conversion. There can be no conversion without the awakening of the psychic being.

Letters on Yoga, p. 1096

What is meant by [the psychic's] coming to the front is simply this. The psychic ordinarily is deep within. Very few people are aware of their souls — when they speak of their soul, they usually mean the vital and mental being or else the (false) soul of desire. The psychic remains behind and acts only through the mind, vital and physical wherever it can. For this reason the psychic being except where it is very much developed has only a small and partial, concealed and mixed or diluted influence on the life of most men. By coming forward is meant that it comes from behind the veil, its presence is felt already in the waking daily consciousness, its influence fills, dominates, transforms the mind and vital and their movements, even the physical. One is aware of one's soul, feels the psychic to be one's true being, the mind and the rest begin to be only instruments of the inmost within us.   *Letters on Yoga, p. 1097*

9
Purusha and Prakriti
Soul and Nature

...we have to begin with a dualism of the thing and its shadow, Purusha and Prakriti, commonly called spirit and matter. Properly speaking, the distinction is illusory, since there is nothing which is exclusively spirit or exclusively matter, nor can the Universe be strictly parcelled out between these; from the point of view of Reality spirit and matter are not different but the same. We may say, if we like, that the entire Universe is matter and spirit does not exist; we may say, if we like that the entire Universe is spirit and matter does not exist. In either case we are merely multiplying words without counsel, ignoring the patent fact visible through the Universe that both spirit and matter exist and are indissolubly welded, precisely because they are simply one thing viewed from two sides. The distinction between them is one of the primary dualisms and a first result of the great Ignorance. Maya works out in name and form as material; Maya works out in the conceiver of name and form as spiritual. Purusha is the great principle or force whose presence is necessary to awake creative energy and send it out working into and on shapes of matter. For this reason Purusha is the name usually applied to the conditioned Brahman in His manifestations; but it is always well to remember that the Primal Existence turned towards manifestation has a double aspect, Male and Female, positive and negative. He is the origin of the birth of things and He is the receptacle of the birth and it is to the Male aspect of Himself that the word Purusha predominatingly applies. The image often applied to these relations is that of the man casting his seed into the woman; his duty is merely to originate the seed and deposit it, but it is the woman's duty to cherish the seed, develop it, bring it forth and start it on its career of manifested life. The seed, says the Upanishad, is the self of the Male, it is spirit, and being cast into the Female, Prakriti, it becomes one with her and therefore does her no hurt; spirit takes the shaping appearance of matter and does not break up the appearances of matter, but develops under their law. The Man and the Woman, universal Adam and Eve, are really one and each is incomplete without the other, barren without the other, inactive without the other. Purusha the Male, God, is that side of the One which gives the impulse toward phenomenal existence; Prakriti the Female, Nature, is that side which is and evolves the material of phenomenal existence; both of them are therefore unborn and eternal.

The Upanishads, pp. 45-46

Existence is composed of Prakriti and Purusha, the consciousness that sees and the consciousness that executes and formalises what we see. The one we call Soul, the other Nature. These are the first double terms from which our Yoga has to start. When we come to look in at our selves instead of out at the world and begin to analyse our subjective experience, we find that there are two parts of our being which can be, to all appearance, entirely separated from each other, one a consciousness which is still and passive and supports, and the other a consciousness which is busy and creative and is supported. The passive and fundamental consciousness is the Soul, the Purusha, Witness or *sākṣī*, the active and superstructural consciousness is Nature, Prakriti, processive or creative energy of the *sākṣī*. But the two seem at first to stand apart and distinct as if they had no share in each other.

The Purusha, still and silent witness of whatever Prakriti chooses to create, not interfering with her works, but reflecting only whatever forms, names and movements she casts on the pure mirror of his eternal existence and the Prakriti restlessly creating, acting, forming and effecting things for the delight of the Purusha, compose the double system of the Sankhyas. But as we continue analysing their relations and accumulate more and more experience of our subjective life, we find that this seeing of the Purusha is in effect a command. Whatever Prakriti perceives it to be the pleasure of the Purusha to see, she tends to preserve in his subjective experience or to establish; whatever she perceives it to be his pleasure to cease to see, she tends to renounce and abolish. Whatever he consents to in her, she forces on him and is glad of her mastery and his submission but whenever he insists, she is bound eventually to obey. Early found to be true in our subjective experience, this ultimate principle of things is eventually discovered by the Yogin to determine even objective phenomena. The Purusha and Prakriti are therefore not only the Witness and the Activity witnessed, but the Lord and his executive energy. The Purusha is Ishwara, the Prakriti is His Shakti. Their play with each other is both the motive and the executive force of all existence in the universe.

The Hour of God and Other Writings, pp. 51-52

This division was made most clearly by the old Indian philosophies; but it bases itself upon the eternal fact of practical duality in unity upon which the world-manifestation is founded. It is given different names according to our view of the universe. The Vedantins spoke of the Self and Maya, meaning according to their predilections by the Self the Immutable and by Maya the power the Self has of imposing on itself the cosmic illusion, or by the Self the Divine Being and by Maya the nature of conscious-being and the conscious-force by which the Divine embodies himself in soul-forms and forms of things. Others spoke of Ishwara and Shakti, the Lord and His force, His cosmic power. The analytic philosophy of the Sankhyas affirmed their eternal duality without any possibility of oneness, accepting only relations of union and separation by which the cosmic action of Prakriti begins, proceeds or ceases for the Purusha; for the Purusha is an inactive conscious existence, — it is the Soul the same in itself and immutable forever, — Prakriti the active force of Nature which by its motion creates and maintains and by its sinking into rest dissolves the phenomenon of the cosmos. Leaving aside these philosophical distinctions, we come to the original psychological experience from which all really take their start, that there are two elements in the existence of living beings, of human beings at least if not of all cosmos, — a dual being, Nature and the soul.

This duality is self-evident. Without any philosophy at all, by the mere force of experience it is what we can all perceive, although we may not take the trouble to define. Even the most thoroughgoing materialism which denies the soul or resolves it into a more or less illusory result of natural phenomena acting upon some ill-explained phenomenon of the physical brain which we call consciousness or the mind, but which is really no more than a sort of complexity of nervous spasms, cannot get rid of the practical fact of this duality. It does not matter at all how it came about; the fact is not only there, it determines our whole existence, it is the one fact which is really important to us as human beings with a will and an intelligence and a subjective existence which makes all our happiness and our suffering. The whole problem of life resolves itself into this one question, — "What are we to do with this soul and nature set face to face with each other, — we who have as one side of our existence this Nature, this personal and cosmic activity, which tries to impress itself upon the soul, to possess, control, determine it, and as the other side this soul which feels that in some mysterious way it has a freedom, a control over itself, a responsibility for what it is and does, and tries therefore to turn upon Nature, its own and the world's, and to control, possess, enjoy, or even, it may be, reject and escape from her?" In order to answer that question we have to know, — to know what the soul can do, to know what it can do with itself, to know too what it can do with Nature and the world. The whole of human philosophy, religion, science is really nothing but an attempt to get at the right data upon which it will be possible to answer the question and solve, as satisfactorily as our knowledge will allow, the problem of our existence. *The Synthesis of Yoga, pp. 409-11*

In its outer appearance the truth of existence is solely what we call Nature or Prakriti, a Force that operates as the whole law and mechanism of being, creates the world which is the object of our mind and senses and creates too the mind and senses as a means of relation between the creature and the objective world in which he lives. In this outer appearance man in his soul, his mind, his life, his body seems to be a creature of Nature differentiated from others by a separation of his body, life and mind and especially by his ego-sense — that subtle mechanism constructed for him that he may confirm and centralise his consciousness of all this strong separateness and difference. All in him, his soul of mind and its action as well as the functioning of his life and body, is very evidently determined by the law of his nature, cannot get outside of it, cannot operate otherwise. He attributes indeed a certain freedom to his personal will, the will of his ego; but that in reality amounts to nothing, since his ego is only a sense which makes him identify himself with the creation that Nature has made of him, with the varying mind and life and body she has constructed. His ego is itself a product of her workings, and as is the nature of his ego, so will be the nature of its will and according to that he must act and he can no other.

This then is man's ordinary consciousness of himself, this his faith in his own being, that he is a creature of Nature, a separate ego establishing whatever relations with others and with the world, making whatever development of himself, satisfying whatever will, desire, idea of his mind may be permissible in her circle and consonant with her intention or law in his existence.

There is, however, something in man's consciousness which does not fall in with the rigidity of this formula; he has a faith, which grows greater as his soul develops, in another and an inner reality of existence. In this inner reality the truth of existence is no longer Nature but Soul and Spirit, Purusha rather than Prakriti. Nature herself is only a power of Spirit, Prakriti the force of the Purusha. A Spirit, a Self, a Being one in all is the master of this world which is only his partial manifestation. That Spirit is the upholder of Nature and her action and the giver of the sanction by which alone her law becomes imperative and her force and its ways operative. That Spirit within her is the Knower who illuminates her and makes her conscient in us; his is the immanent and superconscient Will that inspires and motives her workings. The soul in man, a portion of this Divinity, shares his nature. Our nature is our soul's manifestation, operates by its sanction and embodies its secret self-knowledge and self-consciousness and its will of being in her motions and forms and changes.

The real soul and self of us is hidden from our intelligence by its ignorance of inner things, by a false identification, by an absorption in our outward mechanism of mind, life and body. But if the active soul of man can once draw back from this identification with its natural instruments, if it can see and live in the entire faith of its inner reality, then all is changed to it, life and existence take on another appearance, action a different meaning and character. Our being then becomes no longer this little egoistic creation of Nature, but the largeness of a divine, immortal and spiritual Power. Our consciousness becomes no longer that of this limited and struggling mental and vital creature, but an infinite, divine and spiritual consciousness. And our will and action too are no longer that of this bounded personality and its ego, but a divine and spiritual will and action, the will and power of the Universal, the Supreme, the All-Self and Spirit acting freely through the human figure.

Essays on the Gita, pp. 554-56

In the spiritual truth of our being the power which we call Nature is the power of being, consciousness and will and therefore the power of self-expression and self-creation of the self, soul or Purusha. But to our ordinary mind in the ignorance and to its experience of things the force of Prakriti has a different appearance. When we look at it in its universal action outside ourselves, we see it first as a mechanical energy in the cosmos which acts upon matter or in its own created forms of matter. In matter it evolves powers and processes of life and in living matter powers and processes of mind. Throughout its operations it acts by fixed laws and in each kind of created thing displays varying properties of energy and laws of process which give its character to the genus or species and again in the individual develops without infringing the law of the kind minor characteristics and variations of a considerable consequence. It is this mechanical appearance of Prakriti which has preoccupied the modern scientific mind and made for it its whole view of Nature, and so much so that science still hopes and labours with a very small amount of success to explain all phenomena of life by laws of matter and all phenomena of mind by law of living matter. Here soul or spirit has no place and nature cannot be regarded as power of spirit. Since the whole of our existence is mechanical, physical and bounded by the biological phenomenon of a brief living consciousness and man is a creature and instrument of material energy, the spiritual self-evolution of Yoga can be only a delusion, hallucination, abnormal state of mind or self-hypnosis. In any case it cannot be what it represents itself to be, a discovery of the eternal truth of our being and a passing above the limited truth of the mental, vital and physical to the full truth of our spiritual nature.

But when we look, not at external mechanical Nature to the exclusion of our personality, but at the inner subjective experience of man the mental being, our nature takes to us a quite different appearance. We may believe intellectually in a purely mechanical view even of our subjective existence, but we cannot act upon it or make it quite real to our self-experience. For we are conscious of an I which does not seem identical with our nature, but capable of a standing back from it, of a detached observation and criticism and creative use of it, and of a will which we naturally think of as a free will; and even if this be a delusion, we are still obliged in practice to act as if we were responsible mental beings capable of a free choice of our actions, able to use or misuse and to turn to higher or lower ends our nature. And even we seem to be struggling both with our environmental and with our own present nature and striving to get mastery over a world which imposes itself on and masters us and at the same time to become something more than we now are. But the difficulty is that we are only in command, if at all, over a small part of ourselves, the rest is subconscient or subliminal and beyond our control, our will acts only in a small selection of our activities; the most is a process of mechanism and habit and we must strive constantly with ourselves and surrounding circumstances to make the least advance or self-amelioration. There seems to be a dual being in us; Soul and Nature, Purusha and Prakriti, seem to be half in agreement, half at odds, Nature laying its mechanical control on the soul, the soul attempting to change and master nature. And the question is what is the fundamental character of this duality and what the issue.

The Sankhya explanation is that our present existence is governed by a dual principle. Prakriti is inert without the contact of Purusha, acts only by a junction with it and then too by the fixed mechanism of her instruments and qualities; Purusha, passive and free apart from Prakriti, becomes by contact with her and sanction to her works subject to this mechanism, lives in her limitation of ego-sense and must get free by withdrawing the sanction and returning to its own proper principle. Another explanation that tallies with a certain part of our experience is that there is a dual being in us, the animal and material, or more widely the lower nature-bound, and the soul or spiritual being entangled by mind in the material existence or in world-nature, and freedom comes by escape from the entanglement, the soul returning to its native planes or the self or spirit to its pure existence. The perfection of the soul then is to be found not at all in, but beyond Nature.

But in a higher than our present mental consciousness we

find that this duality is only a phenomenal appearance. The highest and real truth of existence is the one Spirit, the supreme Soul, Purushottama, and it is the power of being of this Spirit which manifests itself in all that we experience as universe. This universal Nature is not a lifeless, inert or unconscious mechanism, but informed in all its movements by the universal Spirit. The mechanism of its process is only an outward appearance and the reality is the Spirit creating or manifesting its own being by its own power of being in all that is in Nature. Soul and Nature in us too are only a dual appearance of the one existence. The universal energy acts in us, but the soul limits itself by the ego-sense, lives in a partial and separate experience of her workings, uses only a modicum and a fixed action of her energy for its self-expression. It seems rather to be mastered and used by this energy than to use it, because it identifies itself with the ego-sense which is part of the natural instrumentation and lives in the ego experience. The ego is in fact driven by the mechanism of Nature of which it is a part and the ego-will is not and cannot be a free will. To arrive at freedom, mastery and perfection we have to get back to the real self and soul within and arrive too thereby at our true relations with our own and with universal nature.

In our active being this translates itself into a replacement of our egoistic, our personal, our separatively individual will and energy by a universal and a divine will and energy which determines our action in harmony with the universal action and reveals itself as the direct will and the all-guiding power of the Purushottama. We replace the inferior action of the limited, ignorant and imperfect personal will and energy in us by the action of the divine Shakti. To open ourselves to the universal energy is always possible to us, because that is all around us and always flowing into us, it is that which supports and supplies all our inner and outer action and in fact we have no power of our own in any separately individual sense, but only a personal formulation of the one Shakti. And on the other hand this universal Shakti is within ourselves, concentrated in us, for the whole power of it is present in each individual as in the universe, and there are means and processes by which we can awaken its greater and potentially infinite force and liberate it to its larger workings.

The Synthesis of Yoga, pp. 724-26

The Conscious Being, Purusha, is the Self as originator, witness, support and lord and enjoyer of the forms and works of Nature. As the aspect of Self is in its essential character transcendental even when involved and identified with its universal and in-dividual becomings, so the Purusha aspect is characteristically universal-individual and intimately connected with Nature even when separated from her. For this conscious Spirit while retain-ing its impersonality and eternity, its universality, puts on at the same time a more personal aspect...it is the impersonal-personal being in Nature from whom it is not altogether detached, for it is always coupled with her: Nature acts for the Purusha and by its sanction, for its will and pleasure; the Conscious Being imparts its consciousness to the Energy we call Nature, receives in that consciousness her workings as in a mirror, accepts the forms which she, the executive cosmic Force, creates and imposes on it, gives or withdraws its sanction from her movements. The experience of Purusha-Prakriti, the Spirit or Conscious Being in its relations to Nature, is of immense pragmatic importance; for on these relations the whole play of the consciousness depends in the embodied being. If the Purusha in us is passive and allows Nature to act, accepting all she imposes on him, giving a constant automatic sanction, then the soul in mind, life, body, the mental, vital, physical being in us, becomes subject to our nature, ruled by its formation, driven by its activities; that is the normal state of our ignorance. If the Purusha in us becomes aware of itself as the Witness and stands back from Nature, that is the first step to the soul's freedom; for it becomes detached, and it is possible then to know Nature and her processes and in all independence, since we are no longer involved in her works, to accept or not to accept, to make the sanction no longer automatic but free and effective; we can choose what she shall do or not do in us, or we can stand back altogether from her works and withdraw easily into the Self's spiritual silence, or we can reject her present formations and rise to a spiritual level of existence and from there re-create our existence. The Purusha can cease to be subject, *aniśa*, and become lord of its nature, *īśvara*.

The Life Divine, pp. 348-49

What is meant by Prakriti or Nature is the outer or executive side of the Shakti or Conscious Force which forms and moves the worlds. This outer side appears here to be mechanical, a play of the forces, Gunas, etc. Behind it is the living Consciousness and Force of the Divine, the divine Shakti. The Prakriti itself is divided into the lower and higher, — the lower is the Prakriti of the Ignorance, the Prakriti of mind, life and Matter separated in consciousness from the Divine; the higher is the Divine Prakriti of Sachchidananda with its manifesting power of supermind, always aware of the Divine and free from Ignorance and its consequences. Man so long as he is in the ignorance is subject to the lower Prakriti, but by spiritual evolution he becomes aware of the higher Nature and seeks to come into contact with it. He can ascend into it and it can descend into him — such an ascent and descent can transform the lower nature of mind, life and Matter.

Letters on Yoga, p. 287

In the experience of yoga the self or being is in essence one with the Divine or at least it is a portion of the Divine and has all the divine potentialities. But in manifestation it takes two aspects, the Purusha and Prakriti, conscious being and Nature. In Nature here the Divine is veiled, and the individual being is subjected to Nature which acts here as the lower Prakriti, a force of Ignorance, Avidya. The Purusha in itself is divine, but exteriorised in the ignorance of Nature it is the individual apparent being imperfect with her imperfection. Thus the soul or psychic essence, which is the Purusha entering into the evolution and supporting it, carries in itself all the divine potentialities; but the individual psychic being which it puts forth as its representative assumes the imperfection of Nature and evolves in it till it has recovered its full psychic essence and united itself with the Self above of which the soul is the individual projection in the evolution. This duality in the being on all its planes — for it is true in different ways not only of the Self and the psychic but of the mental, vital and physical Purushas — has to be grasped and accepted before the experiences of the yoga can be fully understood.

Letters on Yoga, pp. 284-85

In a certain sense the various Purushas or beings in us, psychic, mental, vital, physical are projections of the Atman, but that gets its full truth only when we get into our inner being and know the inner truth of ourselves. On the surface, in the Ignorance, it is the mental, vital, physical Prakriti that acts and the Purusha is disfigured, as it were, in the action of the Prakriti. It is not our true mental being, our true vital being, our true physical being even that we are aware of; these remain behind, veiled and silent. It is the mental, vital, physical ego that we take for our being until we get knowledge.

Letters on Yoga, p. 300

10
The Gunas of Prakriti

The Three Modes of Nature

The idea of the three essential modes of Nature is a creation of the ancient Indian thinkers and its truth is not at once obvious, because it was the result of long psychological experiment and profound internal experience. Therefore without a long inner experience, without intimate self-observation and intuitive perception of the Nature-forces it is difficult to grasp accurately or firmly utilise.... These modes are termed in the Indian books qualities, gunas, and are given the names *sattva, rajas, tamas*. Sattwa is the force of equilibrium and translates in quality as good and harmony and happiness and light; Rajas is the force of kinesis and translates in quality as struggle and effort, passion and action; Tamas is the force of inconscience and inertia and translates in quality as obscurity and incapacity and inaction. Ordinarily used for psychological self-analysis, these distinctions are valid also in physical Nature. Each thing and every existence in the lower Prakriti contains them and its process and dynamic form are the result of the interaction of these qualitative powers.

The Synthesis of Yoga, pp. 220-21

The modes of Nature are all qualitative in their essence and are called for that reason its gunas or qualities. In any spiritual conception of the universe this must be so, because the connecting medium between spirit and matter must be psyche or soul power and the primary action psychological and qualitative, not physical and quantitative; for quality is the immaterial, the more spiritual element in all the action of the universal Energy, her prior dynamics. The predominance of physical Science has accustomed us to a different view of Nature, because there the first thing that strikes us is the importance of the quantitative aspect of her workings and her dependence for the creation of forms on quantitative combinations and dispositions. And yet even there the discovery that matter is rather substance or act of energy than energy a motive power of self-existent material substance or an inherent power acting in matter has led to some revival of an older reading of universal Nature. The analysis of the ancient Indian thinkers allowed for the quantitative action of Nature, *mātrā;* but that it regarded as proper to its more objective and formally executive working, while the innately ideative executive power which disposes things according to the quality of their being and energy, *guṇa, svabhāva,* is the primary determinant and underlies all the outer quantitative dispositions.

Essays on the Gita, pp. 411-12

The metaphysical bearing of this classification [of the three gunas] does not concern us; but in its psychological and spiritual bearing it is of immense practical importance, because these three principles enter into all things, combine to give them their turn of active nature, result, effectuation, and their unequal working in the soul-experience is the constituent force of our active personality, our temperament, type of nature and cast of psychological response to experience. All character of action and experience in us is determined by the predominance and by the proportional interaction of these three qualities or modes of Nature. The soul in its personality is obliged, as it were, to run into their moulds; mostly, too, it is controlled by them rather than has any free control of them. The soul can only be free by rising above and rejecting the tormented strife of their unequal action and their insufficient concords and combinations and precarious harmonies, whether in the sense of a complete quiescence from the half-regulated chaos of their action or in the sense of a superiority to this lower turn of nature and a higher control or transformation of their working. There must be either an emptiness of the gunas or a superiority to the gunas.

The gunas affect every part of our natural being. They have indeed their strongest relative hold in the three different members of it, mind, life and body. Tamas, the principle of inertia, is strongest in material nature and in our physical being. The action of this principle is of two kinds, inertia of force and inertia of knowledge. Whatever is predominantly governed by Tamas, tends in its force to a sluggish inaction and immobility or else to a mechanical action which it does not possess, but is possessed by obscure forces which drive it in a mechanical round of energy; equally in its consciousness it turns to an inconscience or enveloped subconscience or to a reluctant, sluggish or in some way mechanical conscious action which does not possess the idea of its own energy, but is guided by an idea which seems external to it or at least concealed from its active awareness. Thus the principle of our body is in its nature inert, subconscient, incapable of anything but a mechanical and habitual self-guidance and action: though it has like everything else a principle of kinesis and a principle of equilibrium of its state and action, an inherent principle of response and a secret consciousness, the greatest portion of its rajasic motions is contributed by the life-power and all the overt consciousness by the mental being. The principle of rajas has its strongest hold on the vital nature. It is the Life within us that is the strongest kinetic motor power, but the life-power in earthly beings is possessed by the force of desire, therefore rajas turns always to action and desire; desire is the strongest human and animal initiator of most kinesis and action, predominant to such an extent that many consider it the father of all action and even the originator of our being. Moreover, rajas finding itself in a world of matter which starts from the principle of inconscience and a mechanical driven inertia, has to work against an immense contrary force; therefore its whole action takes on the nature of an effort, a struggle, a besieged and an impeded conflict for possession which is distressed in its every step by a limiting incapacity, disappointment and suffering: even its gains are precarious and limited and marred by the reaction of the effort and an after-taste of insufficiency and transience. The principle of sattwa has its strongest hold in the mind; not so much in the lower parts of the mind which are dominated by the rajasic life-power, but mostly in the intelligence and the will of the reason. Intelligence, reason, rational will are moved by the nature of their predominant principle towards a constant effort of assimilation, assimilation by knowledge, assimilation by a power of understanding will, a constant effort towards equilibrium, some stability, rule, harmony of the conflicting elements of natural happening and experience. This satisfaction it gets in various ways and in various degrees of acquisition. The attainment of assimilation, equilibrium and harmony brings with it always a relative but more or less intense and satisfying sense of ease, happiness, mastery, security, which is other than the troubled and vehement pleasures insecurely bestowed by the satisfaction of rajasic desire and passion. Light and happiness are the characteristics of the sattwic guna. The whole nature of the embodied living mental being is determined by these three gunas.

But these are only predominant powers in each part of our complex system. The three qualities mingle, combine and strive in every fibre and in every member of our intricate psychology. The mental character is made by them, the character of our reason, the character of our will, the character of our moral, aesthetic, emotional, dynamic, sensational being. Tamas brings in all the ignorance, inertia, weakness, incapacity which afflicts our nature, a clouded reason, nescience, unintelligence, a clinging to habitual notions and mechanical ideas, the refusal to think and know, the small mind, the closed avenues, the trotting round of mental habit, the dark and the twilit places. Tamas brings in the impotent will, want of faith and self-confidence and initiative, the disinclination to act, the shrinking from endeavour and aspiration, the poor and little spirit, and in our moral and dynamic being the inertia, the cowardice, baseness, sloth, lax subjection to small and ignoble motives, the weak yielding to our lower nature. Tamas brings into our emotional nature insensibility, indifference, want of sympathy and openness, the shut soul, the callous heart, the soon spent affection and languor of the feelings, into our aesthetic and sensational nature the dull aesthesis, the limited range of response, the insensibility to beauty, all that makes in man the coarse, heavy and vulgar spirit. Rajas contributes our normal active nature with all its good and evil; when unchastened by a sufficient element of sattwa, it turns to egoism, self-will and violence, the perverse, obstinate or exaggerating action of the reason, prejudice, attachment to opinion, clinging to error, the subservience of the intelligence to our desires and preferences and not to the truth, the fanatic or the sectarian mind, self-will, pride, arrogance, selfishness, ambition, lust, greed, cruelty, hatred, jealousy, the egoisms of love, all the vices and passions, the exaggerations of the aesthesis, the morbidities and perversions of the sensational and vital being. Tamas in its own right produces the coarse, dull and ignorant type of human nature, rajas the vivid, restless, kinetic man, driven by the breath of action, passion and desire. Sattwa produces a higher type. The gifts of sattwa are the mind of reason and balance, clarity of the disinterested truth-seeking open intelligence, a will subordinated to the reason or guided by the ethical spirit, self-control, equality, calm, love, sympathy, refinement, measure, fineness of the aesthetic and emotional mind, in the sensational being delicacy, just acceptivity, moderation and poise, a vitality subdued and governed by the mastering intelligence. The accomplished types of the sattwic man are the philosopher, saint and sage, of the rajasic man the statesman, warrior, forceful man of action. But in all men there is in greater or less proportions a mingling of the gunas, a multiple personality and in most a good deal of shifting and alternation from the predominance of one to the prevalence of another guna; even in the governing form of their nature most human beings are of a mixed type. All the colour and variety of life is made of the intricate pattern of the weaving of the gunas.   *The Synthesis of Yoga, pp. 656-60*

The individual soul or the conscious being in a form may identify itself with this experiencing Purusha or with this active Prakriti. If it identifies itself with Prakriti, it is not master, enjoyer, and knower, but reflects the modes and workings of Prakriti. It enters by its identification into that subjection and mechanical working which is characteristic of her. And even, by an entire immersion in Prakriti, this soul becomes inconscient or subconscient, asleep in her forms as in the earth and the metal or almost asleep as in plant life. There, in that inconscience, it is subject to the domination of tamas, the principle, the power, the qualitative mode of obscurity and inertia: sattwa and rajas are there, but they are concealed in the thick coating of tamas. Emerging into its own proper nature of consciousness but not yet truly conscious, because there is still too great a domination of tamas in the nature, the embodied being becomes more and more subject to rajas, the principle, the power, the qualitative mode of action and passion impelled by desire and instinct. There is then formed and developed the animal nature, narrow in consciousness, rudimentary in intelligence, rajaso-tamasic in vital habit and impulse. Emerging yet farther from the great Inconscience towards a spiritual status the embodied being liberates sattwa, the mode of light, and acquires a relative freedom and mastery and knowledge and with it a qualified and conditioned sense of inner satisfaction and happiness. Man, the mental being in a physical body, should be but is not, except in a few among this multitude of ensouled bodies, of this nature. Ordinarily he has too much in him of the obscure earth-inertia and a troubled ignorant animal life-force to be a soul of light and bliss or even a mind of harmonious will and knowledge. There is here in man an incomplete and still hampered and baffled ascension towards the true character of the Purusha, free, master, knower and enjoyer. For these are in human and earthly experience relative modes, none giving its single and absolute fruit; all are intermixed with each other and there is not the pure action of any one of them anywhere. It is their confused and inconstant interaction that determines the experiences of the egoistic human consciousness swinging in Nature's uncertain balance.

The Synthesis of Yoga, pp. 91-92

No existence is cast entirely in the single mould of any of these three modes of the cosmic Force; all three are present in everyone and everywhere. There is a constant combining and separation of their shifting relations and interpenetrating influences, often a conflict, a wrestling of forces, a struggle to dominate each other. All have in great or in small extent or degree, even if sometimes in a hardly appreciable minimum, their sattwic states and clear tracts or inchoate tendencies of light, clarity and happiness, fine adaptation and sympathy with the environment, intelligence, poise, right mind, right will and feeling, right impulse, virtue, order. All have their rajasic modes and impulses and turbid parts of desire and passion and struggle, perversion and falsehood and error, unbalanced joy and sorrow, aggressive push to work and eager creation and strong or bold or fiery or fierce reactions to the pressure of the environment and to life's assaults and offers. All have their tamasic states and constant obscure parts, their moments or their points of unconsciousness, their long habit or their temporary velleities of weak resignation or dull acceptance, their constitutional feeblenesses or movements of fatigue, negligence and indolence and their lapses into ignorance and incapacity, depression and fear and cowardly recoil or submission to the environment and to the pressure of men and events and forces. Each one of us is sattwic in some directions of his energy of Nature or in some parts of his mind or character, in others rajasic, tamasic in others. According as one or other of the modes usually dominates his general temperament and type of mind and turn of action, it is said of him that he is the sattwic, the rajasic or the tamasic man; but few are always of one kind and none is entire in his kind. The wise are not always or wholly wise, the intelligent are intelligent only in patches; the saint suppresses in himself many unsaintly movements and the vile are not entirely evil: the dullest has his unexpressed or unused and undeveloped capacities, the most timorous his moments or his way of courage, the helpless and the weakling a latent part of strength in his nature. The dominant gunas are not the essential soul-type of the embodied being but only the index of the formation he has made for this life or during his present existence and at a given moment of his evolution in Time.

The Synthesis of Yoga, pp. 222-23

Transcendence of the Gunas and their Transformation

...richness of life, even a sattwic harmony of mind and nature does not constitute spiritual perfection. There is a relative possible perfection, but it is a perfection of incompleteness, some partial height, force, beauty, some measure of nobility and greatness, some imposed and precariously sustained balance. There is a relative mastery, but it is a mastery of the body by life or of the life by mind, not a free possession of the instruments by the liberated and self-possessing spirit. The gunas have to be transcended if we would arrive at spiritual perfection. Tamas evidently has to be overcome, inertia and ignorance and incapacity cannot be elements of a true perfection; but it can only be overcome in Nature by the force of rajas aided by an increasing force of sattwa. Rajas has to be overcome, egoism, personal desire and self-seeking passion are not elements of the true perfection; but it can only be overcome by force of sattwa enlightening the being and force of tamas limiting the action. Sattwa itself does not give the highest or the integral perfection; sattwa is always a quality of the limited nature; sattwic knowledge is the light of a limited mentality; sattwic will is the government of a limited intelligent force. Moreover, sattwa cannot act by itself in Nature, but has to rely for all action on the aid of rajas, so that even sattwic action is always liable to the imperfections of rajas; egoism, perplexity, inconsistency, a one-sided turn, a limited and exaggerated will, exaggerating itself in the intensity of its limitations, pursue the mind and action even of the saint, philosopher and sage. There is a sattwic as well as a rajasic or tamasic egoism, at the highest an egoism of knowledge or virtue; but the mind's egoism of whatever type is incompatible with liberation. All the three gunas have to be transcended. Sattwa may bring us near to the Light, but its limited clarity falls away from us when we enter into the luminous body of the divine Nature.   *The Synthesis of Yoga, p. 660*

...man as the individual self, owing to his ignorant self-identification with the work and the becoming, as if that were all his soul and not a power of his soul, a power proceeding from it, is bewildered by the ego-sense. He thinks that it is he and others who are doing all; he does not see that Nature is doing all and that he is misrepresenting and disfiguring her works to himself by ignorance and attachment. He is enslaved by the gunas, now hampered in the dull case of tamas, now blown by the strong winds of rajas, now limited by the partial lights of sattwa, not distinguishing himself at all from the nature-mind which alone is thus modified by the gunas. He is therefore mastered by pain and pleasure, happiness and grief, desire and passion, attachment and disgust: he has no freedom. He must, to be free, get back from the Nature action to the status of the Akshara; he will then be *trigunātīta*, beyond the gunas. Knowing himself as the Akshara Brahman, the unchanging Purusha, he will know himself as an immutable impersonal self, the Atman, tranquilly observing and impartially supporting the action, but himself calm, indifferent, untouched, motionless, pure, one with all beings in their self, not one with Nature and her workings.
                                    Essays on the Gita, pp. 220-22

The seeker must learn to distinguish, as an impartial and discerning witness of all that proceeds within this kingdom of his nature, the separate and the combined action of these qualities;

he must pursue the workings of the cosmic forces in him through all the labyrinth of their subtle unseen processes and disguises and know every intricacy of the maze. As he proceeds in this knowledge, he will be able to become the giver of the sanction and no longer remain an ignorant tool of Nature. At first he must induce the Nature-Force in its action on his instruments to subdue the working of its two lower qualities and bring them into subjection to the quality of light and good and, afterwards, he must persuade that again to offer itself so that all three may be transformed by a higher Power into their divine equivalents, supreme repose and calm, divine illumination and bliss, the eternal divine dynamis, Tapas. The first part of this discipline and change can be firmly done in principle by the will of the mental being in us; but its full execution and the subsequent transformation can be done only when the deeper psychic soul increases its hold on the nature and replaces the mental being as its ruler.   *The Synthesis of Yoga, p. 218*

The static freedom of the soul, no longer witness only and knower, is crowned by a dynamic transformation of the nature. The constant mixture, the uneven operation of the three modes acting upon each other in our three instruments ceases from its normal confused, troubled and improper action and movement. Another action becomes possible, commences, grows, culminates, a working more truly right, more luminous, natural and normal to the deepest divine interplay of Purusha and Prakriti although supernatural and supernormal to our present imperfect nature. The body conditioning the physical mind insists no longer on its tamasic inertia that repeats always the same ignorant movement: it becomes a passive field and instrument of a greater force and light, it responds to every demand of the spirit's force, holds and supports every variety and intensity of new divine experience. Our kinetic and dynamic vital parts, our nervous and emotional and sensational and volitional being, expand in power and admit a tireless action and a blissful enjoyment of experience, but learn at the same time to stand on a foundation of wide self-possessed and self-poised calm, sublime in force, divine in rest, neither exulting and excited nor tortured by sorrow and pain, neither harried by desire and importunate impulses nor dulled by incapacity and indolence. The intelligence, the thinking, understanding and reflective mind, renounces its sattwic limitations and opens to an essential light and peace. An infinite knowledge offers to us its splendid ranges, a knowledge not made up of mental constructions, not bound by opinion and idea or dependent on a stumbling uncertain logic and the petty support of the senses, but self-sure, authentic, all-penetrating, all-comprehending, a boundless bliss and peace, not dependent on deliverance from the hampered strenuousness of creative energy and dynamic action, not constituted by a few limited felicities but self-existent and all-including, pour into ever-enlarging fields and through ever-widening and always more numerous channels to possess the nature. A higher force, bliss and knowledge from a source beyond mind and life and body seize on them to remould in a diviner image.

The Synthesis of Yoga, p. 228

The three Gunas become purified and refined and changed into their divine equivalents: *sattva* becomes *jyoti*, the authentic spiritual light; *rajas* becomes *tapas*, the tranquilly intense divine force; *tamas* becomes *śama*, the divine quiet, rest, peace.

Letters on Yoga, pp. 1201-02

11
Self, Ego and Individuality

...this little mind, vital and body which we call ourselves is only a surface movement and not our "self" at all. It is an external bit of personality put forward for one brief life, for the play of the Ignorance. It is equipped with an ignorant mind stumbling about in search of fragments of truth, an ignorant vital rushing about in search of fragments of pleasure, an obscure and mostly subconscious physical receiving the impacts of things and suffering rather than possessing a resultant pain or pleasure. All that is accepted until the mind gets disgusted and starts looking about for the real Truth of itself and things, the vital gets disgusted and begins wondering whether there is not such a thing as real bliss and the physical gets tired and wants liberation from itself and its pains and pleasures. Then it is possible for the little ignorant bit of personality to get back to its real Self and with it to these greater things — or else to extinction of itself, Nirvana.

The real Self is not anywhere on the surface but deep within and above. Within is the soul supporting an inner mind, inner vital, inner physical in which there is a capacity for universal wideness and with it for the things now asked for — direct contact with the truth of self and things, taste of a universal bliss, liberation from the imprisoned smallness and sufferings of the gross physical body.

...the highest spiritual Self is not even behind our personality and bodily existence but is above it and altogether exceeds it.... This Self has two aspects and the results of realising it correspond to these two aspects. One is static, a condition of wide peace, freedom, silence: the silent Self is unaffected by any action or experience; it impartially supports them but does not seem to originate them at all, rather to stand back detached or unconcerned, *udāsīna*. The other aspect is dynamic and that is experienced as a cosmic Self or Spirit which not only supports but originates and contains the whole cosmic action — not only that part of it which concerns our physical selves but also all that is beyond it — this world and all other worlds, the supraphysical as well as the physical ranges of the universe. Moreover, we feel the Self as one in all; but also we feel it as above all, transcendent, surpassing all individual birth or cosmic existence. To get into the universal Self — one in all — is to be liberated from ego; ego either becomes a small instrumental circumstance in the consciousness or even disappears from our consciousness altogether. That is the extinction or Nirvana of the ego. To get into the transcendent self above all makes us capable of transcending altogether even cosmic consciousness and action — it can be the way to that complete liberation from the world-existence which is called also extinction, *laya, mokṣa, nirvāṇa.*

Letters on Yoga, pp. 1164-66

The direct self-consciousness of the mental being, that by which it becomes aware of its own nameless and formless existence behind the flow of a differentiated self-experience, of its eternal soul-substance behind the mental formations of that substance, of its self behind the ego, goes behind mentality to the timelessness of an eternal present; it is that in it which is ever the same and unaffected by the mental distinction of past, present and future. It is also unaffected by the distinctions of space or of circumstance; for if the mental being ordinarily says of itself, "I am in the body, I am here, I am there, I shall be elsewhere", yet when it learns to fix itself in this direct self-consciousness, it very soon perceives that this is the language of its changing self-experience which only expresses the relations of its surface consciousness to the environment and to externalities. Distinguishing these, detaching itself from these, it perceives that the self of which it is directly conscious does not in any way change by these outward changes, but is always the same, unaffected by the mutations of the body or of the mentality or of the field in which these move and act. It is in its essence featureless, relationless, without any other character than that of pure conscious existence self-sufficient and eternally satisfied with pure being, self-blissful. Thus we become aware of the stable Self, the eternal "Am", or rather the immutable "Is" without any category of personality or Time. *The Life Divine, pp. 511-12*

As soon as we become aware of the Self, we are conscious of it as eternal, unborn, unembodied, uninvolved in its workings: it can be felt within the form of being, but also as enveloping it, as above it, surveying its embodiment from above, *adhyakṣa*; it is omnipresent, the same in everything, infinite and pure and intangible for ever. This Self can be experienced as the Self of the individual, the Self of the thinker, doer, enjoyer, but even so it always has this greater character; its individuality is at the same time a vast universality or very readily passes into that, and the next step to that is a sheer transcendence or a complete and ineffable passing into the Absolute. The Self is that aspect of the Brahman in which it is intimately felt as at once individual, cosmic, transcendent of the universe. *The Life Divine, p. 347*

A spiritual knowledge, moved to arrive at the true Self in us, must reject, as the traditional way of knowledge rejects, all misleading appearances. It must discover that the body is not our self, our foundation of existence; it is a sensible form of the Infinite. The experience of Matter as the world's sole foundation and the physical brain and nerves and cells and molecules as the one truth of all things in us, the ponderous inadequate basis of materialism, is a delusion, a half-view taken for the whole, the dark bottom or shadow of things misconceived as the luminous substance, the effective figure of zero for the Integer. The materialist idea mistakes a creation for the creative Power, a means of expression for That which is expressed and expresses. Matter and our physical brain and nerves and body are the field and foundation for one action of a vital force that serves to connect the Self with the form of its works and maintains them by its direct dynamis. The material movements are an exterior notation by which the soul represents its perceptions of certain truths of the Infinite and makes them effective in the terms of Substance. These things are a language, a notation, a hieroglyphic, a system of symbols, not themselves the deepest truest sense of the things they intimate....

And yet Mind also, our mentality, our thinking, understanding part, is not our Self, is not That, not the end or the beginning; it is a half-light thrown from the Infinite. The experience of Mind as the creator of forms and things and of these forms and things existing in the Mind only, the thin subtle basis of idealism, is also a delusion, a half-view taken for the whole, a pale refracted light idealised as the burning body of the Sun and its splendour. This idealist vision also does not arrive at the essence of being, does not even touch it but only an inferior mode of Nature. Mind is the dubious outer penumbra of a conscious existence which is not limited by mentality but exceeds it. The method of the traditional way of knowledge, eliminating all these things arrives at the conception and realisation of a pure conscious existence, self-aware, self-blissful, unconditioned by mind and life and body and to its ultimate positive experience that is Atman, the Self, the original and essential nature of our existence. Here at last there is something centrally true, but in its haste to arrive at it this knowledge assumes that there is nothing between the thinking mind and the Highest, *buddheḥ paratastu saḥ*, and, shutting its eyes in Samadhi, tries to rush through all that actually intervenes without even seeing these great and luminous kingdoms of the Spirit. Perhaps it arrives at its object, but only to fall asleep in the Infinite. Or, if it remains awake, it is in the highest experience of the Supreme into which the self-annulling Mind can enter, but not in the supreme of the Supreme, *Parātpara*. The Mind can only be aware of the Self in a mentalised spiritual thinness, only of the mind-reflected Sachchidananda. The highest truth, the integral self-knowledge is not to be gained by this self-blinded leap into the Absolute but by a patient transit beyond the mind into the Truth-Consciousness where the Infinite can be known, felt, seen, experienced in all the fullness of its unending riches. And there we discover this Self that we are to be not only a static tenuous vacant Atman, but a great dynamic Spirit individual, universal and transcendent. That Self and Spirit cannot be expressed by the mind's abstract generalisations; all the inspired descriptions of the seers and mystics cannot exhaust its contents and its splendour.

The Synthesis of Yoga, pp. 280-82

Since the Self which we come to realise by the path of knowledge is not only the reality which lies behind and supports the states and movements of our psychological being, but also that transcendent and universal Existence which has manifested itself in all the movements of the universal, the knowledge of the Self includes also the knowledge of the principles of Being, its fundamental modes and its relations with the principles of the phenomenal universe. This was what was meant by the Upanishad when it spoke of the Brahman as that which being known all is known.[1] It has to be realised first as the pure principle of Existence, afterwards, says the Upanishad, its essential modes become clear to the soul which realises it. We may indeed, before realisation, try to analyse by the metaphysical reason and even understand intellectually what Being is and what the world is, but such metaphysical understanding is not the Knowledge. Moreover, we may have the realisation in knowledge and vision, but this is incomplete without realisation in the entire soul-experience and the unity of all our being with that which we realise.[2] It is the science of Yoga to know and the art of Yoga to be unified with the Highest so that we may live in the Self and act from that supreme poise, becoming one not only in the

---

[1] *yasmin vijñāte sarvam idam vijñātam.* Shandilya Upanishad.
[2] This is the distinction made in the Gita between Sankhya and Yoga; both are necessary to an integral knowledge.

conscious essence but in the conscious law of our being with the transcendent Divine whom all things and creatures, whether ignorantly or with partial knowledge and experience, seek to express through the lower law of their members. To know the highest Truth and to be in harmony with it is the condition of right being, to express it in all that we are, experience and do is the condition of right living.   *The Synthesis of Yoga, p. 358*

Man is at present a partly self-conscious soul subject to and limited by mind, life and body, who has to become an entirely self-conscious soul master of his mind, life and body. Not limited by their claims and demands, a perfect self-conscious soul would be superior to and a free possessor of its instruments. This effort of man to be master of his own being has been the sense of a large part of his past spiritual, intellectual and moral strivings.

In order to be possessor of his being with any complete reality of freedom and mastery, man must find out his highest self, the real man or highest Purusha in him, which is free and master in its own inalienable power. He must cease to be the mental, vital, physical ego; for that is always the creation, instrument and subject of mental, vital, physical Nature. This ego is not his real self, but an instrumentation of Nature by which it has developed a sense of limited and separate individual being in mind, life and body. By this instrumentation he acts as if he were a separate existence in the material universe. Nature has evolved certain habitual limiting conditions under which that action takes place; self-identification of the soul with the ego is the means by which she induces the soul to consent to this action and accept these habitual limiting conditions. While the identification lasts, there is a self-imprisonment in this habitual round and narrow action, and, until it is transcended, there can be no free use by the soul of its individual living, much less a real self-exceeding. For this reason an essential movement of the Yoga is to draw back from the outward ego sense by which we are identified with the action of mind, life and body and live inwardly in the soul. The liberation from an externalised ego sense is the first step towards the soul's freedom and mastery.

The Synthesis of Yoga, pp. 606-07

...the emergence of the life-ego[3] is... a machinery of cosmic Nature for the affirmation of the individual, for his self-disengagement from the indeterminate mass substance of the subconscient, for the appearance of a conscious being on a ground prepared by the Inconscience; the principle of life-affirmation of the ego is the necessary consequence. The individual ego is a pragmatic and effective fiction, a translation of the secret self into the terms of surface consciousness, or a subjective substitute for the true self in our surface experience: it is separated by ignorance from other-self and from the inner Divinity, but it is still pushed secretly towards an evolutionary unification in diversity; it has behind itself, though finite, the impulse to the infinite. But this in the terms of an ignorant consciousness translates itself into the will to expand, to be a boundless finite, to take everything it can into itself, to enter into everything and possess it, even to be possessed if by that it can feel itself satisfied and growing in or through others or can take into itself by subjection the being and power of others or get thereby a help or an impulse for its life-affirmation, its life-delight, its enrichment of its mental, vital or physical existence.

The Life Divine, p. 624

The formation of a mental and vital ego tied to the body-sense was the first great labour of the cosmic Life in its progressive evolution; for this was the means it found for creating out of matter a conscious individual. The dissolution of this limiting ego is the one condition, the necessary means for this very same Life to arrive at its divine fruition: for only so can the conscious individual find either his transcendent self or his true Person. This double

---

[3] Vital ego. See the Glossary under "Ego". (Ed.)

movement is usually represented as a fall and a redemption or a creation and a destruction, — the kindling of a light and its extinction or the formation first of a smaller temporary and unreal self and a release from it into our true self's eternal largeness. For human thought falls apart towards two opposite extremes: one, mundane and pragmatic, regards the fulfilment and satisfaction of the mental, vital and physical ego-sense individual or collective as the object of life and looks no farther, while the other spiritual, philosophic or religious which regards the conquest of the ego in the interests of the soul, spirit or whatever be the ultimate entity, as the one thing supremely worth doing. Even in the camp of the ego there are two divergent attitudes which divide the mundane or materialist theory of the universe. One tendency of this thought regards the mental ego as a creation of our mentality which will be dissolved with the dissolution of mind by the death of the body; the one abiding truth is eternal Nature working in the race — this or another — and her purpose should be followed, not ours. The fulfilment of the race, the collective ego, and not that of the individual should be the rule of life. Another trend of thought, more vitalistic in its tendencies, fixes on the conscious ego as the supreme achievement of Nature, no matter how transitory, ennobles it into a human representative of the Will-to-be and holds up its greatness and satisfaction as the highest aim of our existence. In the more numerous systems that take their stand on some kind of religious thought or spiritual discipline there is a corresponding divergence. The Buddhist denies the existence of a real self or ego, admits no universal or transcendent Being. The Advaitin declares the apparently individual soul to be none other than the supreme Self and Brahman, its individuality an illusion; the putting off of individual existence is the only true release. Other systems assert, in flat contradiction of this view, the eternal persistence of the human soul; a basis of multiple consciousness in the One or else a dependent but still separate entity, it is constant, real, imperishable.

Amidst these various and conflicting opinions the seeker of

the Truth has to decide for himself which shall be for him the Knowledge. But if our aim is a spiritual release or a spiritual fulfilment, then the exceeding of this little mould of ego is imperative. In human egoism and its satisfaction there can be no divine culmination and deliverance. A certain purification from egoism is the condition even of ethical progress and elevation, for social good and perfection; much more is it indispensable for inner peace, purity and joy. But a much more radical deliverance, not only from egoism but from ego-idea and ego-sense, is needed if our aim is to raise human into divine nature. Experience shows that, in proportion as we deliver ourselves from the limiting mental and vital ego, we command a wider life, a larger existence, a higher consciousness, a happier soul-state, even a greater knowledge, power and scope. Even the aim which the most mundane philosophy pursues, the fulfilment, perfection, satisfaction of the individual, is best assured not by satisfying the same ego but by finding freedom in a higher and larger self. There is no happiness in smallness of the being, says the Scripture, it is with the large being that happiness comes. The ego is by its nature a smallness of being; it brings contraction of the consciousness and with the contraction limitation of knowledge, disabling ignorance, — confinement and a diminution of power and by that diminution incapacity and weakness, — scission of oneness and by that scission disharmony and failure of sympathy and love and understanding, — inhibition or fragmentation of delight of being and by that fragmentation pain and sorrow. To recover what is lost we must break out of the walls of ego. The ego must either disappear in impersonality or fuse into a larger I: it must fuse into the wider cosmic 'I' which comprehends all these smaller selves or the transcendent of which even the cosmic self is a diminished image. *The Synthesis of Yoga, pp. 341-43*

The ego-sense serves to limit, separate and sharply differentiate, to make the most of the individual form and it is there because it is indispensable to the evolution of the lower life. But when we would rise above to a higher divine life we must loosen the force of the ego and eventually get rid of it — as for the lower life the development of ego, so for the higher life this reverse movement of elimination of the ego is indispensable.

The Synthesis of Yoga, p. 734

In the world we act with the sense of egoism; we claim the universal forces that work in us as our own; we claim as the effect of our personal will, wisdom, force, virtue the selective, formative, progressive action of the Transcendent in this frame of mind, life and body. Enlightenment brings to us the knowledge that the ego is only an instrument; we begin to perceive and feel that these things are our own in the sense that they belong to our supreme and integral Self, one with the Transcendent, not to the instrumental ego. Our limitations and distortions are our contribution to the working; the true power in it is the Divine's. When the human ego realises that its will is a tool, its wisdom ignorance and childishness, its power an infant's groping, its virtue a pretentious impurity, and learns to trust itself to that which transcends it, that is its salvation. The apparent freedom and self-assertion of our personal being to which we are so profoundly attached, conceal a most pitiable subjection to a thousand suggestions, impulsions, forces which we have made extraneous to our little person. Our ego, boasting of freedom, is at every moment the slave, toy and puppet of countless beings, powers, forces, influences in universal Nature.

The Synthesis of Yoga, p. 53

This ego or "I" is not a lasting truth, much less our essential part; it is only a formation of Nature, a mental form of thought-centralisation in the perceiving and discriminating mind, a vital form of the centralisation of feeling and sensation in our parts of life, a form of physical conscious reception centralising substance and function of substance in our bodies. All that we internally are is not ego, but consciousness, soul or spirit. All that we externally and superficially are and do is not ego but Nature. An executive cosmic force shapes us and dictates through our temperament and environment and mentality so shaped, through our individualised formulation of the cosmic energies, our actions and their results. Truly, we do not think, will or act but thought occurs in us, will occurs in us, impulse and act occur in us; our ego-sense gathers around itself, refers to itself all this flow of natural activities. It is cosmic Force, it is Nature that forms the thought, imposes the will, imparts the impulse. Our body, mind and ego are a wave of that sea of force in action and do not govern it, but by it are governed and directed. The sadhaka in his progress towards truth and self-knowledge must come to a point where the soul opens its eyes of vision and recognises this truth of ego and this truth of works. He gives up the idea of a mental, vital, physical "I" that acts or governs action; he recognises that Prakriti, Force of cosmic nature following her fixed modes, is in him and in all things and creatures the one and only worker.

The Synthesis of Yoga, p. 203

Our ego is only a face of the universal being and has no separate existence; our apparent separative individuality is only a surface movement and behind it our real individuality stretches out to unity with all things and upward to oneness with the transcendent Divine Infinity. Thus our ego, which seems to be a limitation of existence, is really a power of infinity; the boundless multiplicity of beings in the world is a result and signal evidence, not of limitation or finiteness, but of that illimitable Infinity. Apparent division can never erect itself into a real separateness; there is supporting and overriding it an indivisible unity which division itself cannot divide. This fundamental world-fact of ego and apparent division and their separative workings in the world existence is no denial of the Divine Nature of unity and indivisible being; they are the surface results of an infinite multiplicity which is a power of the infinite Oneness.   *The Life Divine, pp. 401-02*

...Nature invented the ego that the individual might disengage himself from the inconscience or subconscience of the mass and become an independent living mind, life-power, soul, spirit, co-ordinating himself with the world around him but not drowned in it and separately inexistent and ineffective. For the individual is indeed part of the cosmic being, but he is also something more, he is a soul that has descended from the Transcendence. This he cannot manifest at once, because he is too near to the cosmic Inconscience, not near enough to the original Superconscience; he has to find himself as the mental and vital ego before he can find himself as the soul or spirit.

Still, to find his egoistic individuality is not to know himself; the true spiritual individual is not the mind-ego, the life-ego, the body-ego: predominantly, this first movement is a work of will, of power, of egoistic self-effectuation and only secondarily of knowledge. Therefore a time must come when man has to look below the obscure surface of his egoistic being and attempt to know himself; he must set out to find the real man: without that he would be stopping short at Nature's primary education and never go on to her deeper and larger teachings; however great his practical knowledge and efficiency, he would be only a little higher than the animals. First, he has to turn his eyes upon his own psychology and distinguish its natural elements, — ego, mind and its instruments, life, body, — until he discovers that his whole existence stands in need of an explanation other than the working of the natural elements and of a goal for its activities other than an egoistic self-affirmation and satisfaction. He may seek it in Nature and mankind and thus start on his way to the discovery of his unity with the rest of his world: he may seek it in supernature, in God, and thus start on his way to the discovery of his unity with the Divine. Practically, he attempts both paths and, continually wavering, continually seeks to fix himself in the successive solutions that may be best in accordance with the various partial discoveries he has made on his double line of search and finding.

But through it all what he is in this stage still insistently seeking to discover, to know, to fulfil is himself; his knowledge of Nature, his knowledge of God are only helps towards self-knowledge, towards the perfection of his being, towards the attainment of the supreme object of his individual self-existence. Directed towards Nature and the cosmos, it may take upon itself the figure of self-knowledge, self-mastery, — in the mental and vital sense, — and mastery of the world in which we find ourselves: directed towards God, it may take also this figure but in a higher spiritual sense of world and self, or it may assume that other, so familiar and decisive to the religious mind, the seeking for an individual salvation whether in heavens beyond or by a separate immergence in a supreme Self or a supreme Non-self, — beatitude or Nirvana. Throughout, however, it is the individual who is seeking individual self-knowledge and the aim of his separate existence, with all the rest, even altruism and the love and service of mankind, self-effacement or self-annihilation, thrown in, — with whatever subtle disguises, — as helps and means towards that one great preoccupation of his realised individuality. This may seem to be only an expanded egoism, and the separative ego would then be the truth of man's being persistent in him to the end or till at last he is liberated from it by his self-extinction in the featureless eternity of the Infinite. But there is a deeper secret behind which justifies his individuality and its demand, the secret of the spiritual and eternal individual, the Purusha.

It is because of the spiritual Person, the Divinity in the individual, that perfection or liberation, — salvation, as it is called in the West, — has to be individual and not collective; for whatever perfection of the collectivity is to be sought after, can come only by the perfection of the individuals who constitute it. It is because the individual is That, that to find himself is his great necessity. In his complete surrender and self-giving to the Supreme it is he who finds his perfect self-finding in a perfect self-offering. In the abolition of the mental, vital, physical ego, even of the spiritual ego, it is the formless and limitless Individual that has the peace and joy of his escape into his own infinity. In the experience that he is nothing and no one, or everything and everyone, or the One which is beyond all things and absolute, it is the Brahman in the individual that effectuates this stupendous merger or this marvellous joining, Yoga, of its eternal unit of being with its vast all-comprehending or supreme all-transcending unity of eternal existence. To get beyond the ego is imperative, but one cannot get beyond the self, — except by finding it supremely, universally. For the self is not the ego; it is one with the All and the One and in finding it it is the All and the One that we discover in our self: the contradiction, the separation disappears, but the self, the spiritual reality remains, united with the One and the All by that delivering disappearance.

The Life Divine, pp. 694-96

The first difficulty for the reason is that it has always been accustomed to identify the individual self with the ego and to think of it as existing only by the limitations and exclusions of the ego. If that were so, then by the transcendence of the ego the individual would abolish his own existence; our end would be to disappear and dissolve into some universality of matter, life, mind or spirit or else some indeterminate from which our egoistic determinations of individuality have started. But what is this strongly separative self-experience that we call ego? It is nothing fundamentally real in itself but only a practical constitution of our consciousness devised to centralise the activities of Nature in us. We perceive a formation of mental, physical, vital experience which distinguishes itself from the rest of being, and that is what we think of as ourselves in nature — this individualisation of being in becoming. We then proceed to conceive of ourselves as something which has thus individualised itself and only exists so long as it is individualised, — a temporary or at least a temporal becoming; or else we conceive of ourselves as someone who supports or causes the individualisation, an immortal being perhaps but limited by its individuality. This perception and this conception constitute our ego-sense. Normally, we go no farther in our knowledge of our individual existence.

But in the end we have to see that our individualisation, is only a superficial formation, a practical selection and limited conscious synthesis for the temporary utility of life in a particular body, or else it is a constantly changing and developing synthesis pursued through successive lives in successive bodies. Behind it there is a consciousness, a Purusha, who is not determined or limited by his individualisation or by this synthesis but on the contrary determines, supports and yet exceeds it. That which he selects from in order to construct this synthesis, is his total experience of the world-being. Therefore our individualisation exists by virtue of the world-being, but also by virtue of a consciousness which uses the world-being for experience of its possibilities of individuality. These two powers, Person and his world-material, are both necessary for our present experience of individuality. If the Purusha with his individualising syntheses were to disappear, to merge, to annul himself in any way, our constructed individuality would cease because the Reality that supported it would no longer be in presence; if, on the other hand, the world-being were to dissolve, merge, disappear, then also our individualisation would cease, for the material by which it effectuates itself would be wanting. We have then to recognise these two terms of our existence, a world-being and an individualising consciousness which is the cause of all our self-experience and world-experience.

But we see farther that in the end this Purusha, this cause and self of our individuality, comes to embrace the whole world and all other beings in a sort of conscious extension of itself and to perceive itself as one with the world-being. In its conscious extension of itself it exceeds the primary experience and abolishes the barriers of its active self-limitation and individualisation; by its perception of its own infinite universality it goes beyond all consciousness of separate individuality or limited

. very fact the individual ceases to be the self-
ner words, our false consciousness of existing
tion, by rigid distinction of ourselves from the
becoming is transcended; our identification of
.r personal and temporal individualisation in a
par.... .nd body is abolished. But is all truth of individuality and individualisation abolished? Does the Purusha cease
to exist or does he become the world-Purusha and live intimately
in innumerable minds and bodies? We do not find it to be so.
He still individualises and it is still he who exists and embraces
this wider consciousness while he individualises: but the mind
no longer thinks of a limited temporary individualisation as all
ourselves but only as a wave of becoming thrown up from the
sea of its being or else as a form or centre of universality. The
soul still makes the world-becoming the material for individual
experience, but instead of regarding it as something outside and
larger than itself on which it has to draw, by which it is affected,
with which it has to make accommodations, it is aware of it subjectively as within itself; it embraces both its world-material and
its individualised experience of spatial and temporal activities
in a free and enlarged consciousness. In this new consciousness
the spiritual individual perceives its true self to be one in being
with the Transcendence and seated and dwelling within it, and
no longer takes its constructed individuality as anything more
than a formation for world-experience.

Our unity with the world-being is the consciousness of a
Self which at one and the same time cosmicises in the world and
individualises through the individual Purusha, and both in that
world-being and in this individual being and in all individual
beings it is aware of the same Self manifesting and experiencing
its various manifestations. That then is a Self which must be one
in its being, — otherwise we could not have this experience of
unity, — and yet must be capable in its very unity of cosmic differentiation and multiple individuality. The unity is its being, —
yes, but the cosmic differentiation and the multiple individuality

are the power of its being which it is constantly displaying and which it is its delight and the nature of its consciousness to display. If then we arrive at unity with that, if we even become entirely and in every way that being, why should the power of its being be excised and why at all should we desire or labour to excise it? We should then only diminish the scope of our unity with it by an exclusive concentration accepting the divine being but not accepting our part in the power and consciousness and infinite delight of the Divine. It would in fact be the individual seeking peace and rest of union in a motionless identity, but rejecting delight and various joy of union in the nature and act and power of the divine Existence. That is possible, but there is no necessity to uphold it as the ultimate aim of our being or as our ultimate perfection. *The Life Divine, pp. 367-70*

The ordinary existence of man is not only an individual but an egoistic consciousness; it is, that is to say, the individual soul or Jivatman identifying himself with the nodus of his mental, vital, physical experiences in the movement of universal Nature, with his mind-created ego, and, less intimately, with the mind, life, body which receive the experiences; for of these he can say "my mind, life, body," regarding them as himself yet partly as not himself and something which he possesses and uses, but of the ego he says, "It is I". By detaching himself from all identification with mind, life and body, he can get back from his ego to the consciousness of the true Individual, the Jivatman, who is the real possessor of mind, life and body. Looking back from this Individual to that of which it is the representative and conscious figure, he can get back to the transcendent consciousness of pure Self, absolute Existence or absolute Non-being, three poises of the same eternal Reality. *The Synthesis of Yoga, p. 392*

What we usually call by that name [the individual] is a natural ego, a device of Nature which holds together her action in the mind and body. This ego has to be extinguished, otherwise there is no complete liberation possible; but the individual self or soul is not this ego. The individual soul is the spiritual being which is sometimes described as an eternal portion of the Divine, but can also be described as the Divine himself supporting his manifestation as the Many. This is the true spiritual individual which appears in its complete truth when we get rid of the ego and our false separative sense of individuality, realise our oneness with the transcendent and cosmic Divine and with all beings. It is this which makes possible the Divine Life. Nirvana is a step towards it; the disappearance of the false separative individuality is a necessary condition for our realising and living in our true eternal being, living divinely in the Divine. But this we can do in the world and in life.   *Letters on Yoga, pp. 46-47*

...there is a sense in which the view of all as parts of the whole, waves of the sea or even as in a sense separate entities becomes a necessary part of the integral Truth and the integral Knowledge. For if the Self is always one in all, yet we see that for the purposes at least of the cyclic manifestation it expresses itself in perpetual soul-forms which preside over the movements of our personality through the worlds and the aeons. This persistent soul-existence is the real Individuality which stands behind the constant mutations of the thing we call our personality. It is not a limited ego but a thing in itself infinite; it is in truth the Infinite itself consenting from one plane of its being to reflect itself in a perpetual soul-experience. This is the truth which underlies the Sankhya theory of many Purushas, many essential, infinite, free and impersonal souls reflecting the movements of a single cosmic energy. It stands also, in a different way, behind the very different philosophy of qualified Monism which arose as a protest against the metaphysical excesses of Buddhistic Nihilism and illusionist Adwaita. The old semi-Buddhistic, semi-Sankhya theory which saw only the Quiescent and nothing else in the world except a constant combination of the five elements and the three modes of inconscient Energy lighting up their false activity by the consciousness of the Quiescent in which it is reflected, is not the whole truth of the Brahman. We are not a mere mass of changing mind-stuff, life-stuff, body-stuff taking different forms of mind and life and body from birth to birth, so that at no time is there any real self or conscious reason of existence behind all the flux or none except that Quiescent who cares for none of these things. There is a real and stable power of our being behind the constant mutation of our mental, vital and physical personality, and this we have to know and preserve in order that the Infinite may manifest Himself through it according to His will in whatever range and for whatever purpose of His eternal cosmic activity.   *The Synthesis of Yoga, pp. 359-60*

The one thing that can be described as an unreal reality is our individual sense of separativeness and the conception of the finite as a self-existent object in the Infinite. This conception, this sense are pragmatically necessary for the operations of the surface individuality and are effective and justified by their effects; they are therefore real to its finite reason and finite self-experience: but once we step back from the finite consciousness into the consciousness of the essential and infinite, from the apparent to the true Person, the finite or the individual still exists but as being and power and manifestation of the Infinite; it has no independent or separate reality. Individual independence, entire separativeness are not necessary for individual reality, do not constitute it.   *The Life Divine, pp. 465-66*

This individual being of ours is that by which ignorance is possible to the self-conscious mind, but it is also that by which liberation into the spiritual being is possible and the enjoyment of divine immortality. It is not the Eternal in His transcendence or in His cosmic being who arrives at this immortality; it is the individual who rises into self-knowledge, in him it is possessed and by him it is made effective. All life, spiritual, mental or material, is the play of the soul with the possibilities of its nature; for without this play there can be no self-expression and no relative self-experience. Even, then, in our realisation of all as our larger self and in our oneness with God and other beings, this play can and must persist, unless we desire to cease from all self-expression and all but a tranced and absorbed self-experience. But then it is in the individual being that this trance or this liberated play is realised; the trance is this mental being's immersion in the sole experience of unity, the liberated play is the taking up of his mind into the spiritual being for the free realisation and delight of oneness. For the nature of the divine existence is to possess always its unity, but to possess it also in an infinite experience, from many standpoints, on many planes, through many conscious powers or selves of itself, individualities — in our limited intellectual language — of the one conscious being. Each one of us is one of these individualities. To stand away from God in limited ego, limited mind is to stand away from ourselves, to be unpossessed of our true individuality, to be the apparent and not the real individual; it is our power of ignorance. To be taken up into the divine Being and be aware of our spiritual, infinite and universal consciousness as that in which we now live, is to possess our supreme and integral self, our true individuality; it is our power of self-knowledge.

By knowing the eternal unity of these three powers of the eternal manifestation, God, Nature and the individual self, and their intimate necessity to each other, we come to understand existence itself and all that in the appearances of the world now puzzles our ignorance. Our self-knowledge abolishes none of these things, it abolishes only our ignorance and those circumstances proper to the ignorance which made us bound and subject to the egoistic determinations of our nature. When we get back to our true being, the ego falls away from us; its place is taken by our supreme and integral self, the true individuality. As this supreme self it makes itself one with all beings and sees all world and Nature in its own infinity. What we mean by this is simply that our sense of separate existence disappears into a consciousness of illimitable, undivided, infinite being in which we no longer feel bound to the name and form and the particular mental and physical determinations of our present birth and becoming and are no longer separate from anything or anyone in the universe. This was what the ancient thinkers called the Non-birth or the destruction of birth or Nirvana. At the same time we continue to live and act through our individual birth and becoming, but with a different knowledge and quite another kind of experience; the world also continues, but we see it in our own being and not as something external to it and other than ourselves. To be able to live permanently in this new consciousness of our real, our integral being is to attain liberation and enjoy immortality.

The Synthesis of Yoga, pp. 419-20

12
The Superconscient

Gradations of the Higher Consciousness

We become aware, in a certain experience, of a range of being superconscient to all these three [the waking consciousness,
the subconscient and the subliminal], aware too of something,
a supreme highest Reality sustaining and exceeding them all,
which humanity speaks of vaguely as Spirit, God, the Oversoul:
from these superconscient ranges we have visitations and in our
highest being we tend towards them and to that supreme Spirit.
There is then in our total range of existence a superconscience
as well as a subconscience and inconscience, overarching and
perhaps enveloping our subliminal and our waking selves, but
unknown to us, seemingly unattainable and incommunicable.

But with the extension of our knowledge we discover what
this Spirit or Oversoul is: it is ultimately our own highest deepest vastest Self, it is apparent on its summits or by reflection
in ourselves as Sachchidananda creating us and the world by
the power of His divine Knowledge-Will, spiritual, supramental, truth-conscious, infinite. That is the real Being, Lord and
Creator, who, as the Cosmic Self veiled in Mind and Life and
Matter, has descended into that which we call the Inconscient
and constitutes and directs its subconscient existence by His
supramental will and knowledge, has ascended out of the Inconscient and dwells in the inner being constituting and directing
its subliminal existence by the same will and knowledge, has
cast up out of the subliminal our surface existence and dwells
secretly in it overseeing with the same supreme light and mastery
its stumbling and groping movements. If the subliminal and
subconscient may be compared to a sea which throws up the
waves of our surface mental existence, the superconscience may
be compared to an ether which constitutes, contains, overroofs,

inhabits and determines the movements of the sea and its waves. It is there in this higher ether that we are inherently and intrinsically conscious of our self and spirit, not as here below by a reflection in silent mind or by acquisition of the knowledge of a hidden Being within us; it is through it, through that ether of superconscience, that we can pass to a supreme status, knowledge, experience. Of this superconscient existence through which we can arrive at the highest status of our real, our supreme Self, we are normally even more ignorant than of the rest of our being; yet is it into the knowledge of it that our being emerging out of the involution in Inconscience is struggling to evolve. This limitation to our surface existence, this unconsciousness of our highest as of our inmost self, is our first, our capital ignorance.

The Life Divine, p. 561

In the superconscience beyond our present level of awareness are included the higher planes of mental being as well as the native heights of supramental and pure spiritual being. The first indispensable step in an upward evolution would be to elevate our force of consciousness into those higher parts of Mind from which we already receive, but without knowing the source, much of our larger mental movements, those, especially, that come with a greater power and light, the revelatory, the inspirational, the intuitive. On these mental heights, in these largenesses, if the consciousness could succeed in reaching them or maintain and centre itself there, something of the direct presence and power of the Spirit, something even, — however secondary or indirect, — of the Supermind could receive a first expression, could make itself initially manifest, could intervene in the government of our lower being and help to remould it. Afterwards, by the force of that remoulded consciousness, the course of our evolution could rise by a sublimer ascent and get beyond the mental into the supramental and the supreme spiritual nature. It is possible without an actual ascent into these at present superconscient mental planes or without a constant or permanent living in them, by openness to them, by reception of their knowledge and influences, to get rid to a certain extent of our constitutional and psychological ignorance; it is possible to be aware of ourselves as spiritual beings and to spiritualise, though imperfectly, our normal human life and consciousness. There could be a conscious communication and guidance from this greater more luminous mentality and a reception of its enlightening and transforming forces. That is within the reach of the highly developed or the spiritually awakened human being; but it would not be more than a preliminary stage. To reach an integral self-knowledge, an entire consciousness and power of being, there is necessary an ascent beyond the plane of our normal mind. Such an ascent is at present possible in an absorbed superconscience; but that could lead only to an entry into the higher levels in a state of immobile or ecstatic trance. If the control of that highest spiritual being is to be brought into our waking life, there must be a conscious heightening and widening into immense ranges of new being, new consciousness, new potentialities of action, a taking up, — as integral as possible, — of our present being, consciousness, activities and a transmutation of them into divine values which would effect a transfiguration of our human existence. For wherever a radical transition has to be made, there is always this triple movement, — ascent, widening of field and base, integration, — in Nature's method of self-transcendence.

The Life Divine, pp. 736-37

...from the point of view of the ascent of consciousness from our mind upwards through a rising series of dynamic powers by which it can sublimate itself, the gradation can be resolved into a stairway of four main ascents, each with its high level of fulfilment. These gradations may be summarily described as a series of sublimations of the consciousness through Higher Mind, Illumined Mind and Intuition into Overmind and beyond it; there is a succession of self-transmutations at the summit of which lies the Supermind or Divine Gnosis. All these degrees are gnostic in their principle and power; for even at the first we begin to pass from a consciousness based on an original Inconscience and acting in a general Ignorance or in a mixed Knowledge-Ignorance to a consciousness based on a secret self-existent Knowledge and first acted upon and inspired by that light and power and then itself changed into that substance and using entirely this new instrumentation. In themselves these grades are grades of energy-substance of the Spirit: for it must not be supposed, because we distinguish them according to their leading character, means and potency of knowledge, that they are merely a method or way of knowing or a faculty or power of cognition; they are domains of being, grades of the substance and energy of the spiritual being, fields of existence which are each a level of the universal Consciousness-Force constituting and organising itself into a higher status. When the powers of any grade descend completely into us, it is not only our thought and knowledge that are affected, — the substance and very grain of our being and consciousness, all its states and activities are touched and penetrated and can be remoulded and wholly transmuted. Each stage of this ascent is therefore a general, if not a total, conversion of the being into a new light and power of a greater existence. *The Life Divine, p. 938*

(a) Higher Mind

Our first decisive step out of our human intelligence, our normal mentality, is an ascent into a higher Mind, a mind no longer of mingled light and obscurity or half-light, but a large clarity of the Spirit. Its basic substance is a unitarian sense of being with a powerful multiple dynamisation capable of the formation of a multitude of aspects of knowledge, ways of action, forms and significances of becoming, of all of which there is a spontaneous inherent knowledge. It is therefore a power that has proceeded from the Overmind, — but with

⟍ɪe Supermind as its ulterior origin, — as all these greater powers have proceeded: but its special character, its activity of consciousness are dominated by Thought; it is a luminous thought-mind, a mind of Spirit-born conceptual knowledge. An all-awareness emerging from the original identity, carrying the truths the identity held in itself, conceiving swiftly, victoriously, multitudinously, formulating and by self-power of the Idea effectually realising its conceptions, is the character of this greater mind of knowledge. This kind of cognition is the last that emerges from the original spiritual identity before the initiation of a separative knowledge, base of the Ignorance; it is therefore the first that meets us when we rise from conceptive and ratiocinative mind, our best-organised knowledge-power of the Ignorance, into the realms of the Spirit; it is, indeed, the spiritual parent of our conceptive mental ideation, and it is natural that this leading power of our mentality should, when it goes beyond itself, pass into its immediate source.

But here in this greater Thought there is no need of a seeking and self-critical ratiocination, no logical motion step by step towards a conclusion, no mechanism of express or implied deductions and inferences, no building or deliberate concatenation of idea with idea in order to arrive at an ordered sum or outcome of knowledge; for this limping action of our reason is a movement of Ignorance searching for knowledge, obliged to safeguard its steps against error, to erect a selective mental structure for its temporary shelter and to base it on foundations already laid and carefully laid but never firm, because it is not supported on a soil of native awareness but imposed on an original soil of nescience. There is not here, either, that other way of our mind at its keenest and swiftest, a rapid hazardous divination and insight, a play of the searchlight of intelligence probing into the little known or the unknown. This higher consciousness is a Knowledge formulating itself on a basis of self-existent all-awareness and manifesting some part of its integrality, a harmony of its significances put into thought-form. It can freely express itself in single ideas, but its most characteristic movement is a mass ideation, a system or totality of truth-seeing at a single view; the relations of idea with idea, of truth with truth are not established by logic but pre-exist and emerge already self-seen in the integral whole. There is an initiation into forms of an ever-present but till now inactive knowledge, not a system of conclusions from premises or data; this thought is a self-revelation of eternal Wisdom, not an acquired knowledge. Large aspects of truth come into view in which the ascending Mind, if it chooses, can dwell with satisfaction and, after its former manner, live in them as in a structure; but if progress is to be made, these structures can constantly expand into a larger structure or several of them combine themselves into a provisional greater whole on the way to a yet unachieved integrality. In the end there is a great totality of truth known and experienced but still a totality capable of infinite enlargement because there is no end to the aspects of knowledge, *nāstyanto vistarasya me*.

This is the Higher Mind in its aspect of cognition; but there is also the aspect of will, of dynamic effectuation of the Truth: here we find that this greater more brilliant Mind works always on the rest of the being, the mental will, the heart and its feelings, the life, the body, through the power of thought, through the idea-force. It seeks to purify through knowledge, to deliver through knowledge, to create by the innate power of knowledge. The idea is put into the heart or the life as a force to be accepted and worked out; the heart and life become conscious of the idea and respond to its dynamisms and their substance begins to modify itself in that sense, so that the feelings and actions become the vibrations of this higher wisdom, are informed with it, filled with the emotion and the sense of it: the will and the life impulses are similarly charged with its power and its urge of self-effectuation; even in the body the idea works so that, for example, the potent thought and will of health replaces its faith in illness and its consent to illness, or the idea[1] of strength calls in the substance, power, motion, vibration of strength; the idea generates the force and form proper to the idea and imposes it on our substance of Mind, Life or Matter. It is in this way that the first working proceeds; it charges the whole being with a new and superior consciousness, lays a foundation of change, prepares it for a superior truth of existence.

The Life Divine, pp. 939-41

(b) Illumined Mind

The power of the spiritual Higher Mind and its idea-force, modified and diminished as it must be by its entrance into our mentality, is not sufficient to sweep out all these obstacles and create the gnostic being, but it can make a first change, a modification that will capacitate a higher ascent and a more powerful descent and further prepare an integration of the being in a greater Force of consciousness and knowledge.

This greater Force is that of the Illumined Mind, a Mind no longer of higher Thought, but of spiritual light. Here the clarity of the spiritual intelligence, its tranquil daylight, gives place or subordinates itself to an intense lustre, a splendour and illumination of the Spirit: a play of lightnings of spiritual truth and power breaks from above into the consciousness and adds to the calm and wide enlightenment and the vast descent of peace which characterise or accompany the action of the larger conceptual-spiritual principle, a fiery ardour of realisation and a rapturous ecstasy of knowledge. A downpour of inwardly visible Light very usually envelops this action; for it must be noted that, contrary to our ordinary conceptions, light is not primarily a material creation and the sense or vision of light

---

[1] The word expressing the idea has the same power if it is surcharged with the spiritual force; that is the rationale of the Indian use of the *mantra*.

accompanying the inner illumination is not merely a subjective visual image or a symbolic phenomenon: light is primarily a spiritual manifestation of the Divine Reality illuminative and creative; material light is a subsequent representation or conversion of it into Matter for the purposes of the material Energy. There is also in this descent the arrival of a greater dynamic, a golden drive, a luminous "enthousiasmos" of inner force and power which replaces the comparatively slow and deliberate process of the Higher Mind by a swift, sometimes a vehement, almost a violent impetus of rapid transformation.

The Illumined Mind does not work primarily by thought, but by vision; thought is here only a subordinate movement expressive of sight. The human mind, which relies mainly on thought, conceives that to be the highest or the main process of knowledge, but in the spiritual order thought is a secondary and a not indispensable process. In its form of verbal thought, it can almost be described as a concession made by Knowledge to the Ignorance, because that Ignorance is incapable of making truth wholly lucid and intelligible to itself in all its extent and manifold implications except through the clarifying precision of significant sounds; it cannot do without this device to give to ideas an exact outline and an expressive body. But it is evident that this is a device, a machinery; thought in itself, in its origin on the higher levels of consciousness, is a perception, a cognitive seizing of the object or of some truth of things which is a powerful but still a minor and secondary result of spiritual vision, a comparatively external and superficial regard of the self upon the self, the subject upon itself or something of itself as object: for all there is a diversity and a multiplicity of the self. In mind there is a surface response of perception to the contact of an observed or discovered object, fact or truth and a consequent conceptual formulation of it; but in the spiritual light there is a deeper perceptive response from the very substance of consciousness and a comprehending formulation in that substance, an exact figure of revelatory ideograph in the stuff of being, — nothing more, no verbal representation is needed for the precision and completeness of this thought-knowledge. Thought creates a representative image of Truth; it offers that to the mind as a means of holding Truth and making it an object of knowledge; but the body itself of Truth is caught and exactly held in the sunlight of a deeper spiritual sight to which the representative figure created by thought is secondary and derivative, powerful for communication of knowledge, but not indispensable for reception or possession of knowledge.

A consciousness that proceeds by sight, the consciousness of the seer, is a greater power for knowledge than the consciousness of the thinker. The perceptual power of the inner sight is greater and more direct than the perceptual power of thought: it is a spiritual sense that seizes something of the substance of Truth and not only her figure; but it outlines the figure also and at the same time catches the significance of the figure, and it can embody her with a finer and bolder revealing outline and a larger comprehension and power of totality than thought-conception can manage. As the Higher Mind brings a greater consciousness into the being through the spiritual idea and its power of truth, so the Illumined Mind brings in a still greater consciousness through a Truth-sight and Truth-light and its seeing and seizing power. It can effect a more powerful and dynamic integration; it illumines the thought-mind with a direct inner vision and inspiration, brings a spiritual sight into the heart and a spiritual light and energy into its feeling and emotion, imparts to the life-force a spiritual urge, a truth inspiration that dynamises the action and exalts the life-movements; it infuses into the sense a direct and total power of spiritual sensation so that our vital and physical being can contact and meet concretely, quite as intensely as the mind and emotion can conceive and perceive and feel, the Divine in all things; it throws on the physical mind a transforming light that breaks its limitations, its conservative inertia, replaces its narrow thought-power and its doubts by sight and pours luminosity and consciousness into the very cells of the body. In the transformation by the Higher Mind the spiritual sage and thinker would find his total and dynamic fulfilment; in the transformation by the Illumined Mind there would be a similar fulfilment for the seer, the illumined mystic, those in whom the soul lives in vision and in a direct sense and experience: for it is from these higher sources that they receive their light and to rise into that light and live there would be their ascension to their native empire. *The Life Divine, pp. 944-46*

(c) Intuition

But these two stages [Higher Mind and Illumined Mind] of the ascent enjoy their authority and can get their own united completeness only by a reference to a third level; for it is from the higher summits where dwells the intuitional being that they derive the knowledge which they turn into thought or sight and bring down to us for the mind's transmutation. Intuition is a power of consciousness nearer and more intimate to the original knowledge by identity; for it is always something that leaps out direct from a concealed identity. It is when the consciousness of the subject meets with the consciousness in the object, penetrates it and sees, feels or vibrates with the truth of what it contacts, that the intuition leaps out like a spark or lightning-flash from the shock of the meeting; or when the consciousness, even without any such meeting, looks into itself and feels directly and intimately the truth or the truths that are there or so contacts the hidden forces behind appearances, then also there is the outbreak of an intuitive light; or, again, when the consciousness meets the Supreme Reality or the spiritual reality of things and beings and has a contactual union with it, then the spark, the flash or the blaze of intimate truth-perception is lit in its depths. This close perception is more than sight, more than conception: it is the result of a penetrating and revealing touch which carries in it sight and conception as part of itself or as its natural consequence. A concealed or slumbering identity, not yet recovering itself, still remembers or conveys by the intuition its own contents and the intimacy of its self-feeling and self-vision of things, its light of truth, its overwhelming and automatic certitude.

In the human mind the intuition is even such a truth-remembrance or truth-conveyance, or such a revealing flash or blaze breaking into a great mass of ignorance or through a veil of nescience: but... it is subject there to an invading mixture or a mental coating or an interception and substitution; there is too a manifold possibility of misinterpretation which comes in the way of the purity and fullness of its action. Moreover, there are seeming intuitions on all levels of the being which are communications rather than intuitions, and these have a very various provenance, value and character. The infrarational "mystic", so-styled, — for to be a true mystic it is not sufficient to reject reason and rely on sources of thought or action of which one has no understanding, — is often inspired by such communications on the vital level from a dark and dangerous source. In these circumstances we are driven to rely mainly on the reason and are disposed even to control the suggestions of the intuition, — or the pseudo-intuition, which is the more frequent phenomenon, — by the observing and discriminating intelligence; for we feel in our intellectual part that we cannot be sure otherwise what is the true thing and what the mixed or adulterated article or false substitute. But this largely discounts for us the utility of the intuition: for the reason is not in this field a reliable arbiter, since its methods are different, tentative, uncertain, an intellectual seeking; even though it itself really relies on a camouflaged intuition for its conclusions, — for without that help it could not choose its course or arrive at any assured finding, — it hides this dependence from itself under the process of a reasoned conclusion or a verified conjecture. An intuition passed in judicial review by the reason ceases to be an intuition and can only have the authority of the reason for which there is no inner source of direct certitude. But even if the mind became predominantly an intuitive mind reliant upon its portion of the higher faculty, the co-ordination of its cognitions and its separated activities, — for in mind these would always be apt to appear as a series of imperfectly connected flashes, — would remain difficult so long as this new mentality has not a conscious liaison with its suprarational source or a self-uplifting access to a higher plane of consciousness in which an intuitive action is pure and native.

Intuition is always an edge or ray or outleap of a superior light; it is in us a projecting blade, edge or point of a far-off supermind light entering into and modified by some intermediate truth-mind substance above us and, so modified, again entering into and very much blinded by our ordinary or ignorant mind-substance; but on that higher level to which it is native its light is unmixed and therefore entirely and purely veridical, and its rays are not separated but connected or massed together in a play of waves of what might almost be called in the Sanskrit poetic figure a sea or mass of "stable lightnings". When this original or native Intuition begins to descend into us in answer to an ascension of our consciousness to its level or as a result of our finding of a clear way of communication with it, it may continue to come as a play of lightning-flashes, isolated or in constant action; but at this stage the judgment of reason becomes quite inapplicable, it can only act as an observer or registrar understanding or recording the more luminous intimations, judgments and discriminations of the higher power. To complete or verify an isolated intuition or discriminate its nature, its application, its limitations, the receiving consciousness must rely on another completing intuition or be able to call down a massed intuition capable of putting all in place. For once the process of the change has begun, a complete transmutation of the stuff and activities of the mind into the substance, form and power of Intuition is imperative; until then, so long as the process of consciousness depends upon the lower intelligence serving or helping out or using the intuition, the result can only be a survival of the mixed Knowledge-Ignorance uplifted or relieved by a higher light and force acting in its parts of Knowledge.

Intuition has a fourfold power. A power of revelatory truth-seeing, a power of inspiration or truth-hearing, a power of truth-touch or immediate seizing of significance, which is akin to the ordinary nature of its intervention in our mental intelligence, a power of true and automatic discrimination of the orderly and exact relation of truth to truth, — these are the fourfold potencies of Intuition. Intuition can therefore perform all the action of reason, — including the function of logical intelligence, which is to work out the right relation of things and the right relation of idea with idea, — but by its own superior process and with steps that do not fail or falter. It takes up also and transforms into its own substance not only the mind of thought, but the heart and life and the sense and physical consciousness: already all these have their own peculiar powers of intuition derivative from the hidden Light; the pure power descending from above can assume them all into itself and impart to these deeper heart-perceptions and life-perceptions and the divinations of the body a greater integrality and perfection. It can thus change the whole consciousness into the stuff of Intuition; for it brings its own greater radiant movement into the will, into the feelings and emotions, the life-impulses, the action of sense and sensation, the very workings of the body-consciousness; it recasts them in the light and power of truth and illumines their knowledge and their ignorance. A certain integration can thus take place, but whether it is a total integration must depend on the extent to which the new light is able to take up the subconscient and penetrate the fundamental Inconscience. Here the intuitive light and power may be hampered in its task because it is the edge of a delegated and modified Supermind, but does not bring in the whole mass or body of the identity-knowledge. The basis of Inconscience in our nature is too vast, deep and solid to be altogether penetrated, turned into light, transformed by an inferior power of the Truth-nature. *The Life Divine, pp. 946-50*

(d) Overmind

The next step of the ascent brings us to the Overmind; the intu-itional change can only be an introduction to this higher spiritual overture. But... the Overmind, even when it is selective and not total in its action, is still a power of cosmic consciousness, a principle of global knowledge which carries in it a delegated light from the supramental Gnosis. It is, therefore, only by an opening into the cosmic consciousness that the overmind ascent and descent can be made wholly possible: a high and intense individual opening upwards is not sufficient, — to that vertical ascent towards summit Light there must be added a vast hori-zontal expansion of the consciousness into some totality of the Spirit. At the least, the inner being must already have replaced by its deeper and wider awareness the surface mind and its limited outlook and learned to live in a large universality; for otherwise the overmind view of things and the overmind dynamism will have no room to move in and effectuate its dynamic opera-tions. When the Overmind descends, the predominance of the centralising ego-sense is entirely subordinated, lost in largeness of being and finally abolished; a wide cosmic perception and feeling of a boundless universal self and movement replaces it: many motions that were formerly egocentric may still continue, but they occur as currents or ripples in the cosmic wideness. Thought, for the most part, no longer seems to originate indi-vidually in the body or the person but manifests from above or comes in upon the cosmic mind-waves: all inner individual sight or intelligence of things is now a revelation or illumination of what is seen or comprehended, but the source of the revelation is not in one's separate self but in the universal knowledge; the feelings, emotions, sensations are similarly felt as waves from the same cosmic immensity breaking upon the subtle and the gross body and responded to in kind by the individual centre of the universality; for the body is only a small support or even less, a point of relation, for the action of a vast cosmic instrumentation. In this boundless largeness, not only the separate ego but all sense of individuality, even of a subordinated or instrumental individuality, may entirely disappear; the cosmic existence, the cosmic consciousness, the cosmic delight, the play of cosmic forces are alone left: if the delight or the centre of Force is felt in what was the personal mind, life or body, it is not with a sense of personality but as a field of manifestation, and this sense of the delight or of the action of Force is not confined to the person or the body but can be felt at all points in an unlimited consciousness of unity which pervades everywhere.

But there can be many formulations of overmind conscious-ness and experience; for the Overmind has a great plasticity and is a field of multiple possibilities. In place of an uncentred and unplaced diffusion there may be the sense of the universe in oneself or as oneself: but there too this self is not the ego; it is an extension of a free and pure essential self-consciousness or it is an identification with the All, — the extension or the identification constituting a cosmic being, a universal individual. In one state of the cosmic consciousness there is an individual included in the cosmos but identifying himself with all in it, with the things and beings, with the thought and sense, the joy and grief of others; in another state there is an inclusion of beings in oneself and a reality of their life as part of one's own being. Often there is no rule or governance of the immense movement, but a free play of universal Nature to which what was the per-sonal being responds with a passive acceptance or a dynamic identity, while yet the spirit remains free and undisturbed by any bondage to the reactions of this passivity or this universal and impersonal identification and sympathy. But with a strong influence or full action of the Overmind a very integral sense of governance, a complete supporting or overruling presence and direction of the cosmic Self or the Ishwara can come in and become normal; or a special centre may be revealed or created overtopping and dominating the physical instrument, individual in fact of existence, but impersonal in feeling and recognised by a free cognition as something instrumental to the action of a Transcendent and Universal Being. In the transition towards the Supermind this centralising action tends towards the discovery of a true individual replacing the dead ego, a being who is in his essence one with the supreme Self, one with the universe in extension and yet a cosmic centre and circumference of the specialised action of the Infinite.

These are the general first results and create the normal foundation of the overmind consciousness in the evolved spiritual being, but its varieties and developments are innumerable. The consciousness that thus acts is experienced as a consciousness of Light and Truth, a power, force, action full of Light and Truth, an aesthesis and sensation of beauty and delight universal and multitudinous in detail, an illumination in the whole and in all things, in the one movement and all movements, with a constant extension and play of possibilities which is infinite, even in its multitude of determinations endless and indeterminable. If the power of an ordering overmind Gnosis intervenes, then there is a cosmic structure of the consciousness and action, but this is not like the rigid mental structures; it is plastic, organic, something that can grow and develop and stretch into the infinite. All spiritual experiences are taken up and become habitual and normal to the new nature; all essential experiences belonging to the mind, life, body are taken up and spiritualised, transmuted and felt as forms of the consciousness, delight, power of the infinite existence. Intuition, illumined sight and thought enlarge themselves; their substance assumes a greater substantiality, mass, energy, their movement is more comprehensive, global, many-faceted, more wide and potent in its truth-force: the whole nature, knowledge, aesthesis, sympathy, feeling, dynamism become more catholic, all-understanding, all-embracing, cosmic, infinite.

The overmind change is the final consummating movement of the dynamic spiritual transformation; it is the highest possible status-dynamis of the Spirit in the spiritual-mind plane. It takes up all that is in the three steps below it and raises their charateristic workings to their highest and largest power, adding to them a universal wideness of consciousness and force, a harmonious concert of knowledge, a more manifold delight of being. But there are certain reasons arising from its own characteristic status and power that prevent it from being the final possibility of the spiritual evolution. It is a power, though the highest power, of the lower hemisphere; although its basis is a cosmic unity, its action is an action of division and interaction, an action taking its stand on the play of the multiplicity. Its play is, like that of all Mind, a play of possibilities; although it acts not in the Ignorance but with the knowledge of the truth of these possibilities, yet it works them out through their own independent evolution of their powers. It acts in each cosmic formula according to the fundamental meaning of that formula and is not a power for a dynamic transcendence. Here in earth-life it has to work upon a cosmic formula whose basis is the entire nescience which results from the separation of Mind, Life and Matter from their own source and supreme origin. Overmind can bridge that division up to the point at which separative Mind enters into Overmind and becomes a part of its action; it can unite individual mind with cosmic mind on its highest plane, equate individual self with cosmic self and give to the nature an action of universality; but it cannot lead Mind beyond itself, and in this world of original Inconscience it cannot dynamise the Transcendence: for it is the Supermind alone that is the supreme self-determining truth-action and the direct power of manifestation of that

Transcendence. If then the action of evolutionary Nature ended here, the Overmind, having carried the consciousness to the point of a vast illumined universality and an organised play of this wide and potent spiritual awareness of utter existence, force-consciousness and delight, could only go farther by an opening of the gates of the Spirit into the upper hemisphere and a will to enable the soul to depart out of its cosmic formation into Transcendence.

In the terrestrial evolution itself the overmind descent would not be able to transform wholly the Inconscience; all that it could do would be to transform in each man it touched the whole conscious being, inner and outer, personal and universally impersonal, into its own stuff and impose that upon the Ignorance illumining it into cosmic truth and knowledge. But a basis of Nescience would remain; it would be as if a sun and its system were to shine out in an original darkness of Space and illumine everything as far as its rays could reach so that all that dwelt in the light would feel as if no darkness were there at all in their experience of existence. But outside that sphere or expanse of experience the original darkness would still be there and, since all things are possible in an overmind structure, could reinvade the island of light created within its empire. Moreover, since Overmind deals with different possibilities, its natural action would be to develop the separate possibility of one or more or numerous dynamic spiritual formulations to their utmost or combine or harmonise several possibilities together; but this would be a creation or a number of creations in the original terrestrial creation, each complete in its separate existence. The evolved spiritual individual would be there, there might evolve also a spiritual community or communities in the same world as mental man and the vital being of the animal, but each working out its independent existence in a loose relation within the terrestrial formula. The supreme power of the principle of unity taking all diversities into itself and controlling them as parts of the unity, which must be the law of the new evolutionary consciousness, would not as yet be there. Also by this much evolution there could be no security against the downward pull or gravitation of the Inconscience which dissolves all the formations that life and mind build in it, swallows all things that arise out of it or are imposed upon it and disintegrates them into their original matter. The liberation from this pull of the Inconscience and a secured basis for a continuous divine or gnostic evolution would only be achieved by a descent of the Supermind into the terrestrial formula, bringing into it the supreme law and light and dynamis of the Spirit and penetrating with it and transforming the inconscience of the material basis. A last transition from Overmind to Supermind and a descent of Supermind must therefore intervene at this stage of evolutionary Nature.

Overmind and its delegated powers, taking up and penetrating mind and the life and body dependent upon mind, would subject all to a greatening process; at each step of this process a greater power and a higher intensity of gnosis less and less mixed with the loose, diffused, diminishing and diluting stuff of mind could establish itself: but all gnosis is in its origin power of Supermind, so that this would mean a greater and greater influx of a half-veiled and indirect supramental light and power into the nature. This would continue until the point was reached at which Overmind would begin itself to be transformed into Supermind; the supramental consciousness and force would take up the transformation directly into its own hands, reveal to the terrestrial mind, life, bodily being their own spiritual truth and divinity and, finally, pour into the whole nature the perfect knowledge, power, significance of the supramental existence. The soul would pass beyond the borders of the Ignorance and cross its original line of departure from the supreme Knowledge: it would enter into the integrality of the supramental gnosis; the descent of the gnostic Light would effectuate a complete transformation of the Ignorance.

The Life Divine, pp. 950-55

(e) Supermind

It is hardly possible to say what the supermind is in the language of Mind, even spiritualised Mind, for it is a different consciousness altogether and acts in a different way. Whatever may be said of it is likely to be not understood or misunderstood. It is only by growing into it that we can know what it is and this also cannot be done until after a long process by which mind heightening and illuminating becomes pure Intuition (not the mixed thing that ordinarily goes by that name) and masses itself into overmind; after that overmind can be lifted into and suffused with supermind till it undergoes a transformation.

In the supermind all is self-known self-luminously, there are no divisions, oppositions or separated aspects as in Mind whose principle is division of Knowledge into parts and setting each part against another. Overmind approaches this at its top and is often mistaken for supermind, but it cannot reach it — except by uplifting and transformation. *Letters on Yoga, pp. 259-60*

A principle of active Will and Knowledge superior to Mind and creatrix of the worlds is... the intermediary power and state of being between that self-possession of the One and this flux of the Many....

...we have called this state of consciousness the Supermind; but the word is ambiguous since it may be taken in the sense of mind itself super-eminent and lifted above ordinary mentality but not radically changed, or on the contrary it may bear the sense of all that is beyond mind and therefore assume a too extensive comprehensiveness which would bring in even the Ineffable itself. A subsidiary description is required which will more accurately limit its significance....

...we may accept...the subsidiary term "truth-consciousness" to delimit the connotation of the more elastic phrase, Supermind. *The Life Divine, pp. 122-125*

We call it the Supermind or the Truth-Consciousness, because it is a principle superior to mentality and exists, acts and proceeds in the fundamental truth and unity of things and not like the mind in their appearances and phenomenal divisions.

The Life Divine, p. 143

The Supermind is in its very essence a truth-consciousness, a consciousness always free from the Ignorance which is the foundation of our present natural or evolutionary existence and from which nature in us is trying to arrive at self-knowledge and world-knowledge and a right consciousness and the right use of our existence in the universe. The Supermind, because it is a truth-consciousness, has this knowledge inherent in it and this power of true existence; its course is straight and can go direct to its aim, its field is wide and can even be made illimitable. This is because its very nature is knowledge: it has not to acquire knowledge but possesses it in its own right; its steps are not from nescience or ignorance into some imperfect light, but from truth to greater truth, from right perception to deeper perception, from intuition to intuition, from illumination to utter and boundless luminousness, from growing widenesses to the utter vasts and to very infinitude. On its summits it possesses the divine omniscience and omnipotence, but even in an evolutionary movement of its own graded self-manifestation by which it would eventually reveal its own highest heights it must be in its very nature essentially free from ignorance and error: it starts from truth and light and moves always in truth and light. As its knowledge is always true, so too its will is always true; it does not fumble in its handling of things or stumble in its paces. In the Supermind feeling and emotion do not depart from their truth, make no slips or mistakes, do not swerve from the right and the real, cannot misuse beauty and delight or twist away from a divine rectitude. In the Supermind sense cannot mislead or deviate into the grossnesses which are here its natural imperfections and the cause of reproach, distrust and misuse by our ignorance. Even an incomplete statement made by the Supermind is a truth leading to a further truth, its incomplete action a step towards completeness.

The Supramental Manifestation and Other Writings, pp. 41-42

The Infinite, we may say, organises by the power of its self-knowledge the law of its own manifestation of being in the universe, not only the material universe present to our senses, but whatever lies behind it on whatever planes of existence. All is organised by it not under any inconscient compulsion, not according to a mental fantasy or caprice, but in its own infinite spiritual freedom according to the self-truth of its being, its infinite potentialities and its will of self-creation out of those potentialities, and the law of this self-truth is the necessity that compels created things to act and evolve each according to its own nature. The Intelligence — to give it an inadequate name — the Logos that thus organises its own manifestation is evidently something infinitely greater, more extended in knowledge, compelling in self-power, large both in the delight of its self-existence and the delight of its active being and works than the mental intelligence which is to us the highest realised degree and expression of consciousness. It is to this intelligence infinite in itself but freely organising and self-determiningly organic in its self-creation and its works that we may give for our present purpose the name of the divine supermind or gnosis.

The Synthesis of Yoga, pp. 756-57

(f) Sachchidananda — Existence-Consciousness-Bliss

Sachchidananda is the One with a triple aspect. In the Supreme the three are not three but one — existence is consciousness, consciousness is bliss, and they are thus inseparable, not only inseparable but so much each other that they are not distinct at all. In the superior planes of manifestation they become triune

— although inseparable, one can be made more prominent and base or lead the others. In the lower planes below they become separable in appearance, though not in their secret reality, and one can exist phenomenally without the others so that we become aware of what seems to us an inconscient or a painful existence or a consciousness without Ananda. Indeed, without this separation of them in experience pain and ignorance and falsehood and death and what we call inconscience could not have manifested themselves — there could not have been this evolution of a limited and suffering consciousness out of the universal nescience of Matter.   *Letters on Yoga, p. 239*

Existence, Consciousness, Bliss, these are everywhere the three inseparable divine terms. None of them is really separate, though our mind and our mental experience can make not only the distinction, but the separation. Mind can say and think "I was, but unconscious," — for no being can say "I am, but unconscious," — and it can think and feel "I am, but miserable and without any pleasure in existence." In reality this is impossible. The existence we really are, the eternal "I am," of which it can never be true to say "It was," is nowhere and at no time unconscious. What we call unconsciousness is simply other-consciousness; it is the going in of this surface wave of our mental awareness of outer objects into our subliminal self-awareness and into our awareness too of other planes of existence. We are really no more unconscious when we are asleep or stunned or drugged or "dead" or in any other state, than when we are plunged in inner thought oblivious of our physical selves and our surroundings. For anyone who has advanced even a little way in Yoga, this is a most elementary proposition and one which offers no difficulty whatever to the thought because it is proved at every point by experience. It is more difficult to realise that existence and undelight of existence cannot go together. What we call misery, grief, pain, absence of delight is again merely a surface wave of the delight of existence which takes on to our mental experience these apparently opposite tints because of a certain trick of false reception in our divided being — which is not our existence at all but only a fragmentary formulation or discoloured spray of conscious-force tossed up by the infinite sea of our self-existence. In order to realise this we have to get away from our absorption in these surface habits, these petty tricks of our mental being, — and when we do get behind and away from them it is surprising how superficial they are, what ridiculously weak and little-penetrating pin-pricks they prove to be, — and we have to realise true existence, and true consciousness, and true experience of existence and consciousness, Sat, Chit and Ananda.

Chit, the divine Consciousness, is not our mental self-awareness; that we shall find to be only a form, a lower and limited mode or movement. As we progress and awaken to the soul in us and things, we shall realise that there is a consciousness also in the plant, in the metal, in the atom, in electricity, in everything that belongs to physical nature; we shall find even that it is not really in all respects a lower or more limited mode than the mental, on the contrary it is in many "inanimate" forms more intense, rapid, poignant, though less evolved towards the surface. But this also, this consciousness of vital and physical Nature is, compared with Chit, a lower and therefore a limited form, mode and movement. These lower modes of consciousness are the conscious-stuff of inferior planes in one indivisible existence. In ourselves also there is in our subconscious being an action which is precisely that of the "inanimate" physical Nature whence has been constituted the basis of our physical being, another which is that of plant-life, and another which is that of the lower animal creation around us. All these are so much dominated and conditioned by the thinking and reasoning conscious-being in us that we have no real awareness of these lower planes; we are unable to perceive in their own terms what these parts of us are doing, and receive it very imperfectly in the terms and values of the thinking and reasoning mind. Still we know well enough that there is an animal in us as well as that which is characteristically human, — something which is a creature of conscious instinct and impulse, not reflective or rational, as well as that which turns back in thought and will on its experience, meets it from above with the light and force of a higher plane and to some degree controls, uses and modifies it. But the animal in man is only the head of our subhuman being; below it there is much that is also sub-animal and merely vital, much that acts by an instinct and impulse of which the constituting consciousness is withdrawn behind the surface. Below this sub-animal being, there is at a further depth the subvital. When we advance in that ultra-normal self-knowledge and experience which Yoga brings with it, we become aware that the body too has a consciousness of its own; it has habits, impulses, instincts, an inert yet effective will which differs from that of the rest of our being and can resist it and condition its effectiveness. Much of the struggle in our being is due to this composite existence and the interaction of these varied and heterogeneous planes on each other. For man here is the result of an evolution and contains in himself the whole of that evolution up from the merely physical and subvital conscious being to the mental creature which at the top he is.

But this evolution is really a manifestation and just as we have in us these subnormal selves and subhuman planes, so are there in us above our mental being supernormal and superhuman planes. There Chit as the universal conscious-stuff of existence takes other poises, moves out in other modes, on other principles and by other faculties of action. There is above the mind, as the old Vedic sages discovered, a Truth-plane, a plane of self-luminous, self-effective Idea, which can be turned in light and force upon our mind, reason, sentiments, impulses, sensations and use and control them in the sense of the real Truth of things just as we turn our mental reason and will upon our sense-experience and animal nature to use and control them in the sense of our rational and moral perceptions. There

there is no seeking, but rather natural possession; no conflict or separation between will and reason, instinct and impulse, desire and experience, idea and reality, but all are in harmony, concomitant, mutually effective, unified in their origin, in their development and in their effectuation. But beyond this plane and attainable through it are others in which the very Chit itself becomes revealed, Chit the elemental origin and primal completeness of all this varied consciousness which is here used for various formation and experience. There will and knowledge and sensation and all the rest of our faculties, powers, modes of experience are not merely harmonious, concomitant, unified, but are one being of consciousness and power of consciousness. It is this Chit which modifies itself so as to become on the Truth-plane the supermind, on the mental plane the mental reason, will, emotion, sensation, on the lower planes the vital or physical instincts, impulses, habits of an obscure force not in superficially conscious possession of itself. All is Chit because all is Sat; all is various movement of the original Consciousness because all is various movement of the original Being.

When we find, see or know Chit, we find also that its essence is Ananda or delight of self-existence. To possess self is to possess self-bliss; not to possess self is to be in more or less obscure search of the delight of existence. Chit eternally possesses its self-bliss; and since Chit is the universal conscious-stuff of being, conscious universal being is also in possession of conscious self-bliss, master of the universal delight of existence. The Divine whether it manifests itself in All-Quality or in No-Quality, in Personality or Impersonality, in the One absorbing the Many or in the One manifesting its essential multiplicity, is always in possession of self-bliss and all-bliss because it is always Sachchidananda. For us also to know and possess our true Self in the essential and the universal is to discover the essential and the universal delight of existence, self-bliss and all-bliss. For the universal is only the pouring out of the essential existence, consciousness and delight; and wherever and in whatever form that manifests as existence, there the essential consciousness must be and therefore there must be an essential delight.

The individual soul does not possess this true nature of itself or realise this true nature of its experience, because it separates itself both from the essential and the universal and identifies itself with the separate accidents, with the unessential form and mode and with the separate aspect and vehicle. Thus it takes its mind, body, life-stream for its essential self. It tries to assert these for their own sake against the universal, against that of which the universal is the manifestation. It is right in trying to assert and fulfil itself in the universal for the sake of something greater and beyond, but wrong in attempting to do so against the universal and in obedience to a fragmentary aspect of the universal. This fragmentary aspect or rather collection of fragmentary experiences it combines around an artificial centre of mental experience, the mental ego, and calls that itself and it serves this ego and lives for its sake instead of living for the sake of that something greater and beyond of which all aspects, even the widest and most general are partial manifestations. This is the living in the false and not the true self; this is living for the sake of and in obedience to the ego and not for the sake of and in obedience to the Divine.... We have to seize on the practical fact that to such self-division is due the self-limitation by which we have become unable to possess the true nature of being and experience and are therefore in our mind, life and body subject to ignorance, incapacity and suffering. Non-possession of unity is the root cause; to recover unity is the sovereign means, unity with the universal and with that which the universal is here to express. We have to realise the true self of ourselves and of all; and to realise the true self is to realise Sachchidananda.

The Synthesis of Yoga, pp. 370-74

13
Liberation and Transformation

Deep, intense, convincing, common to all who have overstepped a certain limit of the active mind-belt into horizonless inner space, this is the great experience of liberation, the consciousness of something within us that is behind and outside of the universe and all its forms, interests, aims, events and happenings, calm, untouched, unconcerned, illimitable, immobile, free, the uplook to something above us indescribable and unseizable into which by abolition of our personality we can enter, the presence of an omnipresent eternal witness Purusha, the sense of an Infinity or a Timelessness that looks down on us from an august negation of all our existence and is alone the one thing Real. This experience is the highest sublimation of spiritualised mind looking resolutely beyond its own existence. No one who has not passed through this liberation can be entirely free from the mind and its meshes, but one is not compelled to linger in this experience for ever. Great as it is, it is only the Mind's overwhelming experience of what is beyond itself and all it can conceive. It is a supreme negative experience, but beyond it is all the tremendous light of an infinite Consciousness, an illimitable Knowledge, an affirmative absolute Presence.

The Synthesis of Yoga, pp. 278-79

For certain ways of thinking liberation is a throwing off of all nature, a silent state of pure being, a Nirvana or extinction, a dissolution of the natural existence into some indefinable Absolute, *mokṣa*. But an absorbed and immersed bliss, a wideness of actionless peace, a release of self-extinction or a self-drowning in the Absolute is not our aim. We shall give to the idea of liberation, *mukti*, only the connotation of that inner change which is common to all experience of this kind, essential to perfection and indispensable to spiritual freedom. We shall find that it then implies always two things, a rejection and an assumption, a negative and a positive side; the negative movement of freedom is a liberation from the principal bonds, the master-knots of the lower soul-nature, the positive side an opening or growth into the higher spiritual existence. But what are these master-knots — other and deeper twistings than the instrumental knots of the mind, heart, psychic life-force? We find them pointed out for us and insisted on with great force and a constant emphatic repetition in the Gita; they are four, desire, ego, the dualities and the three gunas of Nature; for to be desireless, ego-less, equal of mind and soul and spirit and *nistraigunya* is in the idea of the Gita to be free, *mukta*. We may accept this description; for everything essential is covered by its amplitude. On the other hand, the positive sense of freedom is to be universal in soul, transcendently one in spirit with God, possessed of the highest divine nature, — as we may say, like to God, or one with him in the law of our being. This is the whole and full sense of liberation and this is the integral freedom of the spirit.

The Synthesis of Yoga, pp. 647-48

By transformation I do not mean some change of the nature — I do not mean, for instance, sainthood or ethical perfection or yogic siddhis (like the Tantrik's) or a transcendental (*cinmaya*) body. I use transformation in a special sense, a change of consciousness radical and complete and of a certain specific kind which is so conceived as to bring about a strong and assured step forward in the spiritual evolution of the being of a greater and higher kind and of a larger sweep and completeness than what took place when a mentalised being first appeared in a vital and material animal world. If anything short of that takes place or at least if a real beginning is not made on that basis, a fundamental progress towards this fulfilment, then my object is not accomplished. A partial realisation, something mixed and inconclusive, does not meet the demand I make on life and yoga.

Light of realisation is not the same thing as Descent. Realisation by itself does not necessarily transform the being as a whole; it may bring only an opening or heightening or widening of the consciousness at the top so as to realise something in the Purusha part without any radical change in the parts of Prakriti. One may have some light of realisation at the spiritual summit of the consciousness but the parts below remain what they were. I have seen any number of instances of that. There must be a descent of the light not merely into the mind or part of it but into all the being down to the physical and below before a real transformation can take place. A light in the mind may spiritualise or otherwise change the mind or part of it in one way or another, but it need not change the vital nature; a light in the vital may purify and enlarge the vital movements or else silence and immobilise the vital being, but leave the body and the physical consciousness as it was, or even leave it inert or shake its balance. And the descent of Light is not enough, it must be the descent of the whole higher consciousness, its Peace, Power, Knowledge, Love, Ananda. Moreover, the descent may be enough to liberate, but not to perfect, or it may be enough to make a great change in the inner being, while the outer remains an imperfect instrument, clumsy, sick or unexpressive. Finally, transformation effected by the sadhana cannot be complete unless it is a supramentalisation of the being. Psychicisation is not enough, it is only a beginning; spiritualisation and the descent of the higher consciousness is not enough, it is only a middle term; the ultimate achievement needs the action of the supramental Consciousness and Force. Something less than that may very well be considered enough by the individual, but it is not enough for the earth-consciousness to take the definitive stride forward it must take at one time or another.   *Letters on Yoga, pp. 98-99*

What I mean by the spiritual transformation is something dynamic (not merely liberation of the Self or realisation of the One which can very well be attained without any descent). It is a putting on of the spiritual consciousness, dynamic as well as static, in every part of the being down to the subconscient. That cannot be done by the influence of the Self leaving the consciousness fundamentally as it is with only purification, enlightenment of the mind and heart and quiescence of the vital. It means a bringing down of the Divine Consciousness static and dynamic into all these parts and the entire replacement of the present consciousness by that. This we find unveiled and unmixed above mind, life and body. It is a matter of the undeniable experience of many that this can descend and it is my experience that nothing short of its *full* descent can thoroughly remove the veil and mixture and effect the full spiritual transformation. No metaphysical or logical reasoning in the void as to what the Atman "must" do or can do or needs or needs not to do is relevant here or of any value. I may add that transformation is not the central object of other paths as it is of this yoga — only so much purification and change is demanded by them as will lead to liberation and the beyond-life. The influence of the Atman can no doubt do that — a full descent of a new consciousness into the whole nature from top to bottom to transform life here is not needed at all for the spiritual escape from life.

Letters on Yoga, pp. 115-16

If the redemption of the soul from the physical vesture be the object, then there is no need of supramentalisation. Spiritual Mukti and Nirvana are sufficient. If the object is to rise to supraphysical planes, then also there is no need of supramentalisation. One can enter into some heaven above by devotion to the Lord of that heaven. But that is no progression. The other worlds are typal worlds, each fixed in its own kind and type and law. Evolution takes place on the earth and therefore the earth is the proper field for progression. The beings of the other worlds do not progress from one world to another. They remain fixed to their own type.

The purely monistic Vedantist says, all is Brahman, life is a dream, an unreality, only Brahman exists. One has Nirvana or Mukti, then one lives only till the body falls — after that there is no such thing as life.

They do not believe in transformation, because mind, life and body are an ignorance, an illusion — the only reality is the featureless relationless Self or Brahman. Life is a thing of relations; in the pure Self, all life and relations disappear. What would be the use or the possibility of transforming an illusion that can never be anything else (however transformed) than an illusion? There is no such thing for them as a "Nirvanic life".

It is only some yogas that aim at a transformation of any kind except that of ignorance into knowledge. The idea varies, — sometimes a divine knowledge or power or else a divine purity or an ethical perfection or a divine love.

What has to be overcome is the opposition of the Ignorance that does not want the transformation of the nature. If that can be overcome, then old spiritual ideas will not form an obstacle.

Letters on Yoga, pp. 10-11

By divine realisation is meant the spiritual realisation — the realisation of Self, Bhagwan or Brahman on the mental-spiritual plane or else the overmental plane. That is a thing (at any rate the mental-spiritual) which thousands have done. So it is obviously easier to do than the supramental. Also nobody can have the supramental realisation who has not had the spiritual....

...There are different statuses (*avasthā*) of the Divine Consciousness. There are also different statuses of transformation. First is the psychic transformation, in which all is in contact with the Divine through the individual psychic consciousness. Next is the spiritual transformation in which all is merged in the Divine in the cosmic consciousness. Third is the supramental transformation in which all becomes supramentalised in the divine gnostic consciousness. It is only with the last that there can begin the *complete* transformation of mind, life and body — in my sense of completeness. *Letters on Yoga, pp. 94-95*

supramental were the same thing... then all the
otees and yogis and sadhaks throughout the ages
een supramental beings and all I have written about
ind would be so much superfluous stuff, useless and
nybody who had spiritual experiences would then be
amental being; the Ashram would be chock-full of supramental beings and every other Ashram in India also. Spiritual
experiences can fix themselves in the inner consciousness and
alter it, transform it, if you like; one can realise the Divine everywhere, the Self in all and all in the Self, the universal Shakti
doing all things; one can feel merged in the Cosmic Self or full of
ecstatic bhakti or Ananda. But one may and usually does still go
on in the outer parts of Nature thinking with the intellect or at
best the intuitive mind, willing with a mental will, feeling joy and
sorrow on the vital surface, undergoing physical afflictions and
suffering from the struggle of life in the body with death and disease. The change then only will be that the inner self will watch
all that without getting disturbed or bewildered, with a perfect
equality, taking it as an inevitable part of Nature, inevitable at
least so long as one does not withdraw to the Self out of Nature.
That is not the transformation I envisage. It is quite another
power of knowledge, another kind of will, another luminous
nature of emotion and aesthesis, another constitution of the
physical consciousness that must come in by the supramental
change.   *Letters on Yoga, pp. 18-19*

Transformation means that the higher consciousness or nature
is brought down into the mind, vital and body and takes the
place of the lower. There is a higher consciousness of the true
self, which is spiritual, but it is above; if one rises above into it,
then one is free as long as one remains there, but if one comes
down into or uses mind, vital or body — and if one keeps any
connection with life, one has to do so, either to come down
and act from the ordinary consciousness or else to be in the
self but use mind, life and body, then the imperfections of these

instruments have to be faced and mended — they can only be
mended by transformation.   *Letters on Yoga, p. 1143*

A divine life in a material world implies necessarily a union of
the two ends of existence, the spiritual summit and the material
base. The soul with the basis of its life established in Matter
ascends to the heights of the Spirit but does not cast away its
base, it joins the heights and the depths together. The Spirit
descends into Matter and the material world with all its lights
and glories and powers and with them fills and transforms life
in the material world so that it becomes more and more divine.
The transformation is not a change into something purely subtle
and spiritual to which Matter is in its nature repugnant and by
which it is felt as an obstacle or as a shackle binding the Spirit;
it takes up Matter as a form of the Spirit though now a form
which conceals and turns it into a revealing instrument, it does
not cast away the energies of Matter, its capacities, its methods; it
brings out their hidden possibilities, uplifts, sublimates, discloses
their innate divinity. The divine life will reject nothing that is
capable of divinisation; all is to be seized, exalted, made utterly
perfect. The mind now still ignorant, though struggling towards
knowledge, has to rise towards and into the supramental light
and truth and bring it down so that it shall suffuse our thinking
and perception and insight and all our means of knowing till
they become radiant with the highest truth in their inmost and
outermost movements. Our life, still full of obscurity and confusion and occupied with so many dull and lower aims, must
feel all its urges and instincts exalted and irradiated and become
a glorious counterpart of the supramental super-life above. The
physical consciousness and physical being, the body itself must
reach a perfection in all that it is and does which now we can
hardly conceive. It may even in the end be suffused with a light
and beauty and bliss from the Beyond and the life divine assume
a body divine.

But first the evolution of the nature must have reached a

point at which it can meet the Spirit direct, feel the aspiration towards the spiritual change and open itself to the workings of the Power which shall transform it. A supreme perfection, a total perfection is possible only by a transformation of our lower or human nature, a transformation of the mind into a thing of light, our life into a thing of power, an instrument of right action, right use for all its forces, of a happy elevation of its being lifting it beyond its present comparatively narrow potentiality for a self-fulfilling force of action and joy of life. There must be equally a transforming change of the body by a conversion of its action, its functioning, its capacities as an instrument beyond the limitations by which it is clogged and hampered even in its greatest present human attainment. In the totality of the change we have to achieve, human means and forces too have to be taken up, not dropped but used and magnified to their utmost possibility as part of the new life.

The Supramental Manifestation and Other Writings, pp. 5-7

14
Validity of Supraphysical and Spiritual Experience

It is a fact that mankind almost from the beginning of its existence or so far back as history or tradition can go, has believed in the existence of other worlds and in the possibility of communication between their powers and beings and the human race. In the last rationalistic period of human thought from which we are emerging, this belief has been swept aside as an age-long superstition; all evidence or intimations of its truth have been rejected *a priori* as fundamentally false and undeserving of inquiry because incompatible with the axiomatic truth that only Matter and the material world and its experiences are real; all other experience purporting to be real must be either a hallucination or an imposture or a subjective result of superstitious credulity and imagination or else, if a fact, then other than what it purported to be and explicable by a physical cause: no evidence could be accepted of such a fact unless it is objective and physical in its character; even if the fact be very apparently supraphysical, it cannot be accepted as such unless it is totally unexplainable by any other imaginable hypothesis or conceivable conjecture.

It should be evident that this demand for physical valid proof of a supraphysical fact is irrational and illogical; it is an irrelevant attitude of the physical mind which assumes that only the objective and physical is fundamentally real and puts aside all else as merely subjective. A supraphysical fact may impinge on the physical world and produce physical results; it may even produce an effect on our physical senses and become manifest to them, but that cannot be its invariable action and most normal character or process. Ordinarily, it must produce a direct effect or a tangible impression on our mind and our life-being, which are the parts of us that are of the same order as itself, and can only indirectly and through them, if at all, influence the physical world and physical life. If it objectivises itself, it must be to a subtler sense in us and only derivatively to the outward physical sense. This derivative objectivisation is certainly possible; if there is an association of the action of the subtle body and its sense-organisation with the action of the material body and its physical organs, then the supraphysical can become outwardly sensible to us. This is what happens, for example, with the faculty called second sight; it is the process of all those psychic phenomena which seem to be seen and heard by the outer senses and are not sensed inwardly through representative or interpretative or symbolic images which bear the stamp of an inner experience or have an evident character of formations in a subtle substance. There can, then, be various kinds of evidence of the existence of other planes of being and communication with them; objectivisation to the outer sense, subtle-sense contacts, mind contacts, life contacts, contacts through the subliminal in special states of consciousness exceeding our ordinary range. Our physical mind is not the whole of us nor, even though it dominates almost the whole of our surface consciousness, the best or greatest part of us; reality cannot be restricted to a sole field of this narrowness or to the dimensions known within its rigid circle.

If it be said that subjective experience or subtle-sense images can easily be deceptive, since we have no recognised method or standard of verification and a too great tendency to admit the extraordinary and miraculous or supernatural at its face-value, this may be admitted: but error is not the prerogative of the inner subjective or subliminal parts of us, it is also an appanage of the physical mind and its objective methods and standards, and such liability to error cannot be a reason for shutting out a large and important domain of experience; it is a reason rather for scrutinising it and finding out in it its own true standards and its characteristic appropriate and valid means of verification. Our subjective being is the basis of our objective experience, and it is not probable that only its physical objectivisations are true and the rest unreliable. The subliminal consciousness, when rightly interrogated, is a witness to truth and its testimony is confirmed again and again even in the physical and the objective field; that testimony cannot, then, be disregarded when it calls our attention to things within us or to things that belong to planes or worlds of a supraphysical experience. At the same time belief by itself is not evidence of reality; it must base itself on something more valid before one can accept it. It is evident that the beliefs of the past are not a sufficient basis for knowledge, even though they cannot be entirely neglected: for a belief is a mental construction and may be a wrong building; it may often answer to some inner intimation and then it has a value, but, as often as not, it disfigures the intimation, usually by a translation into terms familiar to our physical and objective experience, such as that which converted the hierarchy of the planes into a physical hierarchy or geographical space-extension, turned the rarer heights of subtle substance into material heights and placed the abodes of the gods on the summits of physical mountains. All truth supraphysical or physical must be founded not on mental belief alone, but on experience, — but in each case experience must be of the kind, physical, subliminal or spiritual, which is appropriate to the order of the truths into which we are empowered to enter; their validity and significance must be scrutinised, but according to their own law and by a consciousness which can enter into them and not according to the law of another domain or by a consciousness which is capable only of truths of another order; so alone can we be sure of our steps and enlarge firmly our sphere of knowledge. *The Life Divine, pp. 771-74*

Not only are there physical realities which are suprasensible, but, if evidence and experience are at all a test of truth, there are also senses which are supraphysical[1] and can not only take

---

[1] *Sūkṣma indriya*, subtle organs, existing in the subtle body (*sūkṣma deha*), and the means of subtle vision and experience (*sūkṣma dṛṣṭi*).

cognisance of the realities of the material world without the aid of the corporeal sense-organs, but can bring us into contact with other realities, supraphysical and belonging to another world — included, that is to say, in an organisation of conscious experiences that are dependent on some other principle than the gross Matter of which our suns and earths seem to be made.

Constantly asserted by human experience and belief since the origins of thought, this truth, now that the necessity of an exclusive preoccupation with the secrets of the material world no longer exists, begins to be justified by new-born forms of scientific research. The increasing evidences, of which only the most obvious and outward are established under the name of telepathy with its cognate phenomena, cannot long be resisted except by minds shut up in the brilliant shell of the past, by intellects limited in spite of their acuteness through the limitation of their field of experience and inquiry, or by those who confuse enlightenment and reason with the faithful repetition of the formulas left to us from a bygone century and the jealous conservation of dead or dying intellectual dogmas.

It is true that the glimpse of supraphysical realities acquired by methodical research has been imperfect and is yet ill-affirmed; for the methods used are still crude and defective. But these rediscovered subtle senses have at least been found to be true witnesses to physical facts beyond the range of the corporeal organs. There is no justification, then, for scouting them as false witnesses when they testify to supraphysical facts beyond the domain of the material organisation of consciousness. Like all evidence, like the evidence of the physical senses themselves, their testimony has to be controlled, scrutinised and arranged by the reason, rightly translated and rightly related, and their field, laws and processes determined. But the truth of great ranges of experience whose objects exist in a more subtle substance and are perceived by more subtle instruments than those of gross physical Matter, claims in the end the same validity as the truth of the material universe.   *The Life Divine, pp. 18-19*

...the results [of the study of psychic phenomena] cannot be conclusive or sufficiently ample because they are sought for by methods of inquiry and experiment and standards of proof proper to the surface mind and its system of knowledge by indirect contact. Under these conditions they can be investigated only in so far as they are able to manifest in that mind to which they are exceptional, abnormal or supernormal, and therefore comparatively rare, difficult, incomplete in their occurrence. It is only if we can open up the wall between the outer mind and the inner consciousness to which such phenomena are normal, or if we can enter freely within or dwell there, that this realm of knowledge can be truly explained and annexed to our total consciousness and included in the field of operation of our awakened force of nature.   *The Life Divine, p. 537*

...the dialectical intellect is not a sufficient judge of essential or spiritual truths; moreover, very often, by its propensity to deal with words and abstract ideas as if they were binding realities, it wears them as chains and does not look freely beyond them to the essential and total facts of our existence. Intellectual statement is an account to our intelligence and a justification by reasoning of a seeing of things which pre-exists in our turn of mind or temperament or in some tendency of our nature and secretly predetermines the very reasoning that claims to lead to it. That reasoning itself can be conclusive only if the perception of things on which it rests is both a true and a whole seeing. Here what we have to see truly and integrally is the nature and validity of our consciousness, the origin and scope of our mentality; for then alone can we know the truth of our being and nature and of world-being and world- nature. Our principle in such an inquiry must be to see and know; the dialectical intellect is to be used only so far as it helps to clarify our arrangement and justify our expression of the vision and the knowledge, but it cannot be allowed to govern our conceptions and exclude truth that does not fall within the rigid frame of its logic. Illusion, knowledge

and ignorance are terms or results of our consciousness, and
it is only by looking deeply into our consciousness that we
can discover and determine the character and relations of the
Knowledge and the Ignorance or of the Illusion, if it exists,
and the Reality. Being is no doubt the fundamental object of
inquiry, things in themselves and things in their nature; but it
is only through consciousness that we can approach Being. Or
if it be maintained that we can only reach Being, enter into
the Real, because it is superconscient, through extinction or
transcendence of consciousness or through its self-transcendence
and self-transformation, it is still through consciousness that we
must arrive at the knowledge of this necessity and the process or
power of execution of this extinction or this self-transcendence,
this transformation: then, through consciousness, to know of the
Superconscient Truth becomes the supreme need and to discover
the power and process of consciousness by which it can pass into
superconscience, the supreme discovery.

The Life Divine, pp. 493-94

The reason has its place especially with regard to certain physical things and general worldly questions — though even there
it is a very fallible judge — or in the formation of metaphysical
conclusions and generalisations; but its claim to be the decisive
authority in matters of yoga or in spiritual things is untenable.
The activities of the outward intellect there lead only to the
formation of personal opinions, not to the discovery of Truth.
It has always been understood in India that the reason and its
logic or its judgment cannot give you the realisation of spiritual
truths but can only assist in an intellectual presentation of ideas;
realisation comes by intuition and inner experience. Reason and
intellectuality cannot make you see the Divine, it is the soul that
sees. Mind and the other instruments can only share in the vision
when it is imparted to them by the soul and welcome and rejoice
in it. But also the mind may prevent it or at least stand long in
the way of the realisation or the vision. For its prepossessions,

preconceived opinions and mental preferences may build a wall of arguments against the spiritual truth that has to be realised and refuse to accept it if it presents itself in a form which does not conform to its own previous ideas: so also it may prevent one from recognising the Divine if the Divine presents himself in a form for which the intellect is not prepared or which in any detail runs counter to its prejudgments and prejudices. One can depend on one's reason in other matters provided the mind tries to be open and impartial and free from undue passion and is prepared to concede that it is not always right and may err; but it is not safe to depend on it alone in matters which escape its jurisdiction, especially in spiritual realisation and in matters of yoga which belong to a different order of knowledge.

Letters on Yoga, p. 1620

European metaphysical thought — even in those thinkers who try to prove or explain the existence and nature of God or of the Absolute — does not in its method and result go beyond the intellect. But the intellect is incapable of knowing the supreme Truth; it can only range about seeking for Truth, and catching fragmentary representations of it, not the thing itself, and trying to piece them together. Mind cannot arrive at Truth; it can only make some constructed figure that tries to represent it or a combination of figures. At the end of European thought, therefore, there must always be Agnosticism, declared or implicit. Intellect, if it goes sincerely to its own end, has to return and give this report: "I cannot know; there is, or at least it seems to me that there may be or even must be Something beyond, some ultimate Reality, but about its truth I can only speculate; it is either unknowable or cannot be known by me." Or, if it has received some light on the way from what is beyond it, it can say too: "There is perhaps a consciousness beyond Mind, for I seem to catch glimpses of it and even to get intimations from it. If that is in touch with the Beyond or if it is itself the consciousness of the Beyond and you can find some way to reach it, then this Something can be known but not otherwise."

Any seeking of the supreme Truth through intellect alone must end either in Agnosticism of this kind or else in some intellectual system or mind-constructed formula. There have been hundreds of these systems and formulas and there can be hundreds more, but none can be definitive. Each may have its value for the mind, and different systems with their contrary conclusions can have an equal appeal to intelligences of equal power and competence. All this labour of speculation has its utility in training the human mind and helping to keep before it the idea of Something beyond and Ultimate towards which it must turn. But the intellectual Reason can only point vaguely or feel gropingly towards it or try to indicate partial and even conflicting aspects of its manifestation here; it cannot enter into and know it. As long as we remain in the domain of the intellect only, an impartial pondering over all that has been thought and sought after, a constant throwing up of ideas, of all the possible ideas, and the formation of this or that philosophical belief, opinion or conclusion is all that can be done. This kind of disinterested search after Truth would be the only possible attitude for any wide and plastic intelligence. But any conclusion so arrived at would be only speculative; it could have no spiritual value; it would not give the decisive experience or the spiritual certitude for which the soul is seeking. If the intellect is our highest possible instrument and there is no other means of arriving at supraphysical Truth, then a wise and large Agnosticism must be our ultimate attitude. Things in the manifestation may be known to some degree, but the Supreme and all that is beyond the Mind must remain forever unknowable.

It is only if there is a greater consciousness beyond Mind and that consciousness is accessible to us that we can know and enter into the ultimate Reality. Intellectual speculation, logical reasoning as to whether there is or is not such a greater consciousness cannot carry us very far. What we need is a way to get the experience of it, to reach it, enter into it, live in it. If we can get that, intellectual speculation and reasoning must fall necessarily into a very secondary place and even lose their reason for existence. Philosophy, intellectual expression of the Truth may remain, but mainly as a means of expressing this greater discovery and as much of its contents as can at all be expressed in mental terms to those who still live in the mental intelligence....

In the East, especially in India, the metaphysical thinkers have tried, as in the West, to determine the nature of the highest Truth by the intellect. But, in the first place, they have not given mental thinking the supreme rank as an instrument in the discovery of Truth, but only a secondary status. The first rank has always been given to spiritual intuition and illumination and spiritual experience; an intellectual conclusion that contradicts this supreme authority is held invalid. Secondly, each philosophy has armed itself with a practical way of reaching to the supreme state of consciousness, so that even when one begins with Thought, the aim is to arrive at a consciousness beyond mental thinking. Each philosophical founder (as also those who continued his work or school) has been a metaphysical thinker doubled with a yogi. Those who were only philosophic intellectuals were respected for their learning but never took rank as truth-discoverers. And the philosophies that lacked a sufficiently powerful means of spiritual experience died out and became things of the past because they were not dynamic for spiritual discovery and realisation.

In the West it was just the opposite that came to pass. Thought, intellect, the logical reason came to be regarded more and more as the highest means and even the highest end; in philosophy, Thought is the be-all and the end-all. It is by intellectual thinking and speculation that the truth is to be discovered; even spiritual experience has been summoned to pass the tests of the intellect, if it is to be held valid — just the reverse of the Indian position. Even those who see that the mental Thought must be overpassed and admit a supramental "Other", do not seem to escape from the feeling that it must be through mental Thought, sublimating and transmuting itself, that this other Truth must be reached and made to take the place of the mental limitation and ignorance. And again Western thought has ceased to be dynamic; it has sought after a theory of things, not after realisation. It was still dynamic amongst the ancient Greeks, but for moral and aesthetic rather than spiritual ends. Later on, it became yet more purely intellectual and academic; it became intellectual speculation only without any practical ways and means for the attainment of the Truth by spiritual experiment, spiritual discovery, a spiritual transformation. If there were not this difference, there would be no reason for seekers like yourself to turn to the East for guidance; for in the purely intellectual field, the Western thinkers are as competent as any Eastern sage. It is the spiritual way, the road that leads beyond the intellectual levels, the passage from the outer being to the inmost Self, which has been lost by the over-intellectuality of the mind of Europe.

Letters on Yoga, pp. 157-60

...these great writings [the Upanishads] are not the record of ideas; they are a record of experiences; and those experiences, psychological and spiritual, are as remote from the superficial psychology of ordinary men as are the experiments and conclusions of Science from the ordinary observation of the peasant driving his plough through a soil only superficially known or the sailor of old guiding his bark by the few stars important to his rudimentary navigation. Every word in the Upanishads arises out of a depth of psychological experience and observation we no longer possess and is a key to spiritual truths which we can no longer attain except by discipline of a painful difficulty.

The Upanishads, pp. 534-35

Yoga ... is scientific to this extent that it proceeds by subjective experiment and bases all its findings on experience; mental intuitions are admitted only as a first step and are not considered as realisation — they must be confirmed by being translated into and justified by experience.   *Letters on Yoga, p. 189*

That brings us straight to the question raised by Professor Sorley, what is the relation of mystic or spiritual experience and is it true, as it is contended, that the mystic must, whether as to the validity of his experience itself or the validity of his expression of it, accept the intellect as the judge. It is very plain that in the experience itself the intellect cannot claim to put its limits or its law on an endeavour whose very aim, principle and matter is to go beyond the domain of the ordinary earth-ruled and sense-ruled mental intelligence. It is as if I were asked to climb a mountain with a rope around my feet attaching me to the terrestrial level or to fly only on condition that I keep my feet on the earth while I do it. It may be the safest thing to walk on earth and be on firm ground always and to ascend on wings or otherwise may be to risk a collapse and all sorts of accidents of error, illusion, extravagance, hallucination or what not — the usual charges of the positive earth-walking intellect against mystic experience; but I have to take the risk if I want to do it at all. The reasoning intellect bases itself on man's normal experience and on the workings of a surface external perception and conception of things which is at its ease only when working on a mental basis formed by terrestrial experience and its accumulated data. The mystic goes beyond into a region where this mental basis falls away, where these data are exceeded, where there is another law and canon of perception and knowledge. His entire business is to break through these borders into another consciousness which looks at things in a different way and though this new consciousness may include the data of the ordinary external intelligence it cannot be limited by them or bind itself to see from the intellectual standpoint or in accordance with its way of conceiving, reasoning, established interpretation of experience. A mystic entering the domain of the occult or of the spirit with the intellect as his only or his supreme light or guide would risk seeing nothing or else arriving only at a mental realisation already laid down for him by the speculations of the intellectual thinker.

There is, no doubt, a strain of spiritual thought in India which compromises with the modern intellectual demand and admits Reason as a supreme judge, but they speak of a Reason which in its turn is prepared to compromise and accept the data of spiritual experience as valid *per se*. That, in a sense, is just what the Indian philosophers have always done; for they have tried to establish generalisations drawn from spiritual experience by the light of metaphysical reasoning, but on the basis of that experience and with the evidence of the spiritual seekers as a supreme proof ranking higher than intellectual speculation or experience. In that way the freedom of spiritual and mystic experience is preserved, the reasoning intellect comes in only on the second line as a judge of the generalised statements drawn from the experience. This is, I presume, something akin to Prof. Sorley's position — he concedes that the experience itself is of the domain of the Ineffable, but as soon as I begin to interpret it, to state it, I fall back into the domain of the thinking mind, I use its terms and ways of thought and expression and must accept the intellect as judge. If I do not, I knock away the ladder by which I have climbed — through mind to Beyond-Mind — and I am left in the air. It is not quite clear whether the truth of my experience itself is supposed to be invalidated by this unsustained position in the air, but it remains at any rate something aloof and incommunicable without support or any consequences for thought or life. There are three propositions, I suppose, which I can take as laid down or admitted here and joined together. First, the spiritual experience is itself of the Beyond-Mind, ineffable and, I presume, unthinkable. Next, in the expression, the interpretation of the experience, you are obliged to fall back into the domain of the consciousness you have left and must abide by its judgments, accept the terms and the canons of its law, submit to its verdict; you have abandoned the freedom of the Ineffable and are no longer your master. Last, spiritual truth may be true in itself, to its own self-experience, but any statement of it is liable to error and here the intellect is the sole judge.

I do not think I am prepared to accept any of these affirmations completely as they are. It is true that spiritual and mystic experience carries one first into domains of Other-Mind (and also Other-Life) and then into the Beyond-Mind; it is true also that the ultimate Truth is described as unthinkable, ineffable, unknowable — speech cannot reach there nor mind arrive to it; I may observe that it is so to human mind, but not to itself — for to itself it is described as self-conscient, in some direct supramental way knowable, known, eternally self-aware. And here the question is not of the ultimate realisation of the ultimate Ineffable which, according to many, can only be reached in a supreme trance, *samādhi*, withdrawn from all outer mental or other awareness, but of an experience in a luminous silence of the mind which looks up into the boundlessness of the last illimitable silence into which it is to pass and disappear, but before that unspeakable experience of the Ultimate or disappearance into it, there is possible a descent of at least some Power or Presence of the Reality into the substance of mind along with a modification of mind-substance, an illumination of it, and of this experience an expression of some kind, a rendering into thought ought to be possible. Or let us suppose the Ineffable and Unknowable may have aspects, presentations of it that are not utterly unthinkable and ineffable.

If it were not so, all account of spiritual truth and experience would be impossible. At most one could speculate about it, but that would be an activity very much in the air, even in a void, without support or data, a mere manipulation of all the possible ideas of what might be the Supreme and Ultimate. Apart from that there could be only a certain unaccountable transition by one way or another from consciousness to an incommunicable Supraconscience. That is indeed what much mystical seeking actually reached both in Europe and India. The Christian mystics spoke of a total darkness, a darkness complete and untouched by any mental lights, through which one must pass into that luminous Ineffable. The Indian Sannyasis sought to shed mind altogether and pass into a thought-free trance from which if one returns, no communication or expression could be brought back of what was there except a remembrance of inexpressible existence and bliss. But still there were previous experiences of the supreme mystery, formulations of the Highest or the occult universal Existence which were held to be spiritual truth and on the basis of which the seers and mystics did not hesitate to formulate their experience and the thinkers to build on it numberless philosophies and books of exegesis. The only question that remains is what creates the possibility of this communication and expression, this transmission of the facts of a different order of consciousness to the mind and what determines the validity of the expression or, even, of the original experience. If no valid account were possible there could be no question of the judgment of the intellect — only the grotesque contradiction of sitting down to speak of the Ineffable, think of the Unthinkable, comprehend the Incommunicable and Unknowable.

Letters on Yoga, pp. 181-84

...the experiences of yoga belong to an inner domain and go according to a law of their own, have their own method of perception, criteria and all the rest of it which are neither those of the domain of the physical senses nor of the domain of rational or scientific enquiry. Just as scientific enquiry passes beyond that of the physical senses and enters the domain of the infinite and infinitesimal about which the senses can say nothing and test nothing — for one cannot see and touch an electron or know by the evidence of the sense-mind whether it exists or not or decide by that evidence whether the earth really turns round the sun and not rather the sun round the earth as our senses and all our physical experience daily tell us — so the spiritual search passes beyond the domain of scientific or rational enquiry and it is impossible by the aid of the ordinary positive reason to test the data of spiritual experience and decide whether those things exist or not or what is their law and nature. As in Science, so here you have to accumulate experience on experience, following faithfully the methods laid down by the Guru or by the systems of the past, you have to develop an intuitive discrimination which compares the experiences, see what they mean, how far and in what field each is valid, what is the place of each in the whole, how it can be reconciled or related with others that at first might seem to contradict it, etc., etc., until you can move with a secure knowledge in the vast field of spiritual phenomena. That is the only way to test spiritual experience. I have myself tried the other method and I have found it absolutely incapable and inapplicable. On the other hand, if you are not prepared to go through all that yourself, — as few can do except those of extraordinary spiritual stature — you have to accept the leading of a Master, as in Science you accept a teacher instead of going through the whole field of Science and its experimentation all by yourself — at least until you have accumulated sufficient experience and knowledge. If that is accepting things *a priori*, well, you have to accept *a priori*. For I am unable to see by what valid tests you propose to make the ordinary reason the judge of what is beyond it.

...how was I to test by the ordinary mind my experience of Nirvana? To what conclusion could I come about it by the aid of the ordinary positive reason? How could I test its validity? I am at a loss to imagine. I did the only thing I could — to accept it as a strong and valid truth of experience, let it have its full play and produce its full experimental consequences until I had sufficient yogic knowledge to put it in its place. Finally, how without inner knowledge or experience can you or anyone else test the inner knowledge and experience of others?

I have often said that discrimination is not only perfectly admissible but indispensable in spiritual experience. But it must be a discrimination founded on knowledge, not a reasoning founded on ignorance. Otherwise you tie up your mind and hamper experience by preconceived ideas which are as much *a priori* as any acceptance of a spiritual truth or experience can be.   *Letters on Yoga, pp. 191-92*

...I will begin... with the demand for the Divine as a concrete certitude, quite as concrete as any physical phenomenon caught by the senses. Now, certainly, the Divine must be such a certitude not only as concrete but more concrete than anything sensed by ear or eye or touch in the world of Matter; but it is a certitude not of mental thought but of essential experience. When the Peace of God descends on you, when the Divine Presence is there within you, when the Ananda rushes on you like a sea, when you are driven like a leaf before the wind by the breath of the Divine Force, when Love flowers out from you on all creation, when Divine Knowledge floods you with a Light which illumines and transforms in a moment all that was before dark, sorrowful and obscure, when all that is becomes part of the One Reality, when the Reality is all around you, you feel at once by the spiritual contact, by the inner vision, by the illumined and seeing thought, by the vital sensation and even by the very physical sense, everywhere you see, hear, touch only the Divine. Then you can much less doubt it or deny it than you can deny or doubt daylight or air or the sun in heaven — for of these physical things you cannot be sure that they are what your senses represent them to be; but in the concrete experiences of the Divine, doubt is impossible.   *Letters on Yoga, p. 168*

Another objection to the mystic and his knowledge is urged, not against its effect upon life but against his method of the discovery of Truth and against the Truth that he discovers. One objection to the method is that it is purely subjective, not true independently of the personal consciousness and its constructions, not verifiable. But this ground of cavil has no great value: for the object of the mystic is self-knowledge and God-knowledge, and that can only be arrived at by an inward and not by an outward gaze. Or it is the supreme Truth of things that he seeks, and that too cannot be arrived at by an outward inquiry through the senses or by any scrutiny or research that founds itself on outsides and surfaces or by speculation based on the uncertain data of an indirect means of knowledge. It must come by a direct vision or contact of the consciousness with the soul and body of the Truth itself or through a knowledge by identity, by the self that becomes one with the self of things and with their truth of power and their truth of essence. But it is urged that the actual result of this method is not one truth common to all, there are great differences; the conclusion suggested is that this knowledge is not truth at all but a subjective mental formation. But this objection is based on a misunderstanding of the nature of spiritual knowledge. Spiritual truth is a truth of the spirit, not a truth of the intellect, not a mathematical theorem or a logical formula. It is a truth of the Infinite, one in an infinite diversity, and it can assume an infinite variety of aspects and formations: in the spiritual evolution it is inevitable that there should be a many-sided passage and reaching to the one Truth, a many-sided seizing of it; this many-sidedness is the sign of the approach of the soul to a living reality, not to an abstraction or a constructed figure of things that can be petrified into a dead or stony formula. The hard logical and intellectual notion of truth as a single idea which all must accept, one idea or system of ideas defeating all other ideas or systems, or a single limited fact or single formula of facts which all must recognise, is an illegitimate transference from the limited truth of the physical field to the much more complex and plastic field of life and mind and spirit.   *The Life Divine, pp. 886-87*

In fact, subjectivity and objectivity are not independent realities, they depend upon each other; they are the Being, through consciousness, looking at itself as subject on the object and the same Being offering itself to its own consciousness as object to the subject. The more partial view concedes no substantive reality to anything which exists only in the consciousness, or, to put it more accurately, to anything to which the inner consciousness or sense bears testimony but which the outer physical senses do not provide with a ground or do not substantiate. But the outer senses can bear a reliable evidence only when they refer their version of the object to the consciousness and that consciousness gives a significance to their report, adds to its externality its own internal intuitive interpretation and justifies it by a reasoned adherence; for the evidence of the senses is always by itself imperfect, not altogether reliable and certainly not final, because it is incomplete and constantly subject to error. Indeed, we have no means of knowing the objective universe except by our subjective consciousness of which the physical senses themselves are instruments; as the world appears not only to that but in that, so it is to us. If we deny reality to the evidence of this universal witness for subjective or for supraphysical objectivities, there is no sufficient reason to concede reality to its evidence for physical objectivities; if the inner or the supraphysical objects of consciousness are unreal, the objective physical universe has also every chance of being unreal. In each case understanding, discrimination, verification are necessary; but the subjective and the supraphysical must have another method of verification than that which we apply successfully to the physical and external objective. Subjective experience cannot be referred to the evidence of the external senses; it has its own standards of seeing and its inner method of verification: so also supraphysical realities by their very nature cannot be referred to the judgment of the physical or sense mind except when they project themselves into the physical, and even then that judgment is often incompetent or subject to caution; they can only be verified by other senses and by a method of scrutiny and affirmation which is applicable to their own reality, their own nature.

There are different orders of reality; the objective and physical is only one order. It is convincing to the physical or externalising mind because it is directly obvious to the senses, while of the subjective and the supraphysical that mind has no means of knowledge except from fragmentary signs and data and inferences which are at every step liable to error. Our subjective movements and inner experiences are a domain of happenings as real as any outward physical happenings; but if the individual mind can know something of its own phenomena by direct experience, it is ignorant of what happens in the consciousness of others except by analogy with its own or such signs, data, inferences as its outward observation can give it. I am therefore inwardly real to myself, but the invisible life of others has only an indirect reality to me except in so far as it impinges on my own mind, life and senses. This is the limitation of the physical mind of man, and it creates in him a habit of believing entirely only in the physical and of doubting or challenging all that does not come into accord with his own experience or his own scope of understanding or square with his own standard or sum of established knowledge.

This ego-centric attitude has in recent times been elevated into a valid standard of knowledge; it has been implicitly or explicitly held as an axiom that all truth must be referred to the judgement of the personal mind, reason and experience of every man or else it must be verified or at any rate verifiable by a common or universal experience in order to be valid. But obviously this is a false standard of reality and of knowledge, since this means the sovereignty of the normal or average mind and its limited capacity and experience, the exclusion of what is supernormal or beyond the average intelligence. In its extreme, this claim of the individual to be the judge of everything is an egoistic illusion, a superstition of the physical mind, in the mass a gross and vulgar error. The truth behind it is that each man has to think for himself, know for himself according to his capacity, but his judgement can be valid only on condition that he is ready to learn and open always to a larger knowledge. It is reasoned that to depart from the physical standard and the principle of personal or universal verification will lead to gross delusions and the admission of unverified truth and subjective phantasy into the realm of knowledge. But error and delusion and the introduction of personality and one's own subjectivity into the pursuit of knowledge are always present, and the physical or objective standards and methods do not exclude them. The probability of error is no reason for refusing to attempt discovery, and subjective discovery must be pursued by a subjective method of enquiry, observation and verification; research into the supraphysical must evolve, accept and test an appropriate means and methods other than those by which one examines the constituents of physical objects and the processes of Energy in material Nature.

To refuse to enquire upon any general ground preconceived and *a priori* is an obscurantism as prejudicial to the extension of knowledge as the religious obscurantism which opposed in Europe the extension of scientific discovery. The greatest inner discoveries, the experience of self-being, the cosmic consciousness, the inner calm of the liberated spirit, the direct effect of mind upon mind, the knowledge of things by consciousness in direct contact with other consciousness or with its objects, most spiritual experiences of any value, cannot be brought before the tribunal of the common mentality which has no experience of these things and takes its own absence or incapacity of experience as a proof of their invalidity or their non-existence. Physical truth of formulas, generalisations, discoveries founded upon physical observation can be so referred, but even there a training of capacity is needed before one can truly understand and judge; it is not every untrained mind that can follow the mathematics of relativity or other difficult scientific truths or judge of the validity either of their result or their process. All reality, all experience must indeed, to be held as true, be capable of verification by a same or similar experience; so, in fact, all men can have a spiritual experience and can follow it out and verify it in themselves, but only when they have acquired the capacity or can follow the inner methods by which that experience and verification are made possible. It is necessary to dwell for a moment on these obvious and elementary truths because the opposite ideas have been sovereign in a recent period of human mentality, — they are now only receding, — and have stood in the way of the development of a vast domain of possible knowledge. It is of supreme importance for the human spirit to be free to sound the depths of inner or subliminal reality, of spiritual and of what is still superconscient reality, and not to immure itself in the physical mind and its narrow domain of objective external solidities; for in that way alone can there come liberation from the Ignorance in which our mentality dwells and a release into a complete consciousness, a true and integral self-realisation and self-knowledge.

An integral knowledge demands an exploration, an unveiling of all the possible domains of consciousness and experience. For there are subjective domains of our being which lie behind the obvious surface; these have to be fathomed and whatever is ascertained must be admitted within the scope of the total reality. An inner range of spiritual experience is one very great domain of human consciousness; it has to be entered into up to its deepest depths and its vastest reaches. The supraphysical is as real as the physical; to know it is part of a complete knowledge. The knowledge of the supraphysical has been associated with mysticism and occultism, and occultism has been banned as a superstition and a fantastic error. But the occult is a part of existence; a true occultism means no more than a research into supraphysical realities and an unveiling of the hidden laws of being and Nature, of all that is not obvious on the surface. It attempts the discovery of the secret laws of mind and mental energy, the secret laws of life and life-energy, the secret laws of the subtle-physical and its energies, — all that Nature has not put into visible operation on the surface; it pursues also the application of these hidden truths and powers of Nature so as to extend the mastery of the human spirit beyond the ordinary operations of mind, the ordinary operations of life, the ordinary operations of our physical existence. In the spiritual domain which is occult to the surface mind in so far as it passes beyond normal and enters into supernormal experience, there is possible not only the discovery of the self and spirit, but the discovery of the uplifting, informing and guiding light of spiritual consciousness and the power of the spirit, the spiritual way of knowledge, the spiritual way of action. To know these things and to bring their truths and forces into the life of humanity is a necessary part of its evolution. Science itself is in its own way an occultism; for it brings to light the formulas which Nature has hidden and it uses its knowledge to set free operations of her energies which she has not included in her ordinary operations and to organise and place at the service of man her occult powers and processes, a vast system of physical magic, — for there is and can be no other magic than the utilisation of secret truths of being, secret powers and processes of Nature. It may even be found that a supraphysical knowledge is necessary for the completion of physical knowledge, because the processes of physical Nature have behind them a supraphysical factor, a power and action mental, vital or spiritual which is not tangible to any outer means of knowledge.

All insistence on the sole or the fundamental validity of the objective real takes its stand on the sense of the basic reality of Matter. But it is now evident that Matter is by no means fundamentally real; it is a structure of Energy: it is becoming even a little doubtful whether the acts and creations of this Energy itself are explicable except as the motions of power of a secret Mind or Consciousness of which its processes and steps of structure are the formulas. It is therefore no longer possible to take Matter as the sole reality. The material interpretation of existence was the result of an exclusive concentration, a preoccupation with one movement of Existence, and such an exclusive concentration has its utility and is therefore permissible; in recent times it has justified itself by the many immense and the innumerable minute discoveries of physical Science. But a solution of the whole problem of existence cannot be based on an exclusive one-sided knowledge; we must know not only what Matter is and what are its processes, but what mind and life are and what are their processes, and one must know also spirit and soul and all that is behind the material surface: only then can we have a knowledge sufficiently integral for a solution of the problem. For the same reason those views of existence which arise from an exclusive or predominant preoccupation with Mind or with Life and regard Mind or Life as the sole fundamental reality, have not a sufficiently wide basis for acceptance. Such a preoccupation of exclusive concentration may lead to a fruitful scrutiny which sheds much light on Mind and Life, but cannot result in a total solution of the problem. It may very well be that an exclusive or predominant concentration on the subliminal being, regarding the surface existence as a mere system of symbols for an expression of its sole reality, might throw a strong light on the subliminal and its processes and extend vastly the powers of the human being, but it would not be by itself an integral solution or lead us successfully to the integral knowledge of Reality. In our view the Spirit, the Self is the fundamental reality of existence; but an exclusive concentration on this fundamental reality to the exclusion of all reality of Mind, Life or Matter except as an imposition on the Self or unsubstantial shadows cast by the Spirit might help to an independent and radical spiritual realisation but not to an integral and valid solution of the truth of cosmic and individual existence.

An integral knowledge then must be a knowledge of the truth of all sides of existence both separately and in the relation of each to all and the relation of all to the truth of the Spirit. Our present state is an Ignorance and a many-sided seeking; it seeks for the truth of all things but, — as is evident from the insistence and the variety of the human mind's speculations as to the fundamental Truth which explains all others, the Reality at the basis of all things, — the fundamental truth of things, their basic reality must be found in some at once fundamental and universal Real; it is that which, once discovered, must embrace and explain all, — for "That being known all will be known": the fundamental Real must necessarily be and contain the truth of all existence, the truth of the individual, the truth of the universe, the truth of all that is beyond the universe. The Mind, in seeking for such a Reality and testing each thing from Matter upwards to see if that might not be It, has not proceeded on a wrong intuition. All that is necessary is to carry the inquiry to its end and test the highest and ultimate levels of experience.

The Life Divine, pp. 648-54

Yoga is not a matter of theory or dogma, like philosophy or popular religion, but a matter of experience. Its experience is that of a conscient universal and supracosmic Being with whom it brings us into union, and this conscious experience of union with the Invisible, always renewable and verifiable, is as valid as our conscious experience of a physical world and of visible bodies with whose invisible minds we daily communicate.

Synthesis of Yoga, p. 531

15
The Psychology of Faith

Religion has opened itself to denial by its claim to determine the truth by divine authority, by inspiration, by a sacrosanct and infallible sovereignty given to it from on high; it has sought to impose itself on human thought, feeling, conduct without discussion or question. This is an excessive and premature claim, although imposed in a way on the religious idea by the imperative and absolute character of the inspirations and illuminations which are its warrant and justification and by the necessity of faith as an occult light and power from the soul amidst the mind's ignorance, doubts, weakness, incertitudes. Faith is indispensable to man, for without it he could not proceed forward in his journey through the Unknown; but it ought not to be imposed, it should come as a free perception or an imperative direction from the inner spirit. A claim to unquestioned acceptance could only be warranted if the spiritual effort had already achieved man's progression to the highest Truth-Consciousness total and integral, free from all ignorant mental and vital mixture. This is the ultimate object before us, but it has not yet been accomplished, and the premature claim has obscured the true work of the religious instinct in man, which is to lead him towards the Divine Reality, to formulate all that he has yet achieved in that direction and to give to each human being a mould of spiritual discipline, a way of seeking, touching, nearing the Divine Truth, a way which is proper to the potentialities of his nature.

The Life Divine, pp. 863-64

...faith in the spiritual sense is not a mental belief which can waver and change. It can wear that form in the mind, but that belief is not the faith itself, it is only its external form. Just as the body, the external form, can change but the spirit remains the same, so it is here. Faith is a certitude in the soul which does not depend on reasoning, on this or that mental idea, on circumstances, on this or that passing condition of the mind or the vital or the body. It may be hidden, eclipsed, may even seem to be quenched, but it reappears again after the storm or the eclipse; it is seen burning still in the soul when one has thought that it was extinguished for ever. The mind may be a shifting sea of doubts and yet that faith may be there within and, if so, it will keep even the doubt-racked mind in the way so that it goes on in spite of itself towards its destined goal. Faith is a spiritual certitude of the spiritual, the divine, the soul's ideal, something that clings to that even when it is not fulfilled in life, even when the immediate facts or the persistent circumstances seem to deny it. This is a common experience in the life of the human being; if it were not so, man would be the plaything of a changing mind or a sport of circumstances.   *Letters on Yoga, p. 616*

This *śraddhā* — the English word faith is inadequate to express it — is in reality an influence from the supreme Spirit and its light a message from our supramental being which is calling the lower nature to rise out of its petty present to a great self-becoming and self-exceeding. And that which receives the influence and answers to the call is not so much the intellect, the heart or the life mind, but the inner soul which better knows the truth of its own destiny and mission. The circumstances that provoke our first entry into the path are not the real index of the thing that is at work in us. There the intellect, the heart, or the desires of the life mind may take a prominent place, or even more fortuitous accidents and outward incentives; but if these are all, then there can be no surety of our fidelity to the call and our enduring perseverance in the Yoga. The intellect may abandon the idea that attracted it, the heart weary or fail us, the desire of the life mind turn to other objectives. But outward circumstances are only a cover for the real workings of the spirit, and if it is the spirit that has been touched, the inward soul that has received the call, the *śraddhā* will remain firm and resist all attempts to defeat or slay it. It is not that the doubts of the intellect may not assail, the heart waver, the disappointed desire of the life mind sink down exhausted on the wayside. That is almost inevitable at times, perhaps often, especially with us, sons of an age of intellectuality and scepticism and a materialistic denial of spiritual truth which has not yet lifted its painted clouds from the face of the sun of a greater reality and is still opposed to the light of spiritual intuition and inmost experience. There will very possibly be many of those trying obscurations of which even the Vedic Rishis so often complained, "long exiles from the light," and these may be so thick, the night on the soul may be so black that faith may seem utterly to have left us. But through it all the spirit within will be keeping its unseen hold and the soul will return with a new strength to its assurance which was only eclipsed and not extinguished, because extinguished it cannot be when once the inner self has known and made its resolution. The Divine holds our hand through all and if he seems to let us fall, it is only to raise us higher. This saving return we shall experience so often that the denials of doubt will become eventually impossible and, when once the foundation of equality is firmly established and still more when the sun of the gnosis has risen, doubt itself will pass away because its cause and utility have ended.   *The Synthesis of Yoga, pp. 746-47*

The enemy of faith is doubt, and yet doubt too is an utility and necessity, because man in his ignorance and in his progressive labour towards knowledge needs to be visited by doubt, otherwise he would remain obstinate in an ignorant belief and limited knowledge and unable to escape from his errors. This utility and necessity of doubt does not altogether disappear when we enter on the path of Yoga.   *The Synthesis of Yoga, p. 744*

...faith is essentially the secret *śraddhā* of the soul, and it is brought more and more to the surface and there satisfied, sustained and increased by an increasing assurance and certainty of spiritual experience.... too the faith in us must be unattached, a faith that waits upon Truth and is prepared to change and enlarge its understanding of spiritual experiences, to correct mistaken or half true ideas about them and receive more enlightening interpretations, to replace insufficient by more sufficient intuitions, and to merge experiences that seemed at the time to be final and satisfying in more satisfying combinations with new experience and greater largenesses and transcendences. And especially in the psychical and other middle domains there is a very large room for the possibility of misleading and often captivating error, and here even a certain amount of positive scepticism has its use and at all events a great caution and scrupulous intellectual rectitude, but not the scepticism of the ordinary mind which amounts to a disabling denial.

The Synthesis of Yoga, p. 750

I do not ask "undiscriminating faith" from anyone, all I ask is fundamental faith, safeguarded by a patient and quiet discrimination — because it is these that are proper to the consciousness of a spiritual seeker and it is these that I have myself used and found that they removed all necessity for the quite gratuitous dilemma of "either you must doubt everything supraphysical or be entirely credulous", which is the stock-in-trade of the materialist argument.   *Letters on Yoga, p. 172*

Faith does not depend upon experience; it is something that is there before experience. When one starts the yoga, it is not usually on the strength of experience, but on the strength of faith. It is so not only in yoga and the spiritual life, but in ordinary life also. All men of action, discoverers, inventors, creators of knowledge proceed by faith and, until the proof is made or the thing done, they go on in spite of disappointment, failure, disproof, denial because of something in them that tells them that this is the truth, the thing that must be followed and done. Ramakrishna even went so far as to say, when asked whether blind faith was not wrong, that blind faith was the only kind to have, for faith is either blind or it is not faith but something else — reasoned inference, proved conviction or ascertained knowledge.

Faith is the soul's witness to something not yet manifested, achieved or realised, but which yet the Knower within us, even in the absence of all indications, feels to be true or supremely worth following or achieving. This thing within us can last even when there is no fixed belief in the mind, even when the vital struggles and revolts and refuses. Who is there that practises the yoga and has not his periods, long periods of disappointment and failure and disbelief and darkness? But there is something that sustains him and even goes on in spite of himself, because it feels that what it followed after was yet true and it more than feels, it knows.   *Letters on Yoga, pp. 572-73*

Until we know the Truth (not mentally but by experience, by change of consciousness) we need the soul's faith to sustain us and hold on to the Truth — but when we live in the knowledge, this faith is changed into knowledge.

Of course I am speaking of direct spiritual knowledge. Mental knowledge cannot replace faith, so long as there is only mental knowledge, faith is still needed.   *Letters on Yoga, p. 576*

The phrase ["blind faith"] has no real meaning. I suppose they mean they will not believe without proof — but the conclusion formed after proof is not faith, it is knowledge or it is a mental opinion. Faith is something which one has before proof or knowledge and it helps you to arrive at knowledge or experience. There is no proof that God exists, but if I have faith in God, then I can arrive at the experience of the Divine.

Letters on Yoga, p. 572

...in his effort here, but most of all in his effort towards the Unseen, mental man must perforce proceed by faith. When the realisation comes, the faith divinely fulfilled and completed will be transformed into an eternal flame of knowledge.

The Synthesis of Yoga, p. 77

The faith in spiritual things that is asked of the sadhak is not an ignorant but a luminous faith, a faith in light and not in darkness. It is called blind by the sceptical intellect because it refuses to be guided by outer appearances or seeming facts, — for it looks for the truth behind, — and because it does not walk on the crutches of proof and evidence. It is an intuition, an intuition not only waiting for experience to justify it, but leading towards experience. If I believe in self-healing, I shall after a time find out the way to heal myself. If I have a faith in transformation, I can end by laying my hand on and unravelling the process of transformation. But if I begin with doubt and go on with more doubt, how far am I likely to go on the journey?

Letters on Yoga, p. 166

I mean by it [faith] a dynamic intuitive conviction in the inner being of the truth of supersensible things which cannot be proved by any physical evidence but which are a subject of experience. My point is that this faith is a most desirable preliminary (if not absolutely indispensable — for there can be cases of experiences not preceded by faith) to the desired experience.

Letters on Yoga, p. 167

...faith is necessary throughout and at every step because it is a needed assent of the soul and without this assent there can be no progress. Our faith must first be abiding in the essential truth and principles of the Yoga, and even if this is clouded in the intellect, despondent in the heart, outwearied and exhausted by constant denial and failure in the desire of the vital mind, there must be something in the innermost soul which clings and returns to it, otherwise we may fall on the path or abandon it from weakness and inability to bear temporary defeat, disappointment, difficulty and peril.   *The Synthesis of Yoga, p. 745*

The perfect faith is an assent of the whole being to the truth seen by it or offered to its acceptance, and its central working is a faith of the soul in its own will to be and attain and become and its idea of self and things and its knowledge, of which the belief of the intellect, the heart's consent and the desire of the life mind to possess and realise are the outward figures. This soul faith, in some form of itself, is indispensable to the action of the being and without it man cannot move a single pace in life, much less take any step forward to a yet unrealised perfection. It is so central and essential a thing that the Gita can justly say of it that whatever is a man's *śraddhā*, that he is, *yo yacchraddhaḥ sa eva saḥ*, and, it may be added, whatever he has the faith to see as possible in himself and strive for, that he can create and become.   *The Synthesis of Yoga, p. 743*

Even a faltering faith and a slow and partial surrender have their force and their result, otherwise only the rare few could do sadhana at all. What I mean by the central faith is a faith in the soul or the central being behind, a faith which is there even when the mind doubts and the vital despairs and the physical wants to collapse, and after the attack is over reappears and pushes on the path again. It may be strong and bright, it may be pale and in appearance weak, but if it persists each time in going on, it is the real thing. Fits of depression and darkness and despair are a tradition in the path of sadhana — in all yogas oriental or occidental they seem to have been the rule. I know all about them myself — but my experience has led me to the perception that they are an unnecessary tradition and could be dispensed with if one chose. That is why whenever they come in you or others I try to lift up before them the gospel of faith. If still they come, one has to get through them as soon as possible and get back into the sun.   *Letters on Yoga, pp. 575-76*

16
States of Consciousness

(a) Waking-State, Dream-State, Sleep-State

...only a small part whether of world-being or of our own being comes into our ken or into our action. The rest is hidden behind in subliminal reaches of being which descend into the profoundest depths of the subconscient and rise to highest peaks of superconscience, or which surround the little field of our waking self with a wide circumconscient existence of which our mind and sense catch only a few indications. The old Indian psychology expressed this fact by dividing consciousness into three provinces, waking-state, dream-state, sleep-state, *jāgrat, svapna, suṣupti;* and it supposed in the human being a waking-self, a dream-self, a sleep-self, with the supreme or absolute self of being, the fourth or Turiya, beyond, of which all these are derivations for the enjoyment of relative experience in the world.

If we examine the phraseology of the old books, we shall find that the waking-state is the consciousness of the material universe which we normally possess in this embodied existence dominated by the physical mind. The dream-state is a consciousness corresponding to the subtler life-plane and mind-plane behind, which to us, even when we get intimations of them, have not the same concrete reality as the things of the physical existence. The sleep-state is a consciousness corresponding to the supramental plane proper to the gnosis, which is beyond our experience because our causal body or envelope of gnosis is not developed in us, its faculties not active, and therefore we are in relation to that plane in a condition of dreamless sleep. The Turiya beyond is the consciousness of our pure self-existence or our absolute being with which we have no direct relations at all, whatever mental reflections we may receive in our dream or our waking or even, irrecoverably, in our sleep consciousness.

The Synthesis of Yoga, pp. 498-99

In the course of this analysis [of elemental states or conditions of matter] they [the old Hindu thinkers] could not help perceiving that consciousness in each world of matter assumed a different form and acted in a different way corresponding to the characteristics of the matter in which it moved. In its operations in gross matter the forms it assumed were more firm, solid and durable but at the same time more slow, difficult and hampered, just as are the motions and acts of a man in his waking state as compared with what he does in his dreams. In its operations in subtle matter the form and consciousness assumed were freer and more rapid, but more volatile, elastic and swiftly mutable, as are the motions and acts of a man in a dreaming state compared to the activities of his waking condition. To consciousness working on gross matter they gave the name of the Waking-State, to consciousness acting on subtle matter the name of the Dream-State. In causal matter they found that consciousness took the shape merely of the pure sense of blissful existence; they could discover no other distinguishing sensation. This therefore they called the Sleep-State. They farther discovered that the various faculties and functions of man belonged properly some to one, some to another of the three states of consciousness and its corresponding state of matter. His vital and physical functions operated only in gross matter, and they determined accordingly that his physical life was the result of consciousness working in the Waking-State on gross matter. His mental and intuitional processes were found to operate freely and perfectly in subtle matter, but in gross matter with a hampered and imperfect activity; they considered therefore that man's mental life belonged properly to the Dream-State and only worked indirectly and under serious limitations in the Waking-State. They determined accordingly that mental life must be the result of consciousness working in the Dream-State on subtle matter. There remained the fundamental energy of consciousness, Will-to-be or shaping Delight of existence: this, they perceived, was free and pure in causal matter, put to work if consciously, yet through a medium and under limitations in subtle matter, in hampered and half effectual fashion when the subtle self acted through the gross, and subconsciously only in gross matter. They considered therefore that man's causal faculty or spiritual life belonged properly to the Sleep-State and worked indirectly and through less and less easy mediums in the Dream and Waking-States; and accordingly determined that it must be the result of Consciousness working in the Sleep-State on causal matter. The whole of creation amounted therefore to a natural outcome from the mutual relations of Spirit and Matter; these two they regarded as two terms, — call them forces, energies, substances, or what you will, — of phenomenal existence; and psychical life only as one result of their interaction. They refused however to accept any dualism in their cosmogony and, as has been previously pointed out, regarded Spirit and Matter as essentially one; and their difference as no more than an apparent duality in one real entity. This one entity is not analysable or intellectually knowable, yet it is alone the real, immutable and sempiternal Self of things.

Supplement, pp. 231-33

...it [ancient psychology] distinguished three strata of the conscient self, the waking, the dream and the sleep selves of Man, — in other words, the superficial existence, the subconscient or subliminal and the superconscient which to us seems the inconscient because its state of consciousness is the reverse of ours: for ours is limited and based on division and multiplicity, but this is "that which becomes a unity"; ours is dispersed in knowledge, but in this other self conscious knowledge is self-collected and concentrated; ours is balanced between dual experiences, but this is all delight, it is that which in the very heart of our being fronts everything with a pure all-possessing consciousness and enjoys the delight of existence. Therefore, although its seat is that stratum of consciousness which to us is a deep sleep, — for the mind there cannot maintain its accustomed functioning and becomes inconscient, — yet its name is He who knows, the

Wise One, *prājña*. "This," says the Mandukya Upanishad, "is omniscient, omnipotent, the inner control, the womb of all and that from which creatures are born and into which they depart." It answers, therefore, closely enough to the modern idea of the subliminal self; for it is inconscient only to the waking mind, precisely because it is superconscient to it and the mind is therefore only able to seize it in its results and not in itself. And what better proof can there be of the depth and truth of the ancient psychology than the fact that when modern thought in all its pride of exact and careful knowledge begins to cast its fathom into these depths, it is obliged to repeat in other language what had already been written nearly three thousand years ago?

The Supramental Manifestation and Other Writings, pp. 262-63

(b) Normal (Ordinary) and Higher (Spiritual) Consciousness

...briefly... there are two states of consciousness in either of which one can live. One is a higher consciousness which stands above the play of life and governs it; this is variously called the Self, the Spirit or the Divine. The other is the normal consciousness in which men live; it is something quite superficial, an instrument of the Spirit for the play of life. Those who live and act in the normal consciousness are governed entirely by the common movements of the mind and are naturally subject to grief and joy and anxiety and desire or to everything else that makes up the ordinary stuff of life. Mental quiet and happiness they can get, but it can never be permanent or secure. But the spiritual consciousness is all light, peace, power, bliss. If one can live entirely in it, there is no question; these things become naturally and securely his. But even if he can live partly in it or keep himself constantly open to it, he receives enough of this spiritual light and peace and strength and happiness to carry him securely through all the shocks of life. What one gains by opening to this spiritual consciousness, depends on what one seeks from it; if it is peace, one gets peace; if it is light or knowledge, one lives in a great light and receives a knowledge deeper and truer than any the normal mind of man can acquire; if it is strength or power, he gets a spiritual strength for the inner life or Yogic power to govern the outer work and action; if it is happiness, he enters into a beatitude far greater than any joy or happiness that the ordinary human life can give.   *Supplement, pp. 415-16*

The ordinary consciousness is that in which one knows things only or mainly by the intellect, the external mind and the senses and knows forces etc. only by their outward manifestations and results and the rest by inferences from these data. There may be some play of mental intuition, deeper psychic seeing or impulsions, spiritual intimations, etc. — but in the ordinary consciousness these are incidental only and do not modify its fundamental character.   *Letters on Yoga, p. 317*

The spiritual consciousness is that in which we enter into the awareness of Self, the Spirit, the Divine and are able to see in all things their essential reality and the play of forces and phenomena as proceeding from that essential Reality.
                    Letters on Yoga, p. 316

The higher consciousness lives always in touch with the Self — the lower is separated from it by the activities of the Ignorance.
                    Letters on Yoga, p. 1129

This Higher Consciousness carrying in it a sense of wide and boundless existence, light, power, peace, Ananda etc. is always there above the head and when something of the spiritual Force comes down to work upon the nature, it is from there that it comes. But nothing like the full descent of the peace, bliss etc. can come so long as the being is not ready. Very usually the first preparation is to work on the mind and vital and physical nature in such a way that the soul, the psychic being can have a chance of manifesting itself and influencing the rest of the nature; for that purpose all the main darknesses in the mind and vital have to be combated and thrown out and the physical also prepared in a material way so that the descent may be possible.... There are two things that take place; an ascent of one's consciousness to the higher levels in and above the head, and a descent of the higher consciousness which is above into one's mind, vital and body. How it is done or by what stages or how long it will take varies with each person. But this new consciousness is very different from the ordinary one and many things happen in its coming which would not happen to the mind and might seem strange to it — e.g. the dissolution of the ego and the opening into a wider self or spirit not limited by the body, to which the body is only a small instrument and nothing more. One must therefore dismiss all fear of new things and accept with calm and confidence each field of new experience....

Letters on Yoga, pp.1207-08

If one can remain always in the higher consciousness, so much the better. But why does not one remain always there? Because the lower is still part of the nature and it pulls you down towards itself. If on the other hand the lower is transformed, it becomes of one kind with the higher and there is nothing lower to pull downward.   *Letters on Yoga, p. 1143*

(c) Samadhi — Yogic Trance

Trance in English is usually used only for the deeper kinds of samadhi; but, as there is no other word, we have to use it for all kinds.   *Letters on Yoga, pp. 742-43*

...since mind-consciousness is the sole waking state possessed by mental being,... it cannot ordinarily quite enter into another without leaving behind completely both all our waking existence and all our inward mind. This is the necessity of the Yogic trance. But one cannot continually remain in this trance; or, even if one could persist in it for an indefinitely long period, it is always likely to be broken in upon by any strong or persistent call on the bodily life. And when one returns to the mental consciousness, one is back again in the lower being. Therefore it has been said that complete liberation from the human birth, complete ascension from the life of the mental being is impossible until the body and the bodily life are finally cast off. The ideal upheld before the Yogin who follows this method is to renounce all desire and every least velleity of the human life, of the mental existence, to detach himself utterly from the world and, entering more and more frequently and more and more deeply into the most concentrated state of Samadhi, finally to leave the body while in that utter in-gathering of the being so that it may depart into the supreme Existence. It is also by reason of this apparent incompatibility of mind and Spirit that so many religions and systems are led to condemn the world and look forward only to a heaven beyond or else a void Nirvana or supreme featureless self-existence in the Supreme.   *The Synthesis of Yoga, pp. 379-80*

Samadhi or Yogic trance retires to increasing depths according as it draws farther and farther away from the normal or waking state and enters into degrees of consciousness less and less communicable to the waking mind, less and less ready to receive a summons from the waking world. Beyond a certain point the trance becomes complete and it is then almost or quite impossible to awaken or call back the soul that has receded into them; it can only come back by its own will or at most by a violent shock of physical appeal dangerous to the system owing to the abrupt upheaval of return. There are said to be supreme states of trance in which the soul persisting for too long a time cannot return; for it loses its hold on the cord which binds it to the consciousness of life, and the body is left, maintained indeed in its set position, not dead by dissolution, but incapable of recovering the ensouled life which had inhabited it. Finally, the Yogin acquires at a certain stage of development the power of abandoning his body definitively without the ordinary phenomena of death, by an act of will,[1] or by a process of withdrawing the pranic life-force through the gate of the upward life-current (*udāna*), opening for it a way through the mystic *brahmarandhra* in the head. By departure from life in the state of Samadhi he attains directly to that higher status of being to which he aspires.

The Synthesis of Yoga, pp. 499-500

"Nirvikalpa Samadhi" properly means a complete trance in which there is no thought or movement of consciousness or awareness of either inward or outward things — all is drawn up into a supracosmic Beyond. *Letters on Yoga, p. 741*

Nirvikalpa Samadhi according to tradition is simply a trance from which one cannot be awakened even by burning or branding — i.e. a trance in which one has gone completely out of the body. In more scientific parlance it is a trance in which there is no formation or movement of the consciousness and one gets lost in a state from which one can bring back no report except that one was in bliss. It is supposed to be a complete absorption in the Sushupti or the Turiya. *Letters on Yoga, pp. 740-41*

Dream-State and Sleep-State of Samadhi

In the dream-state itself there are an infinite series of depths; from the lighter recall is easy and the world of the physical senses is at the doors, though for the moment shut out; in the deeper it becomes remote and less able to break in upon the inner absorption, the mind has entered into secure depths of trance. There is a complete difference between Samadhi and normal

---

[1] *icchā-mṛtyu*

sleep, between the dream-state of Yoga and the physical state of dream. The latter belongs to the physical mind; in the former the mind proper and subtle is at work liberated from the immixture of the physical mentality. The dreams of the physical mind are an incoherent jumble made up partly of responses to vague touches from the physical world round which the lower mind-faculties disconnected from the will and reason, the *buddhi*, weave a web of wandering phantasy, partly of disordered associations from the brain-memory, partly of reflections from the soul travelling on the mental plane, reflections which are, ordinarily, received without intelligence or coordination, wildly distorted in the reception and mixed up confusedly with the other dream elements, with brain-memories and fantastic responses to any sensory touch from the physical world. In the Yogic dream-state, on the other hand, the mind is in clear possession of itself, though not of the physical world, works coherently and is able to use either its ordinary will and intelligence with a concentrated power or else the higher will and intelligence of the more exalted planes of mind. It withdraws from experience of the outer world, it puts its seals upon the physical senses and their doors of communication with material things; but everything that is proper to itself, thought, reasoning, reflection, vision, it can continue to execute with an increased purity and power of sovereign concentration free from the distractions and unsteadiness of the waking mind. It can use too its will and produce upon itself or upon its environment mental, moral and even physical effects which may continue and have their after consequences on the waking state subsequent to the cessation of the trance....

The greatest value of the dream-state of Samadhi lies, however, not in these more outward things, but in its power to open up easily higher ranges and powers of thought, emotion, will by which the soul grows in height, range and self-mastery. Especially, withdrawing from the distraction of sensible things, it can, in a perfect power of concentrated self-seclusion, prepare itself by a free reasoning, thought, discrimination, or more intimately, more finally, by an ever deeper vision and identification, for access to the Divine, the supreme Self, the transcendent Truth, both in its principles and powers and manifestations and in its highest original Being. Or it can by an absorbed inner joy and emotion, as in a sealed and secluded chamber of the soul, prepare itself for the delight of union with the divine Beloved, the Master of all bliss, rapture and Ananda.

The Synthesis of Yoga, pp. 500-01, 503

The sleep-state ascends to a higher power of being, beyond thought into pure consciousness, beyond emotion into pure bliss, beyond will into pure mastery; it is the gate of union with the supreme state of Sachchidananda out of which all the activities of the world are born. But here we must take care to avoid the pitfalls of symbolic language. The use of the words dream and sleep for these higher states is nothing but an image drawn from the experience of the normal physical mind with regard to planes in which it is not at home. It is not the truth that the Self in the third status called perfect sleep, *suṣupti*, is in a state of slumber. The sleep self is on the contrary described as Prajna, the Master of Wisdom and Knowledge, Self of the Gnosis, and as Ishwara, the Lord of being. To the physical mind a sleep, it is to our wider and subtler consciousness a greater waking. To the normal mind all that exceeds its normal experience but still comes into its scope, seems a dream; but at the point where it borders on things quite beyond its scope, it can no longer see truth even as in a dream, but passes into the blank incomprehension and non-reception of slumber. This border-line varies with the power of the individual consciousness, with the degree and height of its enlightenment and awakening. The line may be pushed up higher and higher until it may pass even beyond the mind. Normally indeed the human mind cannot be awake, even with the inner waking of trance, on the supramental levels; but this disability can be overcome. Awake on these levels the soul becomes master of the ranges of gnostic thought, gnostic will, gnostic delight, and if it can do this in Samadhi, it may carry its memory of experience and its power of experience over into the waking state. Even on the yet higher level open to us, that of the Ananda, the awakened soul may become similarly possessed of the Bliss-Self both in its concentration and in its cosmic comprehension. But still there may be ranges above from which it can bring back no memory except that which says, "somehow, indescribably, I was in bliss," the bliss of an unconditioned existence beyond all potentiality of expression by thought or description by image or feature. Even the sense of being may disappear in an experience in which the world-existence loses its sense and the Buddhistic symbol of Nirvana seems alone and sovereignly justified. However high the power of awakening goes, there seems to be a beyond in which the image of sleep, of *suṣupti*, will still find its application.

The Synthesis of Yoga, pp. 504-05

Samadhi in Traditional Yogas

Intimately connected with the aim of the Yoga of Knowledge which must always be the growth, the ascent or the withdrawal into a higher or a divine consciousness not now normal to us, is the importance attached to the phenomenon of Yogic trance, to Samadhi. It is supposed that there are states of being which can only be gained in trance; that especially is to be desired in which all action of awareness is abolished and there is no consciousness at all except the pure supramental immersion in immobile, timeless and infinite being. By passing away in this trance the soul departs into the silence of the highest Nirvana without possibility of return into any illusory or inferior state of existence. Samadhi is not so all-important in the Yoga of devotion, but it still has its place there as the swoon of being into which the ecstasy of divine love casts the soul. To enter into it is the supreme step of the ladder of Yogic practice in Rajayoga and Hathayoga.

The Synthesis of Yoga, p. 498

Samadhi in the Gita

The sign of the man in Samadhi is not that he loses consciousness of objects and surroundings and of his mental and physical self and cannot be recalled to it even by burning or torture of the body, — the ordinary idea of the matter; trance is a particular intensity, not the essential sign. The test is the expulsion of all desires, their inability to get at the mind, and it is the inner state from which this freedom arises, the delight of the soul gathered within itself with the mind equal and still and high-poised above the attractions and repulsions, the alternations of sunshine and storm and stress of the external life. It is drawn inward even when acting outwardly; it is concentrated in self even when gazing out upon things; it is directed wholly to the Divine even when to the outward vision of others busy and preoccupied with the affairs of the world.   *Essays on the Gita, pp. 94-95*

Samadhi from the View of the Integral Yoga

For the integral Yoga this method [of total absorption] of Samadhi may seem to have the disadvantage that when it ceases, the thread is broken and the soul returns into the distraction and imperfection of the outward life, with only such an elevating effect upon that outer life as the general memory of these deeper experiences may produce. But this gulf, this break is not inevitable. In the first place, it is only in the untrained psychic being that the experiences of the trance are a blank to the waking mind; as it becomes the master of its Samadhi, it is able to pass without any gulf of oblivion from the inner to the outer waking. Secondly, when this has been once done, what is attained in the inner state, becomes easier to acquire by the waking consciousness and to turn into the normal experience, powers, mental status of the waking life. The subtle mind which is normally eclipsed by the insistence of the physical being, becomes powerful even in the waking state, until even there the enlarging man is able to live in his several subtle bodies as well as in his physical body, to be aware of them and in them, to use their senses, faculties, powers, to dwell in possession of supra-physical truth, consciousness and experience.

The Synthesis of Yoga, pp. 503-04

...a certain self-gathered state of our whole existence lifted into that superconscient truth, unity and infinity of self-aware, self-blissful existence is the aim and culmination; and that is the meaning we shall give to the term Samadhi. Not merely a state withdrawn from all consciousness of the outward, withdrawn even from all consciousness of the inward into that which exists beyond both whether as seed of both or transcendent even of their seed-state; but a settled existence in the One and Infinite, united and identified with it, and this status to remain whether we abide in the waking condition in which we are conscious of the forms of things or we withdraw into the inward activity which dwells in the play of the principles of things, the play of their names and typal forms or we soar to the condition of static inwardness where we arrive at the principles themselves and at the principle of all principles, the seed of name and form.[2] For the soul that has arrived at the essential Samadhi and is settled in it (*samādhistha*) in the sense the Gita attaches to the word, has that which is fundamental to all experience and cannot fall from it by any experience however distracting to one who has not yet ascended the summit. It can embrace all in the scope of its being without being bound by any or deluded or limited.

The Synthesis of Yoga, p. 307

Experiences in trance have their utility for opening the being and preparing it, but it is only when the realisation is constant in the waking state that it is truly possessed. Therefore in this yoga

---

[2] The Waking, Dream and Sleep states of the soul.

most value is given to the waking realisation and experience.

Letters on Yoga, p. 743

Samadhi is not a thing to be shunned — only it has to be made more and more conscious.

Letters on Yoga, p. 743

It is not necessary to be in samadhi to be in contact with the Divine.

Letters on Yoga, p. 743

Immersion in Sachchidananda is a state one can get in the waking condition without samadhi....

Letters on Yoga, p. 741

What then is the nature of Samadhi or the utility of its trance in an integral Yoga? It is evident that where our objective includes the possession of the Divine in life, a state of cessation of life cannot be the last consummating step or the highest desirable condition: Yogic trance cannot be an aim, as in so many Yogic systems, but only a means, and a means not of escape from the waking existence, but to enlarge and raise the whole seeing, living and active consciousness.

The Synthesis of Yoga, p. 498

(d) Cosmic Consciousness

Man is shut up at present in his surface individual consciousness and knows the world (or rather the surface of it) only through his outward mind and senses and by interpreting their contacts with the world. By yoga there can open in him a consciousness which becomes one with that of the world; he becomes directly aware of a universal Being, universal states, universal Force and Power, universal Mind, Life, Matter and lives in conscious relations with these things. He is then said to have cosmic consciousness.

Letters on Yoga, p. 1070

The ordinary consciousness of man is confined to his own individuality — he can enter into the consciousness of others and of the universe only by indirect means or a superficial and incomplete apprehension, by sense experience, contacts of emotional sympathy, mental concepts, analogy with his own movements, inference. In yoga at a certain point this limitation breaks down, the consciousness enlarges itself, becomes directly aware of the Cosmic Self and knows the individual self to be one with it; of the Cosmic Energy and meets directly the action of the cosmic forces; of the cosmic mind, life, matter and feels first a contact of its individual mind, life, body with them, then a unity in which one's own individual mentality, vitality, physicality is felt as only a part of the universal, a wave of the ocean, a dynamo receiving and formulating the universal forces. Finally, the individual melts into the cosmic Consciousness, the whole world is felt in oneself and oneself suffused through the world — it is the cosmic Consciousness, Mind, Life, material Energy that works through the individual function. The separate ego either does not exist or is only a convenience for the universal Spirit and its action. This is the complete consummation of the cosmic Consciousness, but in its fullness it is not common, belonging properly to what we may call the overmind realisation; but a constant partial and growing experience of it or an increasing contact with the cosmic Consciousness is a normal part of yoga.

Letters on Yoga, pp. 1604-05

When one has the cosmic consciousness, one can feel the cosmic Self as one's own self, one can feel one with other beings in the cosmos, one can feel all the forces of Nature as moving in oneself, all selves as one's own self.   *Letters on Yoga, p. 1071*

The cosmic consciousness is that in which the limits of ego, personal mind and body disappear and one becomes aware of a cosmic vastness which is or filled by a cosmic spirit and aware also of the direct play of cosmic forces, universal mind forces, universal life forces, universal energies of Matter, universal overmind forces. But one does not become aware of all these together; the opening of the cosmic consciousness is usually progressive. It is not that the ego, the body, the personal mind disappear, but one feels them as only a small part of oneself. One begins to feel others too as part of oneself or varied repetitions of oneself, the same self modified by Nature in other bodies. Or, at the least, as living in the larger universal self which is henceforth one's own greater reality. All things in fact begin to change their nature and appearance; one's whole experience of the world is radically different from that of those who are shut up in their personal selves. One begins to know things by a different kind of experience, more direct, not depending on the external mind and the senses. It is not that the possibility of error disappears, for that cannot be so long as mind of any kind is one's instrument for transcribing knowledge, but there is a new, vast and deep way of experiencing, seeing, knowing, contacting things; and the confines of knowledge can be rolled back to an almost unmeasurable degree. The thing one has to be on guard against in the cosmic consciousness is the play of a magnified ego, the vaster attacks of the hostile forces — for they too are part of the cosmic consciousness — and the attempt of the cosmic Illusion (Ignorance, Avidya) to prevent the growth of the soul into the cosmic Truth. These are things that one has to learn from experience; mental teaching or explanation is quite insufficient. To enter safely into the cosmic consciousness and to pass safely through it, it is necessary to have a strong central unegoistic sincerity and to have the psychic being, with its divination of truth and unfaltering orientation towards the Divine, already in front in the nature.

Letters on Yoga, pp. 316-17

The cosmic consciousness has many levels — the cosmic physical, the cosmic vital, the cosmic Mind, and above the higher planes of cosmic Mind there is the Intuition and above that the overmind and still above that the supermind where the Transcendental begins. In order to live in the Intuition plane (not merely to receive intuitions), one has to live in the cosmic consciousness because there the cosmic and individual run into each other as it were, and the mental separation between them is already broken down, so nobody can reach there who is still in the separative ego.

A reflected static realisation of Sachchidananda is possible on any of the cosmic planes, but the full entering into it, the entire union with the Supreme Divine dynamic as well as static, comes with the transcendence.   *Letters on Yoga, pp. 1157-58*

There are in the cosmic consciousness two sides — one the contact with and perception of the ordinary cosmic forces and the beings behind these forces, that is what I call the cosmic Ignorance — the other is the perception of the cosmic Truths, the realisation of the one universal, the one universal Force, all the Vedantic truths of the One in all and all in one, all the various aspects of the Divine in the cosmic and a host of other things can come which do help to realisation and knowledge — provided they are taken in the right way. However all that can be best dealt with when it actually comes. It does not always come as soon as there is the widening — many pass through the widening of the consciousness to what is beyond the cosmic and take the cosmic in detail afterwards — and it is perhaps the safest order.   *Letters on Yoga, pp. 1070-71*

To have the cosmic consciousness without liberation is possible, but then there is no freedom anywhere in the being from the lower nature and one may become in one's extended consciousness the playground of all kinds of forces without being able to be either free or master.

On the other hand, if there has been Self-realisation, there is one part of the being that remains untouched amid the play of the cosmic forces — while if the peace and purity of the self has been established in the whole inner consciousness, then the outer touches of the lower nature can't come in or overpower.

This is the advantage of Self-realisation preceding the cosmic consciousness and supporting it.   *Letters on Yoga, pp. 1073-74*

Now about the cosmic consciousness and Nirvana. Cosmic consciousness is a complex matter. To begin with, there are two sides to it, the experience of the Self free, infinite, silent, inactive, one in all and beyond all, and the direct experience of the cosmic Energy and its forces, workings and formations, this latter experience not being complete till one has the sense of being commensurate with the universe or pervading, exceeding and containing it. Till then there may be direct contacts, communications, interchanges with cosmic forces, beings, movements, but not the full unity of mind with the cosmic Mind, of life with the cosmic Life, of body and physical consciousness with the cosmic material Energy and its substance. Again, there may be a realisation of the Cosmic Self which is not followed by the realisation of the dynamic universal oneness. Or, on the contrary, there may be some dynamic universalising of consciousness without the experience of the free static Self omnipresent everywhere, — the preoccupation with and pleasure of the greater energies that one would thus experience would stop the way to that liberation. Also the identification or universalisation may be more on one plane or level than on another, predominantly mental or predominantly emotional (through universal sympathy or love) or vital of another kind (experience of the universal life forces) or physical. But in any case, even with the full realisation and experience it should be evident that this cosmic play would be something that one would finally feel as limited, ignorant, imperfect from its very nature. The free soul might regard it untouched and unmoved by its imperfections and vicissitudes, do some appointed work, try to help all or be an instrument of the Divine, but neither the work nor the instrumentation would have anything like the perfection or even the full light, power, bliss of the Divine. This could only be gained by an ascension into higher planes of cosmic existence or their descent into one's consciousness — and, if this were not envisaged or accepted, the push to Nirvana would still remain as a way of escape. The other way would be the ascent after death into these higher planes — the heavens of the religions signify after all nothing but such an urge to a greater, luminous, beatific Divine Existence.

But, one might ask, if the higher planes or if the overmind itself were to manifest their consciousness with all their power, light, freedom and vastness and these things were to descend into an individual consciousness here, would not that make unnecessary both the cosmic negation or the Nirvanic push and the urge towards some Divine Transcendence? But in the result though one might live in a union with the Divine in a luminous wide free consciousness embracing the universe in itself and be a channel of great energies or creations, spiritual or external, yet this world here would remain fundamentally the same — there would be a gulf of difference between the Spirit within and its medium and stuff on which it acted, between the inner consciousness and the world in which it is working. The achievement inner, subjective, individual might be perfect, but the dynamic outcome insufficient, disparate, a mixture, not a perfect harmony of the inner and the outer, a new integral rhythm of existence here that could be called truly divine. Only a consciousness like the supramental, unconditioned and in perfect unity with its source, a Truth-Consciousness empowered to create its own free determinations would be able to establish some perfect harmony and rhythm of the higher hemisphere in this lowest rung of the lower hemisphere. Whether it is to do so or not depends on the significance of the evolutionary existence; it depends on whether that existence is something imperfect in its very nature and doomed to frustration — in which case either a negative way of transcendence by some kind of Nirvana or a positive way of transcendence, perhaps by breaking the shining shield of overmind, *hiraṇmaya pātra*, into what is above it, would be the final end of the soul escaping from this meaningless universe; unless indeed like the Amitabha Buddha one were held by compassion or else the Divine Will within to continue helping and sharing the upward struggle towards the Light of those here still in the darkness of the Ignorance. If, on the contrary, this world is a Lila of spiritual involution and evolution in which one power after another up to the highest is to appear, as Matter, Life and Mind have already appeared out of an apparent indeterminate Inconscience, then another culmination is possible.

The push to Nirvana has two motive forces behind it. One is the sense of the imperfection, sorrow, death, suffering of this world — the original motive force of the Buddha. But for escape from these afflictions Nirvana might not be necessary, if there are higher worlds into which one can ascend where there is no such imperfection, sorrow, death or suffering. But this other possibility of escape is met by the idea that these higher worlds too are transient and part of the Ignorance, that one has to return here always till one overcomes the Ignorance, that the Reality and the cosmic existence are as Truth and Falsehood, opposite, incompatible. This brings in the second motive force, that of the call to transcendence. If the Transcendent is not only supracosmic but an aloof Incommunicable, *avyavahāryam*, which one cannot reach except by a negation of all that is here, then some kind of Nirvana, an absolute Nirvana even is inevitable. If, on the other hand, the Divine is transcendent but not incommunicable, the call will still be there and the soul will leave the chequered cosmic play for the beatitude of the transcendent existence, but an absolute Nirvana would not be indispensable; a beatific union with the Divine offers itself as the way before the seeker. This is the reason why the Cosmic Consciousness is not sufficient and the push away from it is so strong, — it is only if the golden lid of the overmind is overpassed and opened and the dynamic contact with the supermind and a descent of its Light and Power here is intended that it can be otherwise.   *Letters on Yoga, pp. 246-49*

(e) Nirvana

What then is Nirvana? In orthodox Buddhism it does mean a disintegration, not of the soul — for that does not exist — but of a mental compound or stream of associations or *saṁskāras* which we mistake for ourself. In illusionist Vedanta it means, not a disintegration but a disappearance of a false and unreal individual self into the one real Self or Brahman; it is the idea and experience of individuality that so disappears and ceases, — we may say a false light that is extinguished (*nirvāṇa*) in the true Light. In spiritual experience it is sometimes the loss of all sense of individuality in a boundless cosmic consciousness; what was the individual remains only as a centre or a channel for the flow of a cosmic consciousness and a cosmic force and action. Or it may be the experience of the loss of individuality in a transcendent being and consciousness in which the sense of cosmos as well as the individual disappears. Or again, it may be in a transcendence which is aware of and supports the cosmic action.   *Letters on Yoga, p. 46*

They [those who have the experience of Nirvana] do not feel as if they had any existence at all. In the Buddhistic Nirvana they feel as if there were no such thing at all, only an infinite zero without form. In the Adwaita Nirvana there is felt only one Vast Existence, no separate being is discernible anywhere. There are forms of course but they are only forms, not separate beings. Mind is silent, thought has ceased, — desires, passions, vital movements there are none. There is consciousness but only a formless elemental consciousness without limits. The body moves and acts, but the sense of the body is not there. Sometimes there is only the consciousness of pure existence, sometimes only pure consciousness, sometimes all that exists is only a ceaseless limitless Ananda. Whether all else is really dissolved or only covered up is a debatable point, but at any rate it is an experience as if of their dissolution.   *Letters on Yoga, pp. 65-66*

[Footnote on Nirvana:] Extinction, not necessarily of all being, but of being as we know it; extinction of ego, desire and egoistic action and mentality. *The Life Divine, p. 23*

It is not possible to situate Nirvana as a world or plane, for the Nirvana push is to a withdrawal from world and world-values; it is therefore a state of consciousness or rather of super-consciousness without habitation or level. There is more than one kind of Nirvana (extinction or dissolution) possible. Man being a mental being in a body, *manomaya puruṣa*, makes this attempt at retreat from the cosmos through the spiritualised mind, he cannot do otherwise and it is this that gives it the appearance of an extinction or dissolution, *laya, nirvaṇā*; for extinction of the mind and all that depends on it including the separative ego in something Beyond is the natural way, almost the indispensable way for such a withdrawal. In a more affirmative yoga seeking transcendence but not withdrawal there would not be this indispensability, for there would be the way already alluded to of self-exceeding or transformation of the mental being. But it is possible also to pass to that through a certain experience of Nirvana, an absolute silence of mind and cessation of activities, constructions, representations, which can be so complete that not only to the silent mind but also to the passive senses the whole world is emptied of its solidity and reality and things appear only as unsubstantial forms without any real habitations or else floating in Something that is a nameless infinite: this infinite or else something still beyond is That which alone is real; an absolute calm, peace, liberation would be the resulting state. Action would continue, but no initiation or participation in it by the silent liberated consciousness; a nameless power would do all until there began the descent from above which would transform the consciousness, making its silence and freedom a basis for a luminous knowledge, action, Ananda. But such a passage would be rare; ordinarily a silence of the mind, a liberation of the consciousness, a renunciation of its belief in the final value or truth of the mind's imperfect representations or constructions would be enough for the higher working to be possible.   *Letters on Yoga, pp. 245-46*

We recognise, then, that it is possible for the consciousness in the individual to enter into a state in which relative existence appears to be dissolved and even Self seems to be an inadequate conception. It is possible to pass into a Silence beyond the Silence. But this is not the whole of our ultimate experience, nor the single and all-excluding truth. For we find that this Nirvana, this self-extinction, while it gives an absolute peace and freedom to the soul within is yet consistent in practice with a desireless but effective action without. This possibility of an entire motionless impersonality and void Calm within doing outwardly the works of the eternal verities, Love, Truth and Righteousness, was perhaps the real gist of the Buddha's teaching, — this superiority to ego and to the chain of personal workings and to the identification with mutable form and idea, not the petty ideal of an escape from the trouble and suffering of the physical birth. In any case, as the perfect man would combine in himself the silence and the activity, so also would the completely conscious soul reach back to the absolute freedom of the Non-Being without therefore losing its hold on Existence and the universe. It would thus reproduce in itself perpetually the eternal miracle of the divine Existence, in the universe, yet always beyond it and even, as it were, beyond itself. The opposite experience could only be a concentration of mentality in the individual upon Non-existence with the result of an oblivion and personal withdrawal from a cosmic activity still and always proceeding in the consciousness of the Eternal Being.   *The Life Divine, pp. 29-30*

...I said once that souls which have passed into Nirvana may (not "must") return to complete the larger upward curve. I have written somewhere, I think, that for this yoga (it might also be added, in the natural complete order of the manifestation) the experience of Nirvana can only be a stage or passage to the complete realisation. I have said also that there are many doors by which one can pass into the realisation of the Absolute (Parabrahman), and Nirvana is one of them, but by no means the only one. You may remember Ramakrishna's saying that the Jivakoti can ascend the stairs, but not return, while the Ishwarakoti can ascend and descend at will. If that is so, the Jivakoti might be those who describe only the curve from Matter through Mind into the silent Brahman and the Ishwarakoti those who get to the integral Reality and can therefore combine the Ascent with the Descent and contain the "two ends" of existence in their single being. *Letters on Yoga, p. 59*

There are a hundred ways of approaching the Supreme Reality and, as is the nature of the way taken, so will be the nature of the ultimate experience by which one passes into That which is ineffable, That of which no report can be given to the mind or expressed by any utterance. All these definitive culminations may be regarded as penultimates of the one Ultimate; they are steps by which the soul crosses the limits of Mind into the Absolute. Is then this realisation of passing into a pure immobile self-existence or this Nirvana of the individual and the universe one among these penultimates, or is it itself the final and absolute re-alisation which is at the end of every journey and transcends and eliminates all lesser experience? It claims to stand behind and supersede, to sublate and to eliminate every other knowledge; if that is really so, then its finality must be accepted as conclu-sive. But, against this pretension, it has been claimed that it is possible to travel beyond by a greater negation or a greater af-firmation, — to extinguish self in Non-Being or to pass through the double experience of cosmic consciousness and Nirvana of world-consciousness in the One Existence to a greater Divine Union and Unity which holds both these realisations in its vast integral Reality. It is said that beyond the duality and the non-duality there is That in which both are held together and find their truth in a Truth which is beyond them. A consummating experience which proceeds by the exceeding and elimination of all other possible but lesser experiences is, as a step towards the Absolute, admissible. A supreme experience which affirms and includes the truth of all spiritual experience, gives to each its own absolute, integralises all knowledge and experience in a supreme reality, might be the one step farther that is at once a largest illuminating and transforming Truth of all things and a highest infinite Transcendence. The Brahman, the supreme Reality, is That which being known all is known; but in the illusionist solution it is That, which being known, all becomes unreal and an incomprehensible mystery: in this other experience, the Reality being known, all assumes its true significance, its truth to the Eternal and Absolute.   *The Life Divine, p. 470*

17
Sleep and Dreams

The physical is not the only world; there are others that we become aware of through dream records, through the subtle senses, through influences and contacts, through imagination, intuition and vision.... In sleep we leave the physical body, only a subconscient residue remaining, and enter all planes and all sorts of worlds. In each we see scenes, meet beings, share in happenings, come across formations, influences, suggestions which belong to these planes. Even when we are awake, part of us moves in these planes, but their activity goes on behind the veil; our waking minds are not aware of it. Dreams are often only incoherent constructions of our subconscient, but others are records (often much mixed and distorted) or transcripts of experiences in these supraphysical planes. When we do sadhana, this kind of dream becomes very common; then subconscious dreams cease to predominate. *Letters on Yoga, pp. 1499-1500*

Ordinarily when one sleeps a complex phenomenon happens. The waking consciousness is no longer there, for all has been withdrawn within into the inner realms of which we are not aware when we are awake, though they exist; for then all that is put behind a veil by the waking mind and nothing remains except the surface self and the outward world — much as the veil of the sunlight hides from us the vast worlds of the stars that are behind it. Sleep is a going inward in which the surface self and the outside world are put away from our sense and vision. But in ordinary sleep we do not become aware of the worlds within; the being seems submerged in a deep subconscience. On the surface of this subconscience floats an obscure layer in which dreams take place, as it seems to us, but, more correctly it may be said, are recorded. When we go very deeply asleep, we have what appears to us as a dreamless slumber; but, in fact, dreams are going on, but they are either too deep down to reach the recording surface or are forgotten, all recollection of their having existed even is wiped out in the transition to the waking consciousness. Ordinary dreams are for the most part or seem to be incoherent, because they are either woven by the subconscient out of deep-lying impressions left in it by our past inner and outer life, woven in a fantastic way which does not easily yield any clue of meaning to the waking mind's remembrance, or are fragmentary records, mostly distorted, of experiences which are going on behind the veil of sleep — very largely indeed these two elements get mixed up together. For, in fact, a large part of our consciousness in sleep does not get sunk into this subconscious state; it passes beyond the veil into other planes of being which are connected with our own inner planes, planes of supraphysical existence, worlds of a larger life, mind or psyche which are there behind and whose influences come to us without our knowledge. Occasionally we get a dream from these planes, something more than a dream, — a dream experience which is a record direct or symbolic of what happens to us or around us there. As the inner consciousness grows by sadhana, these dream experiences increase in number, clearness, coherence, accuracy and after some growth of experience and consciousness, we can, if we observe, come to understand them and their significance to our inner life. Even we can by training become so conscious as to follow our own passage, usually veiled to our awareness and memory, through many realms and the process of the return to the waking state. At a certain pitch of this inner wakefulness this kind of sleep, a sleep of experiences, can replace the ordinary subconscious slumber.

Letters on Yoga, pp. 1023-24

What happens in sleep is that our consciousness withdraws from the field of its waking experiences; it is supposed to be resting, suspended or in abeyance, but that is a superficial view of the matter. What is in abeyance is the waking activities, what is at rest is the surface mind and the normal conscious action of the bodily part of us; but the inner consciousness is not suspended, it enters into new inner activities, only a part of which, a part happening or recorded in something of us that is near to the surface, we remember. There is maintained in sleep, thus near the surface, an obscure subconscious element which is a receptacle or passage for our dream experiences and itself also a dream-builder; but behind it is the depth and mass of the subliminal, the totality of our concealed inner being and consciousness which is of quite another order. Normally it is a subconscient part in us, intermediate between consciousness and pure inconscience, that sends up through this surface layer its formations in the shape of dreams, constructions marked by an apparent inconsequence and incoherence. Many of these are fugitive structures built upon circumstances of our present life selected apparently at random and surrounded with a phantasy of variation; others call back the past, or rather selected circumstances and persons of the past, as a starting-point for similar fleeting edifices. There are other dreams of the subconscious which seem to be pure phantasy without any such initiation or basis; but the new method of psycho-analysis, trying to look for the first time into our dreams with some kind of scientific understanding, has established in them a system of meanings, a key to things in us which need to be known and handled by the waking consciousness; this of itself changes the whole character and value of our dream-experience. It begins to look as if there were something real behind it and as if too that something were an element of no mean practical importance.

But the subconscious is not our sole dream-builder. The subconscious in us is the extreme border of our secret inner existence where it meets the Inconscient, it is a degree of our being in which the Inconscient struggles into a half consciousness; the surface physical consciousness also, when it sinks back from the waking level and retrogresses towards the Inconscient, retires into this intermediate subconscience. Or, from another viewpoint, this nether part of us may be described as the ante-chamber of the Inconscient through which its formations rise into our waking or our subliminal being. When we sleep and the surface physical part of us, which is in its first origin here an output from the Inconscient, relapses towards the originating inconscience, it enters into this subconscious element, ante-chamber or substratum, and there it finds the impressions of its past or persistent habits of mind and experiences, — for all have left their mark on our subconscious part and have there a power of recurrence. In its effect on our waking self this recurrence often takes the form of a reassertion of old habits, impulses dormant or suppressed, rejected elements of the nature, or it comes up as some other not so easily recognisable, some peculiar disguised or subtle result of these suppressed or rejected but not erased impulses or elements. In the dream-consciousness the phenomenon is an apparently fanciful construction, a composite of figures and movements built upon or around the buried impressions with a sense in them that escapes the waking intelligence because it has no clue to the subconscient's system of significances. After a time this subconscious activity appears to sink back into complete inconscience and we speak of this state as deep dreamless sleep; thence we emerge again into the dream-shallows or return to the waking surface.

But, in fact, in what we call dreamless sleep, we have gone into a profounder and denser layer of the subconscient, a state too involved, too immersed or too obscure, dull and heavy to bring to the surface its structures, and we are dreaming there but unable to grasp or retain in the recording layer of subconscience these more obscure dream-figures. Or else, it may be, the part of our mind which still remains active in the sleep of the body has entered into the inner domains of our being, the subliminal mental, the subliminal vital, the subtle-physical, and is there lost to all active connection with the surface parts of us. If we are still in the nearer depths of these regions, the surface subconscient which is our sleep-wakefulness records something of what we experience in these depths; but it records it in its own transcription, often marred by characteristic incoherences and always, even when most coherent, deformed or cast into figures drawn from the world of waking experience. But if we have gone deeper inward, the record fails or cannot be recovered and we have the illusion of dreamlessness; but the activity of the inner dream consciousness continues behind the veil of the now mute and inactive subconscient surface. This continued dream activity is revealed to us when we become more inwardly conscious, for then we get into connection with the heavier and deeper subconscient stratum and can be aware, — at the time or by a retracing or recovering through memory, — of what happened when we sank into these torpid depths. It is possible too to become conscious deeper within our subliminal selves and we are then aware of experiences on other planes of our being or even in supraphysical worlds to which sleep gives us a right of secret entry. A transcript of such experiences reaches us; but the transcriber here is not the subconscious, it is the subliminal, a greater dream-builder.

If the subliminal thus comes to the front in our dream-consciousness, there is sometimes an activity of our subliminal intelligence, — dream becomes a series of thoughts, often strangely or vividly figured, problems are solved which our waking consciousness could not solve, warnings, premonitions, indications of the future, veridical dreams replace the normal subconscious incoherence. There can come also a structure of symbol-images, some of a mental character, some of a vital nature: the former are precise in their figures, clear in their significance; the latter are often complex and baffling to our waking consciousness, but, if we can seize the clue, they reveal their own sense and peculiar system of coherence. Finally, there can come to us the records of happenings seen or experienced by us on other planes of our own being or of universal being into which we enter: these have sometimes, like the symbolic dreams, a strong bearing on our own inner and outer life or the life of others, reveal elements of our or their mental being and life-being or disclose influences on them of which our waking self is totally ignorant; but sometimes they have no such bearing and are purely records of other organised systems of consciousness independent of our physical existence. The subconscious dreams constitute the bulk of our most ordinary sleep-experience and they are those which we usually remember; but sometimes the subliminal builder is able to impress our sleep consciousness sufficiently to stamp his activities on our waking memory. If we develop our inner being, live more inwardly than most men do, then the balance is changed and a larger dream-consciousness opens before us; our dreams can take on a subliminal and no longer a subconscious character and can assume a reality and significance.

It is even possible to become wholly conscious in sleep and follow throughout from beginning to end or over large stretches the stages of our dream-experience; it is found that then we are aware of ourselves passing from state after state of consciousness to a brief period of luminous and peaceful dreamless rest, which is the true restorer of the energies of the waking nature, and then returning by the same way to the waking consciousness. It is normal, as we thus pass from state to state, to let the previous experiences slip away from us; in the return only the more vivid or those nearest to the waking surface are remembered: but this can be remedied, — a greater retention is possible or the power can be developed of going back in memory from dream to dream, from state to state, till the whole is once more before us. A coherent knowledge of sleep-life, though difficult to achieve or to keep established, is possible.   *The Life Divine, pp. 422-25*

In the waking state you are conscious only of a certain limited field and action of your nature. In sleep you can become vividly aware of things beyond this field — a larger mental or vital nature behind the waking state or else a subtle physical or a subconscient nature which contains much that is there in you but not distinguishably active in the waking state.

Letters on Yoga, p. 1487

...it is a well-known psychological law that what is suppressed or rejected in the waking state may still recur in sleep and dream because they are still there in the subconscient being. But if the waking state is thoroughly cleared, these dream-movements must gradually disappear because they lose their food and the impressions in the subconscient are gradually effaced.

Letters on Yoga, p. 1658

It is the waking mind which thinks and wills and controls more or less the life in the waking state. In the sleep that mind is not there and there is no control. It is not the thinking mind that sees dreams etc. and is conscious in a rather incoherent way in sleep. It is usually what is called the subconscient that comes up then. If the waking mind were active in the body, one would not be able to sleep.   *Letters on Yoga, p. 1486*

It is the subconscient that is active in the ordinary dreams. But in the dreams in which one goes out into other planes of consciousness, mental, vital, subtle physical, it is part of the inner being, inner mental or vital or physical that is usually active.

Letters on Yoga, p. 1487

There are such things as dream inspirations — it is rare, however, that these are of any value. For the dreams of most people are recorded by the subconscient. Either the whole thing is a creation of the subconscient and turns out, if recorded, to be incoherent and lacking in any sense, or, if there is a real communication from a higher plane, marked by a sense of elevation and wonder, it gets transcribed by the subconscient and what that forms is either flat or ludicrous.   *The Future Poetry, p. 341*

The consciousness in the night almost always descends below the level of what one has gained by sadhana in the waking consciousness, unless there are special experiences of an uplifting character in the time of sleep or unless the yogic consciousness acquired is so strong in the physical itself as to counteract the pull of the subconscient inertia. In ordinary sleep the consciousness in the body is that of the subconscient physical, which is a diminished consciousness, not awake and alive like the rest of the being. The rest of the being stands back and part of its consciousness goes out into other planes and regions and has experiences which are recorded in dreams....   *Letters on Yoga, pp. 1485-86*

When you practise yoga, the consciousness opens and you become aware — especially in sleep — of things, scenes, beings, happenings of other (not physical) worlds and yourself in sleep go there and act there.   *Letters on Yoga, p. 1504*

In the sleep the consciousness goes into other planes and has experiences there and when these are translated perfectly or imperfectly by the physical mind, they are called dreams. All the time of sleep such dreams take place, but sometimes one remembers and at other times does not at all remember. Sometimes also one goes low down into the subconscient and the dreams are there, but so deep down that when one comes out there is not even the consciousness that one had dreamed.
                                                          Letters on Yoga, p. 1493

When the sleep is more awake, so to say, then one has dreams of all kinds; when there is no such awareness of dreams, it is because the sleep of the body is more deep, — the dreams are there but the body consciousness does not note them or remember that it had them.   *Letters on Yoga, p. 1493*

> [Q: Sometimes one remembers the dreams, sometimes one does not. Why is it so?]

It depends on the connection between the two states of consciousness at the time of waking. Usually there is a turn over of the consciousness in which the dream-state disappears more or less abruptly, effacing the fugitive impression made by the dream events (or rather their transcription) on the physical sheath. If the waking is more composed (less abrupt) or, if the impression is very strong, then the memory remains at least of the last dream. In the last case one may remember the dream for a long time, but usually after getting up the dream memories fade away. Those who want to remember their dreams sometimes make a practice of lying quiet and tracing backwards, recovering the dreams one by one. When the dream-state is very light, one can remember more dreams than when it is heavy.   *Letters on Yoga, pp. 1493-94*

1. ...Dream-consciousness is a vast world in which there are a multitude of provinces and kingdoms, but ordinary dreamers for the most part penetrate consciously only to these first layers which belong to what may properly be called the subconscious belt. When they pass into deeper sleep regions, their recording surface dream-mind becomes unconscious and no longer gives any transcript of what is seen and experienced there; or else in coming back these experiences of the deeper strata fade away and are quite forgotten before one reaches the waking state. But when there is a stronger dream-capacity, or the dream-state becomes more conscious, then one is aware of these deeper experiences and can bring back a transcript which is sometimes a clear record, sometimes a hieroglyph, but in either case possessed of a considerable interest and significance.

2. It is only the subconscious belt that is chaotic in its dream sequences; for its transcriptions are fantastic and often mixed, combining a jumble of different elements: some play with impressions from the past, some translate outward touches pressing on the sleep-mind; most are fragments from successive dream experiences that are not really part of one connected experience — as if a gramophone record were to be made up of snatches of different songs all jumbled together. The vital dreams even in the subconscious range are often coherent in

themselves and only seem incoherent to the waking intelligence because the logic and law of their sequences is different from the logic and law which the physical reason imposes on the incoherences of physical life. But if one gets the guiding clue and if one has some dream-experience and dream-insight, then it is possible to seize the links of the sequences and make out the significance, often very profound or very striking, both of the detail and of the whole. Deeper in, we come to perfectly coherent dreams recording the experience of the inner vital and inner mental planes; there are also true psychic dreams — the latter usually are of a great beauty. Some of these mental or vital plane dream-experiences, however, are symbolic, very many in fact, and can only be understood if one is familiar with or gets the clue to the symbols.   *The Future Poetry, pp. 447-48*

Most people move most in the vital in sleep because it is the nearest to the physical and easiest to remain. One does enter the higher planes but either the transit there is brief or one does not remember. For in returning to the waking consciousness it is again through the lower vital and subtle physical that one passes and as these are the last dreams they are more easily remembered. The other dreams are remembered only if (1) they are strongly impressed on the recording consciousness, (2) one wakes immediately after one of them, (3) one has learned to be conscious in sleep, i.e. follows consciously the passage from plane to plane. Some train themselves to remember by remaining without moving when they wake and following back the thread of the dreams.   *Letters on Yoga, pp. 1494-95*

Those dreams which are formed from subconscient impressions arranged at haphazard (subconscient mind, vital or physical) either have no significance or some meaning which is difficult to find and not very much worth knowing even if it is found. Other dreams are either simply happenings of the mental, vital or subtle physical worlds or else belong to the wider mental, vital or subtle physical planes and have a meaning which the figures of the dream are trying to communicate.   *Letters on Yoga, p. 1491*

It is a very small number of dreams that can be so explained [that they arise by external stimuli] and in many cases the explanation is quite arbitrary or cannot be proved. A much larger number of dreams arise from subconscient impressions of the past without any stimulus from outside. These are the dreams from the subconscient which are the bulk of those remembered by people who live in the external mind mostly. There are also the dreams that are renderings of vital movements and tendencies habitual to the nature, personal formations of the vital plane. But when one begins to live within then the dreams are often transcriptions of one's experiences on the vital plane and beyond that there is a large field of symbolic and other dreams which have nothing to do with memory.   *Letters on Yoga, p. 1496*

There is no solid connection [between the waking and the dream states], but there can be a subtle one. Events of the waking state often influence the dream world, provided they have a sufficient repercussion on the mind or the vital. Formations and activities of the dream planes can project something of themselves or of their influence into the waking physical state, though they seldom reproduce themselves with any exactness there. It is only if the dream consciousness is very highly developed that one can usually see things there that are afterwards confirmed by thoughts, speech or actions of people or events in the physical world.   *Letters on Yoga, pp. 1492-93*

The power to have such dreams is comparatively rare, for ordinarily such previsions come in inner vision but not in sleep. In dreams vital or mental formations often take shape which sometimes fulfil themselves in essence, but not with this accuracy of detail.

It is only a particular class of dreams that do that [indicate the exact past and the future]. Most coherent dreams are either symbolic or indicate things that take place in the mental or vital planes rather than on the physical.   *Letters on Yoga, pp. 1489-90*

> *Q: How can one distinguish between a dream of deeper origin and a vision?*

A: There is no criterion, but one can easily distinguish if one is in the inward condition, not sleep, in which most visions take place, by the nature of the impression made. A vision in a dream is more difficult to distinguish from a vivid dream-experience but one gets to feel the difference.   *The Mother, pp. 393-94*

18
Psychical[1] Phenomena

The range of the psychic consciousness and its experiences is almost illimitable and the variety and complexity of its phenomena almost infinite. Only some of the broad lines and main features can be noted here. The first and most prominent is the activity of the psychic senses of which the sight is the most developed ordinarily and the first to manifest itself with any largeness when the veil of the absorption in the surface consciousness which prevents the inner vision is broken. But all the physical senses have their corresponding powers in the psychical being, there is a psychical hearing, touch, smell, taste: indeed the physical senses are themselves in reality only a projection of the inner sense into a limited and externalised operation in and through and upon the phenomena of gross matter. The psychical sight receives characteristically the images that are formed in the subtle matter of the mental or psychical ether, *cittākāśa*. These may be transcriptions there or impresses of physical things, persons, scenes, happenings, whatever is, was or will be or may be in the physical universe. These images are very variously seen and under all kinds of conditions; in Samadhi or in the waking state, and in the latter with the bodily eyes closed or open, projected on or into a physical object or medium or seen as if materialised in the physical atmosphere or only in a psychical ether revealing itself through this grosser physical atmosphere; seen through the physical eyes themselves as a secondary instrument and as if under the conditions of the physical vision or by the psychical vision alone and independently of the relations of our ordinary sight to space. The real agent is always the psychical sight and the power indicates that the consciousness is more or less awake, intermittently or normally and more or less perfectly, in the

---

[1] See the definition of "psychic(al)" in the Glossary.

psychical body. It is possible to see in this way the transcriptions or impressions of things at any distance beyond the range of the physical vision or the images of the past or the future.

Besides these transcriptions or impresses the psychical vision receives thought images and other forms created by constant activity of consciousness in ourselves or in other human beings, and these may be according to the character of the activity images of truth or falsehood or else mixed things, partly true, partly false, and may be too either mere shells and representations or images inspired with a temporary life and consciousness and, it may be, carrying in them in one way or another some kind of beneficent or maleficent action or some willed or unwilled effectiveness on our minds or vital being or through them even on the body. These transcriptions, impresses, thought images, life images, projections of the consciousness may also be representations or creations not of the physical world, but of vital, psychic or mental worlds beyond us, seen in our own minds or projected from other than human beings. And as there is this psychical vision of which some of the more external and ordinary manifestations are well enough known by the name of clairvoyance, so there is a psychical hearing and psychical touch, taste, smell, — clairaudience, clairsentience are the more external manifestations, — with precisely the same range each in its own kind, the same fields and manner and conditions and varieties of their phenomena.

These and other phenomena create an indirect, a representative range of psychical experience; but the psychical sense has also the power of putting us in a more direct communication with earthly or supra-terrestrial beings through their psychical selves or their psychical bodies or even with things, for things also have a psychical reality and souls or presences supporting them which can communicate with our psychical consciousness. The most notable of these more powerful but rarer phenomena are those which attend the power of exteriorisation of our consciousness for various kinds of action otherwise and elsewhere than in the physical body, communication in the psychical body or some emanation or reproduction of it, oftenest, though by no means necessarily, during sleep or trance and the setting up of relations or communication by various means with the denizens of another plane of existence.

...The physical mind is only a little part of us and there is a much more considerable range of our being in which the presence, influence and powers of the other planes are active upon us and help to shape our external being and its activities. The awakening of the psychical consciousness enables us to become aware of these powers, presences and influences in and around us; and while in the impure or yet ignorant and imperfect mind this unveiled contact has its dangers, it enables us too, if rightly used and directed, to be no longer their subject but their master and to come into conscious and self-controlled possession of the inner secrets of our nature. The psychical consciousness reveals this interaction between the inner and the outer planes, this world and others, partly by an awareness, which may be very constant, vast and vivid, of their impacts, suggestions, communications to our inner thought and conscious being and a capacity of reaction upon them there, partly also through many kinds of symbolic, transcriptive or representative images presented to the different psychical senses. But also there is the possibility of a more direct, concretely sensible, almost material, sometimes actively material communication — a complete though temporary physical materialisation seems to be possible — with the powers, forces and beings of other worlds and planes. There may even be a complete breaking of the limits of the physical consciousness and the material existence. *The Synthesis of Yoga, pp. 844-46*

The psychical consciousness is that of what is now often called the subliminal self, the subtle or dream self of Indian psychology, and its range of potential knowledge, almost infinite... includes a very large power and many forms of insight into both the possibilities and the definite actualities of past, present and future.

Its first faculty, that which most readily attracts attention, is its power of seeing by the psychical sense images of all things in time and space. As exercised by clairvoyants, mediums and others this is often, and indeed usually, a specialised faculty limited though often precise and accurate in action, and implies no development of the inner soul or the spiritual being or the higher intelligence. It is a door opened by chance or by an innate gift or by some kind of pressure between the waking and the subliminal mind and admitting only to the surface or the outskirts of the latter. All things in a certain power and action of the secret universal mind are represented by images, — not only visual but, if one may use the phrase, auditory and other images, — and a certain development of the subtle or psychical senses makes it possible, — if there is no interference of the constructing mind and its imaginations, if, that is to say, artificial or falsifying mental images do not intervene, if the psychical sense is free, sincere and passive, — to receive these representations or transcriptions with a perfect accuracy and not so much predict as see in its correct images the present beyond the range of the physical sense, the past and the future. The accuracy of this kind of seeing depends on its being confined to a statement of the thing seen and the attempt to infer, interpret or otherwise go beyond the visual knowledge may lead to much error unless there is at the same time a strong psychical intuition fine, subtle and pure or a high development of the luminous intuitive intelligence.

The Synthesis of Yoga, pp. 861-62

...in the phenomena of hypnosis not only can the hypnotised subject be successfully forbidden to feel the pain of a wound or puncture when in the abnormal state, but can be prevented with equal success from returning to his habitual reaction of suffering when he is awakened. The reason of this phenomenon is perfectly simple; it is because the hypnotiser suspends the habitual waking consciousness which is the slave of nervous habits and is able to appeal to the subliminal mental being in the depths, the inner mental being who is master, if he wills, of the nerves and the body. But this freedom which is effected by hypnosis abnormally, rapidly, without true possession, by an alien will, may equally be won normally, gradually, with true possession, by one's own will so as to effect partially or completely a victory of the mental being over the habitual nervous reactions of the body. *The Life Divine, pp. 106-07*

...there is an action of the sense-mind which is superior to the particular action of the senses and is aware of things even without imaging them in forms of sight, sound, contact, but which also as a sort of subordinate operation, subordinate but necessary to completeness of presentation, does image in these forms. This is evident in psychical phenomena. Those who have carried the study and experimentation of them to a certain extent, have found that we can sense things known only to the minds of others, things that exist only at a great distance, things that belong to another plane than the terrestrial but have here their effects; we can both sense them in their images and also feel, as it were, all that they are without any definite image proper to the five senses.

This shows, in the first place, that sight and the other senses are not mere results of the development of our physical organs in the terrestrial evolution. Mind, subconscious in all Matter and evolving in Matter, has developed these physical organs in order to apply its inherent capacities of sight, hearing, etc. on the physical plane by physical means for a physical life; but they are inherent capacities and not dependent on the circumstance of terrestrial evolution and they can be employed without the use of the physical eye, ear, skin, palate. Supposing that there are psychical senses which act through a psychical body, and we thus explain these psychical phenomena, still that action also is only an organisation of the inherent functioning of the essential sense, the Sanjnana, which in itself can operate without bodily organs. This essential sense is the original capacity of consciousness to feel in itself all that consciousness has formed and to feel it in all the essential properties and operations of that which has form, whether represented materially by the vibration of sound or images of light or any other physical symbol.

The Upanishads, pp. 194-95

There is indeed an inner sense in the subliminal nature, a subtle sense of vision, hearing, touch, smell and taste; but these are not confined to the creation of images of things belonging to the physical environment, — they can present to the consciousness visual, auditory, tactual and other images and vibrations of things beyond the restricted range of the physical senses or belonging to other planes or spheres of existence. This inner sense can create or present images, scenes, sounds that are symbolic rather than actual or that represent possibilities in formation, suggestions, thoughts, ideas, intentions of other beings, image-forms also of powers or potentialities in universal Nature; there is nothing that it cannot image or visualise or turn into sensory formations. It is the subliminal in reality and not the outer mind that possesses the powers of telepathy, clairvoyance, second sight and other supernormal faculties whose occurrence in the surface consciousness is due to openings or rifts in the wall erected by the outer personality's unseeing labour of individualisation and interposed between itself and the inner domain of our being. It should be noted, however, that owing to this complexity the action of the subliminal sense can be confusing or misleading, especially if it is interpreted by the outer mind to which the secret of its operations is unknown and its principles of sign-construction and symbolic figure-languages foreign; a greater inner power of intuition, tact, discrimination is needed to judge and interpret rightly its images and experiences. It is still the fact that they add immensely to our possible scope of knowledge and widen the narrow limits in which our sense-bound outer physical consciousness is circumscribed and imprisoned.

But more important is the power of the subliminal to enter

into a direct contact of consciousness with other consciousness or with objects, to act without other instrumentation, by an essential sense inherent in its own substance, by a direct mental vision, by a direct feeling of things, even by a close envelopment and intimate penetration and a return with the contents of what is enveloped or penetrated, by a direct intimation or impact on the substance of mind itself, not through outward signs or figures, — a revealing intimation or a self-communicating impact of thoughts, feelings, forces. It is by these means that the inner being achieves an immediate, intimate and accurate spontaneous knowledge of persons, of objects, of the occult and to us intangible energies of world-Nature that surround us and impinge upon our own personality, physicality, mind-force and life-force. In our surface mentality we are sometimes aware of a consciousness that can feel or know the thoughts and inner reactions of others or become aware of objects or happenings without any observable sense-intervention or otherwise exercise powers supernormal to our ordinary capacity; but these capacities are occasional, rudimentary, vague. Their possession is proper to our concealed subliminal self and, when they emerge, it is by a coming to the surface of its powers or operations. These emergent operations of the subliminal being or some of them are now fragmentarily studied under the name of psychic phenomena, — although they have ordinarily nothing to do with the *psyche*, the soul, the inmost entity in us, but only with the inner mind, the inner vital, the subtle-physical parts of our subliminal being;...   *The Life Divine, pp. 535-37*

19
Evolution of Mankind

Psychological and Spiritual Growth of Society

(a) Cycles of Growth

In the history of man everything seems now to point to alternations of a serious character, ages of progression, ages of recoil,
the whole constituting an evolution that is cyclic rather than
in one straight line. A theory of cycles of human civilisation
has been advanced, we may yet arrive at the theory of cycles
of human evolution, the *kalpas* and *manvantaras* of the Hindu
theory. If its affirmation of cycles of world-existence is farther
off from affirmation, it is because they must be so vast in their
periods as to escape not only all our means of observation, but
all our means of deduction or definite inference.

The Supramental Manifestation and Other Writings, p. 229

...there is the beginning of a perception that behind the economic
motives and causes of social and historical development there
are profound psychological, even perhaps soul factors; and in
pre-war Germany, the metropolis of rationalism and materialism
but the home also, for a century and a half, of new thought and
original tendencies good and bad, beneficent and disastrous, a
first psychological theory of history was conceived and presented
by an original intelligence....

The theorist, Lamprecht, basing himself on European and
particularly on German history, supposed that human society
progresses through certain distinct psychological stages which
he terms respectively symbolic, typal and conventional, individualist and subjective. This development forms, then, a sort of
psychological cycle through which a nation or a civilisation is
bound to proceed. Obviously, such classifications are likely to
err by rigidity and to substitute a mental straight line for the coils

and zigzags of Nature. The psychology of man and his societies is too complex, too synthetical of many-sided and intermixed tendencies to satisfy any such rigorous and formal analysis. Nor does this theory of a psychological cycle tell us what is the inner meaning of its successive phases or the necessity of their succession or the term and end towards which they are driving. But still to understand natural laws whether of Mind or Matter it is necessary to analyse their working into its discoverable elements, main constituents, dominant forces, though these may not actually be found anywhere in isolation....

Undoubtedly, wherever we can seize human society in what to us seems its primitive beginnings or early stages, — no matter whether the race is comparatively cultured or savage or economically advanced or backward, — we do find a strongly symbolic mentality that governs or at least pervades its thought, customs and institutions. Symbolic, but of what? We find that this social stage is always religious and actively imaginative in its religion; for symbolism and a widespread imaginative or intuitive religious feeling have a natural kinship and especially in earlier or primitive formations they have gone always together. When man begins to be predominantly intellectual, sceptical, ratiocinative he is already preparing for an individualist society and the age of symbols and the age of conventions have passed or are losing their virtue. The symbol then is of something which man feels to be present behind himself and his life and his activities — the Divine, the Gods, the vast and deep unnameable, a hidden, living and mysterious nature of things. All his religious and social institutions, all the moments and phases of his life are to him symbols in which he seeks to express what he knows or guesses of the mystic influences that are behind his life and shape and govern or at the least intervene in its movements....

From this symbolic attitude came the tendency to make everything in society a sacrament, religious and sacrosanct, but as yet with a large and vigorous freedom in all its forms, — a freedom which we do not find in the rigidity of "savage" communities because these have already passed out of the symbolic into the conventional stage though on a curve of degeneration instead of a curve of growth. The spiritual idea governs all; the symbolic religious forms which support it are fixed in principle; the social forms are lax, free and capable of infinite development. One thing, however, begins to progress towards a firm fixity and this is the psychological type. Thus we have first the symbolic idea of the four orders, expressing — to employ an abstractly figurative language which the Vedic thinkers would not have used nor perhaps understood, but which helps best our modern understanding — the Divine as knowledge in man, the Divine as power, the Divine as production, enjoyment and mutuality, the Divine as service, obedience and work. These divisions answer to four cosmic principles, the Wisdom that conceives the order and principle of things, the Power that sanctions, upholds and enforces it, the Harmony that creates the arrangement of its parts, the Work that carries out what the rest direct. Next, out of this idea there developed a firm but not yet rigid social order based primarily upon temperament and psychic type[1] with a corresponding ethical discipline and secondarily upon the social and economic[2] function. But the function was determined by its suitability to the type and its helpfulness to the discipline; it was not the primary or sole factor. The first, the symbolic stage of this evolution is predominantly religious and spiritual; the other elements, psychological, ethical, economic, physical are there but subordinated to the spiritual and religious idea. The second stage,which we may call the typal, is predominantly psychological and ethical; all else, even the spiritual and religious, is subordinate to the psychological idea and to the ethical ideal which expresses it. Religion becomes then a mystic sanction for the ethical motive and discipline, Dharma; that becomes its chief social utility, and for the rest it takes a more and more other-worldly turn. The idea of the direct expression of the divine

---

[1] *guṇa*   [2] *karma*

Being or cosmic Principle in man ceases to dominate or to be the leader and in the forefront; it recedes, stands in the background and finally disappears from the practice and in the end even from the theory of life....

...the typal passes naturally into the conventional stage. The conventional stage of human society is born when the external supports, the outward expressions of the spirit or the ideal, become more important than the ideal, the body or even the clothes more important than the person....

The tendency of the conventional age of society is to fix, to arrange firmly, to formalise, to erect a system of rigid grades and hierarchies, to stereotype religion, to bind education and training to a traditional and unchangeable form, to subject thought to infallible authorities, to cast a stamp of finality on what seems to it the finished life of man. The conventional period of society has its golden age when the spirit and thought that inspired its forms are confined but yet living, not yet altogether walled in, not yet stifled to death and petrified by the growing hardness of the structure in which they are cased. That golden age is often very beautiful and attractive to the distant view of posterity by its precise order, symmetry, fine social architecture, the admirable subordination of its parts to a general and noble plan. Thus at one time the modern litterateur, artist or thinker looked back often with admiration and with something like longing to the mediaeval age of Europe; he forgot in its distant appearance of poetry, nobility, spirituality the much folly, ignorance, iniquity, cruelty and oppression of those harsh ages, the suffering and revolt that simmered below these fine surfaces, the misery and squalor that was hidden behind that splendid façade. So too the Hindu orthodox idealist looks back to a perfectly regulated society devoutly obedient to the wise yoke of the Shastra, and that is his golden age, — a nobler one than the European in which the apparent gold was mostly hard burnished copper with a thin gold-leaf covering it, but still of an alloyed metal, not the true Satya Yuga. In these conventional periods of society there is much indeed that is really fine and sound and helpful to human progress, but still they are its copper age and not the true golden; they are the age when the Truth we strive to arrive at is not realised, not accomplished,[3] but the exiguity of it eked out or its full appearance imitated by an artistic form, and what we have of the reality has begun to fossilise and is doomed to be lost in a hard mass of rule and order and convention.

For always the form prevails and the spirit recedes and diminishes. It attempts indeed to return, to revive the form, to modify it, anyhow to survive and even to make the form survive; but the time-tendency is too strong. This is visible in the history of religion; the efforts of the saints and religious reformers become progressively more scattered, brief and superficial in their actual effects, however strong and vital the impulse. We see this recession in the growing darkness and weakness of India in her last millennium; the constant effort of the most powerful spiritual personalities kept the soul of the people alive but failed to resuscitate the ancient free force and truth and vigour or permanently revivify a conventionalised and stagnating society; in a generation or two the iron grip of that conventionalism has always fallen on the new movement and annexed the names of its founders. We see it in Europe in the repeated moral tragedy of ecclesiasticism and Catholic monasticism. Then there arrives a period when the gulf between the convention and the truth becomes intolerable and the men of intellectual power arise, the great "swallowers of formulas", who, rejecting robustly or fiercely or with the calm light of reason symbol and type and convention, strike at the walls of the prison-house and seek by the individual reason, moral sense or emotional desire the Truth that society has lost or buried in its whited sepulchres. It is then that the individualistic age of religion and thought and society is created; the Age of Protestantism has begun, the Age

---

[3] The Indian names of the golden age are *Satya*, the Age of the Truth, and *Kṛta*, the Age when the law of the Truth is accomplished.

of Reason, the Age of Revolt, Progress, Freedom. A partial and external freedom, still betrayed by the conventional age that preceded it into the idea that the Truth can be found in outsides, dreaming vainly that perfection can be determined by machinery, but still a necessary passage to the subjective period of humanity through which man has to circle back towards the recovery of his deeper self and a new upward line or a new revolving cycle of civilisation. *Social and Political Thought, pp. 1-3, 6-10*

The cycles of evolution tend always upward, but they are cycles and do not ascend in a straight line. The process therefore gives the impression of a series of ascents and descents, but what is essential in the gains of the evolution is kept or, even if eclipsed for a time, re-emerges in new forms suitable to the new ages. The creation has descended all the degrees of being from the Supermind to Matter and in each degree it has created a world, reign, plane or order proper to that degree. In the creating of the material world there was a plunge of this descending Consciousness into an apparent Inconscience and an emergence of it out of that Inconscience, degree by degree, until it recovers its highest spiritual and supramental summits and manifests their powers here in Matter. *Letters on Yoga, pp. 1-2*

(b) The Three Steps of Nature — Body, Mind, Spirit

The progressive self-manifestation of Nature in man, termed in modern language his evolution, must necessarily depend upon three successive elements. There is that which is already evolved, that which is persistently in the stage of conscious evolution, and that which is to be evolved and may perhaps be already displayed, if not constantly, then occasionally or with some regularity of recurrence, in primary formations or in others more developed and, it may well be, even in some, however rare, that are near to the highest possible realisation of our present humanity. For the march of Nature is not drilled to a regular and mechanical forward stepping. She reaches constantly beyond herself even at the cost of subsequent deplorable retreats. She has rushes; she has splendid and mighty outbursts; she has immense realisations. She storms sometimes passionately forward hoping to take the kingdom of heaven by violence. And these self-exceedings are the revelation of that in her which is most divine or else most diabolical, but in either case the most puissant to bring her rapidly forward towards her goal.

That which Nature has evolved for us and has firmly founded is the bodily life. She has effected a certain combination and harmony of the two inferior but most fundamentally necessary elements of our action and progress upon earth, — Matter, which, however the too ethereally spiritual may despise it, is our foundation and the first condition of all our energies and realisations, and the Life-Energy which is our means of existence in a material body and the basis there even of our mental and spiritual activities. She has successfully achieved a certain stability of her constant material movement which is at once sufficiently steady and durable and sufficiently pliable and mutable to provide a fit dwelling-place and instrument for the progressively manifesting god in humanity....

If the bodily life is what Nature has firmly evolved for us as her base and first instrument, it is our mental life that she is evolving as her immediate next aim and superior instrument. This in her ordinary exaltations is the lofty preoccupying thought in her; this, except in her periods of exhaustion and recoil into a reposeful and recuperating obscurity, is her constant pursuit wherever she can get free from the trammels of her first vital and physical realisations. For here in man we have a distinction which is of the utmost importance. He has in him not a single mentality, but a double and a triple, the mind material and nervous, the pure intellectual mind which liberates itself from the illusions of the body and the senses and a divine mind above intellect which in its turn liberates itself from the imperfect modes of the logically discriminative and imaginative reason. Mind in man is first emmeshed in the life of the body, where in the plant it is entirely involved and in animals always imprisoned. It accepts this life as not only the first but the whole condition of its activities and serves its needs as if they were the entire aim of existence. But the bodily life in man is a base, not the aim, his first condition and not his last determinant. In the just idea of the ancients man is essentially the thinker, the Manu, the mental being who leads the life and the body,[4] not the animal who is led by them. The true human existence, therefore, only begins when the intellectual mentality emerges out of the material and we begin more and more to live in the mind independent of the nervous and physical obsession and in the measure of that liberty are able to accept rightly and rightly to use the life of the body. For freedom and not a skilful subjection is the true means of mastery. A free, not a compulsory acceptance of the conditions, the enlarged and sublimated conditions of our physical being, is the high human ideal.

The mental life thus evolving in man is not, indeed, a common possession. In actual appearance it would seem as if it were only developed to the fullest in individuals and as if there were great numbers and even the majority in whom it is either a small and ill-organised part of their normal nature or not evolved at all or latent and not easily made active. Certainly, the mental life is not a finished evolution of Nature; it is not yet firmly founded in the human animal. The sign is that the fine and full equilibrium of vitality and matter, the sane, robust, long-lived human body is ordinarily found only in races or classes of men who reject the effort of thought, its disturbances, its tensions, or think only with the material mind. Civilised man has yet to establish an equilibrium between the fully active mind and the body; he does not yet normally possess it. Indeed, the increasing effort towards a more intense mental life seems to create,

---

[4] *manomayaḥ prāṇaśarīranetā.* Mundaka Upanishad, II. 2. 7.

frequently, an increasing disequilibrium of the human elements, so that it is possible for eminent scientists to describe genius as a form of insanity, a result of degeneration, a pathological morbidity of Nature. The phenomena which are used to justify this exaggeration, when taken not separately, but in connection with all other relevant data, point to a different truth. Genius is one attempt of the universal Energy to so quicken and intensify our intellectual powers that they shall be prepared for those more puissant, direct and rapid faculties which constitute the play of the supra-intellectual or divine mind. It is not, then, a freak, an inexplicable phenomenon, but a perfectly natural next step in the right line of her evolution. She has harmonised the bodily life with the material mind, she is harmonising it with the play of the intellectual mentality; for that, although it tends to a depression of the full animal and vital vigour, does not or need not produce active disturbances. And she is shooting yet beyond in the attempt to reach a still higher level. Nor are the disturbances created by her process as great as is often represented. Some of them are the crude beginnings of new manifestations; others are an easily corrected movement of disintegration, often fruitful of fresh activities and always a small price to pay for the far-reaching results that she has in view.

We may perhaps, if we consider all the circumstances, come to this conclusion that mental life, far from being a recent appearance in man, is the swift repetition in him of a previous achievement from which the Energy in the race had undergone one of her deplorable recoils. The savage is perhaps not so much the first forefather of civilised man as the degenerate descendant of a previous civilisation. For if the actuality of intellectual achievement is unevenly distributed, the capacity is spread everywhere.... Even in the mass men seem to need, in favourable circumstances, only a few generations to cover ground that ought apparently to be measured in the terms of millenniums. Either, then, man by his privilege as a mental being is exempt from the full burden of the tardy laws of evolution or else he already represents and with helpful conditions and in the right stimulating atmosphere can always display a high level of material capacity for the activities of the intellectual life. It is not mental incapacity, but the long rejection or seclusion from opportunity and withdrawal of the awakening impulse that creates the savage. Barbarism is an intermediate sleep, not an original darkness....

Mind is not the last term of evolution, not an ultimate aim, but, like body, an instrument. It is even so termed in the language of Yoga, the inner instrument.[5] And Indian tradition asserts that this which is to be manifested is not a new term in human experience, but has been developed before and has even governed humanity in certain periods of its development. In any case, in order to be known it must at one time have been partly developed. And if since then Nature has sunk back from her achievement, the reason must always be found in some unrealised harmony, some insufficiency of the intellectual and material basis to which she has now returned, some over-specialisation of the higher to the detriment of the lower existence.

But what then constitutes this higher or highest existence to which our evolution is tending? In order to answer the question we have to deal with a class of supreme experiences, a class of unusual conceptions which it is difficult to represent accurately in any other language than the ancient Sanskrit tongue in which alone they have been to some extent systematised. The only approximate terms in the English language have other associations and their use may lead to many and even serious inaccuracies. The terminology of Yoga recognises besides the status of our physical and vital being, termed the gross body and doubly composed of the food-sheath and the vital vehicle, besides the status of our mental being, termed the subtle body and singly composed of the mind-sheath or mental vehicle,[6] a third, supreme and divine status of supra-mental being, termed

[5] *antaḥkaraṇa*   [6] *manaḥ-koṣa*

the causal body and composed of a fourth and a fifth vehicle[7] which are described as those of knowledge and bliss. But this knowledge is not a systematised result of mental questionings and reasonings, not a temporary arrangement of conclusions and opinions in the terms of the highest probability, but rather a pure self-existent and self-luminous Truth. And this bliss is not a supreme pleasure of the heart and sensations with the experience of pain and sorrow as its background, but a delight also self-existent and independent of objects and particular experiences, a self-delight which is the very nature, the very stuff, as it were, of a transcendent and infinite existence.

Do such psychological conceptions correspond to anything real and possible? All Yoga asserts them as its ultimate experience and supreme aim. They form the governing principles of our highest possible state of consciousness, our widest possible range of existence. There is, we say, a harmony of supreme faculties, corresponding roughly to the psychological faculties of revelation, inspiration and intuition, yet acting not in the intuitive reason or the divine mind, but on a still higher plane, which see Truth directly face to face, or rather live in the truth of things both universal and transcendent and are its formulation and luminous activity. And these faculties are the light of a conscious existence superseding the egoistic and itself both cosmic and transcendent, the nature of which is Bliss. These are obviously divine and, as man is at present apparently constituted, superhuman states of consciousness and activity. A trinity of transcendent existence, self-awareness and self-delight[8] is, indeed, the metaphysical description of the supreme Atman, the self-formulation, to our awakened knowledge, of the Unknowable whether conceived as a pure Impersonality or as a cosmic Personality manifesting the universe. But in Yoga they are regarded also in their psychological aspects as states of subjective existence to which our waking consciousness is now alien,

---

[7] *vijñānakoṣa* and *ānandakoṣa*　　[8] Sachchidananda

but which dwell in us in a superconscious plane and to which, therefore, we may always ascend....

We perceive then, these three steps in Nature, a bodily life which is the basis of our existence here in the material world, a mental life into which we emerge and by which we raise the bodily to higher uses and enlarge it into a greater completeness, and a divine existence which is at once the goal of the other two and returns upon them to liberate them into their highest possibilities. *The Synthesis of Yoga, pp. 5-14*

The Self of man is a thing hidden and occult; it is not his body, it is not his life, it is not, — even though he is in the scale of evolution the mental being, the Manu, — his mind. Therefore neither the fullness of his physical, nor of his vital, nor of his mental nature can be either the last term or the true standard of his self-realisation; they are means of manifestation, subordinate indications, foundations of his self-finding, values, practical currency of his self, what you will, but not the thing itself which he secretly is and is obscurely groping or trying overtly and self-consciously to become. Man has not possessed as a race this truth about himself, does not now possess it except in the vision and self-experience of the few in whose footsteps the race is unable to follow, though it may adore them as Avatars, seers, saints or prophets. For the Oversoul who is the master of our evolution, has his own large steps of Time, his own great eras, tracts of slow and courses of rapid expansion, which the strong, semi-divine individual may overleap, but not the still half-animal race. The course of evolution proceeding from the vegetable to the animal, from the animal to the man, starts in the latter from the subhuman; he has to take up into him the animal and even the mineral and vegetable: they constitute his physical nature, they dominate his vitality, they have their hold upon his mentality. His proneness to many kinds of inertia, his readiness to vegetate, his attachment to the soil and clinging to his roots, to safe anchorages of all kinds, and on the other

hand his nomadic and predatory impulses, his blind servility
to custom and the rule of the pack, his mob-movements and
openness to subconscious suggestions from the group-soul, his
subjection to the yoke of rage and fear, his need of punishment
and reliance on punishment, his inability to think and act for
himself, his incapacity for true freedom, his distrust of novelty,
his slowness to seize intelligently and assimilate, his downward
propensity and earthward gaze, his vital and physical subjection
to his heredity, all these and more are his heritage from the
subhuman origins of his life and body and physical mind. It is
because of this heritage that he finds self-exceeding the most
difficult of lessons and the most painful of endeavours. Yet it
is by exceeding of the lower self that Nature accomplishes the
great strides of her evolutionary process. To learn by what he
has been, but also to know and increase to what he can be, is
the task that is set for the mental being.

Social and Political Thought, pp. 66-67

(c) The Three Stages of Social Evolution — Infrarational, Rational, Suprarational

...there are necessarily three stages of the social evolution or,
generally, of the human evolution in both individual and society.
Our evolution starts with an infrarational stage in which men
have not yet learned to refer their life and action in its principles
and its forms to the judgment of the clarified intelligence; for they
still act principally out of their instincts, impulses, spontaneous
ideas, vital intuitions or else obey a customary response to desire,
need and circumstance, — it is these things that are canalised or
crystallised in their social institutions. Man proceeds by various
stages out of these beginnings towards a rational age in which
his intelligent will more or less developed becomes the judge,
arbiter and presiding motive of his thought, feeling and action,
the moulder, destroyer and re-creator of his leading ideas, aims

and intuitions. Finally, if our analysis and forecast are correct, the human evolution must move through a subjective towards a suprarational or spiritual age in which he will develop progressively a greater spiritual, supra-intellectual and intuitive, perhaps in the end a more than intuitive, a gnostic consciousness. He will be able to perceive a higher divine end, a divine sanction, a divine light of guidance for all he seeks to be, think, feel and do, and able, too, more and more to obey and live in this larger light and power. That will not be done by any rule of infrarational religious impulse and ecstasy, such as characterised or rather darkly illumined the obscure confusion and brute violence of the Middle Ages, but by a higher spiritual living for which the clarities of the reason are a necessary preparation and into which they too will be taken up, transformed, brought to their invisible source.

These stages or periods are much more inevitable in the psychological evolution of mankind than the Stone and other Ages marked out by Science in his instrumental culture, for they depend not on outward means or accidents, but on the very nature of his being. But we must not suppose that they are naturally exclusive and absolute in their nature, or complete in their tendency or fulfilment when they come, or rigidly marked off from each other in their action or their time. For they not only arise out of each other, but may be partially developed in each other and they may come to co-exist in different parts of the earth at the same time. But, especially, since man as a whole is always a complex being, even man savage or degenerate, he cannot be any of these things exclusively or absolutely, — so long as he has not exceeded himself, has not developed into the superman, has not, that is to say, spiritualised and divinised his whole being. At his animal worst he is still some kind of thinking or reflecting animal: even the infrarational man cannot be utterly infrarational, but must have or tend to have some kind of play more or less evolved or involved of the reason and a more or less crude suprarational element, a more or less disguised working of the spirit. At his lucid mental best, he is still not a pure mental being, a pure intelligence; even the most perfect intellectual is not and cannot be wholly or merely rational, — there are vital urgings that he cannot exclude, visits or touches of a light from above that are not less suprarational because he does not recognise their source. No god, but at his highest a human being touched with a ray of the divine influence, man's very spirituality, however dominant, must have, while he is still this imperfectly evolved human, its rational and infrarational tendencies and elements. And as with the psychological life of individuals, so must it be with the ages of his communal existence; these may be marked off from each other by the predominant play of one element, its force may overpower the others or take them into itself or make some compromise, but an exclusive play seems to be neither intended nor possible.

Thus an infrarational period of human and social development need not be without its elements, its strong elements of reason and of spirituality. Even the savage, whether he be primitive or degenerate man, has some coherent idea of this world and the beyond, a theory of life and a religion. To us with our more advanced rationality his theory of life may seem incoherent, because we have lost its point of view and its principle of mental associations. But it is still an act of reason, and within its limits he is capable of a sufficient play of thought both ideative and practical, as well as a clear ethical idea and motive, some aesthetic notions and an understood order of society poor and barbarous to our view, but well enough contrived and put together to serve the simplicity of its objects. Or again we may not realise the element of reason in a primitive theory of life or of spirituality in a barbaric religion, because it appears to us to be made up of symbols and forms to which a superstitious value is attached by these undeveloped minds. But this is because the reason at this stage has an imperfect and limited action and the element of spirituality is crude or undeveloped and not yet self-conscious; in order to hold firmly their workings and make them real and concrete to his mind and spirit primitive man has to give them shape in symbols and forms to which he clings with a barbaric awe and reverence, because they alone can embody for him his method of self-guidance in life. For the dominant thing in him is his infrarational life of instinct, vital intuition and impulse, mechanical custom and tradition, and it is that to which the rest of him has to give some kind of primary order and first glimmerings of light. The unrefined reason and unenlightened spirit in him cannot work for their own ends; they are bond-slaves of his infrarational nature.

At a higher stage of development or of a return towards a fuller evolution, — for the actual savage in humanity is perhaps not the original primitive man, but a relapse and reversion towards primitiveness, — the infrarational stage of society may arrive at a very lofty order of civilisation. It may have great intuitions of the meaning or general intention of life, admirable ideas of the arrangement of life, a harmonious, well-adapted, durable and serviceable social system, an imposing religion which will not be without its profundities, but in which symbol and ceremonial will form the largest portion and for the mass of man will be almost the whole of religion. In this stage pure reason and pure spirituality will not govern the society or move large bodies of men, but will be represented, if at all, by individuals at first few, but growing in number as these two powers increase in their purity and vigour and attract more and more votaries.

This may well lead to an age, if the development of reason is strongest, of great individual thinkers who seize on some idea of life and its origins and laws and erect that into a philosophy, of critical minds standing isolated above the mass who judge life, not yet with a luminous largeness, a minute flexibility of understanding or a clear and comprehensive profundity, but still with power of intelligence, insight, acuteness, perhaps even a preeminent social thinker here and there who, taking advantage of some crisis or disturbance, is able to get the society to modify or reconstruct itself on the basis of some clearly rational and intelligent principle. Such an age seems to be represented by the traditions of the beginnings of Greek civilisation, or rather the beginnings of its mobile and progressive period. Or if spirituality predominates, there will be great mystics capable of delving into the profound and still occult psychological possibilities of our nature who will divine and realise the truth of the self and spirit in man and, even though they keep these things secret and imparted only to a small number of initiates, may yet succeed in deepening with them the crude forms of the popular life. Even such a development is obscurely indicated in the old traditions of the mysteries. In prehistoric India we see it take a peculiar and unique turn which determined the whole future trend of the society and made Indian civilisation a thing apart and of its own kind in the history of the human race. But these things are only a first beginning of light in the midst of a humanity which is still infrarational as well as infra-spiritual and, even when it undergoes the influence of these precursors, responds only obscurely to their inspirations and without any clearly intelligent or awakened spiritual reception of what they impart or impose. It still turns everything into infrarational form and disfiguring tradition and lives spiritually by ill-understood ceremonial and disguising symbol. It feels obscurely the higher things, tries to live them in its own stumbling way, but it does not yet understand; it cannot lay hold either on the intellectual form or the spiritual heart of their significance.

As reason and spirituality develop, they begin to become a larger and more diffused force, less intense perhaps, but wider and more effective on the mass. The mystics become the sowers of the seed of an immense spiritual development in which whole classes of society and even men from all classes seek the light, as happened in India in the age of the Upanishads. The solitary individual thinkers are replaced by a great number of writers, poets, thinkers, rhetoricians, sophists, scientific inquirers, who pour out a profuse flood of acute speculation and inquiry stimulating the thought-habit and creating even in the mass a generalised activity of the intelligence, — as happened in Greece in the age of the sophists. The spiritual development, arising uncurbed by reason in an infrarational society, has often a tendency to outrun at first the rational and intellectual movement. For the greatest illuminating force of the infrarational man, as he develops, is an inferior intuition, an instinctively intuitional sight arising out of the force of life in him, and the transition from this to an intensity of inner life and the growth of a deeper spiritual intuition which outleaps the intellect and seems to dispense with it, is an easy passage in the individual man. But for humanity at large this movement cannot last; the mind and intellect must develop to their fullness so that the spirituality of the race may rise securely upward upon a broad basis of the developed lower nature in man, the intelligent mental being. Therefore we see that the reason in its growth either does away with the distinct spiritual tendency for a time, as in ancient Greece, or accepts it but spins out around its first data and activities a vast web of the workings of the intelligence, so that, as in India, the early mystic seer is replaced by the philosopher-mystic, the religious thinker and even the philosopher pure and simple.

For a time the new growth and impulse may seem to take possession of a whole community as in Athens or in old Aryan India. But these early dawns cannot endure in their purity, so long as the race is not ready. There is a crystallisation, a lessening of the first impetus, a new growth of infrarational forms in which the thought or the spirituality is overgrown with inferior accretions or it is imbedded in the form and may even die in it, while the tradition of the living knowledge, the loftier life and activity remains the property of the higher classes or a highest class. The multitude remains infrarational in its habit of mind, though perhaps it may still keep in capacity an enlivened intelligence or a profound or subtle spiritual receptiveness as its gain from the past. So long as the hour of the rational age has not arrived, the irrational period of society cannot be left behind; and that arrival can only be when not a class or a few but the multitude has learned to think, to exercise its intelligence actively — it matters not at first however imperfectly — upon their life, their needs, their rights, their duties, their aspirations as human beings. Until then we have as the highest possible development a mixed society, infrarational in the mass, but saved for civilisation by a higher class whose business it is to seek after the reason and the spirit, to keep the gains of mankind in these fields, to add to them, to enlighten and raise with them as much as possible the life of the whole.

At this point we see that Nature in her human mass tends to move forward slowly on her various lines of active mind and life towards a greater application of reason and spirituality which shall at last bring near the possibility of a rational and, eventually, a spiritual age of mankind.

Social and Political Thought, pp. 173-78

Human society has in its growth to pass through three stages of evolution before it can arrive at the completeness of its possibilities. The first is a condition in which the forms and activities of the communal existence are those of the spontaneous play of the powers and principles of its life. All its growth, all its formations, customs, institutions are then a natural organic development, — the motive and constructive power coming mostly from the subconscient principle of the life within it, — expressing, but without deliberate intention, the communal psychology, temperament, vital and physical need, and persisting or altering partly under the pressure of an internal impulse, partly under that of the environment acting on the communal mind and temper. In this stage the people is not yet intelligently self-conscious in the way of the reason, is not yet a thinking collective being, and it does not try to govern its whole communal existence by the reasoning will, but lives according to its vital intuitions or their first mental renderings....

A second stage of the society is that in which the communal mind becomes more and more intellectually self-conscious, first in its more cultured minds, then more generally, first broadly, then more and more minutely and in all the parts of its life. It learns to review and deal with its own life, communal ideas, needs, institutions in the light of the developed intelligence and finally by the power of the critical and constructive reason. This is a stage which is full of great possibilities but attended too by serious characteristic dangers. Its first advantages are those which go always with the increase of a clear and under-standing and finally an exact and scientific knowledge and the culminating stage is the strict and armoured efficiency which the critical and constructive, the scientific reason used to the fullest degree offers as its reward and consequence. Another and greater outcome of this stage of social evolution is the emergence of high and luminous ideals which promise to raise man beyond the limits of the vital being, beyond his first social, economic and political needs and desires and out of their customary moulds and inspire an impulse of bold experiment with the communal life which opens a field of possibility for the realisation of a more and more ideal society. This application of the scientific mind to life with the strict, well-finished, armoured efficiency which is its normal highest result, this pursuit of great consciously proposed social and political ideals and the progress which is the index of the ground covered in the endeavour, have been, with whatever limits and drawbacks, the distinguishing advantages of the political and social effort of Europe.

On the other hand the tendency of the reason when it pre-tends to deal with the materials of life as its absolute governor, is to look too far away from the reality of the society as a living growth and to treat it as a mechanism which can be manipu-lated at will and constructed like so much dead wood or iron according to the arbitrary dictates of the intelligence. The sophis-ticating, labouring, constructing, efficient, mechanising reason loses hold of the simple principles of a people's vitality; it cuts it away from the secret roots of its life. The result is an ex-aggerated dependence on system and institution, on legislation and administration and the deadly tendency to develop, in place of a living people, a mechanical State. An instrument of the communal life tries to take the place of the life itself and there is created a powerful but mechanical and artificial organisation; but, as the price of this exterior gain, there is lost the truth of life of an organically self-developing communal soul in the body of a free and living people. It is this error of the scientific reason stifling the work of the vital and the spiritual intuition under the dead weight of its mechanical method which is the weakness of Europe and has deceived her aspiration and prevented her from arriving at the true realisation of her own higher ideals.

It is only by reaching a third stage of the evolution of the collective social as of the individual human being that the ideals first seized and cherished by the thought of man can discover their own real source and character and their true means and conditions of effectuation or the perfect society be anything more than a vision on a shining cloud constantly run after in a circle and constantly deceiving the hope and escaping the embrace. That will be when man in the collectivity begins to live more deeply and to govern his collective life neither primarily by the needs, instincts, intuitions welling up out of the vital self, nor secondarily by the constructions of the reasoning mind, but first, foremost and always by the power of unity, sympathy, sponta-neous liberty, supple and living order of his discovered greater self and spirit in which the individual and the communal exis-tence have their law of freedom, perfection and oneness. That is a rule that has not yet anywhere found its right conditions for even beginning its effort, for it can only come when man's attempt to reach and abide by the law of the spiritual existence is no longer an exceptional aim for individuals or else degraded in its more general aspiration to the form of a popular religion, but is recognised and followed out as the imperative need of his being and its true and right attainment the necessity of the next step in the evolution of the race.

The Foundations of Indian Culture, pp. 336-38

(d) Barbarism, Civilisation, Culture

The time is passing away, permanently — let us hope — for this cycle of civilisation, when the entire identification of the self with the body and the physical life was possible for the general consciousness of the race. That is the primary characteristic of complete barbarism. To take the body and the physical life as the one thing important, to judge manhood by the physical strength, development and prowess, to be at the mercy of the instincts which rise out of the physical inconscient, to despise knowledge as a weakness and inferiority or look on it as a peculiarity and no necessary part of the conception of manhood, this is the mentality of the barbarian. It tends to reappear in the human being in the atavistic period of boyhood, — when, be it noted, the development of the body is of the greatest importance, — but to the adult man in civilised humanity it is ceasing to be possible. For, in the first place, by the stress of modern life even the vital attitude of the race is changing. Man is ceasing to be so much of a physical and becoming much more of a vital and economic animal. Not that he excludes or is intended to exclude the body and its development or the right maintenance of and respect for the animal being and its excellences from his idea of life; the excellence of the body, its health, its soundness, its vigour and harmonious development are necessary to a perfect manhood and are occupying attention in a better and more intelligent way than before. But the first rank in importance can no longer be given to the body, much less that entire predominance assigned to it in the mentality of the barbarian.

Social and Political Thought, pp. 67-68

It is true that the first tendencies of Science have been materialistic and its indubitable triumphs have been confined to the knowledge of the physical universe and the body and the physical life. But this materialism is a very different thing from the old identification of the self with the body. Whatever its apparent tendencies, it has been really an assertion of man the mental being and of the supremacy of intelligence. Science in its very nature is knowledge, is intellectuality, and its whole work has been that of the Mind turning its gaze upon its vital and physical frame and environment to know and conquer and dominate Life and Matter. The scientist is Man the thinker mastering the forces of material Nature by knowing them. Life and Matter are after all our standing-ground, our lower basis and to know their processes and their own proper possibilities and the opportunities they give to the human being is part of the knowledge necessary for transcending them. Life and the body have to be exceeded, but they have also to be utilised and perfected. Neither the laws nor the possibilities of physical Nature can be entirely known unless we know also the laws and possibilities of supraphysical Nature; therefore the development of new and the recovery of old mental and psychic sciences have to follow upon the perfection of our physical knowledge, and that new era is already beginning to open upon us. But the perfection of the physical sciences was a prior necessity and had to be the first field for the training of the mind of man in his new endeavour to know Nature and possess his world.

Social and Political Thought, pp. 70-71

...if Science has thus prepared us for an age of wider and deeper culture and if in spite of and even partly by its materialism it has rendered impossible the return of the true materialism, that of the barbarian mentality, it has encouraged more or less indirectly both by its attitude to life and its discoveries another kind of barbarism, — for it can be called by no other name, — that of the industrial, the commercial, the economic age which is now progressing to its culmination and its close. This economic barbarism is essentially that of the vital man who mistakes the vital being for the self and accepts its satisfaction as the first aim of life. The characteristic of Life is desire and the instinct of possession. Just as the physical barbarian makes the excellence of the body and the development of physical force, health and prowess his standard and aim, so the vitalistic or economic barbarian makes the satisfaction of wants and desires and the accumulation of possessions his standard and aim. His ideal man is not the cultured or noble or thoughtful or moral or religious, but the successful man. To arrive, to succeed, to produce, to accumulate, to possess is his existence. The accumulation of wealth and more wealth, the adding of possessions to possessions, opulence, show, pleasure, a cumbrous inartistic luxury, a plethora of conveniences, life devoid of beauty and nobility, religion vulgarised or coldly formalised, politics and government turned into a trade and profession, enjoyment itself made a business, this is commercialism. To the natural unredeemed economic man beauty is a thing otiose or a nuisance, art and poetry a frivolity or an ostentation and a means of advertisement. His idea of civilisation is comfort, his idea of morals social respectability, his idea of politics the encouragement of industry, the opening of markets, exploitation and trade following the flag, his idea of religion at best a pietistic formalism or the satisfaction of certain vitalistic emotions. He values education for its utility in fitting a man for success in a competitive or, it may be, a socialised industrial existence, science for the useful inventions and knowledge, the comforts, conveniences, machinery of production with which it arms him, its power for organisation, regulation, stimulus to production. The opulent plutocrat and the successful mammoth capitalist and organiser of industry are the supermen of the commercial age and the true, if often occult rulers of its society.

The essential barbarism of all this is its pursuit of vital success, satisfaction, productiveness, accumulation, possession, enjoyment, comfort, convenience for their own sake. The vital part of the being is an element in the integral human existence as much as the physical part; it has its place but must not exceed its place. A full and well-appointed life is desirable for man living in society, but on condition that it is also a true and beautiful life. Neither the life nor the body exist for their own sake, but as vehicle and instrument of a good higher than their own. They must be subordinated to the superior needs of the mental being, chastened and purified by a greater law of truth, good and beauty before they can take their proper place in the integrality of human perfection. Therefore in a commercial age with its ideal, vulgar and barbarous, of success, vitalistic satisfaction, productiveness and possession the soul of man may linger a while for certain gains and experiences, but cannot permanently rest. If it persisted too long, Life would become clogged and perish of its own plethora or burst in its straining to a gross expansion. Like the too massive Titan it will collapse by its own mass, *mole ruet sua.*   *Social and Political Thought, pp. 72-73*

...barbarism is the state of society in which man is almost entirely preoccupied with his life and body, his economic and physical existence, — at first with their sufficient maintenance, not as yet their greater or richer well-being, — and has few means and little inclination to develop his mentality, while civilisation is the more evolved state of society in which to a sufficient social and economic organisation is added the activity of the mental life in most if not all of its parts; for sometimes some of these parts are left aside or discouraged or temporarily atrophied by their inactivity, yet the society may be very obviously civilised and even highly civilised. This conception will bring in all the civilisations historic and prehistoric and put aside all the barbarism, whether of Africa or Europe or Asia, Hun or Goth or Vandal or Turcoman. It is obvious that in a state of barbarism the rude beginnings of civilisation may exist; it is obvious too that in a civilised society a great mass of barbarism or numerous relics of it may exist. In that sense all societies are semi-civilised. How much of our present-day civilisation will be looked back upon with wonder and disgust by a more developed humanity as the superstitions and atrocities of an imperfectly civilised era! But the main point is this that in any society which we can call civilised the mentality of man must be active, the mental pursuits developed and the regulation and improvement of his life by the mental being a clearly self-conscious concept in his better mind.

But in a civilised society there is still the distinction between the partially, crudely, conventionally civilised and the cultured. It would seem therefore that the mere participation in the ordinary benefits of civilisation is not enough to raise a man into the mental life proper; a farther development, a higher elevation is needed. The last generation drew emphatically the distinction between the cultured man and the Philistine and got a fairly clear idea of what was meant by it. Roughly, the Philistine was for them the man who lives outwardly the civilised life, possesses all its paraphernalia, has and mouths the current stock of opinions, prejudices, conventions, sentiments, but is impervious to ideas, exercises no free intelligence, is innocent of beauty and art, vulgarises everything that he touches, religion, ethics, literature, life. The Philistine is in fact the modern civilised barbarian; he is often the half-civilised physical and vital barbarian by his unintelligent attachment to the life of the body, the life of the vital needs and impulses and the ideal of the merely domestic and economic human animal; but essentially and commonly he is the mental barbarian, the average sensational man. That is to say, his mental life is that of the lower substratum of the mind, the life of the senses, the life of the sensations, the life of the emotions, the life of practical conduct — the first status of the mental being. In all these he may be very active, very vigorous, but he does not govern them by a higher light or seek to uplift them to a freer and nobler eminence; rather he pulls the higher faculties down to the level of his senses, his sensations, his unenlightened and unchastened emotions, his gross utilitarian practicality. His aesthetic side is little developed; either he cares nothing for beauty or has the crudest aesthetic tastes which help to lower and vulgarise the general standard of aesthetic creation and the aesthetic sense. He is often strong about morals, far more particular usually about moral conduct than the man of culture, but his moral being is as crude and undeveloped as the rest of him; it is conventional, unchastened, unintelligent, a mass of likes and dislikes, prejudices and current opinions, attachment to social conventions and respectabilities and an obscure dislike — rooted in the mind of sensations and not in the intelligence — of any open defiance or departure from the generally accepted standard of conduct. His ethical bent is a habit of the sense-mind; it is the morality of the average sensational man. He has a reason and the appearance of an intelligent will, but they are not his own, they are part of the group-mind, received from his environment; or so far as they are his own, merely a practical, sensational, emotional reason and will, a mechanical repetition of habitual notions and rules of conduct, not a play of real thought and intelligent determination. His use of them no more makes him a developed mental being than the daily movement to and from his place of business makes the average Londoner a developed physical being or his quotidian contributions to the economic life of the country make the bank-clerk a developed economic man. He is not mentally active, but mentally reactive, — a very different matter.

The Philistine is not dead, — quite the contrary, he abounds, — but he no longer reigns. The sons of Culture have not exactly conquered, but they have got rid of the old Goliath and replaced him by a new giant. This is the sensational man who has got awakened to the necessity at least of some intelligent use of the higher faculties and is trying to be mentally active. He has been whipped and censured and educated into that activity and he lives besides in a maelstrom of new information, new intellectual fashions, new ideas and new movements to which he can no longer be obstinately impervious. He is open to new ideas, he can catch at them and hurl them about in a rather confused fashion; he can understand or misunderstand ideals, organise to get them carried out and even, it would appear, fight and die for them. He knows he has to think about ethical problems, social problems, problems of science and religion, to welcome new political developments, to look with as understanding an eye as he can attain to at all the new movements of thought and inquiry and action that chase each other across the modern field or clash upon it. He is a reader of poetry as well as a devourer of fiction and periodical literature, — you will find in him perhaps a student of Tagore or an admirer of Whitman; he has perhaps no very clear ideas about beauty and aesthetics, but he has heard that Art is a not altogether unimportant part of life. The shadow of this new colossus is everywhere. He is the great reading public; the newspapers and weekly and monthly reviews are his; fiction and poetry and art are his mental caterers, the theatre and the cinema and the radio exist for him: Science hastens to bring her knowledge and discoveries to his doors and equip his life with endless machinery; politics are shaped in his image. It is he who opposed and then brought about the enfranchisement of women, who has been evolving syndicalism, anarchism, the war of classes, the uprising of labour, waging what we are told are wars of ideas, or of cultures, — a ferocious type of conflict made in the very image of this new barbarism, — or bringing about in a few days Russian revolutions which the century-long efforts and sufferings of the intelligentsia failed to achieve. It is his coming which has been the precipitative agent for the reshaping of the modern world. If a Lenin, a Mussolini, a Hitler have achieved their rapid and almost stupefying success, it was because this driving force, this responsive quick-acting mass was there to carry them to victory — a force lacking to their less fortunate predecessors.

The first results of this momentous change have been inspiriting to our desire of movement, but a little disconcerting to the thinker and to the lover of a high and fine culture; for if it has to some extent democratised culture or the semblance of culture, it does not seem at first sight to have elevated or strengthened it by this large accession of the half-redeemed from below. Nor does the world seem to be guided any more directly by the reason and intelligent will of her best minds than before. Commercialism is still the heart of modern civilisation; a sensational activism is still its driving force. Modern education has not in the mass redeemed the sensational man; it has only made necessary to him things to which he was not formerly accustomed, mental activity and occupations, intellectual and even aesthetic sensations, emotions of idealism. He still lives in the vital substratum, but he wants it stimulated from above. He requires an army of writers to keep him mentally occupied and provide some sort of intellectual pabulum for him; he has a thirst for general information of all kinds which he does not care or has not time to co-ordinate or assimilate, for popularised scientific knowledge, for such new ideas as he can catch, provided they are put before him with force or brilliance, for mental sensations and excitation of many kinds, for ideals which he likes to think of as actuating his conduct and which do give it sometimes a certain colour. It is still the activism and sensationalism of the crude mental being, but much more open and free. And the cultured, the intelligentsia find that they can get a hearing from him such as they never had from the pure Philistine, provided they can first stimulate or amuse him; their ideas have now a chance of getting executed such as they never had before. The result has been to cheapen thought and art and literature, to make talent and even genius run in the grooves of popular success, to put the writer and thinker and scientist very much in a position like that of the cultured Greek slave in a Roman household where he has to work for, please, amuse and instruct his master while keeping a careful eye on his tastes and preferences and repeating trickily the manner and the points that have caught his fancy. The higher mental life, in a word, has been democratised, sensationalised, activised with both good and bad results. Through it all the eye of faith can see perhaps that a yet crude but an enormous change has begun. Thought and Knowledge, if not yet Beauty, can get a hearing and even produce rapidly some large, vague, yet in the end effective will for their results; the mass of culture and of men who think and strive seriously to appreciate and to know has enormously increased behind all this surface veil of sensationalism, and even the sensational man has begun to undergo a process of transformation. Especially, new methods of education, new principles of society are beginning to come into the range of practical possibility which will create perhaps one day that as yet unknown phenomenon, a race of men — not only a class — who have to some extent found and developed their mental selves, a cultured humanity.

Social and Political Thought, pp. 78-83

The pursuit of the mental life for its own sake is what we ordinarily mean by culture; but the word is still a little equivocal and capable of a wider or a narrower sense according to our ideas and predilections. For our mental existence is a very complex matter and is made up of many elements. First, we have its lower and fundamental stratum, which is in the scale of evolution nearest to the vital. And we have in that stratum two sides, the mental life of the senses, sensations and emotions in which the subjective purpose of Nature predominates although with the objective as its occasion, and the active or dynamic life of the mental being concerned with the organs of action and the field of conduct in which her objective purpose predominates although with the subjective as its occasion. We have next in the scale, more sublimated, on one side the moral being and its ethical life, on the other the aesthetic; each of them attempts to possess and dominate the fundamental mind stratum and turn its experiences and activities to its own benefit, one for the culture and worship of Right, the other for the culture and worship of Beauty. And we have, above all these, taking advantage of them, helping, forming, trying often to govern them entirely, the intellectual being. Man's highest accomplished range is the life of the reason or ordered and harmonised intelligence with its dynamic power of intelligent will, the *buddhi*, which is or should be the driver of man's chariot.

But the intelligence of man is not composed entirely and exclusively of the rational intellect and the rational will; there enters into it a deeper, more intuitive, more splendid and powerful, but much less clear, much less developed and as yet hardly at all self-possessing light and force for which we have not even a name. But, at any rate, its character is to drive at a kind of illumination, — not the dry light of the reason, nor the moist and suffused light of the heart, but a lightning and a solar splendour. It may indeed subordinate itself and merely help the reason and heart with its flashes; but there is another urge in it, its natural urge, which exceeds the reason. It tries to illuminate the intellectual being, to illuminate the ethical and aesthetic, to illuminate the emotional and the active, to illuminate even the senses and the sensations. It offers in words of revelation, it unveils as if by lightning flashes, it shows in a sort of mystic or psychic glamour or brings out into a settled but for mental man almost a supernatural light a Truth greater and truer than the knowledge given by Reason and Science, a Right larger and more divine than the moralist's scheme of virtues, a Beauty more profound, universal and entrancing than the sensuous or imaginative beauty worshipped by the artist, a joy and divine sensibility which leaves the ordinary emotions poor and pallid, a Sense beyond the senses and sensations, the possibility of a diviner Life and action which man's ordinary conduct of life hides away from his impulses and from his vision. Very various, very fragmentary, often very confused and misleading are its effects upon all the lower members from the reason downward, but this in the end is what it is driving at in the midst of a hundred deformations. It is caught and killed or at least diminished and stifled in formal creeds and pious observances; it is unmercifully traded in and turned into poor and base coin by the vulgarity of conventional religions; but it is still the light of which the religious spirit and the spirituality of man is in pursuit and some pale glow of it lingers even in their worst degradations.

Social and Political Thought, pp. 76-77

The idea of culture begins to define itself for us a little more clearly, or at least it has put away from it in a clear contrast its natural opposites. The unmental, the purely physical life is very obviously its opposite, it is barbarism; the unintellectualised vital, the crude economic or the grossly domestic life which looks only to money-getting, the procreation of a family and its maintenance, are equally its opposites; they are another and even uglier barbarism. We agree to regard the individual who is dominated by them and has no thought of higher things as an uncultured and undeveloped human being, a prolongation of the savage, essentially a barbarian even if he lives in a civilised nation and in a society which has arrived at the general idea and at some ordered practice of culture and refinement. The societies or nations which bear this stamp we agree to call barbarous or semi-barbarous. Even when a nation or an age has developed within itself knowledge and science and arts, but still in its general outlook, its habits of life and thought is content to be governed not by knowledge and truth and beauty and high ideals of living, but by the gross vital, commercial, economic view of existence, we say that that nation or age may be civilised in a sense, but for all its abundant or even redundant appliances and apparatus of civilisation it is not the realisation or the promise of a cultured humanity. Therefore upon even the European civilisation of the nineteenth century with all its triumphant and teeming production, its great developments of science, its achievement in the works of the intellect we pass a certain condemnation, because it has turned all these things to commercialism and to gross uses of vitalistic success. We say of it that this was not the perfection to which humanity ought to aspire and that this trend travels away from and not towards the higher curve of human evolution. It must be our definite verdict upon it that it was inferior as an age of culture to ancient Athens, to Italy of the Renascence, to ancient or classical India. For great as might be the deficiencies of social organisation in those eras and though their range of scientific knowledge and material achievement was immensely inferior, yet they were more advanced in the art of life, knew better its object and aimed more powerfully at some clear ideal of human perfection.

In the range of the mind's life itself, to live in its merely practical and dynamic activity or in the mentalised emotional or sensational current, a life of conventional conduct, average feelings, customary ideas, opinions and prejudices which are not one's own but those of the environment, to have no free and open play of mind, but to live grossly and unthinkingly by the unintelligent rule of the many, to live besides according to the senses and sensations controlled by certain conventions, but neither purified nor enlightened nor chastened by any law of beauty, — all this too is contrary to the ideal of culture. A man may so live with all the appearance or all the pretensions of a civilised existence, enjoy successfully all the plethora of its appurtenances, but he is not in the real sense a developed human being. A society following such a rule of life may be anything else you will, vigorous, decent, well-ordered, successful, religious, moral, but it is a Philistine society; it is a prison which the human soul has to break. For so long as it dwells there, it dwells in an inferior, uninspired and unexpanding mental status; it vegetates infructuously in the lower stratum and is governed not by the higher faculties of man, but by the crudities of the unuplifted sense-mind. Nor is it enough for it to open windows in this prison by which it may get draughts of agreeable fresh air, something of the free light of the intellect, something of the fragrance of art and beauty, something of the large breath of wider interests and higher ideals. It has yet to break out of its prison altogether and live in that free light, in that fragrance and large breath; only then does it breathe the natural atmosphere of the developed mental being. Not to live principally in the activities of the sense-mind, but in the activities of knowledge and reason and a wide intellectual curiosity, the activities of the cultivated aesthetic being, the activities of the enlightened will which make for character and high ethical ideals and a large human action, not to be governed by our lower or our average mentality but by truth and beauty and the self-ruling will is the ideal of a true culture and the beginning of an accomplished humanity.   *Social and Political Thought, pp. 84-86*

Since the infinite, the absolute and transcendent, the universal, the One is the secret summit of existence and to reach the spiritual consciousness and the Divine the ultimate goal and aim of our being and therefore of the whole development of the individual and the collectivity in all its parts and all its activities, reason cannot be the last and highest guide; culture, as it is understood ordinarily, cannot be the directing light or find out the regulating and harmonising principle of all our life and action. For reason stops short of the Divine and only compromises with the problems of life, and culture in order to attain the Transcendent and Infinite must become spiritual culture, something much more than an intellectual, aesthetic, ethical and practical training.   *Social and Political Thought, p. 162*

The normal society treats man essentially as a physical, vital and mental being. For the life, the mind, the body are the three terms of existence with which it has some competence to deal. It develops a system of mental growth and efficiency, an intellectual, aesthetic and moral culture. It evolves the vital side of human life and creates an ever-growing system of economic efficiency and vital enjoyment, and this system becomes more and more rich, cumbrous and complex as civilisation develops. Depressing by its mental and vital overgrowth the natural vigour of the physical and animal man, it tries to set the balance right by systems of physical culture, a cumbrous science of habits and remedies intended to cure the ills it has created and as much amelioration as it can manage of the artificial forms of living that are necessary to its social system. In the end, however, experience shows that society tends to die by its own development, a sure sign that there is some radical defect in its system, a certain proof that its idea of man and its method of development do not correspond to all the reality of the human being and to the aim of life which that reality imposes....

It may be suggested on the contrary and with some chance of knocking at the right door that the radical defect of all our systems is their deficient development of just that which society has most neglected, the spiritual element, the soul in man which is his true being. Even to have a healthy body, a strong vitality and an active and clarified mind and a field for their action and enjoyment, carries man no more than a certain distance; afterwards he flags and tires for want of a real self-finding, a satisfying aim for his action and progress. These three things do not make the sum of a complete manhood; they are means to an ulterior end and cannot be made for ever an aim in themselves. Add a rich emotional life governed by a well-ordered ethical standard, and still there is the savour of something left out, some supreme good which these things mean, but do not in themselves arrive at, do not discover till they go beyond themselves. Add a religious system and a widespread spirit of belief and piety, and still you have not found the means of social salvation. All these things human society has developed, but none of them has saved it from disillusionment, weariness and decay. The ancient intellectual cultures of Europe ended in disruptive doubt and sceptical impotence, the pieties of Asia in stagnation and decline. Modern society has discovered a new principle of survival, progress, but the aim of that progress it has never discovered, — unless the aim is always more knowledge, more equipment, convenience and comfort, more enjoyment, a greater and still greater complexity of the social economy, a more and more cumbrously opulent life. But these things must lead in the end where the old led, for they are only the same thing on a larger scale; they lead in a circle, that is to say, nowhere: they do not escape from the cycle of birth, growth, decay and death, they do not really find the secret of self-prolongation by constant self-renewal which is the principle of immortality, but only seem for a moment to find it by the illusion of a series of experiments each of which ends in disappointment. That so far has been the nature of modern progress. Only in its new turn inwards, towards a greater subjectivity now only beginning, is there a better hope; for by that turning it may discover that the real truth of man is to be found in his soul. It is not indeed certain that a subjective age will lead us there, but it gives us the possibility, can turn in that direction, if used rightly, the more inward movement.

It will be said that this is an old discovery and that it governed the old societies under the name of religion. But that was only an appearance. The discovery was there, but it was made for the life of the individual only, and even for him it looked beyond the earth for its fulfilment and at earth only as the place of his preparation for a solitary salvation or release from the burden of life. Human society itself never seized on the discovery of the soul as a means for the discovery of the law of its own being or on a knowledge of the soul's true nature and need and its fulfilment as the right way of terrestrial perfection....

The true and full spiritual aim in society will regard man not as a mind, a life and a body, but as a soul incarnated for a divine fulfilment upon earth, not only in heavens beyond, which after all it need not have left if it had no divine business here in the world of physical, vital and mental nature. It will therefore regard the life, mind and body neither as ends in themselves, sufficient for their own satisfaction, nor as mortal members full of disease which have only to be dropped off for the rescued spirit to flee away into its own pure regions, but as first instruments of the soul, the yet imperfect instruments of an unseized diviner purpose. It will believe in their destiny and help them to believe in themselves, but for that very reason in their highest and not only in their lowest or lower possibilities. Their destiny will be, in its view, to spiritualise themselves so as to grow into visible members of the spirit, lucid means of its manifestation, themselves spiritual, illumined, more and more conscious and perfect. For, accepting the truth of man's soul as a thing entirely divine in its essence, it will accept also the possibility of his whole being becoming divine in spite of Nature's first patent contradictions of this possibility, her darkened denials of this ultimate certitude, and even with these as a necessary earthly starting-point. And as it will regard man the individual, it will regard too man the collectivity as a soul-form of the Infinite, a collective soul myriadly embodied upon earth for a divine fulfilment in its manifold relations and its multitudinous activities. Therefore it will hold sacred all the different parts of man's life which correspond to the parts of his being, all his physical, vital, dynamic, emotional, aesthetic, ethical, intellectual, psychic evolution, and see in them instruments for a growth towards a diviner living. It will regard every human society, nation, people or other organic aggregate from the same standpoint, subsouls, as it were, means of a complex manifestation and self-fulfilment of the Spirit, the divine Reality, the conscious Infinite in man upon earth. The possible godhead of man because he is inwardly of one being with God will be its one solitary creed and dogma....

The spiritual aim will seek to fulfil itself therefore in a fullness of life and man's being in the individual and the race which will be the base for the heights of the spirit, — the base becoming in the end of one substance with the peaks. It will not proceed by a scornful neglect of the body, nor by an ascetic starving of the vital being and an utmost bareness or even squalor as the rule of spiritual living, nor by a puritanic denial of art and beauty and the aesthetic joy of life, nor by a neglect of science and philosophy as poor, negligible or misleading intellectual pursuits, — though the temporary utility even of these exaggerations as against the opposite excesses need not be denied; it will be all things to all, but in all it will be at once their highest aim and meaning and the most all-embracing expression of themselves in which all they are and seek for will be fulfilled. It will aim at establishing in society the true inner theocracy, not the false theocracy of a dominant Church or priesthood, but that of the inner Priest, Prophet and King. It will reveal to man the divinity in himself as the Light, Strength, Beauty, Good, Delight, Immortality that dwells within and build up in his outer life also the kingdom of God which is first discovered within us. It will show man the way to seek for the Divine in every way of his being, *sarvabhāvena*,[9] and so find it and live in it, that however — even in all kinds of ways — he lives and acts, he shall live and act in that,[10] in the Divine, in the Spirit, in the eternal Reality of his being.   *Social and Political Thought, pp. 208-213, 216-17*

[9] Gita.   [10] Gita. *Sarvathā vartamāno'pi sa yogī mayi vartate.*

20
Towards a Greater Psychology

Materialistic Basis of Modern Psychology

Modern Science, obsessed with the greatness of its physical discoveries and the idea of the sole existence of Matter, has long attempted to base upon physical data even its study of Soul and Mind and of those workings of Nature in man and animal in which a knowledge of psychology is as important as any of the physical sciences. Its very psychology founded itself upon physiology and the scrutiny of the brain and the nervous system.

Social and Political Thought, p. 1

To perceive and have a right view of our way to such a transformation [conversion of the human into a likeness of and a fundamental oneness with the divine nature] we must form some sufficient working idea of the complex thing that this human nature at present is in the confused interminglings of its various principles, so that we may see the precise nature of the conversion each part of it must undergo and the most effective means for the conversion. How to disengage from this knot of thinking mortal matter the Immortal it contains, from this mentalised vital animal man the happy fullness of his submerged hints of Godhead, is the real problem of a human being and living. Life develops many first hints of the divinity without completely disengaging them; Yoga is the unravelling of the knot of Life's difficulty.

First of all we have to know the central secret of the psychological complexity which creates the problem and all its difficulties. But an ordinary psychology which only takes mind and its phenomena at their surface values, will be of no help to us; it will not give us the least guidance in this line of self-exploration and self-conversion. Still less can we find the clue in a scientific psychology with a materialistic basis which assumes that the body and the biological and physiological factors of our nature are not only the starting-point but the whole real foundation and regards human mind as only a subtle development from the life and the body. That may be the actual truth of the animal side of human nature and of the human mind in so far as it is limited and conditioned by the physical part of our being. But the whole difference between man and the animal is that the animal mind, as we know it, cannot get for one moment away from its origins, cannot break out from the covering, the close chrysalis which the bodily life has spun round the soul, and become something greater than its present self, a more free, magnificent and noble being; but in man mind reveals itself as a greater energy escaping from the restrictions of the vital and physical formula of being. But even this is not all that man is or can be: he has in him the power to evolve and release a still greater ideal energy which in its turn escapes out of the restrictions of the mental formula of his nature and discloses the supramental form, the ideal power of a spiritual being. In Yoga we have to travel beyond the physical nature and the superficial man and to discover the workings of the whole nature of the real man. In other words we must arrive at and use a psychophysical knowledge with a spiritual foundation.

Synthesis of Yoga, pp. 597-98

Superficial Nature of Early Psychology

...psychological enquiry in Europe (and without enquiry there can be no sound knowledge) is only beginning and has not gone very far, and what has reigned in men's minds up to now is a superficial statement of the superficial appearances of our consciousness as they look to us at first view and nothing more. But knowledge only begins when we get away from the surface phenomena and look behind them for their true operations and causes. To the superficial view of the outer mind and senses the sun is a little fiery ball circling in mid air round the earth and the stars twinkling little things stuck in the sky for our benefit at night. Scientific enquiry comes and knocks this infantile first-view to pieces. The sun is a huge affair (millions of miles away from our air) around which the small earth circles, and the stars are huge members of huge systems indescribably distant which have nothing apparently to do with the tiny earth and her creatures. All Science is like that, a contradiction of the sense-view or superficial appearances of things and an assertion of truths which are unguessed by the common and the uninstructed reason. The same process has to be followed in psychology if we are really to know what our consciousness is, how it is built and made and what is the secret of its functionings or the way out of its disorder.   *Letters on Yoga, pp. 321-22*

Rediscovery of the Subconscious (Subliminal) Mind

Modern psychology has extended our knowledge and has admitted us to a truth which the ancients already knew but expressed in another language. We know now or we rediscover the truth that the conscious operation of mind is only a surface action. There is a much vaster and more potent subconscious mind which loses nothing of what the senses bring to it; it keeps all its wealth in an inexhaustible store of memory, *akṣitam śravaḥ*. The surface mind may pay no attention, still the subconscious mind attends, receives, treasures up with an infallible accuracy. The illiterate servant-girl hears daily her master reciting Hebrew in his study; the surface mind pays no attention to the unintelligible gibberish, but the subconscious mind hears, remembers and, when in an abnormal condition it comes up to the surface, reproduces those learned recitations with a portentous accuracy which the most correct and retentive scholar might envy. The man or mind has not heard because he did not attend;

the greater man or mind within has heard because he always attends, or rather sub-tends, with an infinite capacity. So too a man put under an anaesthetic and operated upon has felt nothing; but release his subconscious mind by hypnosis and he will relate accurately every detail of the operation and its appropriate sufferings; for the stupor of the physical sense-organ could not prevent the larger mind within from observing and feeling.

Similarly we know that a large part of our physical action is instinctive and not directed by the surface but by the subconscious mind. And we know now that it is a mind that acts and not merely an ignorant nervous reaction from the brute physical brain. The subconscious mind in the catering insect knows the anatomy of the beetle it intends to immobilise and make food for its young and it directs its sting accordingly, as unerringly as the most skilful surgeon, provided the mere limited surface mind with its groping and faltering nervous action does not get in the way and falsify the inner knowledge or the inner will-force.

These examples point us to the truths which western psychology, hampered by past ignorance posing as scientific orthodoxy, still ignores or refuses to acknowledge. The Upanishads declare that the Mind in us is infinite; it knows not only what has been seen but what has not been seen, not only what has been heard but what has not been heard, not only what has been discriminated by the thought but what has not been discriminated by the thought. Let us say, then, in the tongue of our modern knowledge that the surface man in us is limited by his physical experiences; he knows only what his nervous life in the body brings to his embodied mind; and even of those bringings he knows, he can retain and utilise only so much as his surface mind-sense attends to and consciously remembers; but there is a larger subliminal consciousness within him which is not thus limited. That consciousness senses what has not been sensed by the surface mind and its organs and knows what the surface mind has not learned by its acquisitive thought. That in

the insect knows the anatomy of its victim; that in the man outwardly insensible not only feels and remembers the action of the
surgeon's knife, but knows the appropriate reactions of suffering
which were in the physical body inhibited by the anaesthetic and
therefore non-existent; that in the illiterate servant-girl heard
and retained accurately the words of an unknown language and
could, as Yogic experience knows, by a higher action of itself
understand those superficially unintelligible sounds.

The Upanishads, pp. 192-94

The Deeper View of the "New" Psychology and its Limitations

It is true that psychology has made an advance and has begun
to improve its method. Formerly, it was a crude, scholastic and
superficial systematisation of man's ignorance of himself. The
surface psychological functionings, will, mind, senses, reason,
conscience, etc., were arranged in a dry and sterile classification;
their real nature and relation to each other were not fathomed
nor any use made of them which went beyond the limited action Nature had found sufficient for a very superficial mental
and psychic life and for very superficial and ordinary workings.
Because we do not know ourselves, therefore we are unable to
ameliorate radically our subjective life or develop with mastery,
with rapidity, with a sure science the hidden possibilities of our
mental capacity and our moral nature. The new psychology
seeks indeed to penetrate behind superficial appearances, but
it is encumbered by initial errors which prevent a profounder
knowledge, — the materialistic error which bases the study of
mind upon the study of the body; the sceptical error which
prevents any bold and clear-eyed investigation of the hidden
profundities of our subjective existence; the error of conservative distrust and recoil which regards any subjective state or
experience that departs from the ordinary operations of our
mental and psychical nature as a morbidity or a hallucination,

— just as the Middle Ages regarded all new science as magic and a diabolical departure from the sane and right limits of human capacity; finally, the error of objectivity which leads the psychologist to study others from outside instead of seeing his true field of knowledge and laboratory of experiment in himself. Psychology is necessarily a subjective science and one must proceed in it from the knowledge of oneself to the knowledge of others.

But whatever the crudities of the new science, it has at least taken the first capital step without which there can be no true psychological knowledge; it has made the discovery which is the beginning of self-knowledge and which all must make who deeply study the facts of consciousness, — that our waking and surface existence is only a small part of our being and does not yield to us the root and secret of our character, our mentality or our actions. The sources lie deeper. To discover them, to know the nature and the processes of the inconscient or subconscient self and, so far as is possible, to possess and utilise them as physical science possesses and utilises the secret of the forces of Nature ought to be the aim of a scientific psychology.

But here the first difficulty confronts us, the problem whether this other and greater self of which our waking existence is only a surface and a phenomenon, is subconscient or inconscient. And thereon hinges the whole destiny of the human being. For if it is inconscient in its very nature, then we cannot hope to illuminate ourselves with the hidden light of these depths — for light there is none — or to find and to possess ourselves of the secret of its power. On the other hand if it is subconscient, that is to say a concealed consciousness deeper, greater, more powerful than our superficial self, an endless vista of self-enlargement opens out before us and the human race marches towards infinite possibilities.

Modern psychological experiment and observation have proceeded on two different lines which have not yet found their point of meeting. On the one hand psychology has taken for its starting-point the discoveries and the fundamental thesis of the physical sciences and has worked as a continuation of physiology. The physical sciences are the study of inconscient Force working in inconscient Matter and a psychology which accepts this formula as the basis of all existence must regard consciousness as a phenomenal result of the Inconscient working on the inconscient. Mind is only an outcome and as it were a record of nervous reactions. The true self is the inconscient; mental action is one of its subordinate phenomena. The Inconscient is greater than the conscient; it is the god, the magician, the creator whose action is far more unerring than the ambitious but blundering action of the conscious mentality. The tree is more perfectly guided than man in its more limited action, precisely because it lives unambitiously according to Nature and is passive in the hands of the Inconscient. Mind enters in to enlarge the field of activity, but also to multiply errors, perversities, revolts against Nature, departures from the instinctive guiding of the Inconscient Self which generate that vast element of ignorance, falsehood and suffering in human life, — that "much falsehood in us" of which the Vedic poet complains.

Where then lies the hope that mind will repair its errors and guide itself according to the truth of things? The hope lies in Science, in the intelligent observation, utilising, initiation of the forces and workings of the Inconscient. To take only one instance, — the Inconscient operates by the law of heredity and, left to itself, works faultlessly to ensure the survival of good and healthy types. Man misuses heredity in the false conditions of his social life to transmit and perpetuate degeneracy. We must study the law of heredity, develop a science of Eugenics and use it wisely and remorselessly — with the remorseless wisdom of Nature — so as to ensure by intelligence the result that the Inconscient assures by instinctive adaptation. We can see where this idea and this spirit will lead us, — to the replacement of the emotional and spiritual idealism which the human mind has developed by a cold sane materialistic idealism and to an amelioration of mankind attempted by the rigorous mechanism of the scientific expert, no longer by the profound inspiration of genius and the supple aspiration of puissant character and personality. And yet what if this were only another error of the conscient mind? What if the mistaking and the disease, the revolt and departure from Nature were itself a part, a necessary part of the wise and unerring plan of the profound Inconscient Self and all the much falsehood a means of arriving at a greater truth and a more exalted capacity? The fact that genius itself, the highest result of our developing consciousness, flowers so frequently on a diseased branch is a phenomenon full of troubling suggestions. The clear way of ascertained science need not always be the best way; it may stand often in the path of development of a yet greater and deeper Knowledge.

The other line of psychological investigation is still frowned upon by orthodox science, but it thrives and yields its results in spite of the anathema of the doctors. It leads us into by-paths of psychical research, hypnotism, mesmerism, occultism and all sorts of strange psychological gropings. Certainly, there is nothing here of the assured clearness and firmly-grounded positivism of the physical method. Yet facts emerge and with the facts a momentous conclusion, — the conclusion, that there is a "subliminal" self behind our superficial waking mind not inconscient but conscient, greater than the waking mind, endowed with surprising faculties and capable of a much surer action and experience, conscient of the superficial mind though of it the superficial mind is inconscient. And then a question rises. What if there were really no Inconscient at all, but a hidden Consciousness everywhere perfect in power and wisdom, of which our mind is the first slow, hesitating and imperfect disclosure and into the image of which the human mentality is destined progressively to grow? It would at least be no less valid a generalisation and it would explain all the facts that we now know considerably better than the blind and purposeless determinism of the materialistic theory.

In pursuing psychological investigation upon this line we shall only be resuming that which had already been done by our remote forefathers. For they too, the moment they began to observe, to experiment, to look below the surface of things, were compelled to perceive that the surface man is only a form and appearance and that the real self is something infinitely greater and more profound. They too must have passed through the first materialistic stages of science and philosophy. For we read in the Aitareya Upanishad that entering upon possession of the material world and the body, the Purusha, the Conscious Soul, asks himself, "If utterance is by speech and life by the breath, vision by the eye, hearing by the ear, thought by the mind," if in short all the apparent activities of the being can be accounted for by the automatic functioning of Nature, "then what am I?" And the Upanishad says farther, "He being born distinguished only the working of the material elements, for what else was there of which he should discuss and conclude?" Yet in the end "he beheld this conscious being which is Brahman utterly extended and he said to himself, Now have I really seen." So too in the Taittiriya Upanishad Bhrigu Varuni meditating on the Brahman comes first to the conclusion that "Matter is Brahman" and only afterwards discovers Life that is Brahman, — so rising from the materialistic to the vitalistic theory of existence as European thought is now rising, — then Mind that is Brahman and then Knowledge that is Brahman, — so rising to the sensational and the idealistic realisations of the truth — and at last Bliss of Existence that is Brahman. There he pauses in the ultimate spiritual realisation, the highest formulation of knowledge that man can attain.

The Conscient therefore and not the Inconscient was the Truth at which the ancient psychology arrived; and it distinguished three strata of the conscient self, the waking, the dream and the sleep selves of Man, — in other words the superficial existence, the subconscient or subliminal and the superconscient which to us seems the inconscient because its state of consciousness is the reverse of ours: for ours is limited and based on division and multiplicity, but this is "that which becomes a unity"; ours is dispersed in knowledge, but in this other self conscious knowledge is self-collected and concentrated; ours is balanced between dual experiences, but this is all delight, it is that which in the very heart of our being fronts everything with a pure all-possessing consciousness and enjoys the delight of existence. Therefore, although its seat is that stratum of consciousness which to us is a deep sleep, — for the mind there cannot maintain its accustomed functioning and becomes inconscient, — yet its name is He who knows, the Wise One, Prajna. "This" says the Mandukya Upanishad, "is omniscient, omnipotent, the inner control, the womb of all and that from which creatures are born and into which they depart." It answers, therefore, closely enough to the modern idea of the Inconscient corrected by the other modern idea of the subliminal self; for it is inconscient only to the waking mind precisely because it is superconscient to it and the mind is therefore only able to seize it in its results and not in itself. And what better proof can there be of the depth and truth of the ancient psychology than the fact that when modern thought in all its pride of exact and careful knowledge begins to cast its fathom into these depths, it is obliged to repeat in other language what had already been written nearly three thousand years ago?

We find the same idea of this inner control repeated in the Gita; for it is the Lord who "sits in the hearts of all creatures and turns all creatures mounted on an engine by his Maya." At times the Upanishad seems to describe this Self as the "mental being leader of the life and the body", which is really the subliminal mind of the psychical investigators; but this is only a relative description. The Vedantic psychology was aware of other depths that take us beyond this formula and in relation to which the mental being becomes in its turn as superficial as is our waking to our subliminal mind. And now once more in the revolutions of human thought these depths have to be sounded; modern psychology will be led perforce, by the compulsion of the truth that it is seeking, on to the path that was followed by the ancient. The new dawns, treading the eternal path of the Truth, follow it to the goal of the dawns that have gone before, — how many, who shall say?

For this knowledge was not first discovered in the comparatively late antiquity that gave us the Upanishads which we now possess. It is already there in the dateless verses of the Rig Veda, and the Vedic sages speak of it as the discovery of yet more ancient seers besides whom they themselves were new and modern. Emerging from the periods of eclipse and the nights of ignorance which overtake humanity, we assume always that we are instituting a new knowledge. In reality, we are continually rediscovering the knowledge and repeating the achievement of the ages that have gone before us, — receiving again out of the "Inconscient" the light that it had drawn back into its secrecies and now releases once more for a new day and another march of the great journey.

The Supramental Manifestation and Other Writings, pp. 258-63

[To a disciple]

Your practice of psycho-analysis was a mistake. It has, for the time at least, made the work of purification more complicated, not easier. The psycho-analysis of Freud is the last thing that one should associate with yoga. It takes up a certain part, the darkest, the most perilous, the unhealthiest part of the nature, the lower vital subconscious layer, isolates some of its most morbid phenomena and attributes to it and them an action out of all proportion to its true role in the nature. Modern psychology is an infant science, at once rash, fumbling and crude. As in all infant sciences, the universal habit of the human mind — to take a partial or local truth, generalise it unduly and try to explain a whole field of Nature in its narrow terms — runs riot here. Moreover, the exaggeration of the importance of suppressed sexual complexes is a dangerous falsehood and it can have a nasty influence and tend to make the mind and vital more and not less fundamentally impure than before.

It is true that the subliminal in man is the largest part of his nature and has in it the secret of the unseen dynamisms which explain his surface activities. But the lower vital subconscious which is all that this psycho-analysis of Freud seems to know, — and even of that it knows only a few ill-lit corners, — is no more than a restricted and very inferior portion of the subliminal whole. The subliminal self stands behind and supports the whole superficial man; it has in it a larger and more efficient mind behind the surface mind, a larger and more powerful vital behind the surface vital, a subtler and freer physical consciousness behind the surface bodily existence. And above them it opens to higher superconscient as well as below them to lower subconscient ranges. If one wishes to purify and transform the nature, it is the power of these higher ranges to which one must open and raise to them and change by them both the subliminal and the surface being. Even this should be done with care, not prematurely or rashly, following a higher guidance, keeping always the right attitude; for otherwise the force that is drawn down may be too strong for an obscure and weak frame of nature. But to begin by opening up the lower subconscious, risking to raise up all that is foul or obscure in it, is to go out of one's way to invite trouble. First, one should make the higher mind and vital strong and firm and full of light and peace from above; afterwards one can open up or even dive into the subconscious with more safety and some chance of a rapid and successful change.   *Letters on Yoga, pp. 1605-07*

I find it difficult to take these psycho-analysts at all seriously when they try to scrutinise spiritual experience by the flicker of their torch-lights, — yet perhaps one ought to, for half-knowledge is a powerful thing and can be a great obstacle to the coming in front of the true Truth. This new psychology looks to me very much like children learning some summary and not very adequate alphabet, exulting in putting their a-b-c-d of the subconscient and the mysterious underground super-ego together and imagining that their first book of obscure beginnings (c-a-t cat, t-r-e-e tree) is the very heart of the real knowledge. They look from down up and explain the higher lights by the lower obscurities; but the foundation of these things is above and not below, *upari budhna eṣām*. The superconscient, not the subconscient, is the true foundation of things. The significance of the lotus is not to be found by analysing the secrets of the mud from which it grows here; its secret is to be found in the heavenly archetype of the lotus that blooms for ever in the Light above. The self-chosen field of these psychologists is besides poor, dark and limited; you must know the whole before you can know the part and the highest before you can truly understand the lowest. That is the promise of the greater psychology awaiting its hour before which these poor gropings will disappear and come to nothing.   *Letters on Yoga, pp. 1608-09*

Part Two

Essays on Sri Aurobindo's
Psychological Thought

All truths, even those which seem to be in conflict, have their validity, but they need a reconciliation in some largest Truth which takes them into itself.

Sri Aurobindo

1
The Nature and Methodology
of Yoga Psychology

The following account of Sri Aurobindo's first major spiritual experience provides a good starting-point for explicating the nature of yoga psychology:

> ...to reach Nirvana was the first radical result of my own Yoga. It threw me suddenly into a condition above and without thought, unstained by any mental or vital movement; there was no ego, no real world — only when one looked through the immobile senses, something perceived or bore upon its sheer silence a world of empty forms, materialised shadows without true substance. There was no One or many even, only just absolutely That, feature-less, relationless, sheer, indescribable, unthinkable, absolute, yet supremely real and solely real. This was no mental realisation nor something glimpsed somewhere above, — no abstraction, — it was positive, the only positive reality, — although not a spatial physical world, pervading, occupying or rather flooding and drowning this semblance of a physical world leaving no room or space for any reality but itself, allowing nothing else to seem at all actual, positive or substantial.[1]

The illusoriness of the ego and the unreality of the world mentioned in the experience just described are well-known philosophical concepts, associated chiefly with Buddhism and Vedanta. Here, however, the non-existence of the ego and the unreality of the world are not stated as abstract philosophical concepts but as a *direct experience*, devoid of any thought or mental movement: "there was no ego, no real world". Herein lies the first fundamental characteristic of yogic knowledge — it is based on experience, not on thought or reasoning. Thus yoga psychology, like modern psychology, is an empirical science, that is, a body of knowledge based on observed or experiential data;

it is not a philosophy arrived at by speculative thought. Criticizing the inadequate scientific basis of early modern psychology, Sri Aurobindo states;

> The old European system of psychology was... a pseudo-scientific system. Its observations were superficial, its terms and classification arbitrary, its aim and spirit abstract, empty and scholastic.[2]

> A direct experiential and experimental psychology seems to be demanded if psychology is to be a science and not merely a mass of elementary and superficial generalisations with all the rest guesswork or uncertain conclusion or inference. We must see, feel, know directly what we observe; our interpretations must be capable of being sure and indubitable; we must be able to work surely on a ground of sure knowledge.[3]

Sri Aurobindo's assertion that "Yoga... bases all its findings on experience"[4] disaffirms views such as the following that regard Indian psychology — which is based on yogic knowledge — as philosophical rather than scientific:

> There is no empirical psychology in India. Indian Psychology is based on Metaphysics.[5]

> In India there is no psychology in our [European] sense of the word. India is "pre-psychological"... [6]

Explaining the relationship between yogic or supra-intellectual knowledge and philosophical thought through which it is expressed, Sri Aurobindo states:

> ...fundamentally, it [the statement of supra-intellectual things] is not an expression of ideas arrived at by speculative thinking. One has to arrive at spiritual knowledge through experience and a consciousness of things which arises directly out of that experience or else underlies or is involved in it. This kind of knowledge, then, is fundamentally a consciousness and not a thought or formulated idea. For instance, my first major experience... came after and by

the exclusion and silencing of all thought — there was, first, what might be called a spiritually substantial or concrete consciousness of stillness and silence, then the awareness of some sole and supreme Reality in whose presence things existed only as forms but forms not at all substantial or real or concrete; but this was all apparent to a spiritual perception and essential and impersonal sense and there was not the least concept or idea of reality or unreality or any other notion, for all concept or idea was hushed or rather entirely absent in the absolute stillness. These things were known directly through the pure consciousness and not through the mind, so there was no need of concepts or words or names. At the same time this fundamental character of spiritual experience is not absolutely limitative; it can do without thought, but it can do with thought also.[7]

A second characteristic of yoga psychology is that its purview extends beyond the normal or ordinary state of awareness and includes non-ordinary states of consciousness whose view of things often contradicts that of the ordinary consciousness. For example, the ego — that which gives us the sense of being someone who exists in the world and who is separate from everyone and everything else in the world — is an unquestionable fact of experience of our ordinary consciousness. However, in the Nirvana state of consciousness, previously alluded to, the ego is an illusion. According to yoga psychology, the true view of things can be obtained only by going beyond the normal superficial mental consciousness and looking from a deeper or higher consciousness.

> ...knowledge only begins when we get away from the surface phenomena and look behind them for their true operations and causes. To the superficial view of the outer mind and senses the sun is a little fiery ball circling in mid air round the earth and the stars twinkling little things stuck in the sky for our benefit at night. Scientific enquiry comes and knocks this infantile first-view to pieces. The sun is a huge affair (millions of miles away from our air) around

which the small earth circles, and the stars are huge members of huge systems indescribably distant which have nothing apparently to do with the tiny earth and her creatures. All Science is like that, a contradiction of the sense-view or superficial appearances of things and an assertion of truths which are unguessed by the common and the uninstructed reason. The same process has to be followed in psychology if we are really to know what our consciousness is, how it is built and made and what is the secret of its functionings or the way out of its disorder.[8]

The last statement leads up to the definition and scope of psychology from the standpoint of yoga.

Psychology is the science of consciousness and its status and operations in Nature and, if that can be glimpsed or experienced, its status and operations beyond what we know as Nature.

It is not enough to observe and know the movements of our surface nature and the superficial nature of other living creatures just as it [is] not enough for Science to observe and know as electricity only the movements of lightning in the clouds or for the astronomer to observe and know only those movements and properties of the stars that are visible to the unaided eye. Here as there a whole world of occult phenomena have to be laid bare and brought under control before the psychologist can hope to be master of his province.

Our observable consciousness, that which we call ourselves, is only the little visible part of our being. It is a small field below which are depths and farther depths and widths and ever wider widths which support and supply it but to which it has no visible access. All that is our self, our being, — what we see at the top is only our ego and its visible nature.

Even the movements of this little surface nature cannot be understood nor its true law discovered until we know all that is below or behind and supplies it — and know too all that is around it and above.[9]

The yogic view that regards our observable surface self as only a small part of our being is similar to the psychoanalytical view which compares the mind to an iceberg, nine-tenths of which lies below the surface. However, yoga psychology is based on a vastly more comprehensive view of consciousness, distinguishing various levels of consciousness which, in relation to the surface consciousness, are below it (the subconscient and the inconscient), behind it (the subliminal), around it (the circumconscient) and above it (the superconscient).[10]

From the standpoint of yoga psychology, the reductionistic view of psychoanalysis which tries to explain all human motivation, including the pursuit of art, philosophy and religion, in terms of the unconscious is due to an incomplete and lopsided view of consciousness. Commenting on the psychoanalytical reductionism, Sri Aurobindo writes:

> They [the psychoanalysts] look from down up and explain the higher lights by the lower obscurities; but the foundation of these things [spiritual experiences] is above and not below, *upari budhna eṣām*.[11] The superconscient, not the subconscient, is the true foundation of things. The significance of the lotus is not to be found by analysing the secrets of the mud from which it grows here; its secret is to be found in the heavenly archetype of the lotus that blooms for ever in the Light above. The self-chosen field of these psychologists is besides poor, dark and limited; you must know the whole before you can know the part and the highest before you can truly understand the lowest.[12]

Implicit in the statement that one must know the whole before one can know the part is the yogic view that the human being is part of the Being of the universe; therefore in order to understand the psychological nature of the human being, it is necessary to know first the metaphysical reality of the Being of the universe.

> Being or the Self of things can only be known by metaphysical — not necessarily intellectual — knowledge.

.is self-knowledge has two inseparable aspects, a psycholog-
.nowledge of the process of Being, a metaphysical knowledge
.ts principles and essentiality.[13]

A complete psychology cannot be a pure natural science, but must
be a compound of science and metaphysical knowledge.[14]

Thus another characteristic of yoga psychology — in which it
differs from modern psychology — is that it is part of and inseparable from philosophy. Though both yoga psychology and
yoga philosophy are based on experience and constitute a unified
body of knowledge, their provinces and nature of enquiry are
distinctly different.

Metaphysics deals with the ultimate cause of things and all that
lies behind the world of phenomena. As regards mind and consciousness, it asks what they are, how they came into existence,
what is their relation to Matter, Life, etc. Psychology deals with
mind and consciousness and tries to find out not so much their
ultimate nature and relations as their actual workings and the rule
and law of these workings.[15]

The investigation of the workings of consciousness and the
laws governing these workings calls for special processes and
instruments which can be discovered only by yogic practice.

This definition [of psychology as an examination of the nature and
movements of consciousness] at once takes us out of the field of
ordinary psychology and extends the range of our observation to
an immense mass of facts and experiments which exceed the common surface and limited range very much as the vastly extended
range of observation of Science exceeds that of the common man
looking at natural external phenomena only with the help [of] his
unaided mind and senses. The field of Yoga is practically unlimited and its processes and instrumentation have a plasticity and
adaptability and power of expansion to which it is difficult to see
or set any limit.[16]

It is only by Yoga process that one can arrive at an instrumentation which will drive large wide roads into the psychological Unknown and not only obscure and narrow tunnels.... It is through consciousness, by an instrumentation of consciousness only that the nature and laws and movements of consciousness can be discovered — and this is the method of Yoga.[17]

Yoga, by which one discovers the processes and develops the instruments required for the study of consciousness, does not refer to any specific spiritual discipline.

But what precisely do we mean by the word Yoga? It is used here in the most general sense possible as a convenient name including all processes or results of processes that lead to the unveiling of a greater and inner knowledge, consciousness, experience. Any psychic discipline by which we can pass partly or wholly into a spiritual state of consciousness, any spontaneous or systematised approach to the inner Reality or the supreme Reality, any state of union or closeness to the Divine, any entry into a consciousness larger, deeper or higher than the normal consciousness common to humankind, fall automatically within the range of the word Yoga.[18]

When questioned about tests of validity of the knowledge acquired by the processes of yoga, Sri Aurobindo replied:

...the experiences of yoga belong to an inner domain and go according to a law of their own, have their own method of perception, criteria and all the rest of it which are neither those of the domain of the physical senses nor of the domain of rational or scientific enquiry. Just as scientific enquiry passes beyond that of the physical senses and enters the domain of the infinite and infinitesimal about which the senses can say nothing — for one cannot see and touch an electron or know by the evidence of the sense-mind whether it exists or not or decide by that evidence whether the earth really turns round the sun and not rather the sun round the earth as our senses and all our physical experience daily tell us — so the spiritual search passes beyond the domain of scientific[19] or rational enquiry and it is impossible by the aid of the ordinary positive reason to test the data of spiritual experience and decide whether those things exist or not or what is their law and nature. As in Science, so here you have to accumulate experience on experience, following faithfully the methods laid down by the Guru or by the systems of the past, you have to develop an intuitive discrimination which compares the experiences, see what they mean, how far and in what field each is valid, what is the place of each in the whole, how it can be reconciled or related with others that at first might seem to contradict it, etc., etc., until you can move with sure knowledge in the vast field of spiritual phenomena. That is the only way to test spiritual experience. I have myself tried the other method and I have found it absolutely incapable and inapplicable. On the other hand, if you are not prepared to go through all that yourself, — as few can do except those of extraordinary spiritual stature — you have to accept the leading of a Master, as in Science you accept a teacher instead of going through the whole field of Science and its experimentation all by yourself — at least until you have accumulated sufficient experience and knowledge. If that is accepting things *a priori*, well, you have to accept *a priori*. For I am unable to see by what valid tests you propose to make the ordinary reason the judge of what is beyond it.[20]

A Victorian agnostic objection to the claim that yogic knowledge is scientific states that yogic experience is subjective and purely individual; such experience, which is coloured by the individuality of the seer cannot be said to achieve ultimate truth. To this Sri Aurobindo replies:

One might ask whether Science itself has arrived at any ultimate truth; on the contrary, ultimate truth even on the physical plane seems to recede as Science advances. Science started on the assumption that the ultimate truth must be physical and objective — and the objective Ultimate (or even less than that) would explain all subjective phenomena. Yoga proceeds on the opposite view that the ultimate Truth is spiritual and subjective and it is in that ultimate Light that we must view objective phenomena. It is the two opposite poles and the gulf is as wide as it can be.

Yoga, however, is scientific to this extent that it proceeds by subjective experiment and bases all its findings on experience; mental intuitions are admitted only as a first step and are not considered as realisation — they must be confirmed by being translated into and justified by experience. As to the value of the experience itself, it is doubted by the physical mind because it is subjective, not objective. But has the distinction much value? Is not all knowledge and experience subjective at bottom? Objective external physical things are seen very much in the same way by human beings because of the construction of the mind and senses; with another construction of mind and sense quite another account of the physical world would be given — Science itself has made that very clear.... that the yoga experience is individual, coloured by the individuality of the seer... may be true to a certain extent of the precise form or transcription given to the experience in certain domains; but even here the difference is superficial. It is a fact that yogic experience runs everywhere on the same lines. Certainly, there are, not one line, but many; for, admittedly, we are dealing with a many-sided Infinite to which there are and must be many ways of approach; but yet the broad lines are the same everywhere and the intuitions, experiences, phenomena are the same in ages and countries far apart from each other and systems practised quite independently from each other. The experiences of the mediaeval European *bhakta* or mystic are precisely the same in substance, however differing in names, forms, religious colouring, etc., as those of the mediaeval Indian *bhakta* or mystic — yet these people were not corresponding with one another or aware of each other's experiences and results as are modern scientists from New York to Yokohama. That would seem to show that there is something there identical, universal and presumably true — however the colour of the translation may differ because of the difference of mental language.

As for ultimate Truth, I suppose both the Victorian agnostic and, let us say, the Indian Vedantin may agree that it is veiled but there. Both speak of it as the Unknowable; the only difference is that the Vedantin says it is unknowable by the mind and inexpressible by speech, but still attainable by something deeper or higher than the mental perception, while even mind can reflect and speech express the thousand aspects it presents to the mind's outward and inward experience.[21]

The nature of yoga psychology may be made clearer by comparing it with modern psychology and noting some of their similarities and differences. Yoga psychology, like modern psychology, is an empirical science in the sense that both are knowledge based on experience. Both employ observation and experiment as their fundamental methods. However, the field of yoga psychology is much vaster than that of modern psychology since it extends to experiences and phenomena which are beyond the perception of the physical senses or cognizable by the intellect. Therefore, in addition to the physical senses, yoga psychology employs subtler inner senses belonging to the subliminal consciousness. Further, unlike modern psychology which relies solely on intellectual reasoning in drawing conclusions from observations, yoga psychology utilises an intuitive perception for assessing the significance and validity of experiences which pertain to non-ordinary states of consciousness and which are therefore supra-rational. Both modern and yoga psychologies presume the operation of law in the realm of the psyche. However, modern psychology attempts to discover the laws governing psychological phenomena from the study of sample data, therefrom deriving generalisations by statistical inference based on the law of probability. Yoga psychology, on the other hand, shuns generalisations and aims at understanding the human being as a part of the whole universe by proceeding intuitively from the knowledge of the whole, based on self-realisation, to the knowledge of the part. In Sri Aurobindo's words: "...this knowledge [Vijnana, which takes into itself all truth and sees objects of knowledge all at once in their essence, totality and parts or aspects] is not a systematised result of mental questionings and reasonings, not a temporary arrangement of conclusions and opinions in terms of the highest probability, but rather a pure self-existent and *self-luminous Truth*."[22] Such knowledge of the essential nature of things in their totality and parts can be acquired only through spiritual experience and realisation. "The truth of things can only be perceived when one gets to what may be called summarily the spiritual vision of things and even there completely only when there is not only vision but direct experience in the very substance of one's own being and all being."[23] Thus whereas modern psychology consists of intellectual knowledge discovered by the mind, yoga psychology is supra-intellectual knowledge which is discovered by growing into a consciousness beyond that of the mind.

Notes and References

1. Sri Aurobindo, *On Himself*, Sri Aurobindo Birth Centenary Library (hereafter SABCL), (Pondicherry: Sri Aurobindo Ashram, 1970–75), Vol. 26, pp. 101–02.
2. Sri Aurobindo, *Essays Divine and Human* (Pondicherry: Sri Aurobindo Ashram Publication Department, 1994), p. 332.
3. Ibid., pp. 335–36.
4. Sri Aurobindo, *Letters on Yoga*, SABCL Vol. 22, p. 189.
5. Jadunath Sinha, *Indian Psychology*, Vol. 1 (Delhi: Motilal Banarsidass, 1985), p. xviii.
6. C.G. Jung, *Psychology and Religion: West and East*, Collected Works, Vol. XI (Bollingen Series XX, Pantheon Books, 1958), p. 580.
7. Sri Aurobindo, *On Himself*, SABCL Vol. 26, pp. 86–87.
8. Sri Aurobindo, *Letters on Yoga*, SABCL Vol. 22, pp. 321–22.
9. Sri Aurobindo, *Essays Divine and Human*, pp. 333–34.
10. A fuller discussion of the subject will be found in a subsequent

essay in this book ("Sri Aurobindo and the Concept of the Unconscious in Western Psychology").

11. "Their foundation is above." (Rig Veda 1.24.7)
12. Sri Aurobindo, *Letters on Yoga*, SABCL Vol. 24, pp. 1608–09.
13. Sri Aurobindo, *Essays Divine and Human*, p. 323.
14. Ibid., p. 322.
15. Sri Aurobindo, *Letters on Yoga*, SABCL Vol. 24, p. 1281.
16. Sri Aurobindo, *Essays Divine and Human*, p. 339.
17. Ibid., p. 340.
18. Ibid., p. 345.
19. It should be noted that here the term "scientific" is used in its narrow sense, denoting what is based solely on positive reason.
20. Sri Aurobindo, *Letters on Yoga*, SABCL Vol. 22, pp. 190–91.
21. Ibid., pp. 189–90.
22. Sri Aurobindo, *The Synthesis of Yoga — Parts One and Two*, SABCL Vol. 20, p. 12.
23. Sri Aurobindo, *Essays Divine and Human*, p. 337.

2
The Scientific Study of Consciousness
Three Prerequisites for Consciousness Research

> *Having examined and explained Matter by physical methods...*
> *— it is not really explained, but let that pass, — having failed to*
> *carry that way of knowledge into other fields beyond a narrow*
> *limit, we must then at least consent to scrutinise life and mind*
> *by methods appropriate to them.... Adhering still to the essen-*
> *tial rigorous method of science, though not to its purely physical*
> *instrumentation, scrutinising, experimenting, holding nothing for*
> *established which cannot be scrupulously and universally verified,*
> *we shall still arrive at supraphysical certitudes.*[1]
>
> — Sri Aurobindo

During the past nearly three decades, several factors — especially the wide use of psychedelic drugs and the spread of various Eastern psycho-spiritual disciplines in the West — have led an increasing number of Western scientists to view consciousness as something more than what can be learned about from the study of behaviour — the subject-matter of mainstream psychology today. These scientists have been posing certain fundamental questions about consciousness hitherto dealt with only by mystics and philosophers: What is consciousness? What are its major dimensions or levels? What is the nature of the various altered states of consciousness? Is consciousness individual or cosmic? How can the ordinary consciousness, which is fraught with psychological difficulties, be exceeded or transformed? For the majority of scientists who are interested in such questions, however, the interest has been a personal rather than a scientific one. As Charles T. Tart has observed, "...very large numbers of scientists are now personally exploring ASC's [altered states of consciousness], but few have begun to connect the personal exploration with their scientific activities."[2] Consequently, questions about consciousness such as those just mentioned, observes Robert E. Ornstein, "have not yet had a full treatment within academic science."[3] Having begun with a bold redefinition of psychology as the science of consciousness, Ornstein, too, subsequently gave an attenuated definition of psychology as the science of human experience,[4] seemingly stating, in Sri Aurobindo's words: "Psychology ought to be rather than is the science of consciousness."[5] This essay, drawing from Sri Aurobindo and from recent scientific thought, presents some of the chief impediments to the scientific study of consciousness, and explicates some of the requirements for such a study.

As has been pointed out by several scientists during the past nearly twenty years, one of the chief obstacles in pursuing a scientific study of consciousness is the dominant paradigm of modern science. The term 'paradigm', derived from the Greek word *paradeigma*, meaning 'pattern', has been used by Thomas S. Kuhn[6] in his analysis of the history of science to connote "the collective set of attitudes, values, procedures, techniques, etc."[7] that constitute the generally accepted framework of a particular science. Two chief aspects of today's ruling paradigm in science which prevent a scientific study of conciousness consist in its materialistic view of consciousness and its inappropriate methodology vis-à-vis the study of consciousness.

Most neuro-scientists today, states Fritjof Capra, subscribe to the view that matter being the primary reality, consciousness is merely "a property of complex material patterns which emerges at a certain level of biological evolution".[8] (For a recent elaboration of this view as formulated by Daniel C. Dennett, see the next essay on "Consciousness: the Materialistic and the Mystical Views".) Sri Aurobindo has summed up this materialistic view of consciousness as follows:

> In the theory of the sole reality of Matter, consciousness is only an operation of Matter-energy in Matter, a secretion or vibration

of the brain-cells, a physical reception of images and a brain-response, a reflex action or a reaction of Matter to the contacts of Matter.[9]

One crippling consequence of such an epiphenomenal view of consciousness is the attempt to study consciousness — or mind, as it is generally called in Western psychology, — by studying solely its manifestations in the body and its expression in behaviour. However, if consciousness is not an epiphenomenon but the essential reality — as maintained by yoga and as some recent consciousness research[10] and emerging thought based on subatomic physics[11] tend to corroborate — then the attempt to study consciousness through some of its superficial manifestations, whether physiological or behavioural, is, to use an inadequate analogy, like trying to discover the contents of a house by looking at it from outside or trying to understand a book by studying the properties of its paper and ink: one has to go *inside* the house or the book to discover its contents. Regarding an attempt at understanding consciousness by examining some of its superficial appearances, Sri Aurobindo writes:

> Consciousness is not an unaccountable freak or a chance growth or a temporary accident in a material and inconscient universe.
>
> It may so appear on the surface and physical science, since by its very terms it is limited to the examination of appearances and must start from the surface phenomenon, may choose or may have no alternative but to treat it on that basis. But surface appearances are not the reality of things, they may be a part of the truth but they are not the whole reality. One must look beyond the external appearances of things before one can know things in themselves....
>
> Physical science — and psychology in its present methods is only an extension of physical science — conducts its search into things from down upwards; it regards Matter as the foundation and the bottom of things and having searched into that foundation, got as it thinks to the very bottom, it believes, or once believed, it has by that very fact understood their depths, their centre, their

height and top. But this is a naive error. The truth of things is in their depths or at their centre and even at their top. The truth of consciousness also is to be found at its top and in its depths or at its centre.... [12]

It is not sufficient to examine the material, the physiological processes accompanying the functioning of consciousness and attempt to explain the functioning by its physical processes. This leaves consciousness itself unexplained; if it accounts to some extent, but imperfectly, for sense phenomena or mechanical thinking, it does not account in the least for the most important powers of our conscious energy; it does not account for reason, understanding, will, creative thought, conscious selection, the conscious intellectual and spiritual action and self-development of the human being.... To see how the body uses consciousness may be within limits a fruitful science, but it is more important to see how consciousness uses the body and still more important to see how it evolves and uses its own powers. The physiological study of the phenomenon of consciousness is only a side-issue; the psychological study of it independent of all reference to the body except as an instrument is the fruitful line of inquiry. [13]

To be able to "look beyond the external appearances of things" and discover the real nature of consciousness, the first prerequisite is a new paradigm which, as a tentative hypothesis, regards consciousness as a reality in its own right rather than as a byproduct of matter. Such a view, states Sri Aurobindo, can possibly create an opening for undreamed discoveries which have eluded the purely materialistic paradigm.

Its [physical science's] first regard is on Matter as the one principle of being and on Energy only as a phenomenon of Matter; but in the end one questions whether it is not the other way round, all things the action of Energy, and Matter only the field, body and instrument of her workings. The first view is quantitative and purely mechanical, the second lets in a qualitative and a more spiritual element. We do not at once leap out of the materialistic circle, but we see an opening in it which may widen into an outlet when, stirred by this suggestion, we look at life and mind not merely as a phenomenon in Matter but as energies and see that they are quite other energies than the material, with their own peculiar qualities, powers and workings.... Only a limited range of the phenomena of life and mind could be satisfied by a purely bio-physical, psycho-physical or bio-psychical explanation.... To know more we must have studied not only the actual or possible action of body and Matter on mind and life, but explored all the possible action of mind too on life and body; that opens undreamed vistas. And there is always the vast field of the action of mind in itself and on itself, which needs for its elucidation another, a mental, a psychic science.[14]

The second prerequisite for the study of consciousness is an appropriate methodology. The inadequacy of the quantitative and inferential methods of conventional science as applied to psychological studies has been recognised in recent years by several scientists:

> [In the methodology of conventional science]... data are gathered by observation and measurement, and are then interconnected with the help of conceptual models that are expressed, whenever possible, in mathematical language.... Such a science is inadequate for understanding the nature of consciousness and will not be able to deal with any qualities or values.[15]

> [In studies of perception]... scientific methodology in psychology tended to become identified with measurement alone.... This methodological dam has recently been cracked, largely through research in social and clinical psychology, where the effects of subjective factors on perception are especially obvious.[16]

> Blackburn... noted that many of our most talented young people are "turned off" to science: as a solution he proposed that we recognize the validity of a more sensuous-intuitive approach to nature, treating it as complementary to the classical intellectual approach.[17]

We associate "Psychology" with people in laboratories, perform-
ing experiments with quantitative methods. Many... have chal-
lenged the usefulness of a purely quantitative science, arguing
that an entire dimension of man's nature is omitted in such an
attempt.[18]

According to Sri Aurobindo, the fundamental methods of all
science — observation and experiment — are equally applicable
to the science of consciousness. He writes, in the notes entitled
"Towards a True Scientific Psychology":

> When the ancient thinkers of India set themselves to study the
> soul of man in themselves and others, they... proceeded at once
> to a process which resembles exactly enough the process adopted
> by modern science in its study of physical phenomena.... For there
> is no difference of essential law in the physical and the psychical,
> but only a difference and undoubtedly a great difference of energy,
> instrumentation and exact process....
>
>   Exact observation and untrammelled, yet scrupulous experi-
> ment are the method of every true Science. Not mere observation
> by itself — for without experiment, without analysis and new-
> combination observation leads to a limited and erroneous knowl-
> edge; often it generates an empirical classification which does not
> in the least deserve the name of science.[19]

Sri Aurobindo states, however, that the study of consciousness
calls for "intuitive and experimental knowledge"[20] and "a direct
observation of mental operations."[21] Such a direct observation
and a direct or intuitive knowledge of consciousness requires a
yogic or inner development, including the development of inner,
subtler senses[22]; the gross senses and the intellect employed in the
natural sciences can yield only indirect or inferential knowledge.

> ...the greater part of existence is either above or below mind, and
> mind can know only indirectly what is above or what is below
> it. But the one true and complete way of knowing is by direct
> knowledge.[23]

...the intellect sees only the phenomenon, it cannot go back behind it; when it tries, it only arrives at other and more occult phenomena. The truth of things can only be perceived when one gets to what may be called summarily the spiritual vision of things and even there completely only when there is not only vision but direct experience in the very substance of one's own being and all being.[24]

An important point for consciousness research lies in what Sri Aurobindo says about the procedure to be followed in Yoga: "As in Science, so here you have to accumulate experience on experience, following faithfully the methods laid down by the Guru or by the systems of the past...."[25] As Lama Govinda states: "Without the presence of a tradition, in which the experiences and knowledge of former generations are formulated (philosophy), every individual would be compelled to master the entire domain of the psychic, and only a few favoured ones would attain the goal of knowledge."[26] Though self-evident in the natural sciences, the necessity of founding one's research on knowledge already established is hardly recognised in the field of consciousness research. This brings us to the third prerequisite for the study of consciousness — a schema of consciousness derived from the knowledge already acquired in the past. Such a schema is needed to serve both as a map for the exploration of the unknown territory and as a framework into which all findings through personal observation and experiment can be meaningfully fitted.

The need for a framework in the form of a comprehensive theoretical model has been expressed by Charles T. Tart in relation to the study of parapsychological phenomena. He states:

Aside from the effects of paradigm clash, psi phenomena are difficult to accept because there is no comprehensive theory for understanding them.... [27]

A further need for theories and models is to organize the data of parapsychology: there are so many scattered observations and literature that the investigator cannot hope to digest it all.[28]

The need for an integrative conceptual framework in the field of contemporary psychology and psychotherapy has been well stated by Stanislav Grof who remarks:

> All the systems involved may represent more or less accurate descriptions of the aspect or level of the unconscious which they are describing. What we need now is a 'bootstrap psychology' that would integrate the various systems into a collection of maps covering the entire range of human consciousness.[29]

Alluding to the well-known story of the blind men and the elephant, Robert E. Ornstein, besides pointing out the need for an overall view, states further that such an all-embracing perspective requires a different mode of knowledge. He writes:

> ...we cannot understand the nature of an elephant by combining 'scalyness', 'length', 'softness', etc. in any conceivable proportion. Without the development of an overall perspective, we remain lost in individual investigations. Such a perspective is a province of another mode of knowledge and cannot be achieved in the same way that individual parts are explored.[30]

The study of consciousness thus calls for a comprehensive schema of consciousness based on a direct and experiential knowledge already acquired. Such a schema, states Sri Aurobindo, "has to be formulated... the results, though data of experience, being at first taken as a working hypothesis, subject to verification.[31]

Notes and References

1. Sri Aurobindo, "Materialism" in *The Supramental Manifestation and Other Writings*, Sri Aurobindo Birth Centenary Library (hereafter SABCL), (Pondicherry: Sri Aurobindo Ashram, 1970–75), Vol. 16, pp. 255–56.

2. Charles T. Tart, "States of Consciousness and State-Specific Sciences" in Robert E. Ornstein (Ed.), *The Nature of Human Consciousness* (New York: The Viking Press, 1973), p. 60.

3. Robert E. Ornstein (Ed.), *The Nature of Human Consciousness* (New York: The Viking Press, 1973), p. XI.

4. Compare the following:

   "Psychology is, primarily, the science of consciousness. Its researchers deal with consciousness directly when possible and indirectly, through the study of physiology and behaviour, when necessary." (Robert E. Ornstein, *The Psychology of Consciousness*, First Ed., San Francisco: W. H. Freeman & Co., 1972).

   "Psychology is, primarily, the science of human experience. Its researchers study secondary phenomena — such as behaviour, physiology, and 'verbal report' — as they relate to the central questions of consciousness." (Robert E. Ornstein, *The Psychology of Consciousness*, Second Ed., San Diego: Harcourt Bruce Jovanovich Inc., 1977).

5. Sri Aurobindo, *Essays Divine and Human*, (Pondicherry: Sri Aurobindo Ashram Publication Department, 1994), p. 332.

6. Thomas S. Kuhn, *The Structure of Scientific Revolutions* (Chicago: University of Chicago Press. 1970).

7. Arthur S. Reber, *The Penguin Dictionary of Psychology*, 1987, s. v. "paradigm".

8. Fritjof Capra, *Uncommon Wisdom* (London: Fontana Paperbacks, 1989).

9. Sri Aurobindo, *The Life Divine*, SABCL Vol. 18, p. 440.

10. Stanislav Grof, *Realms of the Human Unconscious* (New York: Dutton, 1976).

11. Fritjof Capra, *The Tao of Physics* (Berkeley, Calif.: Shambala, 1975).

12. Sri Aurobindo, *Essays Divine and Human*, pp. 337–38.

13. Ibid., p. 291.

14. Sri Aurobindo, "Materialism" in *The Supramental Manifestation and other Writings*, SABCL Vol. 16, pp. 254–55.

15. Fritjof Capra, *Uncommon Wisdom*, p. 145.

16. Hadley Cantril, Adelber Ames, Jr., Albert H. Hastorf and William H. Itelson, "Psychology and Scientific Research" in Robert E. Ornstein (Ed.), *The Nature of Human Consciousness.*
17. Charles T. Tart, "States of Consciousness and State-Specific Sciences", in Robert E. Ornstein (Ed.), *The Nature of Human Consciousness,* p. 41.
18. Robert E. Ornstein (Ed), *The Nature of Human Consciousness,* p. 213.
19. Sri Aurobindo, *Essays Divine and Human,* pp. 331–32.
20. Ibid., p. 321.
21. Ibid., p. 322.
22. Ibid., p. 340.
23. Ibid., p. 300.
24. Ibid., p. 337.
25. Sri Aurobindo, *Letters on Yoga,* SABCL Vol. 22, pp. 190–91.
26. Lama Govinda, "The Two Types of Psychology" in Robert E. Ornstein (Ed.). *The Nature of Human Consciousness.* p. 236.
27. Charles T. Tart, "Preliminary Notes on the Nature of Psi Processes" in ibid., p. 470.
28. Ibid., p. 492.
29. Quoted in Fritjof Capra, *Uncommon Wisdom,* p. 102.
30. Robert E. Ornstein, *The Psychology of Consciousness,* pp. 11–12.
31. Sri Aurobindo, *Essays Divine and Human,* p. 329.

3
Consciousness: The Materialistic and the Mystical Views

Perhaps the earliest roots of the concept of consciousness lie in ancient Indian thought which, founded on immediate mystical experience, conceived of the Absolute Reality as Sat-Chit-Ananda (Existence-Consciousness-Bliss). In this concept of the triune Reality, Chit or Consciousness stands for the Conscious Force which as Energy creates the universe.

In contrast to this mystical concept of consciousness is the materialistic view which is described by Sri Aurobindo thus:

> ...consciousness in itself does not exist, there are only phenomena of reactions of Matter to Matter or of Energy in Matter to Energy in Matter to which by generalisation we give the name. There is no person who is conscious, thinks, speaks, perceives, wills, acts; it is an organised body in which certain chemical, molecular, cellular, glandular and nerve activities take place and certain material results and reactions of these activities take place in the brain which take the form of these phenomena. It is the body that thinks, perceives, wills, speaks, acts; it is Matter that goes through these operations and becomes aware of them; it may be said that brain-matter makes a record or notation of these actions and this notation is consciousness and this record is memory. There is nothing in the world except Matter and the operations of Matter.[1]

The above-stated mystical and materialistic views of consciousness are diametrically opposed in several respects. First, materialism posits matter as the only reality, consciousness being regarded as its epiphenomenal by-product and a mere characteristic of evolved matter, not a 'thing' in itself; on the other hand, the mystical view regards consciousness as the primary reality, and holds that matter is "by no means fundamentally real" and only "a structure of Energy".[2]

Secondly, according to the materialistic viewpoint, consciousness is a characteristic of only living organisms, the non-living kingdoms of nature being regarded as devoid of it; from the mystical viewpoint, consciousness as "the fundamental thing in existence"[3] pervades the entire universe and even transcends it. Thirdly, the materialist looks upon the functionings of consciousness as mechanical phenomena, explicable in mechanistic terms in contrast to the mystical view, according to which consciousness is the Conscious Force, impregnated with and expressive of purpose and meaning at all levels of its manifestation.

In recent times, attempts have been made to base the materialistic view of consciousness on scientific evidence.[4] However, in essence, any materialistic theory is necessarily a philosophical theory, for it takes its stand on the metaphysical postulate that physical matter is the ultimate reality. Therefore a materialistic theory of consciousness oversteps the limits of science and enters the realm of philosophy; it cannot claim to be a scientific theory. What Sri Aurobindo observed more than half a century ago is perhaps even truer today.

> Most continental scientists have now renounced the idea that Science can explain the fundamentals of existence. They hold that Science is only concerned with process and not with fundamentals. They declare that it is not the business of Science nor is it within its means to decide anything about the great questions which concern philosophy and religion. This is the enormous change which the latest developments of Science have brought about. Science itself nowadays is neither materialistic nor idealistic. The rock on which materialism was built and which in the 19th century seemed unshakable has now been shattered. Materialism has now become a philosophical speculation just like any other theory; it cannot claim to found itself on a sort of infallible Biblical authority, based on the facts and conclusions of Science. This change can be felt by one like myself who grew up in the heyday of absolute rule of scientific materialism in the 19th century. The way which had been

almost entirely barred, except by rebellion, now lies wide open to spiritual truths, spiritual ideas, spiritual experiences. That is the real revolution....The facts of Science do not compel anyone to take any particular philosophical direction. They are now neutral and can even be used on one side or another[5] though most scientists do not consider such a use as admissible.[6]

Thus any scientific theory which bases itself on a philosophy abandons the neutrality of present-day science and harks back to the scientific orthodoxy of the nineteenth century.

According to the materialistic view, consciousness emerges in the course of evolution from primordial unconscious matter. Regarding such a theory of the origin of consciousness, Sri Aurobindo writes:

According to the materialist hypothesis consciousness must be a result of energy in Matter; it is Matter's reaction of reflex to itself in itself, a response of organised inconscient chemical substance that touches upon it, a record of which that inconscient substance through some sensitiveness of cell and nerve becomes inexplicably aware. But such an explanation may account, — if we admit this impossible magic of the conscious response of an inconscient to the inconscient, — for sense and reflex action, [yet it] becomes absurd if we try to explain by it thought and will, the imagination of the poet, the attention of the scientist, the reasoning of the philosopher. Call it mechanical cerebration, if you will, but no mere mechanism of grey stuff of brain can explain these things; a gland cannot write Hamlet or pulp of brain work out a system of metaphysics. There is no parity, kinship or visible equation between the alleged cause or agent on the one side and on the other the effect and its observable process. There is a gulf here that cannot be bridged by any stress of forcible affirmation or crossed by any stride of inference or violent leap of argumentative reason. Consciousness and an inconscient substance may be connected, may interpenetrate, may act on each other, but they are and remain things opposite, incommensurate with each other, fundamentally diverse.[7]

From Sri Aurobindo's viewpoint, the fundamental shortcoming of the materialistic theory is that it attempts to explain the essential nature of consciousness on the basis of ordinary human experience, but the *essential* nature of things is beyond the ken of ordinary experience, for "human consciousness... cannot see what is there, but only speculate, infer or conjecture"[8] thus ending up with abstractions. On the other hand, consciousness as directly experienced by the mystic "is not something abstract, it is like existence itself... something very concrete".[9]

Based on such direct experience of consciousness as a concrete reality, here is an account of its nature in Sri Aurobindo's words.

Consciousness, Reality and Existence

Consciousness is a fundamental thing, the fundamental thing in existence — it is the energy, the motion, the movement of consciousness that creates the universe and all that is in it — not only the macrocosm but the microcosm is nothing but consciousness arranging itself.[10]

In the supreme timeless Existence, as far as we know it by reflection in spiritual experience, existence and consciousness are one. We are accustomed to identify consciousness with certain operations of mentality and sense and, where these are absent or quiescent, we speak of that state of being as unconscious. But consciousness can exist where there are no overt operations, no signs revealing it, even where it is withdrawn from objects and absorbed in pure existence or involved in the appearance of non-existence. It is intrinsic in being, self-existent, not abolished by quiescence, by inaction, by veiling or covering, by inert absorption or involution; it is there in the being, even when its state seems to be dreamless sleep or a blind trance or an annulment of awareness or an absence. In the supreme timeless status where consciousness is one with being and immobile, it is not a separate reality, but simply and purely the self-awareness inherent in existence.[11]

Consciousness is a reality inherent in existence. It is there even when it is not active on the surface, but silent and immobile; it is there even when it is invisible on the surface, not reacting on outward things or sensible to them, but withdrawn and either active or inactive within; it is there even when it seems to us to be quite absent and the being to our view unconscious and inanimate.[12]

...modern materialistic thought... is governed by science and sees consciousness only as a phenomenon that emerges out of in-conscient Matter and consists of certain reactions of the system to outward things. But that is a phenomenon of consciousness, it is not consciousness itself, it is even only a very small part of the possible phenomenon of consciousness and can give no clue to Consciousness the Reality which is of the very essence of existence.[13]

To me, for instance, consciousness is the very stuff of existence and I can feel it everywhere enveloping and penetrating the stone as much as man or the animal.[14]

Consciousness, Mind and Matter

The development of recent research and thought seems to point to a sort of obscure beginning of life and perhaps a sort of inert or suppressed consciousness in the metal and in the earth and in other 'inanimate' forms, or at least the first stuff of what becomes consciousness in us may be there. Only while in the plant can we dimly recognise and conceive the thing that I have called vital consciousness. The consciousness of Matter, of the inert form, is difficult indeed for us to understand or imagine, and what we find it difficult to understand or imagine we consider it our right to deny. Nevertheless, when one has pursued consciousness so far into the depths, it becomes incredible that there should be this sudden gulf in Nature. Thought has a right to suppose a unity where that unity is confessed by all other classes of phenomena and in one class only, not denied, but merely more concealed than in others. And if we suppose the unity to be unbroken, we then arrive at the existence of consciousness in all forms of the Force which is at work in the world. Even if there be no conscient or superconscient Purusha inhabiting all forms, yet is there in those forms a conscious force of being of which even their outer parts overtly or inertly partake.

Necessarily, in such a view, the word consciousness changes its meaning. It is no longer synonymous with mentality but indicates a self-aware force of existence of which mentality is a middle term; below mentality it sinks into vital and material movements which are for us subconscient; above it rises into the supramental which is for us the superconscient. But in all it is one and the same thing organising itself differently. This is, once more, the Indian conception of Chit which, as energy, creates the worlds. Essentially, we arrive at that unity which materialistic Science perceives from the other end when it asserts that Mind cannot be another force than Matter, but must be merely development and outcome of material energy. Indian thought at its deepest affirms on the other hand that Mind and Matter are rather different grades of the same energy, different organisations of one conscious Force of Existence.[15]

Chit, the divine Consciousness, is not our mental self-awareness; that we shall find to be only a form, a lower and limited mode or movement. As we progress and awaken to the soul in us and things, we shall realise that there is a consciousness also in the plant, in the metal, in the atom, in electricity, in everything that belongs to physical nature; we shall find even that it is not really in all respects a lower or more limited mode than the mental, on the contrary it is in many "inanimate" forms more intense, rapid, poignant, though less evolved towards the surface. But this also, this consciousness of vital and physical Nature is, compared with Chit, a lower and therefore a limited form, mode and movement. These lower modes of consciousness are the conscious-stuff of inferior planes in one indivisible existence. In ourselves also there is in our subconscious being an action which is precisely that of the "inanimate" physical Nature whence has been constituted the basis of our physical being, another which is that of plant-life, and another which is that of the lower animal creation around us. All these are so much dominated and conditioned by the thinking and reasoning conscious-being in us that we have no real awareness of these lower planes; we are unable to perceive in their own terms what these parts of us are doing, and receive it very imperfectly in the terms and values of the thinking and reasoning mind.[16]

Consciousness is usually identified with mind, but mental consciousness is only the human range which no more exhausts all the possible ranges of consciousness than human sight exhausts all the gradations of colour or human hearing all the gradations of sound — for there is much above or below that is to man invisible and inaudible. So there are ranges of consciousness above and below the human range, with which the normal human has no contact and they seem to it unconscious, — supramental or overmental and submental ranges.[17]

Ordinarily we mean by it [consciousness] our first obvious idea of a mental waking consciousness such as is possessed by the human being during the major part of his bodily existence, when he is not asleep, stunned or otherwise deprived of his physical and superficial methods of sensation. In this sense it is plain enough that consciousness is the exception and not the rule in the order of the material universe. We ourselves do not always possess it. But this vulgar and shallow idea of the nature of consciousness, though it still colours our ordinary thought and associations, must now definitely disappear out of philosophical thinking. For we know that there is something in us which is conscious when we sleep, when we are stunned or drugged or in a swoon, in all apparently unconscious states of our physical being. Not only so, but we may now be sure that the old thinkers were right when they declared that even in our waking state what we call then our consciousness is only a small selection from our entire conscious being. It is a superficies, it is not even the whole of our mentality. Behind it, much vaster than it, there is a subliminal or subconscient mind which is the greater part of ourselves and contains heights and profundities which no man has yet measured or fathomed.[18]

Most people associate consciousness with the brain or mind because that is the centre for intellectual thought and mental vision, but consciousness is not limited to that kind of thought or vision. It is everywhere in the system and there are several centres of it,...[19]

Consciousness, Body and Brain

Materialism indeed insists that, whatever the extension of consciousness, it is a material phenomenon inseparable from our physical organs and not their utiliser but their result. This orthodox contention, however, is no longer able to hold the field against the tide of increasing knowledge. Its explanations are becoming more and more inadequate and strained. It is becoming always clearer that not only does the capacity of our total consciousness far exceed that of our organs, the senses, the nerves, the brain, but that even for our ordinary thought and consciousness these organs are only their habitual instruments and not their generators. Consciousness uses the brain which its upwards strivings have produced, brain has not produced nor does it use the consciousness. There are even abnormal instances which go to prove that our organs are not entirely indispensable instruments, — that the heart-beats are not absolutely essential to life, any more than is breathing, nor the organised brain-cells to thought. Our physical organism no more causes or explains thought and consciousness than the construction of an engine causes or explains the motive power of steam or electricity. The force is anterior, not the physical instrument.[20]

There is no doubt a connection and interdependence between consciousness and the inconscient substance in which it resides and through which it seems to operate. Consciousness depends upon the body and its functionings, on the brain, nerves, gland-action, right physiological working, for its own firm state and action. It uses them as its instruments and, if they are injured or unable to act, the action of the consciousness may also be in part or whole impaired, impeded or suspended. But this does not prove that the action of consciousness is an action of the body and nothing else.[21]

Body, brain, nervous system are instruments of consciousness, they are not its causes.

Consciousness is its own cause, a producer of objects and images and not their product. We are blinded to this truth because when we think of consciousness, it is of the individual we think.

We look at the world in the way and speak of it in the terms of individual consciousness; but it is of the universal consciousness that the world is a creation.[22]

Conclusion and Summary

Science can only describe the processes of things. To try to explain the essential nature of a thing on the basis of our normal experience is necessarily to go beyond the limits of science into the realm of philosophy. The materialistic and mechanistic theory of consciousness which attempts to explain the essential nature of consciousness in terms of brain processes is such a pseudo-scientific philosophical theory. The only way to arrive at an empirical and scientific theory of consciousness is to transcend normal experience and apprehend consciousness directly through mystical experience.

Speaking from such experience, Sri Aurobindo states that Consciousness, Existence and Reality are one. Consciousness is at once the self-awareness inherent in existence and the conscious Force that builds the universe. Therefore, consciousness is not confined to the human being, but is present in the animal, the plant and also in matter.

Human consciousness is not identical with mind; mental consciousness is only a middle term below which lie levels of consciousness which to us are subconscient, and above which there exist levels of consciousness which to us are superconscient.

Consciousness, the fundamental thing in existence, is its own cause. It is not caused by the brain but precedes it in evolution, though in the human being it is dependent upon the brain as a necessary instrument for its expression.

Notes and References

1. Sri Aurobindo, *Essays Divine and Human*, (Pondicherry: Sri Aurobindo Ashram, 1994), p. 293.
2. Sri Aurobindo, *The Life Divine*, Sri Aurobindo Birth Centenary Library (hereafter SABCL), (Pondicherry: Sri Aurobindo Ashram, 1970–75) Vol. 19, p. 652.
3. Sri Aurobindo, *Letters on Yoga*, SABCL Vol. 22, p. 236.
4. A good example of such an attempt is to be found in Daniel C. Dennett, *Consciousness Explained*, (Boston: Little, Brown and Company, 1991.)
5. Two well-known examples of how recent scientific discoveries can be used to argue against materialism and to support the mystical philosophies are Fritjof Capra, *The Tao of Physics* (Berkeley: Shambhala Publications, 1975) and Gary Zukav, *The Dancing Wu Li Masters* (New York: William Morrow & Co., 1979).
6. Sri Aurobindo, *Letters on Yoga*, SABCL Vol. 22, pp. 206–07.
7. Sri Aurobindo, *Essays Divine and Human*, p. 289.
8. Sri Aurobindo, *Essays Divine and Human*, p. 303.
9. Sri Aurobindo, *Letters on Yoga*, SABCL Vol. 22, p. 479.
10. Ibid., p. 236.
11. Sri Aurobindo, *The Life Divine*, SABCL Vol.18, pp. 544–45.
12. Sri Aurobindo, *Letters on Yoga*, SABCL Vol. 22, p. 234.
13. Ibid., p. 238.
14. Sri Aurobindo, *Savitri*, SABCL Vol. 29, p. 736.
15. Sri Aurobindo, *The Life Divine*, SABCL Vol. 18, pp. 87–88.
16. Sri Aurobindo, *The Synthesis of Yoga*, SABCL Vol. 20, p. 371.
17. Sri Aurobindo, *Letters on Yoga*, SABCL Vol. 22, p. 234.
18. Sri Aurobindo, *The Life Divine*, SABCL Vol. 18, p. 85.
19. Sri Aurobindo, *Letters on Yoga*, SABCL Vol. 23, p. 727.

20. Sri Aurobindo, *The Life Divine*, SABCL Vol. 18, pp. 85–86.
21. Sri Aurobindo, *Essays Divine and Human*, pp. 289–90.
22. Ibid., p. 318.

4
Sri Aurobindo on the Structure and Organisation of the Being
An Integral Map for Self-Discovery

We are not only what we know of ourselves but an immense more which we do not know; our momentary personality is only a bubble on the ocean of our existence.[1] — Sri Aurobindo

Our mind and ego are like the crown and dome of a temple jutting out from the waves while the great body of the building is submerged under the surface of the waters.[2] — Sri Aurobindo

Normally, one feels oneself to be a unitary entity, a single being. Someone who is to some extent conscious of his psychological make-up can somewhat distinguish among its different aspects, physical, emotional and mental. But in our ordinary consciousness or awareness all these elements are mixed up. When one becomes more conscious — usually as a result of the practice of a spiritual discipline — one discovers that one's psychological nature is complex, made up of different distinguishable parts of the being.

Men do not know themselves and have not learned to distinguish the different parts of their being; for these are usually lumped together by them as mind, because it is through a mentalised perception and understanding that they know or feel them; therefore they do not understand their own states and actions, or, if at all, then only on the surface.[3]

...man is not made up of one piece but of many pieces and each part of him has a personality of its own. That is a thing which people yet have not sufficiently realised — the psychologists have begun to glimpse it, but recognise only when there is a marked case of double or multiple personality. But all men are like that, in reality.[4]

Two Systems in the Organisation of the Being

Sri Aurobindo distinguishes "two systems simultaneously active in the organisation of the being and its parts". One system is concentric, like "a series of rings or sheaths"; the other is vertical, "like a flight of steps".[5]

The concentric system consists of the outer or surface being, the inner being, and supporting both of these, the inmost being or the psychic (Fig.1). The outer being and the inner being have three corresponding parts — mental, vital, physical. Thus "There are, we might say, two beings in us, one on the surface, our ordinary exterior mind, life, body consciousness, another behind the veil, an inner mind, an inner life, an inner physical consciousness constituting another or inner self."[6]

Outer being
(Physical, Vital, Mental)

Inner Being
(Physical, Vital, Mental)

Innermost Being
(the Psychic)

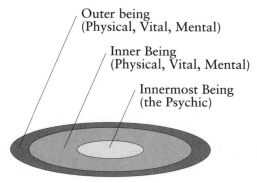

FIGURE 1.

THE CONCENTRIC SYSTEM

The vertical system consists of various levels or gradations of consciousness below and above mental consciousness — the level with which we are most familiar as human beings. The Inconscient, the Subconscient, the Physical, the Vital, Mind, Higher Mind, Illumined Mind, Intuition, Overmind, Supermind and Sachchidananda constitute the chief levels of consciousness in the vertical system (Fig.2).

FIGURE 2.

THE VERTICAL SYSTEM — LEVELS OF CONSCIOUSNESS

Evolution of Consciousness

In Sri Aurobindo's thought, the concept of levels of consciousness is intimately related to the concept of evolution of consciousness.

> ...this One Being and Consciousness is involved here in Matter.
> Evolution is the method by which it liberates itself; consciousness
> appears in what seems to be inconscient, and once having appeared
> is self-impelled to grow higher and higher and at the same time
> to enlarge and develop towards a greater and greater perfection.
> Life is the first step of this release of consciousness; mind is the
> second; but the evolution does not finish with mind, it awaits a
> release into something greater, a consciousness which is spiritual
> and supramental.[7]

In my explanation of the universe I have put forward this cardinal fact of a spiritual evolution as the meaning of our existence here. It is a series of ascents from the physical being and consciousness to the vital, the being dominated by the life-self, thence to the mental being realised in the fully developed man and thence into the perfect consciousness which is beyond the mental, into the supramental Consciousness and the supramental being.... [8]

The Outer Being

The three major divisions in the outer being consist of the mind (the mental), the life-self (the vital) and the body (the physical). Each of these parts has its own distinct type of consciousness, though in our ordinary awareness they are all mixed up.

Each plane of our being — mental, vital, physical — has its own consciousness, separate though interconnected and interacting; but to our outer mind and sense, in our waking experience, they are all confused together. The body, for instance, has its own consciousness and acts from it, even without any mental will of our own or even against that will, and our surface mind knows very little about this body-consciousness, feels it only in an imperfect way, sees only its results and has the greatest difficulty in finding out their causes.[9]

One of the first distinctions that one learns to make as one grows in consciousness is the difference between the mental and the vital.

The "Mind" in the ordinary use of the word covers indiscriminately the whole consciousness, for man is a mental being and mentalises everything; but... "mind" and "mental"... connote specially the part of the nature which has to do with cognition and intelligence, with ideas, with mental or thought perceptions, the reactions of thought to things, with the truly mental movements and formations, mental vision and will, etc., that are part of his intelligence. The vital has to be carefully distinguished from mind, even though it has a mind element transfused into it; the vital is the Life-nature made up of desires, sensations, feelings, passions, energies of action, will of desire, reactions of the desire-soul in man and all that play of possessive and other related instincts, anger, fear, greed, lust, etc., that belong to this field of the nature. Mind and vital are mixed up on the surface of the consciousness, but they are quite separate forces in themselves and as soon as one gets behind the ordinary surface consciousness one sees them as separate, discovers their distinction and can with the aid of this knowledge analyse their surface mixtures.[10]

...mind and vital... are not the same. The thinking mind or *buddhi* lives, however imperfectly in man, by intelligence and reason. Vital, on the other hand, is a thing of desires, impulses, force-pushes, emotions, sensations, seekings after life-fulfilment, possession and enjoyment; these are its functions and its nature; — it is that part of us which seeks after life and its movements for their own sake and it does not want to leave hold of them if they bring it suffering as well as or more than pleasure; it is even capable of luxuriating in tears and suffering as part of the drama of life.[11]

Similarly, the body, which is not mere unconscious Matter, but "a structure of a secretly conscious Energy that has taken form in it",[12] has a consciousness which is different from and independent of the mind.

The body also has a consciousness of its own and, though it is a submental instrument or servant consciousness, it can disobey or fail to obey as well. In many things, in matters of health and illness for instance, in all automatic functionings, the body acts on its own and is not a servant of the mind. If it is fatigued, it can offer a passive resistance to the mind's will. It can cloud the mind with *tamas*, inertia, dullness, fumes of the subconscient so that the mind cannot act. The arm lifts, no doubt, when it gets the suggestion, but at first the legs do not obey when they are asked to walk; they have to learn how to leave the crawling attitude and movement and take up the erect and ambulatory habit. When you first ask the hand to draw a straight line or to play music, it can't do it and won't do it. It has to be schooled, trained, taught and afterwards it does automatically what is required of it. All this proves that there is a body-consciousness which can do things at the mind's order, but has to be awakened, trained, made a good and conscious instrument.[13]

Though separate, the three principal parts of the outer being — the mental, the vital and the physical — are intermixed and interact on one another, giving rise to distinguishable subdivisions within each part of the being. Thus, besides the mind proper (the thinking mind), there is a part of the mind which is intermixed with the vital, called the vital mind. There is also a part of the mind which is interfused with the physical, called the physical mind. Similar subdivisions exist within the vital and the physical. Two of these subdivisions which generally play a prominent role in most human beings are the *vital mind* and the *physical mind*.

The vital mind is the part of the mind which is intermixed and dominated by impulses, desires and feelings of the vital nature. The reasoning of the vital mind is a pseudo-reasoning as is well illustrated by the common act of rationalisation by which the mind, usurped by the vital, provides plausible "rational" explanations and justifications for impulses and desires of the vital.

The physical mind is the part of the mind which is intermingled with and partakes of the characteristics of the physical consciousness. Some of the chief characteristics of the physical, namely, inertia, obscurity, mechanical repetitiveness, automatism, constriction and chaotic activity are reflected in the physical mind in the form of mental torpor, doubt, mechanical reactions to things, habitual modes of thinking, and confusion. The part of the mind which is closest to the physical is referred to as the *mechanical mind*; it is like a machine that goes on turning round and round whatever thoughts occur in it.

The Inner Being (The Subliminal)

Behind the outer being is the inner being, also called the subliminal self.

> There is an inner as well as an outer consciousness all through our being, upon all its levels. The ordinary man is aware only of his surface self and quite unaware of all that is concealed by the surface. And yet what is on the surface, what we know or think we know of ourselves and even believe that that is all we are, is only a small part of our being and by far the larger part of us is below the surface. Or, more accurately, it is behind the frontal consciousness, behind the veil, occult and known only by an occult knowledge.... What we call our mind is only an outer mind, a surface mental action, instrumental for the partial expression of a larger mind behind of which we are not ordinarily aware and can know only by going inside ourselves. So too what we know of the vital in us is only the outer vital, a surface activity partially expressing a larger secret vital which we can only know by going within. Equally, what we call our physical being is only a visible projection of a greater and subtler invisible physical consciousness which is much more complex, much more aware, much wider in its receptiveness, much more open and plastic and free.[14]

Whereas the outer being "receives consciously only the outer touches and knows things indirectly through the outer mind and senses",[15] the inner being is "directly aware of the universal consciousness and the universal forces that play through us and around us."[16] For the inner mind is directly in touch with the universal mind, just as the inner vital is in direct touch with the universal life-forces, and the inner physical with the universal physical forces around us. To illustrate the difference between indirect knowledge through the outer being and direct knowledge through the inner being:

> Take illness. If we live only in the outward physical consciousness, we do not usually know that we are going to be ill until the

symptoms of the malady declare themselves on the body. But if we develop the inward physical consciousness, we become aware of a subtle environmental physical atmosphere and can feel the forces of illness coming towards us through it, feel them even at a distance and, if we have learnt how to do it, we can stop them by the will or otherwise. We sense too around us a vital physical or nervous envelope which radiates from the body and protects it, and we can feel the adverse forces trying to break through it and can interfere, stop them or reinforce the nervous envelope. Or we can feel the symptoms of illness, fever or cold, for instance, in the subtle physical sheath before they are manifest in the gross body and destroy them there, preventing them from manifesting in the body.[17]

Environmental Consciousness (The Circumconscient)

The subliminal has a formation of consciousness which projects itself beyond the body "and forms a circumconscient, an environing part of itself, through which it receives the contacts of the world and can become aware of them and deal with them before they enter."[18] This environmental consciousness surrounding the body is that part of the individual being through which the individual is in inner contact with other beings and with universal forces.

> By environmental consciousness I mean something that each man carries around him, outside his body, even when he is not aware of it, — by which he is in touch with others and with the universal forces. It is through this that the thoughts, feelings, etc. of others pass to enter into one — it is through this also that waves of the universal force — desire, sex, etc. come in and take possession of the mind, vital or body.[19]

> Each man has his own personal consciousness entrenched in his body and gets into touch with his surroundings only through his body and senses and the mind using the senses.

Yet all the time the universal forces are pouring into him without his knowing it. He is aware only of thoughts, feelings, etc., that rise to the surface and these he takes for his own. Really they come from outside in mind waves, vital waves, waves of feeling and sensation, etc., which take particular form in him and rise to the surface after they have got inside.

But they do not get into his body at once. He carries about with him an environmental consciousness (called by the Theosophists the Aura) into which they first enter. If you can become conscious of this environmental self of yours, then you can catch the thought, passion, suggestion or force of illness and prevent it from entering into you. If things in you are thrown out, they often do not go altogether but take refuge in this environmental atmosphere and from there they try to get in again. Or they go to a distance outside but linger on the outskirts or even perhaps far off, waiting till they get an opportunity to attempt entrance.[20]

The Inmost Being (The Psychic)

Supporting mind, life and body is the inmost being, called by Sri Aurobindo the psychic being, the term being derived from a Greek root (*psukhē*) which means the soul. The soul in its essence, called the psyche, is described by Sri Aurobindo as a spark and an eternal portion of the Divine present in all things and beings in the universe. Whereas the Universal Self or Atman stands above the evolutionary process and is unaffected by it, the psyche is the element that develops in the evolution and grows into an individual self called the psychic being.

It is necessary to understand clearly the difference between the evolving soul (psychic being) and the pure Atman, self or spirit. The pure self is unborn, does not pass through death or birth, is independent of birth or body, mind or life or this manifested Nature. It is not bound by these things, not limited, not affected, even though it assumes and supports them. The soul, on the contrary, is something that comes down into birth and passes through death — although it does not itself die, for it is immortal — from one state to another, from the earth plane to other planes and back again to the earth-existence. It goes on with this progression from life to life through an evolution which leads it up to the human state and evolves through it all a being of itself which we call the psychic being that supports the evolution and develops a physical, a vital, a mental human consciousness as its instruments of world-experience and of a disguised, imperfect, but growing self-expression.[21]

A distinction must be made also between the true soul (psychic being) and the desire-soul (the vital being) which is often mistaken for the real soul.

In most men the soul is hidden and covered over by the action of the external nature; they mistake the vital being for the soul, because it is the vital which animates and moves the body. But this vital being is a thing made up of desires and executive forces, good and bad; it is the desire-soul, not the true thing. It is when the true soul (psyche) comes forward and begins first to influence and then govern the actions of the instrumental nature that man begins to overcome vital desire and grow towards a divine nature.[22]

Purusha and Prakriti

Developing the concepts of the Sankhya philosophy, Sri Aurobindo distinguishes between the soul or spirit side of the Being called Purusha (Person or Conscious Being), which is the essential or true being, and the Nature side of Being called Prakriti (Nature), which is the phenomenal or instrumental being. Both the outer being and the inner being described previously belong to Prakriti. Behind the outer mind and the inner mind, the outer vital and the inner vital, the outer physical and the inner physical, lies the true being, the Purusha, in the form of "an inmost mental, vital, physical, more specifically called the true mind, the true vital, the true physical consciousness".[23] The psychic being behind the outer being and the inner being and supporting them both is also a Purusha (Fig. 3).

FIGURE 3.

PURUSHA AND PRAKRITI

Explaining the nature of Purusha and Prakriti, Sri Aurobindo writes:

> The Being is one throughout, but on each plane of Nature, it is represented by a form of itself which is proper to that plane, the mental Purusha in the mental plane, the vital Purusha in the vital, the physical Purusha in the physical.[24]

> The Purusha is the silent witness consciousness which observes the actions of Prakriti — Prakriti is the Force of Nature which one feels as doing all the actions, when one gets rid of the sense of the ego as doer.[25]

When we come to look in at our selves instead of out at the world and begin to analyse our subjective experience, we find that there are two parts of our being which can be, to all appearance, entirely separated from each other, one a consciousness which is still and passive and supports, and the other a consciousness which is busy and creative and is supported. The passive and fundamental consciousness is the Soul, the Purusha, Witness or *sākṣī*, the active and superstructural consciousness is Nature, Prakriti, processive or creative energy of the *sākṣī*.[26]

In our ordinary consciousness we are unable to distinguish our true self, the Purusha, from the Nature side of our being, Prakriti, because Purusha is identified with Prakriti. In the state of identification, the Self is bound and governed by its instrumental nature — body, life and mind.

If the Purusha in us is passive and allows Nature to act, accepting all she imposes on him, giving a constant automatic sanction, then the soul in mind, life, body, the mental, vital, physical being in us, becomes subject to our nature, ruled by its formation, driven by its activities; that is the normal state of our ignorance. If the Purusha in us becomes aware of itself as the Witness and stands back from Nature, that is the first step to the soul's freedom.... [27]

The experience of the separation of Purusha from Prakriti may take place on any plane of the being.

Usually it is in the inner mental that this separation first happens and it is the inner mental Purusha who remains silent, observing the Prakriti as separate from himself. But it may also be the inner vital Purusha or inner physical or else without location simply the whole Purusha consciousness separate from the whole Prakriti. Sometimes it is felt above the head, but then it is usually spoken of as the Atman and the realisation is that of the silent Self.[28]

The true being may be realised in one or both of two aspects — the individual soul (psychic being) or the Universal Self (Atman).

Being (Individual and Universal)

When we think of the being, we normally think of the individual being, just as when we think of consciousness, we generally think of the consciousness of the individual. But Being or Consciousness — two aspects of the One Reality — is all-embracing and includes the universe as well as the individual. Seen from a spiritual consciousness "both individual and universe are simultaneous and interrelated expressions of the same transcendent Being".[29] "Universe is a diffusion of the Divine All in infinite Space and Time, the individual its concentration within limits of Space and Time."[30] It is the ego that creates a wall and sense of separation between the individual being and the universal being.

> In the lower nature man is an ego making a clean cut in conception between himself and all other existence; the ego is to him self, but all the rest not-self, external to his being. His whole action starts from and is founded upon this self-conception and world-conception. But the conception is in fact an error. However sharply he individualises himself in mental idea and mental or other action, he is inseparable from the universal being, his body from universal force and matter, his life from the universal life, his mind from universal mind, his soul and spirit from universal soul and spirit.[31]

Thus each part of the individual being corresponds to a plane of the universal being.

Ego and Individuality

In our normal consciousness, as stated previously, we are not conscious of our true being; we are aware only of our outer being — body, life and mind — with which we identify our self. This identification of the true being with the outer being gives rise to an ego — physical, vital, and mental — which gives us the sense of I-ness, an individuality separate from the rest of the universe.

...the ego is mental, vital, physical. Ego implies the identification of our existence with outer self, the ignorance of the true self above and our psychic being within us.[32]

The ego is only a provisional individuality, "a device of Nature which holds together her action in the mind and body"[33] until the true individual — the psychic being — is discovered.

The "I" or the little ego is constituted by Nature and is at once a mental, vital and physical formation meant to aid in centralising and individualising the outer consciousness and action. When the true being is discovered, the utility of the ego is over and the formation has to disappear — the true being is felt in its place.[34]

This persistent soul-existence is the real Individuality which stands behind the constant mutations of the thing we call our personality. It is not a limited ego but a thing in itself infinite.... [35]

The Subconscient and the Inconscient

Whereas the subliminal or inner being is *behind* the outer being of mind, life and body, the subconscient and the Inconscient constitute the nether being *below* the physical consciousness. All upon earth is based on the Inconscient which is not really devoid of consciousness, as the term would imply, but is the nethermost level of the involution of consciousness from which the evolution of consciousness starts.

The Inconscience is an inverse reproduction of the supreme super-conscience: it has the same absoluteness of being and automatic action, but in a vast involved trance; it is being lost in itself, plunged in its own abyss of infinity. Instead of a luminous absorption in self-existence there is a tenebrous involution in it, the darkness veiled within darkness of the Rig Veda, *tama āsīt tamasā gūḍham*, which makes it look like Non-Existence; instead of a luminous inherent self-awareness there is a consciousness plunged into an abyss of self-oblivion, inherent in being but not awake in being.[36]

The subconscient is the antechamber of the Inconscient, and lies between the Inconscient and the conscious mind, life and body.

In the subconscient there is an obscure mind full of obstinate Sanskaras, impressions, associations, fixed notions, habitual reactions formed by our past, an obscure vital full of the seeds of habitual desires, sensations and nervous reactions, a most obscure material which governs much that has to do with the condition of the body. It is largely responsible for our illnesses; chronic or repeated illnesses are indeed mainly due to the subconscient and its obstinate memory and habit of repetition of whatever has impressed itself upon the body-consciousness.[37]

...all that is consciously experienced sinks down into the subconscient, not as precise though submerged memories but as obscure yet obstinate impressions of experience, and these can come up at any time as dreams, as mechanical repetitions of past thought, feelings, action, etc., as "complexes" exploding into action and event, etc., etc. The subconscient is the main cause why all things repeat themselves and nothing ever gets changed except in appearance. It is the cause why people say character cannot be changed, the cause also of the constant return of things one hoped to have got rid of for ever.... All too that is suppressed without being wholly got rid of sinks down there and remains as seed ready to surge up or sprout up at any moment.[38]

Matter is under the control of this power [the subconscient], because it is that out of which it has been created — that is why matter seems to us to be quite unconscious. The material body is very much under the influence of this power for the same reason; it is why we are not conscious of what is going on in the body, for the most part. The outer consciousness goes down into this subconscient when we are asleep, and so it becomes unaware of what is going on in us when we are asleep except for a few dreams.[39]

During the waking state, the mind lives largely in impressions rising up from the subconscient. In ordinary sleep most dreams are formations made from subconscient impressions. Thus, in most human beings, the outer self of mind, life and body is to a great extent an instrument of the upsurging irrational, mechanical and repetitive movements of the subconscious during both waking and sleep.

The Superconscient

Just as the subconscient is what lies *below* the physical consciousness from which things come up into the physical, the vital and the mental parts of the being, so the superconscient, consisting of higher levels of consciousness, lies *above* normal mind, and from these higher ranges, things descend into the lower parts of the being. Whereas the subconscient is the basis of our material being and supports all that comes up in the physical nature, the superconscient supports all our spiritual possibilities and nature. "The role of the superconscient has been to evolve slowly the spiritual man out of the mental half-animal."[40]

The superconscient has generally been referred to as the capital "M" Mind, the Deeper Mind, Cosmic Consciousness, the Higher Self, Spirit and other similar global terms. Sri Aurobindo, however, distinguishes various distinct levels of consciousness among these higher planes of being which lie above the ordinary mind.

> There are above us... successive states, levels or graded powers of being overtopping our normal mind, hidden in our own superconscient parts, higher ranges of Mind, degrees of spiritual consciousness and experience.... [41]

...from the point of view of the ascent of consciousness from our mind upwards through a rising series of dynamic powers by which it can sublimate itself, the gradation can be resolved into a stairway of four main ascents, each with its high level of fulfilment. These gradations may be summarily described as a series of sublimations of the consciousness through Higher Mind, Illumined Mind and Intuition into Overmind and beyond it; there is a succession of self-transmutations at the summit of which lies the Supermind or Divine Gnosis.[42]

There are many layers in each of the main gradations between mind and Supermind, and each of these layers can be regarded as a gradation in itself.

In all the series of the planes or grades of consciousness there is nowhere any real gulf, always there are connecting gradations and one can ascend from step to step.[43]

Higher Mind

Higher mind is the first and lowest of the superconscient planes above the level of the ordinary mind.

I mean by the Higher Mind a first plane of spiritual consciousness where one becomes constantly and closely aware of the Self, the One everywhere and knows and sees things habitually with that awareness; but it is still very much on the mind level although highly spiritual in its essential substance; and its instrumentation is through an elevated thought-power and comprehensive mental sight — not illumined by any of the intenser upper lights but as if in a large strong and clear daylight. It acts as an intermediate state between the Truth-Light above and the human mind; communicating the higher knowledge in a form that the Mind intensified, broadened, made spiritually supple, can receive without being blinded or dazzled by a Truth beyond it.[44]

Illumined Mind

> ...greater Force [than the Higher Mind] is that of the Illumined Mind, a Mind no longer of higher Thought, but of spiritual light. Here the clarity of the spiritual intelligence, its tranquil daylight, gives place or subordinates itself to an intense lustre, a splendour and illumination of the Spirit: a play of lightnings of spiritual truth and power breaks from above into the consciousness and adds to the calm and wide enlightenment and the vast descent of peace which characterise or accompany the action of the larger conceptual-spiritual principle, a fiery ardour of realisation and a rapturous ecstasy of knowledge. A downpour of inwardly visible Light very usually envelops this action; for it must be noted that, contrary to our ordinary conceptions, light is not primarily a material creation and the sense or vision of light accompanying the inner illumination is not merely a subjective visual image or a symbolic phenomenon: light is primarily a spiritual manifestation of the Divine Reality illuminative and creative; material light is a subsequent representation or conversion of it into Matter for the purposes of the material Energy. There is also in this descent the arrival of a greater dynamic, a golden drive, a luminous "enthousiasmos" of inner force and power which replaces the comparatively slow and deliberate process of the Higher Mind by a swift, sometimes a vehement, almost a violent impetus of rapid transformation.[45]

Intuition

In common usage, intuition means the power of understanding things immediately, without the need for conscious reasoning. In this sense, intuition may be based on a feeling, or it may be a rapid "subconscious reasoning", based on subtle cues which are not consciously apprehended. Sri Aurobindo, however, uses the term "intuition" in a much deeper sense when he refers to a certain gradation of consciousness.

> [The Higher Mind and the Illumined Mind] enjoy their authority

and can get their own united completeness only by a reference to a third level; for it is from the higher summits where dwells the intuitional being that they derive the knowledge which they turn into thought or sight and bring down to us for the mind's transmutation. Intuition is a power of consciousness nearer and more intimate to the original knowledge by identity; for it is always something that leaps out direct from a concealed identity. It is when the consciousness of the subject meets with the consciousness in the object, penetrates it and sees, feels or vibrates with the truth of what it contacts, that the intuition leaps out like a spark or lightning-flash from the shock of the meeting; or when the consciousness, even without any such meeting, looks into itself and feels directly and intimately the truth or the truths that are there or so contacts the hidden forces behind appearances, then also there is the outbreak of an intuitive light; or, again, when the consciousness meets the Supreme Reality or the spiritual reality of things and beings and has a contactual union with it, then the spark, the flash or the blaze of intimate truth-perception is lit in its depths. This close perception is more than sight, more than conception: it is the result of a penetrating and revealing touch which carries in it sight and conception as part of itself or as its natural consequence. A concealed or slumbering identity, not yet recovering itself, still remembers or conveys by the intuition its own contents and the intimacy of its self-feeling and self-vision of things, its light of truth, its overwhelming and automatic certitude.[46]

Intuition sees the truth of things by a direct inner contact, not like the ordinary mental intelligence by seeking and reaching out for indirect contacts through the senses etc. But the limitation of the Intuition as compared with the supermind is that it sees things by flashes, point by point, not as a whole. Also in coming into the mind it gets mixed with the mental movement and forms a kind of intuitive mind activity which is not the pure truth, but something in between the higher Truth and the mental seeking. It can lead the consciousness through a sort of transitional stage and that is practically its function.[47]

Overmind

Between the supermind and the human mind are a number of ranges, planes or layers of consciousness — one can regard it in various ways — in which the element or substance of mind and consequently its movements also become more and more illumined and powerful and wide. The overmind is the highest of these ranges; it is full of lights and powers; but from the point of view of what is above it, it is the line of the soul's turning away from the complete and indivisible knowledge and its descent towards the Ignorance. For although it draws from the Truth, it is here that begins the separation of aspects of the Truth, the forces and their working out as if they were independent truths and this is a process that ends, as one descends to ordinary Mind, Life and Matter, in a complete division, fragmentation, separation from the indivisible Truth above.[48]

It is (sometimes directly, sometimes indirectly) by the power of the overmind releasing the mind from its close partitions that the cosmic consciousness opens in the seeker and he becomes aware of the cosmic spirit and the play of the cosmic forces.

It is from or at least through the overmind plane that the original pre-arrangement of things in this world is effected; for from it the determining vibrations originally come.[49]

The overmind has to be reached and brought down before the supermind descent is at all possible — for the overmind is the passage through which one passes from Mind to supermind.

It is from the overmind that all these different arrangements of the creative Truth of things originate. Out of the overmind they come down to the Intuition and are transmitted from it to the Illumined and Higher Mind to be arranged there for our intelligence. But they lose more and more of their power and certitude in the transmission as they come down to the lower levels. What energy of directly perceived Truth they have is lost in the human mind; for to the human intellect they present themselves only as speculative ideas, not as realised Truth, not as direct sight, a dynamic vision coupled with a concrete undeniable experience.[50]

Supermind

Sri Aurobindo does not use the term Supermind in the sense of "mind itself super-eminent and lifted above ordinary mentality but not radically changed".[51] He means by the term a plane of consciousness which is not only above mind and the superconscient planes of consciousness just described, but is radically different from them all. For whereas even the superconscient levels of mind — Higher Mind, Illumined Mind, Intuition and Overmind — are varying blends of Knowledge-Ignorance, Supermind is the Truth-Consciousness.

> We call it the Supermind or the Truth-Consciousness, because it is a principle superior to mentality and exists, acts and proceeds in the fundamental truth and unity of things and not like the mind in their appearances and phenomenal divisions.[52]

> The Supermind is in its very essence a truth-consciousness, a consciousness always free from the Ignorance which is the foundation of our present natural or evolutionary existence and from which nature in us is trying to arrive at self-knowledge and world-knowledge and a right consciousness and the right use of our existence in the universe. The Supermind, because it is a truth-consciousness, has this knowledge inherent in it and this power of true existence; its course is straight and can go direct to its aim, its field is wide and can even be made illimitable. This is because its very nature is knowledge: it has not to acquire knowledge but possesses it in its own right; its steps are not from nescience or ignorance into some imperfect light, but from truth to greater truth, from right perception to deeper perception, from intuition to intuition, from illumination to utter and boundless luminousness, from growing widenesses to the utter vasts and to very infinitude. On its summits it possesses the divine omniscience and omnipotence,

but even in an evolutionary movement of its own graded self-manifestation by which it would eventually reveal its own highest heights it must be in its very nature essentially free from ignorance and error: it starts from truth and light and moves always in truth and light.[53]

The Divine — Sachchidananda (Existence-Consciousness-Bliss)

Sachchidananda is the supracosmic Reality, the Divine, the Supreme Being who "manifests Himself as infinite existence of which the essentiality is consciousness, of which again the essentiality is bliss, is self-delight...."[54]

[Sachchidananda] is one eternal Existence that we then are, one eternal Consciousness which sees its own works in us and others, one eternal Will or Force of that Consciousness which displays itself in infinite workings, one eternal Delight which has the joy of itself and all its workings, — itself stable, immutable, timeless, spaceless, supreme and itself still in the infinity of its workings, not changed by their variations, not broken up by their multiplicity, not increased or diminished by their ebbings and flowings in the seas of Time and Space, not confused by their apparent contrarieties or limited by their divinely-willed limitations. Sachchidananda is the unity of the many-sidedness of manifested things, the eternal harmony of all their variations and oppositions, the infinite perfection which justifies their limitations and is the goal of their imperfections.[55]

Supermind is between the Sachchidananda, the One who is above all manifestation, and this flux of the Many in the manifested universe. For an integral self-knowledge, states Sri Aurobindo, it is not enough to go beyond mind and take a straight plunge into Sachchidananda as aimed at by the traditional Path of Knowledge: it is necessary to attain the Supermind during the ascension beyond mind to Sachchidananda.

The method of the traditional way of knowledge, eliminating all these things [body, life, mind] arrives at the conception and re-alisation of a pure conscious existence, self-aware, self-blissful, unconditioned by mind and life and body, and to its ultimate positive experience that is Atman, the Self, the original and essential nature of our existence. Here at last there is something centrally true, but in its haste to arrive at it this knowledge assumes that there is nothing between the thinking mind and the Highest,... and, shutting its eyes in Samadhi, tries to rush through all that actually intervenes without even seeing these great and luminous kingdoms of the Spirit. Perhaps it arrives at its object, but only to fall asleep in the Infinite. Or, if it remains awake, it is in the highest experience of the Supreme into which the self-annulling Mind can enter but not in the supreme of the Supreme, *Parātpara*. The Mind can only be aware of the Self in a mentalised spiritual thinness, only of the mind-reflected Sachchidananda. The highest truth, the integral self-knowledge is not to be gained by this self-blinded leap into the Absolute but by a patient transit beyond the mind into the Truth-Consciousness where the Infinite can be known, felt, seen, experienced in all the fullness of its unending riches.[56]

References

1. Sri Aurobindo, *The Life Divine*, Sri Aurobindo Birth Centenary Library (hereafter SABCL), (Pondicherry: Sri Aurobindo Ashram, 1970–75), Vol. 18, p. 555.
2. Ibid., p. 556.
3. Sri Aurobindo, *Letters on Yoga*, SABCL Vol. 22, p. 233.
4. Ibid., p. 303.
5. Ibid., p. 251.
6. Sri Aurobindo, *Letters on Yoga*, SABCL Vol. 23, pp. 1020–21.
7. Sri Aurobindo, *On Himself*, SABCL Vol. 26, p. 95.
8. Sri Aurobindo, *Letters on Yoga*, SABCL Vol. 22, p. 47.
9. Ibid., p. 347.
10. Ibid., pp. 320–21.
11. Ibid., p. 323.

12. Sri Aurobindo, *The Life Divine*, SABCL Vol. 18, p. 305.
13. Sri Aurobindo, *Letters on Yoga*, SABCL Vol. 22, pp. 323–24.
14. Ibid., pp. 348–49.
15. Ibid., p. 350.
16. Ibid.
17. Ibid.
18. Sri Aurobindo, *The Life Divine*, SABCL Vol. 18, p. 541.
19. Sri Aurobindo, *Letters on Yoga*, SABCL Vol. 24, p. 1602.
20. Sri Aurobindo, *Letters on Yoga*, SABCL Vol. 22 pp. 313–14.
21. Ibid., p. 438.
22. Ibid., p. 300.
23. Sri Aurobindo, *Letters on Yoga*, SABCL Vol. 22, p. 349.
24. Ibid., p. 285.
25. Ibid., p. 301.
26. Sri Aurobindo, *The Hour of God and Other Writings*, SABCL Vol. 17, p. 51.
27. Sri Aurobindo, *The Life Divine*, SABCL Vol. 18, p. 348.
28. Sri Aurobindo, *Letters on Yoga*, SABCL Vol. 23, p. 1005.
29. Sri Aurobindo, *The Life Divine*, SABCL Vol. 19, p. 974.
30. Sri Aurobindo, *The Life Divine*, SABCL Vol. 18, p. 45.
31. Sri Aurobindo, *The Synthesis of Yoga*, SABCL Vol. 21, pp. 613–14.
32. Sri Aurobindo, *Letters on Yoga*, SABCL Vol. 22, p. 300.
33. Ibid., p. 46.
34. Ibid., p. 278.
35. Sri Aurobindo, *The Synthesis of Yoga*, SABCL Vol. 20, p. 360.
36. Sri Aurobindo, *The Life Divine*, SABCL Vol. 18, p. 550.
37. Sri Aurobindo, *Letters on Yoga*, SABCL Vol. 22, p. 353.
38. Ibid., pp. 354–55.
39. Sri Aurobindo, *Letters on Yoga*, SABCL Vol. 24, p. 1597.
40. Sri Aurobindo, *Letters on Yoga*, SABCL Vol. 22, p. 360.
41. Sri Aurobindo, *The Life Divine*, SABCL Vol.19, pp. 932–33.
42. Ibid., p. 938.
43. Sri Aurobindo, *Letters on Yoga*, SABCL Vol. 22, p. 250.
44. Sri Aurobindo, *The Future Poetry*, SABCL Vol. 9, p. 342.

45. Sri Aurobindo, *The Life Divine*, SABCL Vol. 19, p. 944.
46. Ibid., pp. 946–47.
47. Sri Aurobindo, *Letters on Yoga*, SABCL Vol. 22, p. 264.
48. Ibid., p. 257.
49. Ibid., p. 260.
50. Ibid., p. 261.
51. Sri Aurobindo, *The Life Divine*, SABCL Vol. 18, p. 124.
52. Ibid., p. 143.
53. Sri Aurobindo, *The Supramental Manifestation and Other Writings*, SABCL Vol. 16, pp. 41-42.
54. Sri Aurobindo, *The Upanishads*, SABCL Vol. 12, p. 96.
55. Sri Aurobindo, *The Synthesis of Yoga*, SABCL Vol. 20, p. 395.
56. Ibid., p. 281.

5
Sri Aurobindo on the Self as Experienced in Yoga

The self contains the universe.[1]   —Sri Aurobindo

But this knowledge is valueless for Yoga if it is only an intellectual and metaphysical notion void of life and barren of consequence; a mental realisation alone cannot be sufficient for the seeker. For what Yoga searches after is not truth of thought alone or truth of mind alone, but the dynamic truth of a living and revealing spiritual experience.[2]   —Sri Aurobindo

"Whatever I may be thinking of, I am always at the same time more or less aware of *myself*, of my *personal existence*."[3] In these words, William James states one of the most dominant aspects of human experience, the sense of one's unique existence as a self who is distinct and separate from everyone and everything else in the world. Such an experience of the self as a distinct and independent entity is universally shared by all "normal" human beings. The sense of such a separate self — or ego, as it is generally referred to in psychology — emerges through three overlapping stages: a physical or bodily self, an emotional self, and a mental self. Thus what we regard as our self is experienced by us as having three main aspects — physical, emotional and mental.

Yoga leads to certain great discoveries regarding the self as commonly experienced by us. First, the self, which we ordinarily experience as a single unitary entity, is in fact a complex being consisting of many personalities which are more or less independent.

The practice of Yoga brings us face to face with the extraordinary complexity of our own being, the stimulating but also embarrassing multiplicity of our personality, the rich endless confusion

of Nature. To the ordinary man who lives upon his own waking surface, ignorant of the self's depths and vastnesses behind
the veil, his psychological existence is fairly simple. A small but
clamorous company of desires, some imperative intellectual and
aesthetic cravings, some tastes, a few ruling or prominent ideas and
a great current of unconnected or ill-connected and mostly trivial
thoughts, a number of more or less imperative vital[4] needs, alternations of physical health and disease, a scattered and inconsequent
succession of joys and griefs, frequent minor disturbances and
vicissitudes and rarer strong searchings and upheavals of mind or
body, and through it all Nature, partly with the aid of his thought
and will, and partly without or in spite of it, arranging these things
in some rough practical fashion, some tolerable disorderly order —
this is the material of his existence. The average human being even
now is in his inward existence as crude and undeveloped as was
the bygone primitive man in his outward life. But as soon as we
go deep within ourselves, — and Yoga means a plunge into all the
multiple profundities of the soul, — we find ourselves subjectively,
as man in his growth has found himself objectively, surrounded by
a whole complex world which we have to know and to conquer.

The most disconcerting discovery is to find that every part of
us — intellect, will, sense-mind, nervous or desire self, the heart,
the body — has each, as it were, its own complex individuality and
natural formation independent of the rest; it neither agrees with
itself nor with the others nor with the representative ego which
is the shadow cast by some central and centralising self on our
superficial ignorance. We find that we are composed not of one
but many personalities and each has its own demands and differing
nature.[5]

The second discovery through yoga is that the surface self which
is all that we are ordinarily aware of is only the superficial stratum of our being; there are other vaster strata of being *below*,
behind and *above* the surface consciousness. These are, respectively, the subconscient, the subliminal and the superconscient
parts of the being.

...what we know of ourselves, our present conscious existence, is only a representative formation, a superficial activity, a changing external result of a vast mass of concealed existence.... our existence is something much larger than this apparent frontal being which we suppose ourselves to be and which we offer to the world around us. This frontal and external being is a confused amalgam of mind-formations, life-movements, physical functionings of which even an exhaustive analysis into its component parts and machinery fails to reveal the whole secret. It is only when we go behind, below, above into the hidden stretches of our being that we can know it; ... For below even our most obscure physical consciousness is a subconscious being in which as in a covering and supporting soil are all manner of hidden seeds that sprout up, unaccountably to us, on our surface and into which we are constantly throwing fresh seeds that prolong our past and will influence our future, — a subconscious being, obscure, small in its motions, capriciously and almost fantastically subrational, but of immense potency for the earth-life. Again behind our mind, our life, our conscious physical there is a large subliminal consciousness, — there are inner mental, inner vital, inner more subtle physical reaches supported by an inmost psychic existence which is the connecting soul of all the rest.... Yet again above our human mind are still greater reaches superconscient to it and from there secretly descend influences, powers, touches which are the original determinants of things here and, if they were called down in their fullness, could altogether alter the whole make and economy of life in the material universe.[6]

The third discovery to which one is led through the practice of yoga is that the personal self does not live, as we feel in our surface consciousness, in a private and solitary inner world circumscribed by the physical body and separated from all that is beyond the body, but is connected with the entire cosmos.

The individual is not limited to the physical body — it is only the external consciousness which feels like that. As soon as one gets over this feeling of limitation, one can feel first the inner consciousness which is connected with the body, but does not belong to it, afterwards the planes of consciousness above the body, also a consciousness surrounding the body, but part of oneself, part of the individual being, through which one is in contact with the cosmic forces and with other beings.[7]

Each man has his own personal consciousness entrenched in his body and gets into touch with his surroundings only through his body and senses and the mind using the senses.

Yet all the time the universal forces are pouring into him without his knowing it. He is aware only of thoughts, feelings, etc., that rise to the surface and these he takes for his own. Really they come from outside in mind waves, vital waves, waves of feeling and sensation, etc. which take particular form in him and rise to the surface after they have got inside.[8]

Moreover, we find that inwardly too, no less than outwardly, we are not alone in the world; the sharp separateness of our ego was no more than a strong impression and delusion; we do not exist in ourselves, we do not really live apart in an inner privacy or solitude. Our mind is a receiving, developing and modifying machine into which there is being constantly passed from moment to moment a ceaseless foreign flux, a streaming mass of disparate materials from above, from below, from outside. Much more than half our thoughts and feelings are not our own in the sense that they take form out of ourselves; of hardly anything can it be said that it is truly original to our nature. A large part comes to us from others or from the environment, whether as raw material or as manufactured imports; but still more largely they come from universal Nature here or from other worlds and planes and their beings and powers and influences; for we are overtopped and environed by other planes of consciousness, mind planes, life planes, subtle matter planes, from which our life and action are fed, or fed on, pressed, dominated, made use of for the manifestation of their forms and forces.[9]

The fourth discovery to which yoga leads is that the make-up of physical, emotional and mental constituents which we regard as our self is only the apparent self of our external personality, concealing the real Self within.

> ...this little mind, vital and body which we call ourselves is only a surface movement and not our "self" at all. It is an external bit of personality put forward for one brief life, for the play of the Ignorance.[10] It is equipped with an ignorant mind stumbling about in search of fragments of truth, an ignorant vital rushing about in search of fragments of pleasure, an obscure and mostly subconscious physical receiving the impacts of things.... All that is accepted until the mind gets disgusted and starts looking about for the real Truth of itself and things, the vital gets disgusted and begins wondering whether there is not such a thing as real bliss and the physical gets tired and wants liberation from itself and the pains and pleasures. Then it is possible for the little ignorant bit of personality to go back to its real Self and with it to these greater things — or else to the extinction of itself, Nirvana.[11]

> For our real self is not the individual mental being, that is only a figure, an appearance; our real self is cosmic, infinite, it is one with all existence and the inhabitant of all existence. The self behind our mind, life and body is the same as the self behind the mind, life and body of all our fellow-beings, and if we come to possess it, we shall naturally, when we turn to look out again upon them, tend to become one with them in the common basis of our consciousness.[12]

The experience of the real Self brings about the dissolution of the apparent self, for the apparent self or ego arises from an illusory identification by which one regards the body, the vital and the mind as the self. Before the real Self is discovered, the ego is a necessity, for the ego serves to centralise the diverse elements of the external personality so as to give it a sense of individuality.

The "I" or the little ego is constituted by Nature and is at once a mental, vital and physical formation meant to aid in centralising and individualising the outer consciousness and action. When the true being is discovered, the utility of the ego is over and this formation has to disappear — the true being is felt in its place.[13]

Whereas the apparent self is experienced on the surface of our consciousness, the real Self is experienced either deep within or high above the surface being. Deep within, the real Self is experienced as our individual soul, distinct from and yet one with all other beings. Like the apparent self or the ego, the self within, too, is experienced as having an individual existence, but whereas the ego feels itself to be separate from the rest of the universe, the individual soul — or the psychic being as Sri Aurobindo terms it — feels itself to be one with all existence. "There is individuality in the psychic being, but not egoism."[14]

High above, the real Self is experienced as the Universal or Cosmic Self which is the core of all things and beings in the cosmos, and also as the Transcendent Self beyond the cosmos. Describing the experience of the universal and the transcendent aspects of the highest Self, Sri Aurobindo writes:

> This Self has two aspects and the results of realising it correspond to these two aspects. One is static, a condition of wide peace, freedom, silence: the silent Self is unaffected by any action or experience; it impartially supports them but does not seem to originate them at all, rather to stand back detached or unconcerned, *udāsīna*. The other aspect is dynamic and that is experienced as a cosmic Self or Spirit which not only supports but originates and contains the whole cosmic action — not only that part of it which concerns our physical selves but also all that is beyond it — this world and all other worlds, the supraphysical as well as the physical ranges of the universe. Moreover, we feel the Self as one in all; but also we feel it as above all, transcendent, surpassing all individual birth or cosmic existence. To get into the universal Self — one in all — is to be liberated from ego; ego either becomes a small instrumental circumstance in the consciousness or even disappears from our

consciousness altogether. That is the extinction or Nirvana of the ego. To get into the transcendent self above all makes us capable of transcending altogether even cosmic consciousness and action — it can be the way to that complete liberation from world-existence which is called also extinction, *laya, mokṣa, nirvāṇa*.[15]

For on the other side of the cosmic consciousness there is, attainable to us, a consciousness yet more transcendent, — transcendent not only of the ego, but of the Cosmos itself, — against which the universe seems to stand out like a petty picture against an immeasurable background. That supports the universal activity, — or perhaps only tolerates it; It embraces Life with Its vastness, — or else rejects it from Its infinitude.[16]

Speaking of the need of realising all the three statuses of the Self — individual, universal and transcendent — Sri Aurobindo states:

The Transcendent, the Universal, the Individual are three powers over-arching, underlying and penetrating the whole manifestation.... In the unfolding of consciousness also, these are the three fundamental terms and none of them can be neglected if we would have the experience of the whole Truth of existence. Out of the individual we wake into a vaster freer cosmic consciousness; but out of the universal too with its complex forms and powers we must emerge by a still greater self-exceeding into a consciousness without limits that is founded on the Absolute. And yet in this ascension we do not really abolish but take up and transfigure what we seem to leave; for there is a height where the three live eternally in each other, on that height they are blissfully joined in a nodus of their harmonised oneness.[17]

The highest spiritual state has been described both as a state of Non-Being resulting from extinction of all selfhood and as a state in which one becomes identified with all Being on discovering one's true Self. Thus the Vedantic seers who described the absolute Reality as Sat-Chit-Ananda (Existence-Consciousness-Bliss) also described it as Asat (Non-Existence, Non-Being). Buddhism, too, which looks upon the notion of self as illusory, regards the state of liberation (Nirvana) as one in which there is an extinction of selfhood in a transcendent Permanence which is Non-Being. Reconciling this contradiction, Sri Aurobindo states:

> Non-being is only a word. When we examine the fact it represents, we can no longer be sure that absolute non-existence has any better chance than the infinite Self of being more than an ideative formation of the mind. We really mean by this Nothing something beyond the last term to which we can reduce our purest conception and our most abstract or subtle experience of actual being as we know or conceive it while in this universe. This Nothing then is merely a something beyond positive conception.... [18]

Notes and References

1. Sri Aurobindo, *Letters on Yoga*, Sri Aurobindo Birth Centenary Library (hereafter SABCL), (Pondicherry: Sri Aurobindo Ashram, 1970–75), Vol. 23 p. 1071.
2. Sri Aurobindo, *The Synthesis of Yoga*, SABCL Vol. 20, p. 107.
3. William James, *Psychology — The Briefer Course* (Notre Dame, Indiana: Univ. of Notre Dame Press, 1985), p. 43.
4. Sri Aurobindo uses the term "vital" to designate the part of our psychological make-up which lies between the mental consciousness above it and the physical consciousness below it. The vital part of our being — often referred to simply as "the vital" — represents the Life-Nature, made up of sensations, instincts and impulses, desires, etc.
5. Sri Aurobindo, *The Synthesis of Yoga*, SABCL Vol. 20, pp. 68–69.
6. Ibid., pp. 170–72.
7. Sri Aurobindo, *Letters on Yoga*, SABCL, Vol. 22, p. 313.
8. Ibid., pp. 313–14.
9. Sri Aurobindo, *The Synthesis of Yoga*, SABCL Vol. 20, pp. 69–70.

10. The "Ignorance" is a translation of the Vedantic concept of Avidya, ignorance of the One Reality due to the consciousness of Multiplicity.

11. Sri Aurobindo, *Letters on Yoga*, SABCL Vol. 24, p. 1164.

12. Sri Aurobindo, *The Synthesis of Yoga*, SABCL Vol. 20, p. 354.

13. Sri Aurobindo, *Letters on Yoga*, SABCL Vol. 22, p. 278.

14. Sri Aurobindo, *Letters on Yoga*, SABCL Vol. 24, p. 1368.

15. Ibid., p. 1165.

16. Sri Aurobindo, *The Life Divine*, SABCL Vol. 18, p. 17.

17. Sri Aurobindo, *The Synthesis of Yoga*, SABCL Vol. 20, p. 247.

18. Sri Aurobindo, *The Life Divine*, SABCL Vol. 18, p. 28.

6
Self, Ego and Individuality
Sri Aurobindo's Integral View

*When we have passed beyond individualising, then we shall be real
Persons. Ego was the helper; Ego is the bar.*[1]   — Sri Aurobindo

Self, Ego and Individuality in Ordinary Consciousness

A fundamental characteristic of our ordinary or "normal" state
of consciousness is the sense of I-ness, of being an individual
who has an independent existence, who is distinct and separate
from other individuals and things in the universe. In its basic
connotation, the term "ego" (derived from the Latin word for
"I") is applied to this core of our being as we experience it in
our ordinary consciousness and which we refer to as "I". The
ego is what we regard as the agent of our thoughts, feelings and
actions; thus we say "I think", "I feel", etc.

We may note four features of the ego which appear self-
evident to us in our ordinary state of consciousness:

(i) The ego is experienced as the self; "I" and "myself" are
felt to be the same. Hence, generally the terms "ego" and "self"
are used synonymously by most writers.[2]

(ii) The ego or self is felt as a living reality, existing in a
physical body. As Assagioli states, "...man's basic existential
experience... is being a living self."[3] And as William James remarks, "No psychology... can question the existence of personal
selves."[4] An impairment of the sense of one's personal reality is
generally associated with depersonalisation, a state denoting a
psychiatric disorder.

(iii) The ego or self is experienced as an entity who is
separate from all other beings and things in the universe. All
that is other than oneself is experienced as the not-self. Part of
normal psychological development consists in establishing an

"ego-boundary" which separates one's self from everything else — the not-self. As Ken Wilber observes,

> So fundamental is the primary boundary between self and not-self that all our other boundaries depend on it. We can hardly distinguish boundaries between things until we have distinguished ourselves *from* things. Every boundary you create depends upon your separate existence, that is, your primary boundary of self vs. not-self.[5]

(iv) The ego or self is experienced as being distinct from everyone else, that is, as having an individuality. The sense of ego or self is bound up with the sense of individuality as well as of separateness.

Self, Ego and Individuality in Cosmic Consciousness

In sharp contrast to our ordinary state of consciousness as regards our perceptions of ego, self and individuality stated above are certain non-ordinary states of consciousness, which have been described as mystical or spiritual, in which these perceptions are almost totally reversed.

R. M. Bucke, the first writer who published a scientific and comprehensive account of such mystical states, called them states of "cosmic consciousness", of which he gave fifty instances evidenced by personalities in different epochs, from the Buddha and Christ to Francis Bacon and Walt Whitman.[6] Since Bucke's classic publication, diverse types of mystical states have been more or less loosely described as states of cosmic consciousness. Sri Aurobindo uses the term "cosmic consciousness" in a more specific sense:

> The cosmic consciousness is that of the universe, of the cosmic spirit and cosmic Nature with all the beings and forces within it. All that is as much conscious as a whole as the individual separately is, though in a different way. The consciousness of the individual

is part of this, but a part feeling itself as a separate being. Yet all the time most of what he is comes into him from the cosmic consciousness. But there is a wall of separative ignorance between. Once it breaks down he becomes aware of the cosmic Self, of the consciousness of the cosmic Nature, of the forces playing in it, etc. He feels all that as he now feels physical things and impacts. He finds it all to be one with his larger or universal self.[7]

The cosmic consciousness is that in which the limits of ego, personal mind and body disappear and one becomes aware of a cosmic vastness which is or filled by a cosmic spirit and aware also of the direct play of cosmic forces,... It is not that the ego, the body, the personal mind disappear, but one feels them as only a small part of oneself. One begins to feel others too as part of oneself or varied repetitions of oneself, the same self modified by Nature in other bodies. Or, at the least, as living in the larger universal self which is henceforth one's own greater reality.[8]

Regarding the way in which ego, self and individuality are experienced in the cosmic consciousness as described above we may note the following:

(i) Ego and self are not felt to be the same as in the ordinary consciousness; the ego is perceived as only a small part of one's self; the larger universal self is felt to be one's greater reality.

(ii) The sense of separateness based on the ego-boundary which, in the ordinary consciousness, distinguishes self from not-self disappears; one feels all others as part of oneself.

(iii) Though there is an implicit sense of individuality, enabling one to distinguish oneself from others, the sense of individuality in the cosmic consciousness, unlike individuality in the ordinary state of consciousness, co-exists with a sense of unity: all others are perceived as "part of oneself" or "varied repetitions of oneself". In other words, the self is perceived as being both an individual self and a cosmic self.

Self, Ego and Individuality in Transcendent Consciousness

A more radical disaffirmation of our ordinary perceptions of self, ego and individuality is found in some theories based on the experience of a state transcending that of cosmic consciousness, termed variously Nirvana (Extinction), Laya (Dissolution), Mukti or Moksha (Liberation). About this transcendent state of liberation, Sri Aurobindo writes:

> ...on the other side of the cosmic consciousness there is, attainable to us a consciousness yet more transcendent, — transcendent not only of the ego, but of the Cosmos itself, — against which the universe seems to stand out like a petty picture against an immeasurable background.[9]

> Deep, intense, convincing, common to all who have overstepped a certain limit of the active mind-belt into the horizonless inner space, this is the great experience of liberation, the consciousness of something within us that is behind and outside of the universe and all its forms, interests, aims, events and happenings, calm, untouched, unconcerned, illimitable, immobile, free, the uplook to something above us indescribable and unseizable into which by abolition of our personality we can enter, the presence of an omnipresent eternal witness Purusha,[10] the sense of an Infinity or a Transcendence that looks down on us from an august negation of all our existence and is alone the one thing Real.[11]

Two prominent philosophical theories have each constructed a radical view of reality as well as of the nature of self, ego and individuality on the basis of the experience of Nirvana or Moksha. The two theories are Nagarjuna's Buddhist theory of Nihilism and Shankara's theory of Mayavada (Illusionism), a version of the Vedantic philosophy of Adwaita (Monism).

According to Nihilism, what we experience as our ego or self is not a real entity but an illusion. There is no such thing as a real self but only a stream of experience, ideas, sensations and associations (Sanskaras). The self is merely a name for the continuity of the flow of experience, like the continuous river which is yet never the same river, or the persistent flame which is yet never the same flame. Behind the flux of experience is Nihil, the Void, Non-Being, Non-Existence, an infinite Zero (Shunya), which alone is the enduring Reality. The continuity of experience is maintained by the successions of energies of Action (Karma), kept in motion by desire (Kama) which is the root cause of suffering (Duhkha). The cessation of desire breaks up the continuity of the painful flow of energies by bringing about the disintegration of the bundle of Sanskaras. This produces the extinction of the ego and the disappearance of the idea of selfhood, leading to Nirvana, the state of Non-Existence or Non-Being, the ultimate Reality. Thus from the viewpoint of Nihilism, all sense of ego, self and individuality is an illusion, consisting in an imposition (Adhyaropa) of our ignorance on eternal Non-Existence.

According to Monism, on which Illusionism bases itself, Reality is an infinite and eternal Supreme Being and Absolute Existence (Brahman) whose nature is that of Sat-Chit-Ananda (Existence-Consciousness-Bliss), the One besides whom nothing else exists. By its essentiality the Supreme Being is also the Self (Atman); therefore the Supreme is our own true and highest Self. According to Illusionism, the universe is a creation of Maya, the power of self-illusion in the Brahman by which the Brahman imposes on itself the cosmic illusion; the cosmos is, as it were, a dream that takes place in the Absolute. Ahamkara, the separative ego-sense which makes each being conceive of itself as an independent personality, is a creation of the cosmic illusion. Monism does admit of a Jivatman, an individual self, but the Jivatman is regarded as simply an appearance of the Brahman in illusory Maya. With the attainment of knowledge in the state of Moksha, the individual self is extinguished in the Reality. There is thus no real, eternal self of the individual, even no real eternal universal self, but only the One Self, the One Reality. Therefore, from the viewpoint of Illusionism, both ego and individuality are unreal, the One Self alone is real.

Integral View of Reality

The theories of Nihilism and Illusionism show that the view regarding the nature of self is inextricably tied up with the view of Reality. The two theories view Reality in seemingly opposite ways and consequently assert opposite views regarding the nature of self. Nihilism regards Reality as Absolute Non-Existence and Non-Being, and therefore looks upon the self as an illusion. On the other hand, Illusionism sees Reality as Absolute Existence and Being, and so regards the One Self as identical with Reality.

Regarding the philosophical differences in explaining the nature of the ultimate reality, Sri Aurobindo states: "The overmind[12] presents the truth of things in all sorts of aspects and mind, even the spiritual mind, fastens on one or the other as the very truth, the one real truth of the matter. It is the mind that makes these differences...."[13] Reconciling the mutually exclusive theories of Nihilism and Illusionism in the light of a more comprehensive view of Reality, Sri Aurobindo writes:

> The impressions in the approach to Infinity or the entry into it are not always the same; much depends on the way in which the mind approaches it.... If certain schools of Buddhists felt it in their experience as a limitless Shunya, the Vedantists, on the contrary, see it as a positive Self-Existence featureless and absolute. No doubt, the various experiences were erected into various philosophies, each putting its conception as definitive; but behind each conception there was such an experience.[14]

> Buddha, it must be remembered, refused always to discuss what was beyond the world. But from the little he said it would appear that he was aware of a Permanent beyond equivalent to the Vedantic Para-Brahman, but which he was quite unwilling to describe. The denial of anything beyond the world except a negative state of Nirvana was a later teaching, not Buddha's.[15]

> The universe is only a partial manifestation and Brahman as its foundation is the Sat.[16] But there is also that which is not

manifested and beyond manifestation and is not contained in the
basis of manifestation. The Buddhists and others got from that the
conception of Asat[17] as the ultimate thing.[18]

> The feeling of the Self as a vast peaceful Void, a liberation from
> existence as we know it, is one that one can always have, Buddhist
> or no Buddhist. It is the negative aspect of Nirvana — it is quite
> natural for the mind, if it follows the negative movement of with-
> drawal, to get that first, and if you lay hold on that and refuse to
> go farther, being satisfied with this liberated Non-Existence, then
> you will naturally philosophise like the Buddhists that Shunya is
> the eternal truth. Lao Tse is more perspicacious when he spoke
> of it as the Nothing that is All. Many of course have the pos-
> itive experience of the Atman first, not as a void but as pure
> unrelated Existence like the Adwaitins (Shankara) or as the one
> Existent.[19]

The experience of Nirvana, on which the theories of Nihilism
and Illusionism are based, was for Sri Aurobindo only the beginning of his realisation.

> I cannot say there was anything exhilarating or rapturous in the
> experience [of Nirvana], as it then came to me, — (the ineffable
> Ananda[20] I had years afterwards), — but what it brought was an
> inexpressible Peace, a stupendous silence, an infinity of release and
> freedom. I lived in that Nirvana day and night before it began to
> admit other things into itself or modify itself at all, and the inner
> heart of experience, a constant memory of it and its power to
> return remained until in the end it began to disappear into a greater
> Superconsciousness from above. But meanwhile realisation added
> itself to realisation and fused itself with this original experience.
> At an early stage the aspect of an illusionary world gave place to
> one in which illusion[21] is only a small surface phenomenon with
> an immense Divine Reality behind it and a supreme Divine Reality
> above it and an intense Divine Reality in the heart of everything
> that had seemed at first only a cinematic shape or shadow. And this
> was no reimprisonment in the senses, no diminution or fall from

supreme experience, it came rather as a constant heightening and widening of the Truth; it was the spirit that saw objects, not the senses, and the Peace, the Silence, the freedom in Infinity remained always, with the world or all worlds as a continuous incident in the timeless eternity of the Divine.

...Nirvana in my liberated consciousness turned out to be the beginning of my realisation, a first step towards the complete thing, not the sole true attainment possible or even a culminating finale. It came unasked, unsought for, though quite welcome.... It just happened and settled in as if for all eternity or as if it had been really there always. And then it slowly grew into something not less but greater than its first self.[22]

Whereas Sri Aurobindo's first major spiritual experience — that of Nirvana — confirmed the basic views of Nihilism and of Illusionism (unreality of the ego and illusoriness of the world), his subsequent realisations fusing with the original experience brought a deeper view according to which he saw Nirvana to be an extinction not necessarily of all being but of being as we know it — the being of ego and desire; he found it to be *not* the end of the Path with nothing beyond to explore; but the end merely of the Path through the lower Nature, and a beginning of a Higher Evolution. He came to see the illusoriness of the world as not a feature of the world itself but as consisting in a false interpretation of the world by the mind and senses. Stating his view of reality, he wrote:

The world is a manifestation of the Real and therefore is itself real. The reality is the infinite and eternal Divine.... This Divine by his power has created the world or rather manifested it in his own infinite Being. But here in the material world or at its basis he has hidden himself in what seem to be his opposites, Non-Being, Inconscience and Insentience.... The Being which is hidden in what seems to be an inconscient void emerges in the world first in Matter, then in Life, then in Mind and finally as the Spirit.... This is what we call evolution which is an evolution of Consciousness and an evolution of the Spirit in things and only outwardly an evolution of species.[23]

The Shankara knowledge is... only one side of the Truth; it is the knowledge of the Supreme as realised by the spiritual Mind through the static silence of the pure Existence. It was because he went by this side only that Shankara was unable to accept or explain the origin of the universe except as illusion, a creation of Maya. Unless one realises the Supreme on the dynamic as well as the static side, one cannot experience the true origin of things and the equal reality of the active Brahman.... This other side was developed by the Shakta[24] Tantriks. The two together, the Vedantic and the Tantric truth unified, can arrive at the integral knowledge.[25]

For me all is Brahman and I find the Divine everywhere.... In my Yoga also I found myself moved to include both worlds in my purview — the spiritual and the material — and to try to establish the Divine Consciousness and the Divine Power in men's hearts and earthly life, not for a personal salvation only but for a life divine here.... This at least has always been my view and experience of the reality and nature of the world and things and the Divine.... [26]

Sri Aurobindo's views regarding the nature of self, ego and individuality stem from his view of reality just stated.

Integral View of Self

Identity of Reality and Self

...all this that is... is the Brahman, the Reality. The Brahman becomes all these beings, all beings must be seen in the Self, the Reality, and the Reality must be seen in them, the Reality must be seen as being actually all these beings; for not only the Self is Brahman, but all is the Self, all this that is is the Brahman, the Reality.[27]

Our supreme Self and the supreme Existence which has become the universe are one spirit, one self and one existence.[28]

Brahman is, subjectively, Atman, the Self or immutable existence of all that is in the universe.[29]

The Self is that aspect of the Brahman in which it is intimately felt as at once individual, cosmic, transcendent of the universe.[30]

Aspects of the Self

Sri Aurobindo states that both for philosophical understanding and spiritual experience it is highly important to distinguish among different aspects of the Self, otherwise the nature of the Self is blurred and a confusion arises both in intellectual understanding and inner experience.

The word 'Atman' like 'spirit' in English is popularly used in all kinds of senses, but both for spiritual and philosophical knowledge it is necessary to be clear and precise in one's use of terms so as to avoid confusion of thought and vision by confusion in the words we use to express them.[31]

The Self or Atman, states Sri Aurobindo, is experienced as the true being or self of the individual and as the Self of the cosmos. It has also an existence above the individual and transcending the cosmos in its aspect of Paramatma, the Supreme Being, the Divine. The individual, the cosmic and the transcendent are the three statuses of the Self.

As the Self is at once one and many, the universal Self manifests also as the individual self, the Jivatman, which presides over individual birth and evolution, though the Jivatman itself is unborn, unevolving, above the manifestation. What comes down into the manifestation, descending into the individual being as the representative of the Jivatman, evolving from life to life is the Antaratman, the soul or psychic being.

Jivatman, the individual self, feels his oneness with the universal Atman, but at the same time feels also his distinctness as an individual centre of the universal Self. The Jivatman therefore sees everything in itself or itself in everything or both together according to its state of consciousness. But the Jivatman is one of the centres of the One, not the One itself. If one does not make this distinction, and if there is the least vestige of egoism in the lower nature of one's being, then upon discovering the Jivatman one may think of oneself as an Avatar, an embodiment of the One.

Whereas the Jivatman presides over individual manifestation from above, its representative below in the manifestation — the psychic being — supports from within the evolution of the individual, standing behind and guiding the parts of the outer instrumental being — mental, vital and physical, receiving the essence of all their experiences and growing by these experiences, carrying the consciousness from life to life. When the psychic being realises its oneness with the Jivatman in the state of liberation, it does not disappear or change into the Jivatman. On attaining liberation the Jivatman may choose to merge into the One and pass into the state of Nirvana, Moksha or Laya (Dissolution); but it can also choose to remain in the universe to carry on the evolution beyond liberation.

Integral View of Ego

Ego and the Ignorance

...to the how of the fall into the Ignorance as opposed to the why, the effective cause, there is a substantial agreement in all spiritual experience. It is the division, the separation, the principle of isolation from the Permanent and One that brought it about; it is because the ego set up for itself in the world emphasising its own desire and self-affirmation in preference to its unity with the Divine and its oneness with all; it is because instead of the one supreme

Force, Wisdom, Light determining the harmony of all forces each Idea, Force, Form of things was allowed to work itself out as far as it could in the mass of infinite possibilities by its separate will and inevitably in the end by conflict with others. Division, ego, the imperfect consciousness and groping and struggle of a separate self-affirmation are the efficient cause of the suffering and ignorance of this world.[32]

Of the world he [man] regards only one little foam-bubble, his life and body, as himself. But when we get into our subliminal consciousness, we find it extending itself to be commensurate with its world; when we get into our superconscient Self, we find that the world is only its manifestation and that all in it is the One, all in it is our self. We see that there is one indivisible Matter of which our body is a knot, one indivisible Life of which our life is an eddy, one indivisible Mind of which our mind is a receiving and recording, forming or translating and transmitting station, one indivisible Spirit of which our soul and individual being are a portion or a manifestation. It is the ego-sense which clinches the division and in which the ignorance we superficially are finds its power to maintain the strong though always permeable walls it has created to be its own prison. Ego is the most formidable of the knots which keep us tied to the Ignorance.[33]

Ego: Provisional Substitute for Self

Ego implies the identification of our existence with outer self, the ignorance of our true self above and our psychic being within us.[34]

In the Ignorance Nature centres the order of her psychological movements, not around the secret spiritual self, but around its substitute, the ego-principle; a certain ego-centrism is the basis on which we bind together our experiences and relations in the midst of the complex contacts, contradictions, dualities, incoherences of the world in which we live; this ego-centrism is our rock of safety against the cosmic and the infinite, our defence.[35]

...this constant outer ego-building is only a provisional device... so that the secret individual, the spirit within, may establish a representative and instrumental formation of itself in physical nature, a provisional individualisation in the nature of the Ignorance, which is all that can at first be done in a world emerging out of a universal Inconscience.[36]

The individual ego is a pragmatic and effective fiction, a translation of the secret self into the terms of surface consciousness, or a subjective substitute for the true self in our surface experience: it is separated by ignorance from other-self and from the inner Divinity, but it is still pushed secretly towards an evolutionary unification in diversity; it has behind itself, though finite, the impulse to the infinite. But this in the terms of an ignorant consciousness translates itself into the will to expand, to be a boundless finite, to take everything it can into itself.... [37]

Utility and Necessity of Ego

...Nature invented the ego that the individual might disengage himself from the inconscience or subconscience of the mass and become an independent living mind, life-power, soul, spirit, co-ordinating himself with the world around him but not drowned in it and separately inexistent and ineffective. For the individual is indeed part of the cosmic being, but he is also something more, he is a soul that has descended from the Transcendence. This he cannot manifest at once, because he is too near to the cosmic Inconscience not near enough to the original Superconscience; he has to find himself as the mental and vital ego before he can find himself as the soul or spirit.[38]

The 'I' or the little ego is constituted by Nature and is at once a mental, vital and physical formation meant to aid in centralising and individualising the outer consciousness and action. When the true being is discovered, the utility of the ego is over.... [39]

I suppose the ego came there first as a means of the outer consciousness individualising itself in the flux of Nature and, secondly, as an incentive for tamasic[40] animal man to act and get something done. Otherwise he might merely have contented himself with food and sleep and done nothing else. With that incentive of ego (possession, vanity, ambition, eagerness for power etc. etc.) he began doing all sorts of things he might never otherwise have done.[41]

In the evolution of the lower consciousness here ego and selfishness were a necessity. So long as the higher consciousness above ordinary mind does not descend, ego remains a necessity even in aspiring towards the Divine.... [42]

...the ego is the lynch-pin invented to hold together the motion of our wheel of nature. The necessity of centralisation around the ego continues until there is no longer need of any such device or contrivance because there has emerged the true self, the spiritual being, which is at once wheel and motion and that which holds all together, the centre and the circumference.[43]

Liberation from Ego

As our consciousness changes into the height and depth and wideness of the spirit, the ego can no longer survive there: it is too small and feeble to subsist in that vastness and dissolves into it; for it exists by its limits and perishes by the loss of its limits. The being breaks out of its imprisonment in a separated individuality, becomes universal, assumes a cosmic consciousness in which it identifies itself with the self and spirit, the life, the mind, the body of all beings. Or it breaks out upward into a supreme pinnacle and infinity and eternity of self-existence independent of its cosmic or its individual existence. The ego collapses, losing its wall of separation, into the cosmic immensity; or it falls into nothingness, unable to breathe in the heights of the spiritual ether.[44]

Without the liberation of the psychic and the realisation of the true Self the ego cannot go, both are necessary.[45]

The sense of ego can disappear into that of the Self or the Purusha but that of itself does not bring about the disappearance of the ego-reactions in the Prakriti. The Purusha has to get rid of these by a process of constant rejection and remoulding.[46]

Without persistent rejection it [liberation from the ego] cannot be done. Going up into the Self liberates the higher parts, but the ego remains in the lower parts. The most effective force for this liberation is the psychic control along with steady rejection.[47]

Integral View of Individuality

Distinction between Two Individualities

What we usually call by that name [individuality] is a natural ego, a device of Nature which holds together her action in the mind and body...; but the individual self or soul is not this ego. The individual soul is the spiritual being which is described as an eternal portion of the Divine, but can also be described as the Divine himself supporting his manifestation as the Many. This is the true spiritual individual which appears in its complete truth when we get rid of the ego and our false separative sense of individuality, realise our oneness with the transcendent and cosmic Divine and with all beings.[48]

...the ego is the individual only in the ignorance; there is a true individual who is not the ego and still has an eternal relation with all other individuals which is not egoistic or self-separative, but of which the essential character is practical mutuality founded on essential unity.[49]

Eternal Reality of True Individuality

An eternal infinite self-existence is the supreme reality, but the supreme transcendent eternal Being, Self and Spirit, — an infinite Person, we may say, because his being is the essence and source of all personality, — is the reality and meaning of self-existence; so too the cosmic Self, Spirit, Being, Person is the reality and meaning of cosmic existence; the same Self, Spirit, Being or Person manifesting its multiplicity is the reality and meaning of individual existence.[50]

...the Self is always one in all, yet we see that for the purposes at least of the cyclic manifestation it expresses itself in perpetual soul-forms which preside over the movements of our personality through the worlds and the aeons. This persistent soul-existence is the real Individuality which stands behind the constant mutations of the thing we call our personality. It is not a limited ego but a thing in itself infinite; it is in truth the Infinite itself consenting from one plane of its being to reflect itself in a perpetual soul-experience.... We are not a mere mass of changing mind-stuff, life-stuff, body-stuff taking different forms of mind and life and body from birth to birth, so that at no time is there any real self or conscious reason of existence behind all the flux.... There is a real and stable power of our being behind the constant mutation of our mental, vital and physical personality, and this we have to know and preserve in order that the Infinite may manifest Himself through it according to His will in whatever range and for whatever purpose of His eternal cosmic activity.[51]

Importance and Necessity of Individuality

The immense importance of the individual being, which increases as he rises in the scale, is the most remarkable and significant fact of a universe which started without consciousness and without individuality in an undifferentiated Nescience. This importance can only be justified if the Self as individual is no less real than the Self as cosmic being or Spirit and both are powers of the Eternal. It is only so that can be explained the necessity for the growth of the individual and his discovery of himself as a condition for the discovery of the cosmic Self and Consciousness and of the supreme Reality.[52]

...the World-Transcendent embraces the universe, is one with it and does not exclude it, even as the universe embraces the individual, is one with him and does not exclude him. The individual is a centre of the whole universal consciousness; the universe is a form and definition which is occupied by the entire immanence of the Formless and Indefinable.

This is always the true relation, veiled from us by our ignorance or our wrong consciousness of things. When we attain to knowledge or right consciousness, nothing essential in the eternal relation is changed.... The individual is still necessary to the action of the Transcendent in the universe and that action in him does not cease to be possible by his illumination. On the contrary, since the conscious manifestation of the Transcendent in the individual is the means by which the collective, the universal is also to become conscious of itself, the continuation of the illumined individual in the action of the world is an imperative need of the world-play.[53]

Recapitulation of Sri Aurobindo's Views

The ordinary existence of man is not only an individual but an egoistic consciousness; it is, that is to say, the individual soul or Jivatman identifying himself with the nodus of his mental, vital, physical experiences in the movement of universal Nature, with his mind-created ego and, less intimately, with the mind, life, body which receive the experiences; for of these he can say "my mind, life, body," regarding them as himself yet partly as not himself and something which he possesses and uses, but of the ego he says, "It is I". By detaching himself from all identification with mind, life and body he can get back from his ego to the consciousness of the true Individual, the Jivatman, who is the real possessor of mind, life and body. Looking back from this Individual to that of which it is the representative and conscious figure, he can get back to the transcendent consciousness of pure Self, absolute Existence or absolute Non-Being, three poises of the same eternal Reality.[54]

In the abolition of the mental, vital, physical ego, even of the spiritual ego, it is the formless and limitless Individual that has the peace and joy of his escape into his own infinity. In the experience that he is nothing and no one, or everything and everyone, or the One which is beyond all things and absolute, it is the Brahman in the individual that effectuates this stupendous merger or this marvellous joining, Yoga, of its eternal unit of being with its vast all-comprehending or supreme all-transcending unity of eternal existence. To get beyond the ego is imperative, but one cannot get beyond the self, — except by finding it supremely, universally. For the self is not the ego; it is one with the All and the One and in finding it it is the All and the One that we discover in our self: the contradiction, the separation disappears, but the self, the spiritual reality remains, united with the One and the All by that delivering disappearance.[55]

Notes and References

1. Sri Aurobindo, "Thoughts and Glimpses" in *The Suparmental Manifestation and Other Writings*, Sri Aurobindo Birth Centenary Library (hereafter SABCL), (Pondicherry: Sri Aurobindo Ashram, 1970–75), Vol. 16, p. 377.
2. The majority of psychologists tend to eschew the term "self" which is regarded as somewhat philosophical, and prefer to use the more phenomenological term "ego".
3. Roberto Assagioli, *The Act of Will* (Penguin Books, 1987), p. 126.
4. William James, *Psychology: Briefer Course*, (New York: Henry Holt & Co., 1926), p. 153.
5. Ken Wilber, *No Boundary* (Boston & London: Shambhala, 1979), p. 46.
6. R.M. Bucke, *Cosmic Consciousness* (New York: E.P. Dutton, 1969).
7. Sri Aurobindo, *Letters on Yoga*, SABCL Vol. 22, p. 315.
8. Ibid., p. 316.
9. Sri Aurobindo, *The Life Divine*, SABCL Vol. 18, p. 17.
10. Conscious Being.
11. Sri Aurobindo, *The Synthesis of Yoga*, SABCL Vol. 20, p. 278.
12. Sri Aurobindo speaks of various levels of Mind above the ordinary

mind. The Overmind is the highest of these levels, above which is Supermind, the principle *beyond* Mind, and radically different from it.

13. Sri Aurobindo, *Letters on Yoga*, SABCL Vol. 22, p. 271.
14. Ibid., p. 63.
15. Ibid., p. 62.
16. The Existent.
17. The Non-Existent.
18. Sri Aurobindo, *Letters on Yoga*, SABCL Vol. 22, p. 65.
19. Ibid.
20. Bliss.
21. Sri Aurobindo's footnote: "In fact it is not an illusion in the sense of an imposition of something baseless and unreal on the consciousness, but a misinterpretation by the conscious mind and sense and a falsifying misuse of manifested existence."
22. Sri Aurobindo, *On Himself*, SABCL Vol. 26, pp. 101–02.
23. Ibid., p. 105.
24. Worshippers of Shakti, the dynamic Power of the Eternal.
25. Sri Aurobindo, *Letters on Yoga*, SABCL Vol. 22, p. 39.
26. Sri Aurobindo, *On Himself*, SABCL Vol. 26, p. 98.
27. Sri Aurobindo, *The Life Divine*, SABCL Vol. 18, p. 451.
28. Sri Aurobindo, *The Synthesis of Yoga*, SABCL Vol. 20, p. 282.
29. Sri Aurobindo, *The Upanishads*, SABCL Vol. 12, p. 87.
30. Sri Aurobindo, *The Life Divine*, SABCL Vol. 18, p. 347.
31. Sri Aurobindo, *Letters on Yoga*, SABCL Vol. 22, p. 276.
32. Sri Aurobindo, *Letters on Yoga*, SABCL Vol. 22, p. 27.
33. Sri Aurobindo, *The Life Divine*, SABCL Vol. 18, pp. 563–64.
34. Sri Aurobindo, *Letters on Yoga*, SABCL Vol. 22, p. 300.
35. Sri Aurobindo, *The Life Divine*, SABCL Vol. 18, p. 229.
36. Ibid., p. 531.
37. Ibid., p. 624.
38. Sri Aurobindo, *The Life Divine*, SABCL Vol. 19, p. 694.
39. Sri Aurobindo, *Letters on Yoga*, SABCL Vol. 22, p. 278.
40. Governed by Tamas, principle of inertia.
41. Sri Aurobindo, *Letters on Yoga*, SABCL Vol. 24, p. 1376.

42. Ibid.
43. Sri Aurobindo, *The Life Divine*, SABCL Vol. 18, p. 554.
44. Sri Aurobindo, *The Life Divine*, SABCL Vol. 19, p. 740.
45. Sri Aurobindo, *Letters on Yoga*, SABCL Vol. 24, p. 1379.
46. Ibid., p. 1378.
47. Ibid.
48. Sri Aurobindo, *Letters on Yoga*, SABCL Vol. 22, pp. 46–47.
49. Sri Aurobindo, *The Life Divine*, SABCL Vol. 18, p. 372.
50. Ibid., p. 353.
51. Sri Aurobindo, *The Synthesis of Yoga*, SABCL Vol. 20, p. 360.
52. Sri Aurobindo, *The Life Divine*, SABCL Vol. 19, p. 755.
53. Sri Aurobindo, *The Life Divine*, SABCL Vol. 18, p. 37.
54. Sri Aurobindo, *The Synthesis of Yoga*, SABCL Vol. 20, p. 392.
55. Sri Aurobindo, *The Life Divine*, SABCL Vol. 19, p. 696.

7
Sri Aurobindo on Human Development
A Transpersonal Perspective

A study based on a survey of definitions of Transpersonal Psychology published in the literature between 1968 and 1991 identified five themes which occur most frequently in the forty definitions yielded by the survey.[1] The authors of the study state the themes as follows:
1. States of consciousness.
2. Highest or ultimate potential.
3. Beyond ego or personal self.
4. Transcendence.
5. Spiritual.

A few of the forty definitions are given below (some only in part) to illustrate the above-mentioned themes:

> Many definitions of transpersonal psychology exist. Some common features in them include the following ideas: that a transcendent reality underlies and binds together all phenomena, that individuals can experience directly this reality related to the spiritual dimension of human life, that doing so involves expansion of consciousness beyond ordinary conceptual boundaries and ego awareness.... [2] (Transpersonal Psychology Interest Group, 1982, p. 1.)

> The main features of the transpersonal approach include: a focus on the whole person, including body, intellect, emotions and spirit; an interest in states of consciousness, including an assumption that waking consciousness is not the highest or most satisfying state; an interest in ultimate values and principles.... [3](R. Frager)

> Transpersonal psychology investigates the evolution of consciousness and experiences which lie beyond the personal, including the

highest visions, goals and aspirations of human beings.[4] (Institute of Transpersonal Psychology)

Transpersonal psychology is the study of human nature and development that proceeds on the assumption that human beings possess potentialities that surpass the limits of the normally developed ego. It is an enquiry that presupposes that the ego, as ordinarily constituted, can be transcended and that a higher, transegoic plane or stage of life is possible.[5] (M. Washburn)

What truly defines the transpersonal orientation is a model of the human psyche that recognizes the importance of the spiritual or cosmic dimensions and the potential for consciousness evolution.[6] (S. Grof)

As will be apparent in the presentation that follows, Sri Aurobindo's integral view of human growth incorporates all the five themes just mentioned, and weaves them around a central concept — the evolution of consciousness — which is found in two of the definitions quoted above.

Sri Aurobindo deals with the human being in relation to the Reality as a whole, and speaks of human development in the context of the evolution of the universe, viewed essentially as the evolution of consciousness.

The Nature of Reality and Evolution of Consciousness

Sri Aurobindo's experience confirms the perennial spiritual realisation of the seers of all times that behind the manifold, ever-changing and evanescent appearances of the universe there is an abiding Reality which has been conceived variously as God, Brahman, the Divine, or the Cosmic Buddha, the fundamental triune aspects of which are expressed in the Vedantic concept of Sat-Chit-Ananda (Existence-Consciousness-Bliss). All things and creatures are united in the One Reality, though they appear to be separate and divided to mental consciousness which is an ignorance-consciousness. Through a process of involution, the One Existence and Consciousness is plunged in the universe into its opposite — the Inconscient, the seeming total absence of consciousness. Evolution is the process by which the Supreme Consciousness liberates itself from Inconscience, resulting in the manifestation of progressively higher levels of consciousness. The scientific theory of physical evolution, states Sri Aurobindo, deals only with the outward and visible machinery of a process which is fundamentally a spiritual evolution, an evolution of consciousness. The first emergence from the Inconscient is Matter. Matter is not inert substance as it appears to be, but a form of consciousness which is closest to Inconscience.[7] Life or vital consciousness is the second emergence in the evolutionary process. Mind, the highest level of consciousness which has evolved up to now in the collectivity, has been the third step of the release from Inconscience. Evolution has not come to an end with the appearance of mind; it awaits a release into higher, spiritual levels of consciousness of which there are many gradations, ranging from Higher Mind through Illumined Mind, Intuition and Overmind up to Supermind. The present-day trends towards spiritual growth are the sign that the human race is preparing for the next evolutionary leap — the emergence of the spiritual and supramental being. The structural-hierarchical aspect of Wilber's model of development reflects Sri Aurobindo's concept of the evolutionary gradations of consciousness from Inconscience to the Supreme Consciousness.

Sri Aurobindo's concept of Supermind has been misconstrued by some as representing a superior level of the Mind principle. But in Sri Aurobindo's experience, Supermind, unlike the other higher gradations of mind just mentioned, is not a superior level of mind but an altogether different evolutionary principle transcending mind.

> The supermind is an entirely different consciousness not only from the spiritualised Mind, but from the planes above spiritualised

Mind which intervene between it and the supramental plane. Once one passes beyond overmind to supermind, one enters into a consciousness to which the norms of the other planes do not at all apply and in which the same Truth, e.g. Sachchidananda and truth of this universe, is seen in quite a different way and has a different dynamic consequence. This necessarily results from the fact that supermind has an indivisible knowledge, while overmind proceeds by union in division and Mind by division taking division as the first fact, for that is the natural process of knowledge.[8]

The supramental being, therefore, is not a Nietzschean edition of the human being magnified into a spiritual colossus, but a new evolutionary species as different from the human being as the human being differs from the animal.

The Purpose, Goal and Dynamics of Evolution

In the Vedantic concept of the One Reality as Sat-Chit-Ananda, Chit (Consciousness) is not only the power of awareness of self and things but is also the dynamic and creative Energy — Chit-Shakti (Consciousness-Force). It is this Energy of consciousness that creates the universe and all that is in it, and is thus the one dynamism behind all evolution. The urge towards growth and evolution, inherent in the whole universe, is the inner driving of the Consciousness-Force, the progressive manifestation of the Spirit being the innate intention behind evolution.

> Even in the Inconscient there seems to be at least an urge of inherent necessity producing the evolution of forms and in the forms a developing Consciousness, and it may well be held that this urge is the evolutionary will of a secret Conscious-Being and its push of progressive manifestation the evidence of an innate intention in the evolution...; the teleology, the element of purpose in the nisus is the translation of self-operative Truth of Being into terms of self-effective Will-Power of that Being, and, if consciousness is there, such a Will-Power must also be there and the translation is normal

and inevitable. Truth of Being inevitably fulfilling itself would be the fundamental fact of the evolution, but Will and its purpose must be there as part of the instrumentation,... [9]

To fulfil the evolutionary intent, spiritual growth needs to be a double movement of ascent and descent; the individual consciousness must ascend to progressively higher levels of consciousness and then must bring down the dynamism of the higher levels into the mental, vital and physical consciousness so as to transform these lower levels. The aim of the spiritual disciplines of the past generally stopped short at ascent to the highest level of consciousness and attainment of liberation.

Liberation is indeed an indispensable step and the initial goal of spiritual development, but the farther goal of evolution, states Sri Aurobindo, is transformation — a concept which, like that of Supermind, has not been adequately grasped by some scholars.

> I use transformation in a special sense, a change of consciousness radical and complete and of a certain specific kind which is so conceived as to bring about a strong and assured step forward in the spiritual evolution of the being of a greater and higher kind and of a larger sweep and completeness than what took place when a mentalised being first appeared in a vital and material animal world. [10]

> What I mean by the spiritual transformation is something dynamic (not merely liberation of the Self or realisation of the One which can very well be attained without any descent). It is a putting on of the spiritual consciousness, dynamic as well as static, in every part of the being down to the subconscient.... It means a bringing down of the Divine Consciousness static and dynamic into all these parts and the entire replacement of the present consciousness by that. This we find unveiled and unmixed above mind, life and body. It is a matter of the undeniable experience of many that this can descend and it is my experience that nothing short of its *full*

descent can thoroughly remove the veil and mixture and effect the full spiritual transformation.[11]

As stated earlier, the dynamic power behind all evolution is the Consciousness-Force of the Cosmic Spirit. At each stage, evolution takes place by the double process of the upsurging of the Consciousness-Force from its involution in the Inconscience and a descent of the Consciousness-Force pressing from the planes of consciousness above seeking for manifestation. It is the pressure of the Consciousness-Force from the plane of Life above the material universe that assisted the emergence of life from Matter in which life already lay involved. It is a pressure from the Mind-plane that helped the emergence of mind which was already there involved in Life and Matter. It is the pressure of the spiritual worlds above Mind which is now preparing the manifestation of the Spirit yet slumbering in Mind, Life and Matter. The growing urge towards spiritual growth in humanity today is the push of the Consciousness-Force towards the next higher rung of evolution.

Prior to the appearance of the human being, evolution from Matter to Life and from Life to Mind was effected by the Consciousness-Force without a conscious will in the plant and the animal. The human being, endowed with mind and conscious will, can now aid and consciously collaborate in the evolutionary process. The aim of all systems of yoga or spiritual growth is to bring about conscious evolution towards a principle above Mind.

The past has been the history of a slow and difficult subconscious working with effects on the surface, — it has been an unconscious evolution; the present is a middle stage, an uncertain spiral in which the human intelligence is used by the secret evolutionary Force of being and participates in its action without being fully taken into confidence, — it is an evolution slowly becoming conscious of itself; the future must be a more and more conscious evolution of the spiritual being until it is fully delivered into a self-aware action by the emergent gnostic principle.[12]

An important dynamic in the evolution of spiritual consciousness stems from the strife which takes place as the forces of the higher planes of consciousness encounter the opposition and resistance of the energies of the lower levels of consciousness which one is attempting to outgrow.

> ...these higher forces are not in their descent immediately all-powerful as they would naturally be in their own plane of action and in their own medium. In the evolution in Matter they have to enter into a foreign and inferior medium and work upon it; they encounter there the incapacities of our mind and life and body, meet with the unreceptiveness or blind refusal of the Ignorance, experience the negation and obstruction of the Inconscience.... There is thus ready-formed a power of resistance which opposes or minimises the effects of the descending Light... and it is therefore that in a world of Ignorance all is achieved not only through a complexus but through a collision and struggle and intermixture of Forces.[13]

The strife of forces is all the more severe if the attempt is towards not only the liberation from the lower consciousness but its transformation.

The Process of Evolution

The movement of evolution towards "a progressive self-manifestation of the Spirit in a material universe"[14] is characterised by a triple process: first, an evolution of increasingly more complex forms of Matter which can embody and express increasingly greater powers of consciousness; this is the physical aspect of evolution; secondly, after the emergence of Mind, a spiritual evolution consisting in an ascent towards progressively higher gradations of consciousness above the ordinary mind; thirdly, an integration of what has already evolved into each successive higher level of consciousness so as to bring about a total change of the whole being and nature.

In the evolution of consciousness as well as the evolution of physical forms, there are apparent gaps or "missing links" between successive stages of development which seem to be radically different. The transition from one definitive stage to the next appears to be a sudden transformation rather than a gradual passage. These leaps in the evolutionary process are due to the fact that at each definitive stage of evolution there is a rise of consciousness to another quite different principle of being, resulting in a reversal of consciousness.

> Such a reversal has been made in each radical transition of Nature: Life-Force emerging turns upon Matter, imposes a vital content on the operations of material Energy while it develops also its own new movements and operations; Life-Mind emerges in Life-Force and Matter and imposes its content of consciousness on their operations while it develops also its own action and faculties; a new greater emergence and reversal, the emergence of humanity, is in line with Nature's precedents....[15]

In order to accomplish the leap beyond mind, it is necessary to grow inwards and enter the consciousness of the inner being and discover the inner Person behind the outer personality, or to grow upwards and ascend to the higher planes above the mind. Only thus can a radical change be brought about in human consciousness, transforming the human being from a mental into a spiritual being.

> ...if we can live thus deeper within and put out steadily the inner forces into the outer instrumentation or raise ourselves to dwell on higher and wider levels and bring their powers to bear on physical existence... there could begin a heightening of our force of conscious being so as to create a new principle of consciousness....[16]

Ego and Human Development

All transpersonal views of human growth regard ego development as a necessary stage prior to ego-transcendence. In Wilber's words: "...it is... ridiculous to speak of realizing the transpersonal until the personal has been formed."[17] The differences lie in the concepts of the ego and of the ego-transcendent state. Regarding the ego and its evolutionary significance Sri Aurobindo states:

> ...Nature invented the ego that the individual might disengage himself from the inconscience or subconscience of the mass and become an independent living mind, life-power, soul, spirit, co-ordinating himself with the world around him but not drowned in it.... For the individual is indeed part of the cosmic being, but he is also something more, he is a soul that has descended from the Transcendence. This he cannot manifest at once, because he is too near to the cosmic Inconscience, not near enough to the original Superconscience; he has to find himself as the mental and vital ego before he can find himself as the soul or spirit.[18]

According to Sri Aurobindo, the ego is not fundamentally real in itself but a temporary formation devised by the Consciousness-Force to hold together its action in the body, life and mind in order to aid in centralising the experiences of the outer consciousness, giving one a sense of a separate individuality which is mistaken for one's true self. The ego, which is felt as the "I", is thus a physical, vital and mental formation. It disappears when the true self is discovered.

However, Sri Aurobindo's experience, like that of many other sages in the past, affirms that behind the illusory individuality of the ego is the true spiritual Individual. Unlike the ego which feels itself to be separate from the rest of the universe, the true spiritual individual is one with the cosmic and transcendent Reality.

...what do we mean by the individual? What we usually call by that name is a natural ego... but the individual self or soul is not this ego. The individual soul is the spiritual being which is sometimes described as an eternal portion of the Divine, but can also be described as the Divine himself supporting his manifestation as the Many. This is the true spiritual individual which appears in its complete truth when we get rid of the ego and our false separative sense of individuality, realise our oneness with the transcendent and cosmic Divine and with all beings.[19]

Therefore, according to Sri Aurobindo, liberation from the ego and its consequent extinction does not necessarily lead to a loss of individuality. The sense of individuality disappears only if, with the extinction of the ego, the true spiritual individual chooses to merge into the transcendent Reality, as occurs in the experience of Nirvana. But instead of choosing merger into the One, the spiritual individual *can* choose to continue existence in the cosmic manifestation — as the Buddha is said to have done[20] — to further the cosmic evolutionary process.

...the liberation and transcendence need not necessarily impose a disappearance, a sheer dissolving out from the manifestation; it can prepare a liberation into action of the highest Knowledge and an intensity of Power that can transform the world and fulfil the evolutionary urge.[21]

...the liberated soul extends its perception of unity horizontally as well as vertically. Its unity with the transcendent One is incomplete without its unity with the cosmic Many. And the lateral unity translates itself by a multiplication, a reproduction of its own liberated state at other points in the Multiplicity.... [22]

The idea of individual progress beyond the state of liberation has been beautifully expressed by Wilber: "That [coming to rest in God] is not the end of the story, but the beginning of post-Enlightenment unfolding as the sage enters the market-place with open hands."[23]

Notes and References

1. Denise H. Lajoie & S.I. Shapiro, "Definitions of transpersonal psychology: The first twenty-three years", *The Journal of Transpersonal Psychology*, Vol. 24 (1992), No.1, pp. 71–98.
2. quoted in ibid., p. 84.
3. quoted in ibid.
4. quoted in ibid., p. 86.
5. quoted in ibid., p. 87.
6. quoted in ibid., p. 85.
7. "Matter is *jada* [inert, inconscient] only in appearance. As even modern Science admits, Matter is only energy in action, and, as we know in India, energy is force of consciousness in action." Sri Aurobindo, *Letters on Yoga*, Sri Aurobindo Birth Centenary Library (hereafter SABCL), (Pondicherry: Sri Aurobindo Ashram, 1970–75), Vol. 22, p. 222.
8. Sri Aurobindo, *Letters on Yoga*, SABCL Vol. 22, pp. 240–41.
9. Sri Aurobindo, *The Life Divine*, SABCL Vol. 19, p. 834.
10. Sri Aurobindo, *Letters on Yoga*, SABCL Vol. 22, p. 98.
11. Ibid., pp. 115–16.
12. Sri Aurobindo, *The Life Divine*, SABCL Vol. 19, p. 707.
13. Ibid., pp. 941–42.
14. Ibid., p. 706.
15. Sri Aurobindo, *The Life Divine*, SABCL Vol. 19, p. 839.
16. Ibid., pp. 722–23.
17. Ken Wilber, "A Developmental Model of Consciousness" in Roger N. Walsh and Frances Vaughan (Eds.), *Beyond Ego: Transpersonal Dimensions in Psychology* (Los Angeles: Jeremy P. Tarcher, 1980), pp. 110–11.
18. Sri Aurobindo, *The Life Divine*, SABCL Vol. 19, p. 694.
19. Sri Aurobindo, *Letters on Yoga*, SABCL Vol. 22, pp. 46–47.
20. "Is it not altogether a legend", asks Sri Aurobindo by way of a rhetorical question, "which says of the Buddha that as he stood on the threshold of Nirvana, of the Non-Being, his soul turned back and took the vow never to make the irrevocable crossing so long as there was a single being upon earth undelivered from the knot

of the suffering, from the bondage of the ego?" — Sri Aurobindo, *The Life Divine*, SABCL Vol. 18, p. 40.

21. Sri Aurobindo, *Letters on Yoga*, SABCL Vol. 22, p. 30.
22. Sri Aurobindo, *The Life Divine*, SABCL Vol. 18, p. 40.
23. Ken Wilber, *The Eye of Spirit* (Boston & London: Shambhala, 1997), p. 228.

ANTHOLOGY SOURCES

The passages in the anthology have been drawn from the following volumes of Sri Aurobindo Birth Centenary Library series published by Sri Aurobindo Ashram, Pondicherry (1970–75).

Vol. 12:   *The Upanishads*
Vol. 13:   *Essays on the Gita*
Vol. 14:   *The Foundations of Indian Culture*
Vol. 16:   *The Supramental Manifestation and Other Writings*
Vol. 17:   *The Hour of God and Other Writings*
Vol. 18:   *The Life Divine – Book One and Book Two Part One*
           (pp. 1–632)
Vol. 19:   *The Life Divine – Book Two Part Two* (pp. 633–1070)
Vol. 20:   *The Synthesis of Yoga – Parts One and Two* (pp. 1–520)
Vol. 21:   *The Synthesis of Yoga – Parts Three and Four*
           (pp. 521–872)
Vol. 22:   *Letters on Yoga – Part One* (pp. 1–502)
Vol. 23:   *Letters on Yoga – Parts Two and Three* (pp. 503–1090)
Vol. 24:   *Letters on Yoga – Part Four* (pp. 1091–1775)
Vol. 25:   *The Mother*
Vol. 27:   *Supplement*

The particular source of a passage is indicated at the end of each passage.

ANTHOLOGY FOOTNOTES

In the anthology, footnotes by the editor are indicated by (Ed.) at the end of the footnote to distinguish them from Sri Aurobindo's footnotes.

Glossary of Names and Terms

The Glossary includes Sanskrit terms, certain proper names and special terms found in Sri Aurobindo's writings.

Explanations of philosophical and psychological terms have generally been given in Sri Aurobindo's own words. Some of the terms defined below have more than one meaning, and may have different connotations in different contexts. The meanings given below apply to the terms as used in this book.

the Absolute — the supreme reality of that transcendent Being which we call God. Indian thought calls it Brahman, European thought the Absolute because it is a self-existent which is absolved of all bondage to relativities.

Advaitin — a Vedantic Monist.

Akshara — the Immobile, the Immutable.

akṣitaṃ śravaḥ — inexhaustible store of memory.

Akshara Brahman — the immutable Brahman.

Ananda — bliss, delight; the essential principle of delight.

antaḥ-karaṇa — the inner instrument; mind.

Asat — Non-being; non-existence; something beyond the last term to which we can reduce our purest conception and our most abstract or subtle experience of actual being as we know or can conceive of it while in this universe. This Nothing is merely a something beyond positive conception.

Atman — the Self; the Spirit; the original and essential nature of our existence; the spiritual being above the mind. In its nature the Atman is transcendent or universal (Paramatma, Atma); when it individualises and becomes a central being, it is then the Jivatman.

Avidya — ignorance; the Ignorance of oneness; the consciousness of Multiplicity.

avyavahāryam — the incommunicable.

Bhagwan — the Lord, God.

Bhrighu Varuni — a Vedic sage.

bhakti — love for the Divine; devotion to the Divine.

Brahman — the Absolute; the Supreme Being; the One besides whom there is nothing else existent.

brahmarandhra — (in *yoga*) the opening at the top of the skull

the Buddha — Gautama Buddha also known as Tathāgata (*c.* 563 – *c.*483 BC), the renowned father of Buddhism. His personal name was Siddhartha. After realising the Truth, he became known as the "Buddha" ("the Enlightened").

buddeḥ paratastu saḥ — that which is supreme over the intelligent will is He. [*Gītā 3.42*]

Buddhi — the thinking mind proper; the mental power of understanding; the discerning intelligence and enlightened will; the discriminating principle of mind, at once intelligence and will.

caitya puruṣa — psychic Person; the psychic being.

Central Being — the term is generally applied to the portion of the Divine in us which supports all the rest and survives through death and birth. It has two forms: the Jivatman, which is above the manifestation in life and presides over it; and the psychic being which stands behind mind, life and body in the manifestation and uses them as its instruments.

Centres of Consciousness — "[The soul] is, according to our psychology, connected with the small outer personality by certain centres of consciousness of which we become aware by yoga....The inner centres are for the most part closed or asleep — to open them and make them awake and active is one aim of yoga." — *Sri Aurobindo*

"The centres or Chakras are seven in number: —

1. The thousand-petalled lotus on the top of the head.
2. In the middle of the forehead — the Ajna Chakra — (will, vision, dynamic thought).
3. Throat centre — externalising mind.
4. Heart-lotus — emotional centre. The psychic is behind it.
5. Navel — higher vital (proper).
6. Below navel — lower vital.
7. Muladhara — physical.

"All these centres are in the middle of the body; they are supposed to be attached to the spinal cord; but in fact all these things
are in the subtle body, *sūkṣma deha*, though one has the feeling of
their activities as if in the physical body when the consciousness
is awake." — *Sri Aurobindo*

"In the process of our yoga the centres have each a fixed
psychological use and general function which base all their
special powers and functionings. The *mūlādhāra* governs the
physical down to the subconscient; the abdominal centre —
svādhiṣṭhāna — governs the lower vital; the navel centre —
nābhipadma or *maṇipūra* — governs the larger vital; the heart
centre — *hṛt-padma* or *anāhata* — governs the emotional being;
the throat centre — *viśuddha* — governs the expressive and externalising mind; the centre between the eyebrows — *ājñācakra*
— governs the dynamic mind, will, vision, mental formation; the
thousand-petalled lotus — *sahasradala* — above commands the
higher thinking mind, houses the still higher illumined mind and
at the highest opens to the intuition through which or else by
an overflooding directness the overmind can have with the rest
communication or an immediate contact." — *Sri Aurobindo*

Chakras — *see* Centres of Consciousness.

Chit — pure consciousness; the essential consciousness of the Spirit;
the free and all-creative self-awareness of the Absolute.

Chitta — the basic stuff of mental consciousness; the stuff of mixed
mental-vital-physical consciousness out of which arise the movements of thought, emotion, sensation, impulse, etc.

"Chitta really means the ordinary consciousness including
the mind, vital and physical — but practically it can be taken to
mean something central in the consciousness." — *Sri Aurobindo*

"Chitta is ordinarily used for the mental consciousness in
general, thought, feeling, etc. taken together with a stress now on
one side or another, sometimes on the feelings..., sometimes on
the thought-mind — 'heart and mind' in its wider sense...." — *Sri
Aurobindo*

Chit Shakti — Consciousness-Force.

cinmaya — consisting of pure consciousness; transcendental.

Circumconscient — the subliminal has a formation of consciousness which projects itself beyond the mental, vital, subtle physical and gross physical sheaths and forms a circumconscient, an environing part of itself, through which it receives the contacts of the world outside us.

cittākāśa — mental or psychical ether.

Consciousness-Force, the Force — the Conscious Force that builds the worlds; a universal Energy that is the power of the Cosmic Spirit working out the cosmic and individual truth of things.

Desire-soul — the surface soul in us, which works in our vital cravings, our emotions, aesthetic faculty and mental seeking for power, knowledge and happiness; the true soul is the subliminal psychic essence.

the Divine — the Supreme Being from which all comes and in which all lives. In its supreme Truth the Divine is absolute and infinite peace, consciousness, existence, power and delight. The Transcendent, the Cosmic (Universal) and the Individual are three powers of the Divine, overarching, underlying and penetrating the whole of manifestation.

Ego — the "I" constituted by a mental, vital and physical formation which serves to centralise and individualise the outer consciousness and action; when the true self is discovered, the utility of the ego ceases, this formation disappears and the true individuality is felt in its place.

Environmental consciousness — *see* Circumconscient.

the Force — *see* Consciousness-Force

the Gita — short form of Bhagavad Gita, "the Song of the Blessed Lord", being the spiritual teachings of Sri Krishna to Arjuna on the battlefield of Kurukshetra; it occurs as an episode in the Mahabharata.

Gnosis — a supreme totally self-aware and all-aware Intelligence; the Divine Gnosis is the Supermind.

Gradations between Mind and Supermind — higher ranges of Mind overtopping our normal Mind and leading to Supermind; these successive states, levels or graded powers of being are hidden in our own superconscious parts. In an ascending order the gradations of spiritualised mind are:

Higher Mind: a luminous thought-mind whose instrumentation is through an elevated thought-power and comprehensive mental sight. In the Higher Mind one becomes constantly and closely aware of the Self, the One everywhere and knows and sees habitually with that awareness.

Illumined Mind: a mind no longer of higher thought, but of spiritual light; here the clarity of the intelligence, its tranquil daylight, gives place or subordinates itself to an intense lustre, a splendour and illumination of the Spirit.

Intuition: a power of consciousness nearer and more intimate than the above-mentioned gradations to the original knowlege by identity. What is thought-knowledge in the Higher Mind becomes illumination in the Illumined Mind and direct intimate vision in the Intuition. This true and authentic intuition must be distinguished from a power of the ordinary mental reason which is too easily confused with it, that power of involved reasoning that reaches its conclusion by a bound and does not need the ordinary steps of the logical mind.

Overmind: The Overmind is a delegate of the Supramental Consciousness, its delegate to the cosmic Ignorance. The Supramental is the total Truth-Consciousness; the Overmind draws down the truths separately and gives them a separate identity.

guṇa, **Guna** — quality, character, property; the three Gunas of Nature, her qualities or modes, are Sattwa, Rajas, and Tamas.

Hemispheres, Higher and Lower — "The higher hemisphere is the perfect and eternal reign of the Spirit; for there it manifests without cessation or diminution of its infinities, deploys the unconcealed glories of its illimitable existence, its illimitable consciousness and knowledge, its illimitable force and power, its illimitable beatitude. The lower hemisphere belongs equally to the Spirit; but here it is veiled, closely, thickly, by its inferior self-expression of limiting mind, confining life and dividing body." — *Sri Aurobindo*

Higher Mind — *see under* Gradations between Mind and Supermind.

hiraṇmaya pātra — golden lid.

Horace — (65 – 08 BC) Latin poet.

icchā-mṛtyu — the power of abandoning the body definitively without the ordinary phenomena of death, by an act of will.

Idea-force — the power in the idea — a force of which the idea is a shape.

the Ignorance — *see* Avidya.

Illumined Mind — *see under* Gradations between Mind and Supermind.

the Inconscient, Inconscience — the most involved state of the Superconscience; all powers of the Superconscience progressively evolve and emerge out of the Inconscient, the first emergence being Matter.

the Intraconscient — the subliminal.

Intuition — 1. Insight without conscious reasoning. 2. Plane of consciousness between Illumined Mind and Overmind. *See under* Gradations between Mind and Supermind.

Ishwara — Lord, Master, the Divine, God.

Ishwarakoti — a human being who in losing himself in God yet keeps himself and is able to lean down again to humanity. *See also* Jivakoti.

jāgrat — the waking state, the consciousness of the material world.

Jivakoti — a human being who, once immersed in the Reality, cannot return; he is lost in God and lost to humanity. *See also* Ishwarakoti.

Jivatma — *see* Atman and Central Being.

jyoti — (the authentic spiritual) light.

kalpa — aeon.

karma, **Karma** — action, work; the work or function of a man; action entailing its consequences, the chain of act and consequence.

the Knowledge — the knowledge of the One Reality, the consciousness of Unity. *See* Vidya.

laya — dissolution; annullation of the individual soul in the Infinite.

Life — "The English word life does duty for many very different shades of meaning; but the word Prana familiar in the Upanishad and in the language of Yoga is restricted to the life-force whether viewed in itself or in its functionings;" — *Sri Aurobindo*

"Life is an energy of spirit subordinated to action of mind and body, which fulfils itself through mentality and physicality and acts as a link between them." — *Sri Aurobindo*

Life-mind — *see* vital mind *under* mind.

Manas — mind, the mind proper [as distinct from the intellect (*buddhi*)], sense-mind.

manomaya puruṣa — mental Person; the mental being.

manvantara — an age or period of a *Manu*, an extremely long period. of time, one-fourteenth of a day of *Brahmā*.

mātrā — measure, the quantitative action of Nature.

Maya — illusion; the power of self-illusion in Brahman.

Menes — (fl. *c.* 3100 BC) first historic ruler of the first dynasty of unified Egypt.

mind — "mind" and "mental" connote specially that part of the nature which has to do with cognition and intelligence, with ideas, with mental or thought perceptions, the reactions of thought to things, with the truly mental movements and formations, mental vision and will, etc. that are part of man's intelligence. The ordinary mind has three main parts: mind proper, vital mind, and physical mind.

The **mind proper** is divided into three parts: the thinking mind or intellect, concerned with ideas and knowledge in their own right; the dynamic mind, concerned with the putting out of mental forces for the realisation of the ideas; and the externalising mind, concerned with the expression of ideas in life.

The **vital mind** or desire mind is a mind of dynamic will, action, desire; it is occupied with force and achievement and satisfaction and possession, with enjoyment and suffering, giving and taking, growth and expansion, etc.

The **physical mind** is that part of the mind which is concerned with physical things only; limited by the physical view and experience of things, it mentalises the experience brought by the contact of outward life and things, but does not go beyond that. The mechanical mind, closely connected with the physical mind, goes on repeating without use whatever has happened.

Overtopping the ordinary mind, hidden in our own superconscient parts, there are higher ranges of Mind, gradations of spiritualised mind leading to the Supermind. In ascending order they are: Higher Mind, Illumined Mind, Intuition and Overmind. *See* Gradations between Mind and Supermind.

mokṣa, **Moksha** — spiritual liberation.

mole ruet sua — (Latin) will collapse by its own mass.

Mukta — free.

Muladhar — "root vessel or chamber"; the physical consciousness centre (Chakra); *see also Centres of Consciousness.*

Mukti — spiritual liberation, the release of the soul from the bondage of Ignorance.

nāstyanto vistrarasya me — there is no end to my self-extension. [*Gītā* 10.19]

Nature, Nature Force — the outer or executive side of the Conscious Force which forms and moves the worlds. The higher, divine Nature (Para Prakriti) is free from Ignorance and its consequences; the lower Nature (Apara Prakriti) is a mechanism of active Force put forth for the working of the evolutionary Ignorance. The lower nature of an individual — mind, life and body — are part of Prakriti.

Nescience — Inconscience.

Nihilism — Nagarjuna's (Buddhist) philosophy according to which the ultimate Reality is nihil, Void, Non-Being or Non-Existence.

Nirvana, *nirvāṇa* — extinction (not necessarily of all the being, but of being as we know it, extinction of ego, desire and egoistic action and mentality).

Nirvikalpa Samadhi — complete trance, in which there is no thought or movement of consciousness or awareness of either inner or outer things.

nistraiguṇya — a state in which one is free from the three *guṇas*.

Overmind — *see under* Gradations Between Mind and Supermind.

parātparam — the Supreme beyond the Most High, the supreme of the Supreme.

Physical mind — *it see under* mind.

Prajna — 1. (*prajñā*) — the all-wise Intelligence. 2. (*prājña*) — the Self situated in deep sleep (*suṣupti*), the lord and creator of things; the Master of Wisdom and Knowledge.

Prakriti — Nature; Nature-Force, the Lord's executive force; the outer or executive side of the Conscious Force which forms and moves the worlds. *See also* Nature.

prāṇa, **Prana** — life energy; one of the five workings of the life-force.

the Psychic — the soul; spark of the Divine before it has evolved into an individualised being; the divine essence in the individual. In the course of the evolution, the soul grows and evolves in the form of a soul-personality, the psychic being. The term is also often used for the soul-personality or the psychic being. *See also* Psychic Being *and* Soul.

Psychic(al) — ordinarily, the term, used as an adjective, means: 1. mental as opposed to physical; 2. outside physical or natural laws. In his earlier writings Sri Aurobindo used the term in similar senses. Thus he spoke about "psychic(al) Prana", meaning Prana which is subtler and more inward than the physical Prana; and he referred to clairvoyance, telepathy, etc. as psychic(al) phenomena. However, subsequently he stated: "The word psychic is indeed used in English to indicate anything that is other or deeper than the external mind, life and body or it indicates sometimes anything occult or supraphysical: but that is a use which brings confusion and error and we have almost entirely to discard it." Explaining the meaning of the term as used in his later writings, he wrote: "I use the word psychic for the soul as distinguished from the mind and the vital. All movements and experiences of the soul would in that sense be called psychic, those which arise from or directly touch the psychic being.... " He continued to use the word "psychical" to refer to phenomena connected with the subliminal (inner mind, inner vital, inner physical), such as clairvoyance, telepathy, etc.

Psychical consciousness — the consciousness of the subliminal or inner being.

Psychic being — the divine portion in the individual which evolves from life to life, growing, by its experiences until it becomes a fully conscious being. The term "soul" is often used as a synonym for "psychic being", but strictly speaking, the soul is the undifferentiated psychic essence, whereas the psychic being isthe individualised soul-personality developed by the psychic essence in the course of evolution. *See also* the Psychic, Soul, *and* Soul-personality.

Psychic entity — psychic essence.

Psychic essence — the soul in its essence; the divine essence in the individual, the divine spark which supports the evolution of the being in Nature. In the course of the evolution the psychic essence grows and takes form as the psychic being.

Psychicisation — the psychic change in which the psychic being comes forward to dominate the mind, vital and physical and change the lower nature.

Purusha — Conscious Being; Conscious-Soul; essential being supporting the play of Prakriti (Nature); a Consciousness behind that is the lord, witness, enjoyer, upholder and source of sanction for Nature's works; the Purusha represents the true being on whatever plane it manifests — physical, vital, mental, psychic.

Purushottama — the supreme divine Person; the Supreme Being who is superior both to the mutable Being and the Immutable.

the Quiescent — Inactive Brahman. (The Inactive and the Active Brahman are two aspects of the one Brahman.)

rajas, **Rajas** — the quality that energises and drives to action; the quality of action and passion and struggle impelled by desire and instinct; the force of kinesis. Rajas is one of the three Gunas or modes of Nature.

Ramakrishna — Sri Ramakrishna Paramahansa (1836-1886), a spiritual teacher of modern India.

rasa — taste, liking, pure taste of enjoyment; the response of the mind, the vital feeling and the sense to a certain "taste" in things.

Rig Veda — the most ancient of the sacred books of India.

Rishi — a seer.

Sachchidananda (Sat-Chit-Ananda) — the One Divine Being with a triple aspect of Existence (Sat), Consciousness (Chit) and Delight (Ananda).

Sadhana — the practice of yoga.

śama — the divine quiet, peace, rest.

Samadhi, *Samādhi* — yogic trance (in which the mind acquires the capacity of withdrawing from its limited waking activities into freer and higher states of consciousness).

samādhistha — arrived at the essential *samādhi* and settled in it.

Sanjnana, *samjñāna* — essential sense; contact of consciousness with its object; the inbringing movement of apprehensive consciousness which draws the object placed before it back to itself so as to possess it in conscious substance, to feel it.

Sankhya — one of the six systems of orthodox Hindu philosophy whose method is based on analysis, enumeration and discriminitive setting forth of the principles of our being.

Sanskara — association, impression, fixed notion, habitual reaction formed by one's past.

sarvabhāvena — in every way of his being. (Gita).

Sat — Being, Existence; Pure Existence.

sattva, Sattwa — the quality that illumines and clarifies; the quality of light, harmony, purity and peace; the force of equilibrium. Sattwa is one of the three Gunas or modes of Nature.

the Self — the Atman, the universal Spirit, the self-existent Being, the conscious essential Existence, one in all. (The Self is being, not a being.)

Shakti — Force, Power; the Divine Power; the Power of the other; the consciousness and power of the Divine; the Mother and Energy of the worlds.

Shunya — void; the Nothing which is All.

Sorley, Prof. — William Ritchie Sorley (1855-1935), professor of philosophy at Cambridge.

Soul — the psychic essence or entity, the divine essence in the individual; a spark of the Divine that comes down into the manifestation to support the evolution of the individual. In the course of the evolution, the soul grows and evolves in the form of a soul-personality, the psychic being. The term "soul" is also often used as a synonym for "psychic being." *See also* the Psychic *and* Psychic Being.

Soul-personality — the psychic being or soul-form developing through evolution and passing from life to life. *See* Psychic being.

spark-soul — *see* the Psychic *and* Soul.

Spirit — the Consciousness above mind, the Atman or universal Self which is always in oneness with the Divine.

Spiritualisation — the spiritual change in which there is the established descent of the divine peace, light, knowledge, power, bliss from above, the awareness of the Self and the Divine and of a higher cosmic consciousness and the change of the whole nature to that.

śraddhā — faith.

the Subconscient — the part of the being which is below the level of the mental, vital and physical consciousness; in the average person, it includes the larger part of the physical mind, the vital being and the body-consciousness.

Subconscious mind — the inner or subliminal mind.

the Subliminal — comprises the inner being, taken in its entirety of inner mind, inner life, inner physical with the soul or psychic entity supporting them; (sometimes) all that lies outside the surface consciousness, including the subconscient, the subliminal proper and the superconscient.

the Superconscient; Superconscience — consciousness above and beyond our present level of awareness in which are included the higher planes of mental being as well as the supramental and spiritual.

Supermind — the Supramental, the Truth-Consciousness, the Divine Gnosis, the highest divine consciousness and force operative in the universe. A principle of consciousness superior to mentality, it exists, acts and proceeds in the fundamental truth and unity of things and not like the mind in their appearances and phenomenal divisions. Its fundamental character is knowledge by identity, by which the Self is known, the Divine Sachchidananda is known, but also the truth of manifestation is known because this too is that.

suṣupti, **Sushupti** — deep sleep; the Sleep-State, a consciousness corresponding to the supramental plane proper to the gnosis, which is beyond our experience because our causal body or envelope of gnosis is not developed in us, its faculties not active, and therefore we are in relation to that plane in a state of dreamless sleep.

svabhāva — "own being", "own becoming"; the essential nature and self-principle of being of each becoming.

svapna — the dream-state, a consciousness correponding to the subtler life-plane and mind-plane beyond.

svayaṁprakāśa — supreme existence supremely aware of itself; direct or essential knowledge.

tamas, **Tamas** — the quality that hides or darkens; the quality of ignorance, inertia and obscurity, of incapacity and inaction; the force of inconscience. Tamas is one of the three Gunas or modes of Nature.

Tantra — a yogic system based on the principle of Consciousness-Power (conceived of as the Divine Mother) as the Supreme Reality; its method of discipline is to raise Nature in man into manifest power of Spirit.

Tantrik — relating to Tantra; a follower of the Tantra system of philosophy and yoga.

tapas, **Tapas** — the essential principle of energy.

Transcendence, the Transcendent — the seat of the Transcendent Consciousness is above in an absoluteness of divine Existence of which our mentality can form no conception and of which even our greatest spiritual experience is only a divine reflection. *See also* the Divine.

triguṇātīta — above or beyond the three Gunas.

Truth-Consciousness — *see* Supermind.

Turiya — the fourth plane of our consciousness; the superconscient; the Absolute.

udāna — one of the five *prāṇas* it moves upward from the body to the crown of the head and is a regular channel of communication between the physical life and the greater life of the spirit. *See also prāṇa*.

Upanishads — a class of Hindu sacred writings, regarded as the source of the Vedanta philosophy.

upari budhna eṣām — their foundation is above. (Rig Veda)

Veda — generic name for the most ancient Indian sacred literature.

Vedanta — the "end or culmination of the Veda"; a system of philosophy based on the Upanishads (which occur at the end of the Veda), teaching the culminating knowledge of the Absolute.

Vedantin, Vedantist — an advocate of Vedanta.

Vedic — pertaining to the Veda.

Vidya — knowledge; Knowledge in its highest spiritual sense; the consciousness of Unity.

the Vital — the Life-nature made up of desires, sensations, feelings, passions, energies of action and of all the play of possessive and other related instincts, such as anger, fear, greed, lust, etc. The vital has three main parts:

higher vital: the mental vital and emotional vital taken together. The mental vital gives a mental expression by thought, speech or otherwise to the emotions, desires, passions, sensations or other movements of the vital being; the emotional vital is the seat of various feelings, such as love, joy, sorrow, hatred and the rest.

central vital or **vital proper:** dynamic, sensational and passionate, it is the seat of the stronger vital longings and reactions, such as ambition, pride, fear, love of fame, attractions and repulsions, desires and passions of various kinds and the field of many vital energies.

lower vital: made up of the smaller movements of human life-desire and life-reactions, it is occupied with small desires and feelings, such as food desire, sexual desire, small likings, dislikings, vanity, quarrels, love of praise, anger at blame, little wishes of all kinds, etc.

Vital mind — *see* mind.

Vivekananda, Swami — monastic name of Narendranath Dutta (1863-1902), the most famous disciple of Sri Ramakrishna and one of the great spiritual teachers of modern India.

Yajnavalkya — a famous Rishi who figures prominently in the Brihadaranyaka Upanishad.

Yoga — 1. joining, union; union with the Divine and the conscious seeking for this union. Yoga is in essence the union of the soul with the immortal being and consciousness and bliss of the Divine, effected through the human nature with a result of development into the divine nature of the being. Yoga is a generic name for any discipline by which one attempts to pass out of the limits of one's ordinary mental consciousness into a greater spiritual consciousness. 2. one of the six systems of orthodox Indian philosophy systematised by Patanjali.

Index